Third Edition

Public Relations in Schools

Theodore J. Kowalski
University of Dayton

Upper Saddle River, New Jersey
Columbus, Ohio

Library of Congress Cataloging-in-Publication Data

Public relations in schools / [edited by] Theodore J. Kowalski.—3rd ed.
    p. cm.
    Includes bibliographical references and index.
    ISBN 0-13-046265-9
    1. Schools—Public relations. 2. Schools—Public relations—Case studies. 3. School
management and organization. 4. School management and organization—Case studies. 5.
Community and school. 6. Community and school—Case studies. I. Kowalski, Theodore J.

    LB2847.P82 2004
    659.2'9371—dc21

                    2002044463

Vice President and Executive Publisher: Jeffery W. Johnston
Executive Editor: Debra A. Stollenwerk
Editorial Assistant: Mary Morrill
Assistant Editor: Daniel J. Parker
Production Editor: Kris Robinson
Production Coordination: Amy Gehl, Carlisle Publishers Services
Design Coordinator: Diane C. Lorenzo
Cover Designer: Jason Moore
Cover image: SuperStock
Production Manager: Pamela D. Bennett
Director of Marketing: Ann Castel Davis
Marketing Manager: Darcy Betts Prybella
Marketing Coordinator: Tyra Poole

This book was set in Goudy by Carlisle Communications, Ltd. It was printed and bound by R.R. Donnelley &
Sons Company. The cover was printed by The Lehigh Press, Inc.

Pearson Education Ltd.
Pearson Education Singapore Pte. Ltd.
Pearson Education Canada, Ltd.
Pearson Education—Japan

Pearson Education Australia Pty. Limited
Pearson Education North Asia Ltd.
Pearson Education de Mexico, S.A. de C.V.
Pearson Education Malaysia Pte. Ltd.

10 9 8 7 6 5 4 3 2
ISBN: 0-13-046265-9

Preface

Although studying the relationship between schools and the communities has long been part of the curriculum completed by aspiring administrators, concerns about this essential association not only persist, they actually have increased. Reasons for the disjunction between theory and practice are many and varied. Some relate to demographic patterns. For example, schools have gotten larger at the same time that the communities they serve have grown more diverse. Other underlying reasons are less discernible and deeply rooted in the organizational culture of districts and schools. For instance, once in practice administrators often must choose between two contradictory dispositions toward community involvement. One, commonly studied in graduate school, posits that broad participation in public education policy and decision making is both morally correct and politically sound. The other, transmitted during socialization to the workplace, posits that external interventions and power sharing cause conflict and subsequently prevent managerial efficiency. Regrettably, the latter outlook remains dominant.

Although traditional management beliefs and values toward community involvement persisted in education for many decades, the debilities of this disposition were not challenged widely until the 1980s and 1990s. America's transition from a manufacturing society to an information-based society provided both an infrastructure for rapid and frequent communication and an expectation that this infrastructure would be employed by administrators to engage the public. At the same time, demands for school improvement intensified. Over these two decades, the school reform agenda evolved, ultimately focusing on restructuring local districts and individual schools—a strategy that clearly favors citizen participation and relies on community acceptance. Given this social and political context, the need for administrators to adopt new values and beliefs toward communication and participation would appear axiomatic. Instead, many school officials continue to cling to outdated notions of efficiency, albeit more covertly than in the past. As a result, their interactions with parents, the media, and community leaders remain limited. For them, communication is a one-way process in which they disseminate information to their chosen audiences as they deem necessary.

Communication behavior has both symbolic and real consequences. One-way approaches have not only hindered necessary organizational adaptations, but they also have reinforced convictions among policy elites that many administrators are either insecure about bringing all segments of the school's community together to engage in reform or philosophically opposed to doing so. Constructing a shared vision and implementing a strategic plan—arguably essential restructuring tasks—require broad-based participation. Therefore, this text focuses heavily on explaining communication alternatives and evaluating them in the context of modern technology, prevailing social conditions, and political demands for change.

Two other noteworthy conditions inhibiting both effective school and community relations and meaningful school reform are given considerable attention in this book. The first is persisting misinterpretations of public relations. Unless administrators and the general public understand the concept of public relations and its vital role in organizational development, they are unlikely to support its core functions. Second, relationships between school officials and media representatives have often been counterproductive. In the aftermath of critical reform reports, administrators and school board members often blamed reporters for sensationalizing public education's shortcomings while purposefully ignoring its accomplishments. Consequently, at the time when image and relationship building are imperative, many education personnel view reporters as the enemy and they anticipate that their contacts with them will be confrontational.

Clearly, the quest for school reform in the context of an information-based society has redefined effective practice in school administration. Today, outstanding principals and superintendents are not only competent managers, they are dynamic leaders. They value democratic processes, respect the professional status of teachers, and see diversity as a potential asset. They understand that schools are most effective when they maintain a symbiotic relationship with the communities they serve. As they seek to lead and facilitate positive change, principals and superintendents utilize modern communication technology to access and disseminate information. They model two-way communication as an effective approach to identifying and solving problems.

PURPOSE OF THIS BOOK

The primary objective of this book is to examine the potentialities of educational relations in the context of contemporary societal conditions. More precisely, the process of public relations is examined in relation to (a) life in an information age, (b) practice in social institutions, (c) the use of technology in the practice of school administration, and (d) sustained demands for school improvement. The following features are relevant to this goal:

- ◆ A broad perspective of public relations is presented—one that integrates theory and craft knowledge in promoting two-way communication procedures and extended uses of information.
- ◆ Public relations is defined as an essential and pervasive administrative function. Consequently, every administrator, regardless of assignment, requires a complete understanding of how communication and community relations affect organizational behavior, and, ultimately, organizational effectiveness.

◆ The functions embedded in a comprehensive public relations program are deemed especially vital to school reform. Current strategies, such as state deregulation, district decentralization, and school restructuring, depend on schools identifying real needs and making appropriate adaptations based on those needs. Functions nested in public relations are integral to this task.

◆ The book's content is structured to encourage professional reflection. The case studies, questions and suggested activities, and suggested readings at the end of each chapter are designed to promote critical thinking in problem solving.

The book is divided into three parts. Part I, "Contemporary Conditions," provides a foundation for understanding the applications of public relations in educational institutions. The topics addressed include

◆ A historical perspective of public relations and modern definitions
◆ An analysis of contemporary social conditions and their effect on education
◆ The role of public opinion in prevailing political contexts
◆ The legal and ethical aspects of communication activities
◆ An in-depth discussion of verbal and nonverbal communication in the delivery of public relations programs

Part II, "Public Relations in Districts and Schools," focuses more directly on the applications of public relations in schools. The discussion begins with an examination of districts and schools as social institutions—a discussion that magnifies the importance of communication. Then, the development and delivery of public relations programs are examined at the district and individual school levels. The last chapter in this section addresses public relations in private and nontraditional public schools.

Part III, "Administrator Responsibilities," is devoted to specific duties assumed by administrative personnel engaged in public relations activities. These duties include

◆ Planning
◆ Media relations
◆ Crisis management
◆ Collecting and analyzing data
◆ Funding campaigns
◆ Evaluating public relations activities

All 15 chapters conclude with a case study. The cases are purposely not taken to conclusion so that you may place yourself in the role of decision maker. This allows you to integrate chapter content with a contemporary problem faced by a school administrator.

Perspectives presented in this book represent a rich background of practitioner and academic experiences. Whereas many of the chapter authors specialize in educational leadership, others are highly respected scholars in communication, business, and public relations. The collective experiences and knowledge of the contributors result in a unique book—one that integrates theory and practice from multiple disciplines to provide school administrators with emerging perspectives about communication, information, technology, and human relationships.

NEW TO THIS EDITION

The third edition provides a balance of theory and practice. Special attention is given to prevailing reform strategies, especially state deregulation, district decentralization, teacher professionalization, and parental choice. As an example, the chapter on private schools has been expanded to include discussion of public schools of choice, namely charter schools, alternative schools, vocational schools, and magnet schools.

Diversity is another topic that receives added attention in this edition. Most communities, and hence most schools, have become increasingly diverse. Demographic projections suggest that this trend will continue and result in minority-majorities in many local districts in the next few decades.

Suggested readings and references, and most of the case studies from the second edition, have either been replaced or revamped to reflect changing conditions in education. Last, the topics of technology and public relations theory are infused across the chapters rather than discussed separately. This modification provides a more integrated discussion of contemporary public relations.

Three new authors are contributors to the third edition. Professors Patti Chance (University of Nevada–Las Vegas) and Lars Björk (University of Kentucky) are coauthors of Chapter 6 on the social dimensions of schools. Professor George Perreault (University of Nevada–Reno) is a coauthor of Chapter 8 on programming at the school level.

ACKNOWLEDGMENTS

Many individuals contributed to this project. I am most grateful to the contributing authors. Special mention is given to two colleagues who authored material in previous editions, Professors Edward Chance and Robert Woodroof. Regrettably, both passed away shortly after the second edition was finished.

Sincere gratitude is also expressed to my office assistant Elizabeth Pearn. Her dedication and hard work contributed in countless ways. Appreciation is also extended to my doctoral assistant, Father Charles Kanai, who aided with research and literature reviews, and to Debbie Stollenwerk, my editor at Merrill/Prentice Hall, for guidance and encouragement. Finally, I thank my family for their moral support.

I would also like to thank the reviewers of this manuscript for their candid comments and suggestions: Martha Bruckner, University of Nebraska at Omaha; Christina M. Dawson; Antioch University Seattle; Larry W. Hughes, University of Houston; and Linda C. Tillman, Wayne State University.

About the Authors

Robert H. Beach is a professor of policy and planning and program coordinator for a new doctoral program in Educational Leadership, Policy and Law at Alabama State University. He is a board member of the International Society for Educational Administration and former member and chair of the National Policy Board for Educational Administration.

Lars G. Björk is an associate professor in the Department of Administration and Supervision at the University of Kentucky, codirector of the University Council for Educational Administration's Joint Program Center for the Study of the Superintendency, and a senior associate editor of *Educational Administration Quarterly*. He has coedited several books, including *Higher Education Research and Public Policy* (1988), *Minorities in Higher Education* (1994), and *The New Superintendency: Advances in Research and Theories of School Management and Educational Policy* (2001). He coauthored *The Study of the American Superintendency 2000: A Look at the Superintendent of Education in the New Millennium* (2000).

Patti L. Chance is an assistant professor in the Department of Educational Leadership at the University of Nevada–Las Vegas and serves as program coordinator for PK–12 Educational Leadership. Her areas of expertise include instructional leadership, school improvement, and the principalship. She has served as a building-level principal, assistant principal, and coordinator for K–12 gifted education programs. Dr. Chance serves on editorial boards for several national journals devoted to educational leadership. She has written articles and chapters related to instructional leadership, organizational theory, and educational administration preparation programs and coauthored a textbook for educational administration titled *Introduction to Educational Leadership and Organizational Behavior: Theory Into Practice* (2002).

Margaret M. Clements is a doctoral student in educational leadership and policy studies at Indiana University and is a research assistant at the Indiana Education Policy Center. Her research interests include education finance.

Thomas Glass is a professor in the Department of Leadership at the University of Memphis. He is a former school superintendent and faculty member at Northern Illinois University and Washington State University. In 2000, he directed a national study of superintendents for the American Association of School Administrators that resulted in the publication of *The Study of the American School Superintendency: A Look at the Superintendent of Education in the New Millennium.*

Glenn Graham is professor of educational research at Wright State University. He and Gordon Wise founded the Center for School Tax Levies and Bond Issues at Wright State. They are the authors of the Phi Delta Kappa Fastback on passing tax levies and two books on the same topic published by the Ohio School Boards Association.

Theodore J. Kowalski is the Kuntz Family Chair in Educational Administration at the University of Dayton. A former teacher, principal, and superintendent, he previously served as dean of the Teachers College at Ball State University. He is the author of 14 books and numerous research articles, editor of the *Journal of School Public Relations,* and a member of three other editorial boards. He has delivered over 80 invited lectures at universities throughout the world and has served as a consultant to schools, universities, and businesses.

Joseph R. McKinney holds a law degree from Indiana University–Bloomington School of Law and a doctorate in educational administration from Virginia Tech. He is a member of three state bars, and serves as chair and a professor in the Department of Education at Ball State University. He is an adjunct professor of law at the Indiana University–Bloomington School of Law. Dr. McKinney is the author of three books and more than 40 research-based articles. He is a member of the Authors Committee for West's Educational Law Reporter and has been an Independent Hearing Officer for special education appeals for 10 years.

James F. McNamara is a professor at Texas A&M University, with graduate faculty appointments in the departments of Educational Administration and Educational Psychology in the College of Education and the Department of Statistics in the College of Science. He is a noted authority on survey research methodology. His most recent book is *Surveys and Experiments in Educational Research* (1994).

Maryanne McNamara is a research associate and program evaluator in the Danforth Foundation School Leadership Program at Texas A&M University. Prior to her current appointment, she supervised student teachers at Texas A&M and was director of an alternative high school.

Richard Kent Murray is an associate professor of educational leadership in the School of Education at The Citadel. His current research focus is the use of school uniforms to reduce violence.

Doug Newsom is the coauthor of three textbooks: *Media Writing* (with the late James Wollert); *This Is PR* (with Judy VanSlyke Turk and Dean Kruckeberg); and *Public Relations Writing* (with the late Bob Carrell). She is coeditor of a book of women's colloquium papers, *Silent Voices* (also with Bob Carrell). She is a professor at Texas Christian University in Fort Worth and a public relations practitioner.

Mary John O'Hair is a professor in the Department of Educational Leadership and Policy Studies at the University of Oklahoma and founding director of the Center for Educational and Community Renewal. The center is a consortium of school-university-community partnerships representing over 800 elementary, middle, and high schools in Oklahoma whose purpose is to improve student achievement and democratic citizenship through systemic reform involving leadership for authentic teaching, technology integration, and cooperative networking. Dr. O'Hair is the author of seven books, including *Foundations of Democratic Education* (Wadsworth, 2000), and dozens of articles and other professional publications. She has received professional awards from the American Education Research Association, the International Society for Teacher Education, and the International Communication Association.

George Perreault teaches in the Department of Educational Leadership at the University of Nevada. He previously served as a principal and superintendent in Florida and New Mexico, as well as on the faculty of New Mexico Highlands University, Gonzaga University, and East Carolina University. Professor Perreault has published numerous professional articles and has authored or coauthored seven books, including *The Changing World of School Administration* (2002). In addition, he is associate editor of the *Journal of School Public Relations* and serves on the editorial board of two other national journals.

A. William Place is director of doctoral studies and associate professor of educational administration at the University of Dayton, where he teaches courses in public relations and personnel administration. He is a former teacher, administrator, and teacher association representative in public education. His research interests are in the areas of teacher recruitment and selection.

Edward P. St. John is a professor in the Department of Educational Leadership and Policy Studies at Indiana University, where he also serves as director of the Indiana Education Policy Center. His research on school reform has resulted in a coedited book, *Accelerated Schools in Action* (1996), and a coauthored book, *Families in Schools* (1997). At the policy center, he coauthored *State Policy on Professional Development: Rethinking the Linkages to Student Outcomes* (1999). More recently, he completed two coedited volumes: *Reinterpreting Urban School Reform: A Critical-Empirical Review* (forthcoming from SUNY Press) and *Improving Early Reading and Literacy in Grades 1–5: A Guide for Developing Research-Based Programs That Work* (in press).

Edward H. Seifert is assistant dean in the College of Education and Human Services at Texas A&M University–Commerce. Seifert is a former teacher, principal, superintendent, and university faculty member, and has served in several administrative positions in higher education. He has published more than 60 articles and book chapters, edited two books, wrote two books, and served as a consultant to PK–12 schools in several states. His current focus is on the principalship.

Angela McNabb Spaulding is an associate professor of educational leadership at West Texas A&M University (WTAMU) in Canyon, Texas, where she coordinates the educational leadership program and teaches courses in leadership and curriculum. She is also the project director of the A&M University System Regents' Initiative at WTAMU. She is a sponsor for Alpha Chi, is an academy member of the Regent's Initiative for Excellence in Education, and has been the recipient of the WTAMU Outstanding Professor Award. Dr. Spaulding's research interests include topics emerging from leadership and group dynamics, communication, conflict management, and the micropolitics of life in the classroom. She has numerous publications and presentations in these areas. Dr. Spaulding has been an early childhood classroom teacher and administrator.

Arthur Stellar is president and chief executive officer of the High/Scope Educational Research Foundation in Ypsilanti, Michigan. He formerly served as superintendent of schools for Kingston, New York; Boston; Cobb County, Georgia; Oklahoma City; and Mercer County, West Virginia. He also served as an administrator for the Shaker Heights, Ohio, Schools and Montgomery County Public Schools, Maryland, among others. Stellar has served as president of several professional organizations, including the Horace Mann League and the Association of Supervision and Curriculum Development. He has written extensively on school public relations.

Gordon Wise is professor emeritus of marketing at Wright State University. He and Glenn Graham founded the Center for School Tax Levies and Bond Issues at Wright State. They are the authors of the Phi Delta Kappa Fastback on passing levies and two books on the same topic published by the Ohio School Boards Association.

Brief Contents

Contents

5   Public Relations in a Communication Context: Listening, Nonverbal, and Conflict-Resolution Skills   96

Angela Spaulding
Mary John O'Hair

8   Effective Programming at the School Level   174

George Perreault
Richard Kent Murray

15   Evaluating Public Relations Programs   341
Doug Newsom

Note: Every effort has been made to provide accurate and current Internet information in this book. However, the Internet and information posted on it are constantly changing, so it is inevitable that some of the Internet addresses listed in this textbook will change.

Part I
Contemporary Conditions

1

School Public Relations
A New Agenda

Theodore J. Kowalski

The political context of policy making is largely responsible for public relations (PR) becoming a part of school administration during the first half of the 20th century. Even in local communities, citizens often held different philosophies and expressed different needs. Consequently, administrators who wanted to remain in office attempted to garner support for their preferred policy initiatives. They did this by crafting messages carefully and communicating them selectively—techniques that they borrowed from managers in business and industry.

Unfortunately, many taxpayers continue to view PR solely as a persuasion activity even though the scope of modern practice is much broader, especially as described in the professional knowledge base. Accessing information in a timely manner, exchanging information, providing information to empower other decision makers, and using information to identify and solve problems exemplify elements of today's expanded agenda. Clearly then, the practice of PR has become increasingly more indispensable and more pervasive in administrative work, and equally important, it has become a cogent responsibility for teachers.

The primary purposes of this chapter are to explain the effects of societal and institutional change on education and to provide a foundation for exploring school public relations in depth. The discovery process begins with an analysis of differing perspectives of PR. This is followed by a discussion of the application of PR in districts and schools; applications are discussed with respect to meaning, goals, barriers, and escalating importance. The final part of the chapter explores four essential themes for modern practice:

♦ Dynamics of school reform
♦ Technology
♦ Leadership and communication
♦ Reflective practice

The first two are associated with the context in which school PR is applied; the last two focus on ideal administrative behaviors.

PERSPECTIVES OF PUBLIC RELATIONS

Unfortunately, many stakeholders, policy makers, and educators do not recognize the scope of the purposes and functions associated with school PR. These individuals usually view the process solely as a manipulative activity intended to influence opinions and feelings. Their narrow perspective misses some of the most essential elements of modern practice. As an example, information management and communication, essential elements of PR, are indispensable to organizational development—and organizational development is critical to organizational renewal. In addition, PR touches the entire communication process, both within the organization and between the organization and its ecosystems.[1]

---

[1]An ecosystem is the network of social relationships in which an organization is embedded (McElreath, 1993).

Generally speaking, public relations is a social science—though some consider it an art as well. As a profession, PR practice has not been controlled as have other professions such as law, medicine, or teaching: professions that require practitioners to complete a prescribed course of study and possess a license (Seitel, 1992). This does not mean, however, that PR specialists do not have access to a growing body of research and theory that can be used to guide practice. A growing number of universities are offering undergraduate and graduate degrees in this specialization.

The term *public relations* has many connotations. This is to be expected since it is used at varying times to describe a concept, a profession, a process, and even a goal. Further, the intended meaning may be affected by the context(s) in which it is used. For example, a large manufacturing company and a public school district are both organizations, but their missions and objectives are distinctively different. In the former, profit is critical to organizational survival, and this reality touches the structure and decision-making processes of every department in the company. The effectiveness of public schools, by contrast, is not determined by profits but rather by the extent to which services satisfy the needs and wants of stakeholders and society in general. Because of the critical nature of connotation and context, no one definition adequately and accurately conveys the complete meaning of PR. This does not infer, however, that such interpretations are unimportant.

Many scholars and practitioners continue to explore the basic question, "What is public relations?" (Gordon, 1997). The product of their inquiry has been multiple definitions indicating that the process is getting progressively broader and more complex. An understanding of PR and subsequently of school PR begins with a review of these differing perspectives.

Erroneous Perspectives

A first step to understanding public relations is to examine popular misrepresentations. The most distorted image of modern practice is that it entails nothing more than press agentry. Press agents are specialists whose work is typically confined to publicity functions; they concentrate on disseminating carefully crafted messages intended to benefit their clients (either individuals or corporations). Another common error is to treat *PR* as a synonym for *advertising* or *marketing*. Advertising, like press agentry, entails the preparation of carefully controlled messages and their transmission to the public. In the case of advertising, the messages almost always are sent through purchased mechanisms (e.g., paid ads on television or in a newspaper). Marketing, however, involves promoting, selling, or distributing a product or service. Although press agentry, advertising, and marketing are PR elements, especially in the business world, none standing alone is the equivalent of PR for at least two reasons. First, PR is broader than any of these functions, and second, many PR products are subject to media interpretation, thus they cannot be totally controlled by the issuer (Cohen, 1987). For example, one can control the content of a paid ad in a newspaper, but press releases, a common PR function, are subjected to reporter interpretation.

Another common misrepresentation is that PR is a propaganda tool. Propaganda involves creating and spreading ideas, facts, or allegations in an effort to deliberately influence public opinion. Frequently propagandists employ misinformation to manipulate opinions and actions, both in the organization and in society. Commonly the propagandist's goal is either to enhance his or her organization's image or to destroy the image of competitor organizations. In part, a proclivity to equate PR with propaganda stems largely from historical depictions of PR in its formative years. During this period, PR personnel often "played fast and loose with the truth" (Dilenschneider, 1996, p. xxi). In the current context of practice, the basic function of propaganda—to deceive through one-way communication (only disseminating information)—is not an acceptable PR practice.

Yet another misrepresentation is that *PR* is a synonym for *communication*. Commenting on this error, Haywood (1991) wrote, "Effective public relations is much more than communications: it should be more fundamental to the organization. Public relations should begin before the decision-making stage—when attitudes towards the issues are being developed by management and policies are being formulated" (p. 4). As Haywood suggests, PR is a comprehensive activity intended to influence leadership values and behaviors as well as shaping communication channels.

Multiple Definitions and Models

As noted, connotation and context largely explain why there are so many different definitions of public relations. One way to sift through them is to use a classification system. Definitions of public relations can be broadly categorized as either *descriptive* or *normative*. Descriptive definitions are intended to explain what actually occurs under the rubric of public relations. Even when these definitions are not completely accurate, they play a part in shaping a sense of reality. Gordon (1997) observed, "Many communication scholars agree that definitions are inherently rhetorical and that the formations of definitions are social processes that shape reality" (p. 58).

Descriptive definitions can be general or specific. Dilenschneider (1996), for example, concluded that in its most simple terms, PR is described as the art of influence. Another popular definition is that PR is all about communication. Greater specificity is provided in this definition that identifies the process as a "multiphased function of communication management that is involved in researching, analyzing, affecting, and reevaluating the relationships between an organization and any aspect of its environment" (Crable & Vibbert, 1986, p. 5). Descriptions of reality vary because organizational context and intent are not constant and because persons attempting to describe reality are usually affected by their biases. This is why descriptive definitions should be considered in light of conditions under which they were developed.

Normative definitions, by comparison, focus on identifying goals that describe how publics should be affected or how practitioners should behave (Grunig & Hunt, 1984). They are intended to influence practitioner values and beliefs and delineate acceptable patterns of behavior. Normative definitions focus on desired practitioner behaviors (e.g., candidness, accessibility), desired outcomes (e.g., perceptions, attitudes), or both. In recent years, efforts to create a positive image for the PR function have included the formation of ideal behaviors to serve as a moral, ethical, and professional compass for practitioners.

Organizational goals in normative definitions are usually characterized by several recurring themes. Two of them are *intent* and *relationships between the organization and its many publics*. Some writers (e.g., Lovell, 1982) stress that the general purpose of PR is to promote goodwill toward the organization; others (e.g., Lesly, 1983; McElreath, 1993) view PR as a management function intended to facilitate relationships and understanding between the organization and its ecosystems.

Although definitions of public relations have evolved to reflect the growing complexity of both the concept and its application, some of the earliest definitions still endure in the mainstream literature. Bernay's definition, constructed nearly 60 years ago, remains among the most widely referenced. It has three critical dimensions:

◆ To *inform* the public
◆ To *persuade*, that is, to modify attitudes and opinions
◆ To *integrate* the actions and attitudes of an organization with those of its publics and the actions and attitudes of its publics with those of the organization (Cohen, 1987)

In 1978, when the First World Assembly of Public Relations Associations convened in Mexico City, the participants defined public relations as "the art and social science of analyzing trends, predicting their consequences, counseling organizational leaders, and implementing planned programs of action which will serve both the organization and the public interest" (Newsom, Scott, & VanSlyke Turk, 1989, p. 6). This conceptualization promotes public relations as a core process in leadership and decision making.

Interestingly, modern definitions and descriptions almost always fail to mention *persuasion*. In large measure, this conspicuous omission is attributable to a sensitivity of the Marxist worldview that suggests anything other than a "two-way symmetrical model (in forms that attempt persuasion of others while disallowing reciprocal persuasion of self) is an agent of domination and, therefore, unethical" (Gordon, 1997, p. 62). Although there are other more acceptable perspectives of persuasion, writers have preferred to describe PR as influence (e.g., Dilenschneider, 1996).

Recognizing the problems associated with having myriad definitions, some scholars have tried to clarify the meaning of public relations by using key descriptors. Wilcox, Ault, and Agee (1992), for instance, suggested that students and practitioners focus on recurring key words to enhance their understanding. They identified six of these key words or phrases:

◆ Deliberate
◆ Planned
◆ Performance
◆ Public interest
◆ Two-way communication
◆ Management function

For purposes of school public relations, the last phrase, "management function," should be "administrative function." In this and other school administration texts, a distinction is made between "management" and "leadership." *Management* is defined as a process of implementing strategies and controlling resources (human and material) in order to achieve organizational objectives. *Leadership* is a process that focuses on the determination of organizational objectives and strategies, entails building consensus for meeting those objectives, and involves influencing others to work toward those objectives. Administration encompasses both management and leadership responsibilities and functions (Kowalski, 2003). Nevertheless, many writers, especially in business journals and texts, continue to use *management* as a synonym for *administration*.

Table 1–1 contains an analysis of key words that give meaning to PR. Several writers believe that a nexus between activities and intended outcomes facilitates comprehension of this process. An example of this normative approach, developed by Sharpe, is shown in Figure 1–1.

Public relations practice also can be examined in the context of communication indices. Grunig (1984) developed the most widely used tool for this purpose. He used two

TABLE 1–1
Key Words in Defining Public Relations

Key Word or Phrase	Meaning
Deliberate	PR does not occur by chance; it is a purposeful activity.
Planned	PR does not occur randomly; it is an organized activity.
Performance	PR is shaped and made effective by both policies and practices; process (i.e., how it is applied) is critically important.
Public interest	PR serves multiple publics including those within districts and schools and those within the community.
Two-way communication	PR extends beyond the dissemination of information to include information exchanges.
Management function	PR involves the application of resources to achieve organizational goals.

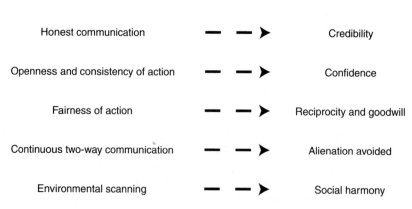

FIGURE 1–1
Sharpe's Five Links in Effective Programs (*Source:* Adapted from Seitel, 1992, p. 10)

factors, *communication direction* (pertaining to the flow of information) and *symmetry* (pertaining to intended benefits), to describe four models of public relations:

- *One-way asymmetrical.* This model is used to disseminate positive publicity and restrict unfavorable information; it is a form of propaganda associated with press agentry intended to benefit the organization.
- *One-way symmetrical.* This model is used to disseminate accurate public information without volunteering negative information; it is more neutral than press agentry and is intended to benefit both the organization and society.
- *Two-way asymmetrical.* This model is used to persuade publics, but information about publics is used to structure communication to increase the probability of influencing the behaviors of the publics (e.g., doing a community interest survey before announcing a strategy for a new building program); it is designed to benefit the organization.
- *Two-way symmetrical.* This model is used for establishing mutual understanding and resolving conflict between the organization and its publics; it requires extensive knowledge and understanding of publics and is intended to benefit both the organization and society (Dozier, 1995; Grunig, 1989).

In summary, there are multiple PR perspectives that vary primarily in two ways: describing process versus outcomes, and describing real behavior versus normative behavior. All are addressed within a framework of three recurring themes: *management, organization,* and *publics* (Gordon, 1997). That is, the concept inevitably involves an administrative function that occurs within an organization and involves contact with external publics. This relationship is illustrated in Figure 1–2.

FIGURE 1–2
Variability in Definitions of Public Relations

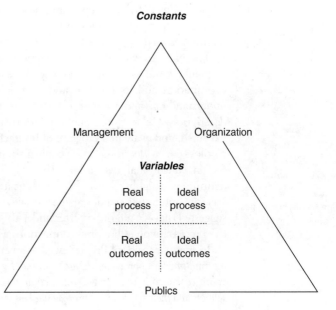

SCHOOL PUBLIC RELATIONS

School public relations refers to the application of PR in the context of organizations having the primary mission of delivering educational services. This includes public and private institutions at both the precollegiate and collegiate levels. The largest subcategory within this organizational family includes public elementary and secondary schools. School PR is examined here with respect to meaning, goals, persistent barriers, and current importance.

Meaning

Historically, education writers and practitioners have preferred to refer to school PR as "community relations." Their reasons were predominately political; that is, these individuals were reluctant to admit that educators seek to shape public opinion. Such an admission, they feared, would cause taxpayers to see them as Madison Avenue persuasion specialists (West, 1985). This fear was well founded, since many taxpayers have treated PR as "synonymous with words like cover-up, obfuscate, misinterpret, and lie" (Martinson, 1995, p. 85).

In this book, school PR is viewed as a broad and positive construct that encompasses many critical communication functions within an organization and between an organization and its ecosystems. These functions are intended to produce and maintain a positive organizational image, to ensure collaboration between school and community, and to ensure organizational effectiveness. Community relations, by comparison, is seen as both a basic PR component and a primary objective for schools.

Definitions of school PR vary in focus and length. They usually allude to using information to influence perceptions and decision making (e.g., Knezevich, 1969; Saxe, 1984) and to enhancing the relationship between the school and community through two-way communication (e.g., Jones, 1966; Lutz & Merz, 1992). Several authors have characterized school PR as both philosophy and process. Walling (1982), for instance, wrote that the concept incorporated values and beliefs about communication and embodied management techniques used by schools to communicate with their constituents.

The National School Public Relations Association (1986) defined educational PR as "a planned and systematic two-way process of communications between an educational organization and its internal and external publics designed to build morale, goodwill, understanding, and support for that organization" (p. 28). West (1985) offered this description: "Educational public relations is a systematically and continuously planned, executed, and evaluated program of interactive communication and human relations that employs paper, electronic, and people mediums to attain internal as well as external support for an educational institution" (p. 23). The focus on human relations in these two definitions is highly relevant because educational PR addresses how people feel about issues, services, and individual or organizational personalities. Alluding to this fact, Norris (1984) suggested that PR might be better understood if it were called "public relationship" because the process involves building connections with a great many different publics.

In summary, school PR is viewed as *an evolving social science and leadership process utilizing multimedia approaches designed to build goodwill, enhance the public's attitude toward the value of education, augment interaction and two-way symmetrical communication between schools and their ecosystems, provide vital and useful information to the public and employees, and serve as an integral part of the planning and decision-making functions.* Its use is justified by three major propositions cogent to all governmental agencies:

1. A democratic government is best served by a free two-way flow of ideas and accurate information so citizens and their government can make informed choices.
2. A democratic government must report and be accountable to the citizens it serves.
3. Citizens, as taxpayers, have a right to government information—but with some exceptions (exceptions to disclosing information may be predicated on laws and administrative judgments about balancing public interests with citizens' rights) (Baker, 1997, p. 456).

School PR also is influenced by the philosophical dispositions of those who exercise power and control important education decisions—for example, governors, state legislators, and school boards.

Goals

Like any administrative function, PR should be guided by goals and objectives identified in an organizational PR plan—a document that helps ensure that goals remain focused and effective. Goals represent desired ends or purposes, and they are usually broad, long-term (i.e., extending beyond 2 or 3 years), philosophical statements providing a normative perspective. In addition to the PR plan, goals also may be found in policy manuals, planning documents, and annual reports. There can be, and often is, a substantial difference between *stated* and *real* goals. For example, the policy manual in one school district states that the purposes of the PR program are to foster open communication and improve community relations, but in reality the program has focused exclusively on efforts to influence the taxpayers to support selective district initiatives.

Although the foci of a PR program may vary from institution to institution depending on contextual needs, several goals are pervasive for schools.

- ◆ *Improving the quality of education.* Every administrative, instructional, and support service provided by public education agencies has as its ultimate goal the improvement of student learning. Public relations is not an exception. All PR activities should either produce or influence activities and outcomes that contribute to improved educational services (Armistead, 2000).
- ◆ *Encouraging open political communication.* Although public employees and taxpayers expect school officials to advocate their own ideas and recommendations, they desire to be a part of open and fair debates about these ideas (Baker, 1997). Denied this opportunity, they may resort to covert political activities that further divide the community in multiple and competing interest groups. School PR should be a mechanism that allows advocates of rival ideas to express themselves via a symmetrical two-way communication system (Martinson, 1999).
- ◆ *Enhancing the image of the school or district.* Two interrelated issues summarize the importance of imaging. First, the public's confidence in elementary and secondary schools has been diminished by a multitude of negative stories appearing in the news media over the past two decades (Peck & Carr, 1997). These reports, often based on conditions in the nation's most troubled schools, have had a cumulative

effect of creating a negative image. This is especially troubling because taxpayers often exhibit a proclivity toward seeing all schools as being alike. Second, public schools are unique entities—a condition stemming from the fact that clientele, educational philosophy, needs and problems, resources, and instructional strategies are less than uniform across institutions. Imaging helps to overcome the negative effects produced by generalizations by exhibiting uniqueness and by establishing a separate identity for local districts and schools (Pfeiffer & Dunlap, 1988). Imaging also allows school officials to emphasize strengths while pointing out needs and problems.

◆ *Building support for change.* Organizational development, including school improvement, requires change. Frequently, efforts to do things differently encounter resistance, both inside (e.g., from teachers or students) and outside (e.g., from parents or pressure groups) the organization. Occasionally, opposition to change is philosophical, reflecting differences in values and beliefs. More often, however, resistance is produced by misinformation, misunderstandings, and rumors. Consequently, successful school reform almost always requires administrators to explain the need for change and to engage the public in discourse about the proposed changes. These actions allow citizens to make informed rather than emotional judgments about reform initiatives.

◆ *Managing information.* Information management is more than controlling data or determining who gets to see data. In two-way communication systems, it also includes seeking and obtaining information—from employees, students, parents, governmental agencies, other educational institutions, and the community at large. It extends to storing, analyzing, and distributing information, especially with respect to visioning, planning, and decision making.

◆ *Marketing programs.* The growing popularity of reform initiatives such as school choice, charter schools, and vouchers has prompted administrators to pay more attention to marketing. The primary characteristics of this function include creating a voluntary exchange of values, the identification of targeted audiences, and sensitivity to consumers (Kotler, 1975). Hanson (2003) noted that educational marketing involves "developing or refining *specific* school programs in response to the needs and desires of specific target-markets (e.g., 'at risk' families, parents of pre-school children, voters)" (p. 235). More generally, marketing includes building public confidence for both new and existing programs.

◆ *Establishing goodwill and a sense of ownership.* In the current political climate, a substantial number of taxpayers have a negative perception of public education. They see their relationship with these institutions as one-sided; that is, they are forced to support schools financially but receive little or nothing in return. Such negative attitudes are especially prevalent among taxpayers without children enrolled in the local schools. Public relations programs should attempt to recapture goodwill and to engage a broad base of citizens in school activities. Engaging them in open discussions and allowing them to participate in the process of making critical decisions are effective ways to rekindle a sense of collective responsibility.

◆ *Providing evaluation data.* Generating information that facilitates assessing and evaluating the organization's effectiveness is one of the most overlooked administrative functions. A well-rounded PR program facilitates this task by providing feedback from various publics. Data may be gathered formally or informally; written community surveys conducted by administrators and open telephone lines encouraging unsolicited comments exemplify common data-gathering methods.

To help ensure that PR goals are pursued, administrators develop performance objectives. These are rather specific statements containing behavioral criteria. They inform employees of expected behaviors, set benchmarks for performance, and provide a framework for summative and formative evaluations. In the case of the former, judgments are made about the amount of progress and about the necessity of adding, deleting, or altering goals. Performance objectives should be sufficiently specific to communicate behavioral expectations and to provide a basis for evaluation, but not so specific that they restrict creativity or dehumanize administrative work. Examples of possible performance objectives and their relationship to goals are shown in Table 1–2.

Persistent Barriers

Administrators often encounter myriad obstacles in trying to implement a PR program, especially in situations where this function has been very limited in the past. A first step in combating this situation is categorizing the nature of the barrier so that corrective action

TABLE 1–2

Examples of Performance Objectives for Administrators

General Goal	Possible Performance Objectives
Enhancing learning	Establish partnerships; involve parents and other citizens on curriculum committees, textbook selection committees; enlist community members as volunteers.
Communicating politically	Manage conflict; hold open discussions to debate competing views; respect minority opinions; prepare communications for multiple publics.
Enhancing image	Celebrate accomplishments; highlight strengths; provide accurate and relevant information to the media and general public.
Supporting change	Engage the public in visioning and planning activities; hold open meetings to explain planned change; provide speakers for civic groups; educate the public about the need for change and the nature of recommended changes.
Managing information	Establish procedures for obtaining, analyzing, and storing data; create channels for accessing and distributing data; provide a mechanism for storing databases.
Marketing programs	Provide information about programs to the community on a regular basis; conduct periodic needs assessments to ascertain changing conditions.
Sharing responsibility	Create school councils that include citizen representatives; create advisory councils; invite employees and the public to suggest improvements; praise successful collaboration.
Obtaining evaluation data	Conduct employee, parent, and community surveys; encourage unsolicited comments; monitor the quantity and quality of complaints, concerns, and problems.

can be taken. All efforts to change organizational operations may be curtailed by three groups of impediments:

- *Those related to understanding*—for example, individuals may not understand the true meaning of PR or they may not understand why this process is necessary for districts and schools.
- *Those related to accepting*—for example, individuals may philosophically reject the purposes of PR or its applications in districts and schools.
- *Those related to acting*—for example, the district or school may have insufficient human and material resources to implement the program (Connor & Lake, 1988).

In the case of public schools, real obstacles often span all three categories. Consequently, administrators need to recognize that educating the public to understand the purposes of PR, getting the public to accept a PR program, and finding the resources to operate the program are equally essential tasks.

Current Importance

Experts believe that schools benefit from a well-conceived PR program even in the best of times because information management and communication are incessant core activities in any organization. In troubled times, the stakes are higher because the stability or status of schools is usually threatened. Whether this peril comes from within the schools or from the wider environment, administrators are expected to protect the well-being of the institution and the interests of its stakeholders. As previously noted, several reform initiatives already have moved some public schools into a market environment in which they must compete more directly with other public or private schools. Under these conditions, organizational image, communication, marketing, and information management assume new levels of importance (Hanson, 2003).

As the future of education gets more uncertain, the PR function becomes more essential to administrative decision making, especially when the decisions involve organizational change. Two issues exemplify this reality; the first is the public's declining confidence and the second is reaching consensus about purposes, programs, and outcomes. School reform is especially difficult in a democratic society because different values and beliefs produce conflicting evaluations of effectiveness and conflicting recommendations for improvement. In this political environment, administrators are expected to educate the public on matters such as student performance and realistic alternatives for school restructuring (Lashway, 2002).

Several education writers (e.g., Berliner & Biddle, 1995; Bracey, 1997) have pointed out that misconceptions about public education have been pervasive among education's chief critics. Commenting on the seemingly endless chain of reform ideas generated during the decade following the publishing of *A Nation at Risk* in 1983, Berliner (1993) observed that schools in this country were unfairly damaged by unsubstantiated claims that public education is expensive and wasteful; that students are lazy and unproductive; and that America's productivity has fallen as a result of inadequate education. Regrettably, rebuttals to these claims frequently have not changed public opinion nor have they placed real needs in their proper context.

The public's concern with high school graduation rates during the 1990s illustrates how erroneous opinions often conceal real societal problems. At that time, many citizens believed that graduation rates were in decline when in fact they were increasing. In the mid-1990s, approximately 75 to 80% of all eligible students in this country were graduating from high school—a substantial increase over the 1950 rate of approximately 50% (Amundson, 1996). In addition to being incorrect, this conclusion distracted policy makers from framing the problem of school failure correctly. That is, policy makers failed to evaluate graduation rates in the context of prevailing social and economic conditions. Students who did not finish high school in the 1990s faced much more limited job prospects than did students in the 1950s (Schlechty, 1990). In essence, both the critics who incorrectly argued that graduation rates had declined and educators who simply corrected the record failed to frame the real dilemma facing schools and society. Because dropping out of school was more consequential in the 1990s than it was in the 1950s, even an 80% graduation rate was not acceptable.

Although most administrators recognize that responding to criticism has become an inevitable part of their practice, they often are uncertain about the best strategy for doing it. This is true for the following reasons:

♦ The critics often have substantial credibility with the public or they possess considerable political power. Elected officials, business leaders, and media representatives are prime examples.
♦ The critics often espouse positions that are politically popular. For example, they frequently blame schools for social problems but avoid blaming society for education's lack of productivity—even though pervasive problems such as poverty and child abuse unquestionably are critical variables.
♦ The critics often believe that they are standing on the high moral ground; they pretend that their positions toward school reform are unaffected by political and economic self-interests.

Amundson (1996) suggested that administrators have three choices with respect to responding to criticism, including those embedded in media coverage:

1. They could ignore the criticism. This alternative requires little risk or energy, but it usually fuels perceptions that administrators are indifferent or incompetent.
2. They could take a defensive posture. This alternative is precarious because simply refuting criticism creates the perception that administrators are denying the need for reform.
3. They could communicate openly and honestly. This alternative prompts administrators to educate the public and to enlist support and assistance in positive ways. It also is the only choice that allows administrators rather than the critics to manage the issues. Engaging the community in discussions about educational purposes, programs, and outcomes is the first step toward meaningful school renewal.

School reform is not the only issue that has elevated the importance of public relations as an element of administrative practice in the past 50 years. For example, the image of public education has been damaged by incessant conflict between teacher unions and school boards (Campbell, Corbally, & Nystrand, 1983). In addition, political and educational philosophies that divide the public—for example, conflict between the values of excellence and equity—often produce divergent and incompatible agendas for local districts. The range of contemporary conditions associated with a greater need for school PR is presented in Table 1–3.

TABLE 1–3
Selected Contemporary Conditions Intensifying the Need for Public Relations

Condition	Ramifications
Public dissatisfaction	Economic and political support for public education suffer as negative images are reinforced.
Life in an information-based society	Accessing and using information rapidly is crucial to identifying and solving problems. An organization's competitiveness is partially determined by information and communication systems.
Life in a pluralistic culture	Groups place conflicting demands on schools. School officials must be able to craft messages for targeted audiences; compromise becomes an important tool for resolving conflict.
Decentralization of governance	Efforts to reform schools from the bottom-up lead to broader participation in critical organizational functions.
Lifelong learning	Learning is no longer considered a youth activity. Administrators are expected to provide learning opportunities for employees and adult patrons.
Demographic changes	The percentage of families having children in the public schools continues to decline. Building goodwill and support require special efforts to reach taxpayers who have no direct link to the schools.
Expanded demands and shrinking resources	As demands for educational services increase, available resources either remain constant or decline. As a consequence, competition for scarce resources becomes more intense.
Market-driven reform ideas	Initiatives such as vouchers, choice, and charter schools require public schools to compete with other institutions for students.
Acceleration of change	The pace of change continues to accelerate. Organizational development entails continuous efforts to scan the environment, restate needs, and alter delivery systems.
Global economy	Expectations that schools will contribute to economic growth by adequately preparing students for the world of work are increasing.
Social and economic conditions	Because many public students are being reared in poverty conditions, greater pressures are being placed on public schools to provide medical, nutritional, psychological, and social services.
Funding concerns	As costs rise and demand for additional programs increases, administrators must spend more time competing for scarce tax dollars.
Philosophical ambiguity	School reform in the context of competing philosophies is extremely difficult. Administrators are expected to educate the public and to facilitate visioning and planning activities that involve a broad spectrum of the community.

DOMINANT THEMES

Four dominant themes frame present-day administrative practice in districts and schools (see Figure 1–3). They are school reform, technology, leadership and communication, and reflective practice. These themes are highly relevant to PR applications, and therefore, reference to them recurs throughout the book. A brief summary of each theme follows.

Dynamics of School Reform

Over the past two centuries, there have been multiple educational reform movements, each trying to answer the same fundamental questions (Parker & Parker, 1995): What are the purposes of public education? Who should pay for this service? To what extent should public education solve societal problems? The protracted effort to change schools that began in approximately 1983 is no exception.

In order to appreciate the present challenges facing administrators, one must understand how the current school reform movement has evolved. The first wave of changes occurred in early to mid-1980s. Students were the primary targets, and making them do more of what they were already doing was the dominant strategy. Laws extending the length of the school year, the length of the school day, and high school graduation requirements are prime examples of policies promulgated during this period. The same strategy of intensification mandates was used in the late 1980s as teachers and administrators were also placed in the

School Reform
Educating, involving, and listening to the public; resolving conflict over needs and wants; engaging the public in school restructuring

Technology
Acquiring and using tools that facilitate communication and information management

PR Themes for Administrators

Leadership and Communication
Facilitating cultural change through continuous two-way communication and symbolic behavior

Reflective Practice
Growing professionally by integrating theoretical knowledge and practical experiences to increase competence

FIGURE 1–3
Dominant Themes for Practice in School Public Relations

reformers' crosshairs (Hanson, 1991). During this second wave, policy makers pressured schools of education to make their programs more rigorous and they increased licensing standards, partly by requiring licensing examinations and partly by initiating new continuing education requirements.

By 1990, however, reformers faced the reality that getting tough with students and educators had produced only modest gains. In addition, their actions had only intensified the relevance of two gnawing queries: Could public schools simultaneously pursue excellence and equity? Could centralized "one size fits all" policies produce desired levels of improvement? Many reformers either began searching outside mainstream education for solutions (e.g., proposing charter schools, choice, and vouchers) or focused on redesigning the organizational structure of existing schools.

The third and current wave of school reform has included a mix of economics, philosophy, politics, and pedagogy. Underlying these strategies are two foundational beliefs. The first is that public schools will improve if they are forced to compete with other schools; vouchers, charter schools, and choice programs are indicative of this perspective. The other is that reform is likely to occur and be more effective if it is tailored to the real student needs; state deregulation and district decentralization, strategies designed to promote reform at the micro level, are indicative of this perspective (Kowalski, 2003).

Both market-based concepts forcing competition and organizational concepts stressing individualization make PR a more essential function. In the case of the former, imaging and marketing clearly are pivotal functions. In the case of the latter, administrators are required to educate the public and to engage a broad spectrum of the community in complex tasks such as visioning, planning, and evaluation. Discussing the current wave of reforms, Wadsworth (1997) concluded that reaching public consensus on change requires an ongoing planning process, leaders who listen, diverse participants, choices, and productive communication. Studies of decentralization reforms carried out in Kentucky during the early 1990s have found that communication between the school and community was critical to forging a local reform agenda (Murray, 1993). Consequently, applications of PR in schools are clearly affected by the continuing efforts to achieve school restructuring.

Technology

Because of the nature of PR activities, practitioners must continuously embrace new technologies to remain competitive and effective. Nearly 25 years ago, for example, typewriters were replaced by microcomputers, and more recently, tools such as the facsimile machine, e-mail, electronic databases, voice mail, digital copiers, and cellular telephones have affected the communication behaviors of administrators. Today, principals, superintendents, and other school leaders have the ability to access and use information very quickly.

As far back as the late 1970s, several scholars were predicting that technology would improve access to information and increase the value of information—a prediction that was not lost on organizational leaders (Lipinski, 1978). West (1981) was one of the first to articulate the public relations potential of technology in school settings. Noting how previous efforts to generate high levels of interaction between school and community had routinely failed, he predicted that technology would make a new model for practice possible. The paradigm shift he envisioned centered on a combination of communication and technorelations—a process utilizing electronic options devoid of physical contact. West warned that technology did not ensure that school and communication relations would be vastly improved. Rather, he argued that this outcome depended on the ability of administrators to use technology in a way that did not sacrifice human interaction for efficiency (West, 1985).

The potential for technology to affect school public relations is extensive. Consider the following examples:

- ◆ Amassing and maintaining extensive databases that facilitate critical functions such as strategic planning and policy development
- ◆ Producing quality visual and printed materials in limited time periods
- ◆ Conducting videoconferences
- ◆ Providing information on demand
- ◆ Developing Web sites for districts and schools
- ◆ Using cable television to broadcast meetings and other school functions
- ◆ Personalizing messages to targeted audiences

Expectations for communication between school officials and the community changed as citizens acquired their own computers and became connected to the Internet. More specifically, parents and other taxpayers now demand more information about schools and they anticipate that school officials will respond quickly to their questions, concerns, and suggestions. Today, many administrators are even evaluated formally with respect to their ability to capitalize on using technologies (Lare & Cimino, 1998).

Leadership and Communication

In this rapidly changing world, information and integrated communication programs are essential to both management and leadership functions (Caywood, 1997). Even so, the greater attention being given to organizational leadership is resulting in new role expectations for administrators. Zaleznik (1989) observed, "Communication is important to both managers and leaders, but the modes differ. Managers communicate in signals, whereas leaders prefer clearly stated messages" (p. 24). Managers are less apt to use information directly; they rely more on sending symbolic messages to others. This approach is often impersonal and derives from the belief that information is supposed to be controlled by those with legitimate authority. Leaders, by comparison, are more likely to strive for harmony between the detached nature of management and the moral dimensions of dealing with people (Sergiovanni, 2001). Put another way, leaders treat information and communication as instruments of empowerment allowing members of the school's community to collectively seek reform.

Scholars who have studied organizational change in business (e.g., Schein, 1999) and in schools (e.g., Fullan & Stiegelbauer, 1991; Hall & Hord, 2001) conclude that new ideas are likely to be rejected if they are incongruous with deeply rooted assumptions shared by the people who will be affected. These shared beliefs, values, and norms constitute a school's culture—the glue that binds people in the school together (Hanson, 2003).

Historically, management literature has treated culture as a cause and communication as an effect. That is, communicative behaviors were viewed as manifestations of culture. More recently, enlightened communication scholars have viewed the relationship between culture and communication as reciprocal. Conrad (1994) wrote, "Cultures are communicative creations. They emerge and are sustained by the communicative acts of all employees, not just the conscious persuasive strategies of upper management. Cultures do not exist separately from people communicating with one another" (p. 27). Axley (1996) described the bond between culture and communication this way: "Communication gives rise to organizational culture, which gives rise to communication, which perpetuates culture" (p. 153). This association implies that communication cannot be understood sufficiently by reducing it to a loop of linear steps or by focusing research exclusively on the transmissions between senders and receivers (Katz & Kahn, 1978). Instead, communication should be seen as a process through which organizational members express their collective inclination to coordinate beliefs, behaviors, and attitudes. Put more simply, communication is the act that people use to give meaning to their organizational lives by sharing perceptions of reality (Kowalski, 1998). A negotiated order evolves from both internal and external interactions among individuals and groups, and this interplay occurs in the informal as well as formal organization. When viewed from this social system perspective, communication is a process that shapes, transmits, and reinforces a socially constructed culture (Mohan, 1993).

If administrators are to lead others in reshaping school cultures, they must know how others perceive reality, and they must use this information to erect mutual understandings about a school's purposes and practices. This objective is unlikely to be met, however, by administrators who either intentionally or unintentionally restrict the debate of values, discourage conflict, or limit access to information (Deetz, 1992; Sarason, 1996). Nor is it likely to be met by administrators unable to communicate effectively across racial and economic lines (Walker-Dalhouse & Dalhouse, 2001).

Regrettably, managers in many organizations continue to treat information as power, and they restrict access to it as a means of protecting personal power (Burgess, 1996). Superintendents and principals who fall into this category are incapable of actualizing the primary function of transformational leadership—shaping and developing new norms in the school (Carlson, 1996). When an administrator appropriately recognizes that organization does not precede communication and becomes subsequently supported by it, he or she is more inclined to view organization as an effect of communication (Taylor, 1993). For example, structure and programs do not produce credibility and trust (essential characteristics of leaders who assume the role of change agent); rather, these qualities are erected through human interactions. Unless leaders accurately evaluate the effects of communication on underlying assumptions, and unless they properly dissect the language of a school, they probably cannot determine the extent to which culture facilitates or obstructs change.

Clearly then, school PR is inextricably tied to the need for leaders to be effective communicators. Communication is both the backbone of a successful PR program (Newsom, Scott, & VanSlyke Turk, 1989) and an indispensable tool for organizational development. Within districts and schools, the communication aspects of PR facilitate accurate understandings of culture and change; outside of districts and schools, it expands community involvement and political support for needed reform (Schlechty, 1997). As leadership becomes an increasingly important part of administration, PR and its core activities, information management and communication, become more central to best practice.

Reflective Practice

In his enlightening book, *The Reflective Practitioner,* Schön (1983) observed that technical knowledge is insufficient to resolve the problems encountered in most professions. Technical knowledge consists of "theory and technique derived from systematic, preferably scientific knowledge" (p. 3). Technical rationality is the foundation for most professions where practice evolves from a positivist philosophy (Schön, 1987). A school administrator's practice, however, is neither totally rational nor highly predictable. Consequently, theory is a valuable but fallible guide for practice. Administrators, like all other professionals, occasionally confront situations that do not fit the neat textbook examples they studied in college. But if they are inflexible or nonanalytical, they routinely apply theoretical constructs or systematic rules even though problems, needs, and other challenges are dynamic and context specific.

A problem's contextual variations are multifaceted; they may be environmental (i.e., conditions outside of the organization), organizational, or personal (i.e., conditions associated with individuals). Even slight contextual variations in a problem's conditions may diminish the effectiveness of technical knowledge. For example, a principal in a rural elementary school had found that using praise was an effective way to motivate teachers who needed to improve their performance. She had learned this technique while studying motivation theory as a graduate student, and she applied it successfully with three different teachers in the rural school. Later in her career she became principal in an affluent suburban community. When she used the same motivational approach with a teacher in that school, she was dismayed to discover that it was not effective. What caused her tried-and-true approach to fail? Was it the difference between a rural and suburban setting? Was it the teacher? Or did she do something differently? Unless the principal is able to analyze contextual variations and their ability to attenuate technical knowledge, situations such as this one are both enigmatic and stressful. Reflective practice is a concept used by professionals to deal with problems of practice, and especially those problems that defy textbook solutions. Given the nature of school administrative work, the process is anchored in a rationality that promotes reasonableness in learning through practice (Hoy, 1996).

Reflection is an acquired skill allowing you to synthesize professional knowledge (what you think will occur) and experience (what actually occurs). The process is especially valuable when outcomes do not meet your expectations based on past experiences, even when the conditions surrounding the current action are not notably unique. For the reflective practitioner, unexpected results trigger both reflection-in-action and reflection-on-action; that is, he or she thinks about the causes of the unanticipated outcomes as they are occurring and later, after the heat of the moment has dissipated. The current event is compared with past similar experiences, and the similarities and differences in contextual variables are assessed and evaluated (Kowalski, 2003). More precisely, reflection can occur in three distinct time frames: during the period when an administrator is planning an action, during the period in which the action is taken, and during the period following the action (Reitzug & Cornett, 1991).

Imagine a superintendent who must inform the media that a teacher is being dismissed for incompetence. Before he releases the information, he may reflect on (a) his previous experiences with reporters, (b) the content of his intended message, (c) potential outlets for the message, (d) potential legal ramifications, and (e) implications for relations with the teachers' union. When he actually communicates the message, questions by reporters may lead to further reflection. He may ask himself: How do I answer the questions? Should I give more information than I originally intended? After the message has been delivered, the third stage of reflection can occur as he contemplates the results and assesses the relationship between his actions and observed outcomes. Did things turn out as he had expected? If not, why not? This last stage is especially meaningful in augmenting the superintendent's professional knowledge base—that is, in determining if and how experience altered his professional convictions.

The open-ended case studies at the end of each chapter in this book provide opportunities for you to develop your reflective practice skills. By assuming the role of a practicing administrator facing PR-related problems, you have opportunities to meld the professional knowledge contained in this book with your professional and personal experiences. In so doing, you are able to plan and test alternative responses to the problems presented in the case studies.

SUMMARY

This chapter explored the meanings of public relations. Multiple perspectives were reviewed showing how definitions differ based on two primary foci: process versus outcomes and real versus normative behaviors. Virtually all PR descriptions, nevertheless, are framed by three recurring themes: *management, organization,* and *publics* (Gordon, 1997). Public relations also was identified as both an art and a science, and it was broadly defined to include goodwill, public opinion, community interaction, two-way communication, employee relations, and planning and decision making.

School PR was defined in this chapter as *an evolving social science and leadership process utilizing multimedia approaches designed to build goodwill, enhance the public's attitude toward the value of education, augment interaction and two-way symmetrical communication between schools and their ecosystems, provide vital and useful information to the public and employees, and serve as an integral part of the planning and decision-making functions.* The value of PR to modern school administration was premised on the following assumptions:

- The two-way flow of ideas and accurate information is essential to school improvement.
- School administrators are accountable to the public.
- The public has a right to information about schools.
- In a democratic society, the publics served by a school should participate in making critical decisions.

Also discussed were possible obstacles to school PR that were broadly categorized as barriers to understanding, barriers to accepting, and barriers to acting. The current importance of school PR programs was linked to changes in the social, political, legal, and economic framework of American society. These evolving conditions have made key facets of PR (e.g., public opinion, information management, and communication) integral to leadership and school renewal.

Last, four themes pertaining to the application of school public relations were summarized. They include school reform, technology, leadership and communication, and reflection. The first two addressed contextual issues; the last two addressed normative leadership behaviors.

CASE
STUDY

The New Superintendent's Plan

When Janet Ferriter became superintendent of the Boswell School District, it marked the first time this farming community had employed a female in an administrative position. The five school board members chose her for three reasons:

1. They were impressed with her self-confidence.
2. She seemed to be highly energetic and enthusiastic.
3. She believed that the community should be highly involved in the schools.

During her employment interview, Dr. Ferriter said that the relationship between the school district and the community should be based on mutual trust and shared responsibility. She added that the community should have input into all major decisions. Rather than asking her to define "community input," the board members concluded that she was referring to their involvement as the community's elected representatives in district governance.

Shortly after becoming superintendent, Dr. Ferriter was surprised to learn that communication between school district personnel and the community had been very limited. The only media coverage the district received was provided by a newspaper and a radio station located about 25 miles away in the county seat. Reporters attended only a few board meetings each year, usually when agenda items were potentially controversial. The district did not publish a newsletter and there were no pamphlets or brochures. Student handbooks and occasional letters written by principals to parents were the only official documents provided by the district's administrators. Dr. Ferriter also observed that communication within the school district relied primarily on informal channels that had been developed by the employees. One principal commented to her, "This is a small town. Before any official message is distributed, everyone already has the information."

After examining what had been done to enhance school-community relations in the past, the superintendent assumed that the board shared her concern about the limited amount of communication that had occurred. Moreover, she was convinced that the board's positive reactions to her interview statements about community involvement constituted a clear signal that she was expected to improve the situation.

Over the next 7 months, Dr. Ferriter, with input from the district's five other administrators, developed a PR plan that was to be presented to the school board for their approval. The plan's primary goals were to improve communication and to increase community participation in the district. Specific initiatives included the following:

1. A public relations advisory committee—consisting of three teachers, two administrators, and these patrons—was to be formed. The committee's primary responsibilities were to oversee implementation of the PR plan, to evaluate outcomes, and to recommend improvements to the superintendent.
2. District administrators were to create several formal channels that would encourage two-way communication between district employees and patrons.
3. The formal channel for communication among district employees would be redesigned and e-mail would be encouraged as the preferred medium for internal two-way communication.
4. The superintendent would be responsible for publishing a monthly school district newsletter.
5. Principals would be encouraged to develop school newsletters that would be published at least once each semester.
6. District officials would conduct an opinion survey among district residents annually; the purpose would be to obtain information for strategic planning and specific projects that may evolve.
7. The PR committee's chairperson would make a verbal report to the school board every other month.

The superintendent projected that implementation of the plan would cost about $63,000 in the first year.

The PR plan was presented to the school board 5 days before the May board meeting, and approval of the plan was placed on the meeting's agenda under new business. The document was called, "A Public Relations Plan for the Boswell School District." Although Dr. Ferriter had told the board that she was working on such a plan way back in January, she had not really disclosed any of the goals and objectives prior to distributing it in preparation for the May meeting.

Dan Jackson, board president, called Dr. Ferriter the day before the board meeting and suggested that there might be some concerns voiced about the plan at the meeting. He added that there might be a motion to table the matter. The superintendent was surprised and disappointed. She explained that approval of the plan was essential so that implementation funds could be placed in the next fiscal-year budget. Jackson suggested that the item remain on the agenda so that it could be discussed openly at the board meeting.

When the superintendent presented the plan to the board for approval, silence fell over the meeting room. Jackson indicated that a motion and a second were necessary to place the item on the table for discussion. His comment prompted two board members to comply. Then Jackson spoke again.

"Well, I'll go first. This plan has some real good ideas and I appreciate all the work Dr. Ferriter did to put it together. Nevertheless, the plan is going to cost quite a bit of money—and I'm not sure this is where we should be spending our dollars."

Wilbur Stines, a farmer who was serving his fourth consecutive term on the board, spoke next. He agreed with Jackson's comments and voiced another objection.

"I have to tell you, Ms. Ferriter. I don't see any reason why tax dollars should be spent on public relations. We're not Sears or General Motors. People here know we have a fine school system. We don't need to spend their money to convince them of that."

The superintendent sat silently hoping that one of the board members would take a different position. Her hopes were raised when Ella Chambers asked to be recognized next. Chambers owned a restaurant in Boswell and she had been Dr. Ferriter's most vocal supporter.

"Janice, I think you have some great ideas here, but I don't think there is much chance people in this community are going to support allocating over $60,000 for public relations. First of all, many of them think schools don't have any business getting involved in this function. And second, this district has a pretty good image already."

The other two board members also made comments indicating that they were unlikely to vote for approval. One of them raised yet another concern. He indicated that the superintendent's plan ignored the fact that the board members already were selected to represent the community. He saw no need to appoint other patrons to district committees.

Dr. Ferriter waited until all the board members had commented before speaking.

"This plan has two important goals—improving communication and increasing community involvement. When I arrived in Boswell last July, I studied what had occurred in these two areas. Based on my observations, I moved forward to develop the plan with the assistance of the other administrators. I know that the cost seems high, but these are important goals. I ask all of you to take another look at the plan and to talk to your neighbors to see what they think. Therefore, I respectfully request that this matter be tabled until the July meeting."

Chambers asked to be recognized. "Mr. Jackson, I move to table this matter for at least 6 months. It is clear that it will not be approved for the next fiscal year, so let's take our time and study this matter in greater detail." The motion was approved unanimously.

After the board meeting ended, the superintendent sat alone in her office trying to figure out what went wrong. She jotted down several questions:

- Did I use the right approach in presenting the program?
- Should I have been more aggressive in stressing the need for the program?
- Should I have talked to individual board members about the program before formally presenting it to them?
- Should I just forget about the program and move on to something else?
- Is there any chance that the board will ever approve the program?

QUESTIONS AND SUGGESTED ACTIVITIES

CASE STUDY

1. Using the categories for barriers presented in this chapter, how would you classify the board's unwillingness to approve the PR plan?
2. Is it possible for the board members to be *for* better school-community relations and *against* PR? Why or why not?
3. The PR plan was developed by the superintendent with input from other administrators. Would it have been beneficial to involve others in the planning process? If so, who?

4. If the school district already has a positive image as claimed by the board members, is a PR plan really necessary? Why or why not?
5. If the superintendent had identified the plan as a community relations initiative, would the board have reacted differently in your opinion? Why or why not?
6. Is the superintendent's PR plan overly ambitious?
7. What changes might make the plan acceptable to the board members?
8. If you were the superintendent, would you continue to fight for the plan's approval? Why or why not?

CHAPTER

9. Definitions of public relations and school public relations are broadly categorized as descriptive or normative. Why is it important for school administrators to understand both?
10. This chapter identified and explained three categories of potential barriers to school public relations (understanding, accepting, acting). Provide two examples of obstacles in each category.
11. How has transition from a manufacturing era to an information age affected citizen expectations about exchanging information with their social institutions?
12. What potential problems are associated with using modern technologies for communication?
13. Four models of public relations based on symmetry and communication direction were discussed in this chapter. Which of these models is most desirable for the modern school administration? Which is least desirable?
14. What conditions have spawned expectations that school administrators be leaders as well as managers? What role does communication play in leadership?
15. What is reflective practice? Why is the process important for professional practice in PR?

SUGGESTED READINGS

Armistead, L. (2000). Public relations: Harness your school's power. *High School Magazine, 7*(6), 24–27.

Ashbaugh, C. R., & Kasten, K. (1993). Educating the reflective school leader. *Journal of School Leadership, 3*(2), 152–164.

Cannon, C. L., & Barham, F. E. (1993). Are you and your public polls apart? *Executive Educator, 15*(10), 41–42.

Cutlip, S. M. (1994). *The unseen power: Public relations, a history.* Hillsdale, NJ: Lawrence Erlbaum Associates.

Decker, L. E. (2001). Allies in education. *Principal Leadership, 2*(1), 42–46.

Eisentadt, D. (1994). After the ball: High-tech PR in the no-nonsense '90s. *Public Relations Quarterly, 39*(2), 23–25.

Flynn, P. D. (2002). School public relations and the principalship: An interview with Steven Mulvenon. *Journal of School Public Relations, 23*(1), 14–18.

Goble, N. (1993). School-community relations: New for the '90s. *Education Digest, 59*(4), 45–48.

Gordon, J. C. (1997). Interpreting definitions of public relations: Self-assessment and a symbolic interactionism-based alternative. *Public Relations Review, 23*(1), 57–66.

Hart, A. W. (1993). Reflection: An instructional strategy in educational administration. *Educational Administration Quarterly, 29*(3), 339–363.

Holiday, A. E. (1994). The ultimate guide to school community relations. *Journal of Educational Public Relations, 15*(4), 3–16.

Kowalski, T. J., & Wiedmer, T. (1994). A study of public relations practices in school districts. *Journal of Educational Public Relations, 60*(1), 21–29.

Lashley, J. E. (1989). Attitude and communication build public relations. *NASSP Bulletin, 73*(513), 34–35.

Leverett, L. (1999). Connecting the disconnected. *School Administrator, 56*(8), 18–22.

Loveless, T. (1997). The structure of public confidence in education. *American Journal of Education, 105*(2), 127–159.

Martinson, D. (1995). School public relations: Do it right or don't do it at all! *Contemporary Education, 66*(2), 82–85.

Ramsey, S. A. (1993). Issues management and the use of technologies in public relations. *Public Relations Review, 19*(3), 261–275.

Reigeluth, C. M. (1999). Visioning public education in America. *Educational Technology, 39*(5), 50–55.

Sparks, S. D. (1993). Public relations: Is it dangerous to use the term? *Public Relations Quarterly, 38*(3), 27–28.

Sweetland, S. R., & Cybulski, T. G. (2002). School public relations and the principalship: An interview with Joseph Murphy. *Journal of School Public Relations, 23*(1), 7–13.

VanMeter, E. J. (1993). Setting new priorities: Enhancing the school-community relations program. *NASSP Bulletin, 77*(554), 22–27.

REFERENCES

Amundson, K. (1996). *Telling the truth about America's public schools.* Arlington, VA: American Association of School Administrators.

Armistead, L. (2000). Public relations: Harness your school's power. *High School Magazine, 7*(6), 24–27.

Axley, S. R. (1996). *Communication at work: Management and the communication-intensive organization.* Westport, CT: Quorum Books.

Baker, B. (1997). Public relations in government. In C. L. Caywood (Ed.), *The handbook of strategic public relations and integrated communication* (pp. 453–480). New York: McGraw-Hill.

Berliner, D. C. (1993). Education's present misleading myths undermine confidence in one of America's most cherished institutions. *Journal of Educational Public Relations, 15*(2), 4–11.

Berliner, D. C., & Biddle, B. J. (1995). *The manufactured crises: Myths, fraud and the attack on America's public schools.* Reading, MA: Addison-Wesley.

Bracey, G. (1997). *Setting the record straight: Responses to misconceptions about public education in the United States.* Alexandria, VA: Association for Supervision and Curriculum Development.

Burgess, J. C. (1996). *Corporate culture: Friend or foe of change?* Paper presented at the Academy of Human Resource Development, Minneapolis.

Campbell, R. F., Corbally, J. E., & Nystrand, R. O. (1983). *Introduction to educational administration* (6th ed.). Boston: Allyn & Bacon.

Carlson, R. V. (1996). *Reframing and reform: Perspectives on organization, leadership, and school change.* New York: Longman.

Caywood, C. L. (1997). The future of integrated communications and public relations. In C. L. Caywood (Ed.), *The handbook of strategic public relations and integrated communication* (pp. 564–566). New York: McGraw-Hill.

Cohen, P. M. (1987). *A public relations primer: Thinking and writing in context.* Upper Saddle River, NJ: Prentice Hall.

Connor, P., & Lake, L. (1988). *Managing organizational change.* New York: Praeger.

Conrad, C. (1994). *Strategic organizational communication: Toward the twenty-first century* (3rd ed.). Fort Worth, TX: Harcourt Brace College Publishers.

Crable, R. E., & Vibbert, S. L. (1986). *Public relations as communication management.* Edina, MN: Bellwether Press.

Deetz, S. A. (1992). *Democracy in an age of corporate colonization: Developments in communication and the politics of everyday life.* Albany: State University of New York Press.

Dilenschneider, R. L. (1996). Public relations: An overview. In R. L. Dilenschneider (Ed.), *Public relations handbook* (pp. xix–xxix). Chicago: The Dartnell Corporation.

Dozier, D. M. (with L. A. Grunig & J. E. Grunig). (1995). *Manager's guide to excellence in public relations and communication management.* Mahwah, NJ: Lawrence Erlbaum Associates.

Fullan, M. G., & Stiegelbauer, S. (1991). *The new meaning of educational change* (2nd ed.). New York: Teachers College Press.

Gordon, J. C. (1997). Interpreting definitions of public relations: Self-assessment and a symbolic interactionism-based alternative. *Public Relations Review, 23*(1), 57–66.

Grunig, J. E. (1984). Organizations, environments, and models of public relations. *Public Relations Research and Education, 1,* 6–29.

Grunig, J. E. (1989). Symmetrical presuppositions as a framework for public relations theory. In C. H. Botan (Ed.), *Public relations theory* (pp. 17–44). Hillsdale, NJ: Lawrence Erlbaum Associates.

Grunig, J. E., & Hunt, T. (1984). *Managing public relations.* New York: Holt, Rinehart and Winston.

Hall, G. E., & Hord, S. M. (2001). *Implementing change: Patterns, principles, and problems.* Boston: Allyn & Bacon.

Hanson, E. M. (1991). Educational restructuring in the USA: Movements of the 1980s. *Journal of Educational Administration, 29*(4), 30–38.

Hanson, E. M. (2003). *Educational administration and organizational behavior* (5th ed.). Boston: Allyn & Bacon.

Haywood, R. (1991). *All about public relations* (2nd ed.). New York: McGraw-Hill.

Hoy, W. K. (1996). Science and theory in the practice of educational administration: A pragmatic perspective. *Educational Administration Quarterly, 32*(3), 366–378.

Jones, J. J. (1966). *School public relations.* New York: Center for Applied Research in Education.

Katz, D., & Kahn, R. (1978). *The social psychology of organizations* (2nd ed.). New York: John Wiley.

Knezevich, S. J. (1969). *Administration of public education* (2nd ed.). New York: Harper & Row.

Kotler, P. (1975). *Marketing for nonprofit organizations.* Upper Saddle River, NJ: Prentice Hall.

Kowalski, T. J. (1998). The role of communication in providing leadership for school restructuring. *Mid-Western Educational Researcher, 11*(1), 32–40.

Kowalski, T. J. (2003). *Contemporary school administration* (2nd ed.). Boston: Allyn & Bacon.

Lare, D., & Cimino, E. (1998). Not by print alone. *American School Board Journal, 185*(12), 40–41.

Lashway, L. (2002). The accountability challenge. *Principal, 81*(3), 14–16.

Lesly, P. (1983). The nature and role of public relations. In P. Lesly (Ed.), *Lesly's public relations handbook* (3rd ed., pp. 3–13). Upper Saddle River, NJ: Prentice Hall.

Lipinski, A. J. (1978). Communicating the future. *Futures, 10*(2), 126–127.

Lovell, R. P. (1982). *Inside public relations.* Boston: Allyn & Bacon.

Lutz, F. W., & Merz, C. (1992). *The politics of school/community relations.* New York: Teachers College Press.

Martinson, D. L. (1995). School public relations: Do it right or don't do it at all. *Contemporary Education, 66*(2), 82–85.

Martinson, D. L. (1999). School public relations: The public isn't always right. *NASSP Bulletin*, 83(609), 103–109.

McElreath, M. P. (1993). *Managing systematic and ethical public relations*. Madison, WI: WCB Brown & Benchmark.

Mohan, M. L. (1993). *Organizational communication and cultural vision: Approaches and analysis*. Albany: State University of New York Press.

Murray, G. J. (1993). KERA and community linkages. *Equity and Excellence in Education, 26*(3), 65–68.

National School Public Relations Association. (1986). *School public relations: The complete book*. Arlington, VA: Author.

Newsom, D., Scott, A., & VanSlyke Turk, J. (1989). *This is PR: The realities of public relations* (4th ed.). Belmont, CA: Wadsworth.

Norris, J. S. (1984). *Public relations*. Upper Saddle River, NJ: Prentice Hall.

Parker, F., & Parker, B. J. (1995). A historical perspective on school reform. *Educational Forum, 59*(3), 278–287.

Peck, K. L., & Carr, A. A. (1997). Restoring public confidence in schools through systems thinking. *International Journal of Educational Reform, 6*(3), 316–323.

Pfeiffer, I. L., & Dunlap, J. B. (1988). Advertising practices to improve school–community relations. *NASSP Bulletin, 72*(506), 14–17.

Reitzug, U. C., & Cornett, J. W. (1991). Teacher and administrator thought: Implications for administrator training. *Planning and Changing, 21*(3), 181–192.

Sarason, S. B. (1996). *Revisiting the culture of the school and the problem of change*. New York: Teachers College Press.

Saxe, R. W. (1984). *School–community relations in transition*. Berkeley, CA: McCutchan.

Schein, E. H. (1999). *The corporate culture survival guide: Sense and nonsense about culture change*. San Francisco: Jossey-Bass.

Schlechty, P. C. (1990). *Schools for the 21st century: Leadership imperatives for educational reform*. San Francisco: Jossey-Bass.

Schlechty, P. C. (1997). *Inventing better schools: An action plan for educational reform*. San Francisco: Jossey-Bass.

Schön, D. A. (1983). *The reflective practitioner*. New York: Basic Books.

Schön, D. A. (1987). *Educating the reflective practitioner*. San Francisco: Jossey-Bass.

Seitel, F. P. (1992). *The practice of public relations* (5th ed.). New York: Macmillan.

Sergiovanni, T. J. (2001). *The principalship: A reflective practice perspective* (4th ed.). Boston: Allyn & Bacon.

Taylor, J. R. (1993). *Rethinking the theory of organizational communication: How to read an organization*. Norwood, NJ: Ablex.

Wadsworth, D. (1997). Building a strategy for successful public engagement. *Phi Delta Kappan, 78*(10), 749–752.

Walker-Dalhouse, D., & Dalhouse, A. D. (2001). Parent-school relations: Communicating more effectively with African American parents. *Young Children, 56*(4), 75–80.

Walling, D. R. (1982). *Complete book of school public relations: An administrator's manual and guide*. Upper Saddle River, NJ: Prentice Hall.

West, P. T. (1981). Imagery and change in the twenty-first century. *Theory into Practice, 20*(4), 229–236.

West, P. T. (1985). *Educational public relations*. Beverly Hills, CA: Sage Publications.

Wilcox, D., Ault, P., & Agee, W. (1992). *Public relations: Strategies and tactics* (3rd ed.). New York: HarperCollins.

Zaleznik, A. (1989). *The managerial mystique: Restoring leadership in business*. New York: Harper & Row.

2

Changes in Society and Schools

Thomas Glass

"The need for community is universal. A sense of belonging, continuity, of being connected to others and to ideas and values that make our lives meaningful and significant. . . ."

Thomas Sergiovanni, 1994, p. xiii

Problems confronting educational leaders are a complex mix of political, social, and economic topics that exist in schools and in society. For example, employee unionization and the development of technology exemplify internal developments; a loss of community and the decline of the traditional family structure are evolving external conditions. These matters are central to the practice of administration because they reflect the reality that society and the public schools are inextricably intertwined. Despite this fact, school administrators for much of the 20th century were guided by management principles that considered democratic administration inefficient.

Today, however, the practice of school administration is focused on both leadership and management. Principals and superintendents are not only expected to manage resources, they also are counted on to facilitate key decisions about institutional directions. This broader role obligates them to have a deeper understanding of society, organizational behavior, and communication; it also requires them to use information to identify and solve problems that prevent schools from making necessary improvements.

This chapter explores several topics that are axial to the relationship between society and schools. They are broadly divided into two parts: those relating to society and those relating more directly to schools. These conditions set the context for contemporary applications of school public relations.

SOCIETAL CHANGE

The demographic profile of the typical public school student has changed considerably in the last 50 years. As an example, the population in many cities and towns has become increasingly diverse. In addition, more children are now living in poverty, more come from one-parent families, and more come to school with emotional, physical, and psychological problems. Despite such realities, some would-be reformers continue to blame only the public schools for the nation's educational problems. Moreover, these critics contend that districts and schools should be able to make themselves more productive without additional political and economic support. Such denials of social and economic dimensions of public education serve to limit reasonable reform efforts, and they perpetuate the myth that schools are basically detached from society.

Community and Government

No period in history has witnessed such dramatic and sweeping changes in the basic context of society than the second half of the 20th century. In the early 1900s, American communities were nearly all rural, with many being so tiny and isolated that families had to depend on one another for essentials. These small and detached communities were usually without electricity, telephones, paved roads, automobiles, and regular mail delivery. For the most part, these communities remained static from the first decades of the 19th century to the Industrial Revolution.

Today, by contrast, most Americans live in urban or suburban settings that have been shaped substantially by the industrial and technological products of the 20th century—products such as automobiles, trains, airplanes, radio, television, computers, and biotechnology. In the 21st century, even fewer American households are located in rural communities and many families remaining in these settings are apt to face the harsh realities of poverty. That is, they will be living in impoverished areas such as Appalachia, the Rio Grande valley, or on Native American reservations.

A loss of community has been apparent in all types of cities and towns ranging from America's great cities to affluent suburbs. Consider contemporary conditions in relation to those that existed just several decades ago. The feeling of belonging—not only to a nuclear family group but also to a communitywide extended family—is no longer a positive social experience for America's children. In today's typical suburban environment, neighbors do not have *interlocking* relationships. Few families have social ties that bind them to other families in their neighborhoods; neighbors usually do not attend the same church, belong to the same clubs, shop at the same stores, share the same recreation activities, or work for the same employer. Often, the only common social experience in suburbia is public education, and reform-related ideas such as vouchers and charter schools may eradicate this unifying characteristic in the future.

The decline of *community* between and within social institutions, such as the church and the extended family, has resulted in significant changes in local government and schooling. Although the erosion of community life has had subtle effects on most schools, its impact on American politics has been visible and pronounced. Consider, for example, the traditional small rural community. In the first half of the 20th century, political participation was usually inclusive, allowing citizens to voice opinions and to participate directly in community decisions. Today, this form of participative democracy is found only in select parts of the country, for example, in sectors of rural New England. Factors such as substantial population growth and a loss of community have contributed to the development of *representative* democracy. Consequently, a few officials may represent thousands or hundreds of thousands of citizens. This growing social distance between politicians and citizens is perhaps one of the most serious challenges facing contemporary American democracy and the local control of public education. At a time when many citizens suffer from a detachment from community life, they also feel increasingly alienated from their government.

Community and Schools

Creation of secure and nurturing communities should be a key goal for America in the 21st century, since it can hardly be argued that children in vibrant and cohesive communities do not do well in school. Even though the critics of education are correct in asserting that the nation's children are much of its future, they are incorrect in suggesting that only schools determine whether children become productive citizens. Seldom do large numbers of students achieve academically when they live in environments saturated with crime, poverty, and social upheaval. Children, more so than others, need strong and purposeful communities providing them human and social capital (Sergiovanni, 1994). This fact is especially evident when one correctly defines educational success broadly rather than basing success solely on a single criterion, such as standardized test scores.

Current economic and political trends are creating a bipolar nation in which the rich and poor are increasingly separated. Instead of recognizing the obvious relationship between human capital level and social and economic attainment, many critics of public education have demanded that schools become the economic leveling force in society (Becker, 1993). In essence, the critics ignore the fact that living in poverty seriously restricts a student's ability to learn.

Whether America's schools can meet myriad challenges in the 21st century depends on both the nation's political and educational leaders. Both groups must envision and pursue reform that addresses multiculturalism and poverty, and they must do so in a manner that integrates the community and school. At the beginning of the 21st century, nearly 12% of the nation's school children were attending school in 1 of the 12 largest urban districts (National Center for Education Statistics [NCES], 2001). Nearly half of these children live below the poverty line (Stratton, 1995, p. 10), and a surprising number of them will be members of homeless families (Blau, 1992).

Those who study contemporary American communities constantly note that the vanishing extended family, the destruction of social networks, and the lack of participative democracy have had a negative effect on social institutions such as the school. Until the nation's political leaders reach consensus on how to socially balance economics in America, and until the critics of education accept the fact that both schools and communities need to be reformed, the likelihood of quality schooling for the increasing number of poor children will probably not occur. If larger numbers of children living in poverty are not successfully prepared for adulthood, the cities and towns in which they live can be expected to continue their decline.

The Changing Family

The foundation of the American school system is both in the community and the family. The community provides a broad base of support, and the family provides the day-to-day interaction with the school. The quality of community support and the family resources a student brings to school influence whether the school and the students are successful. In 2000, approximately 4 of every 10 public school students were members of an identifiable minority group. A majority of these students lived in families with minimal fiscal resources (NCES, 2001). Most lived in communities with few resources to support after-school social and learning activities.

As communities changed in the 1990s, so did family groups. In 1995, 25% of the nation's children under the age of 18 lived in single-parent households; in 1970, only 11% did so. For African American children, the percentage living in single-parent homes during the mid-1990s was an alarming 60%, for Hispanic children it was 29%, and for White children it was only 11% (NCES, 1997).

Poverty is also a major concern. Consider the following statistics:

- In 1995, one out of five American children under the age of 18 was a member of a poverty-level family.
- In 2000, 36% of public school children qualified for free or reduced lunch (NCES, 2001).
- African American and Hispanic children were in 1995, and still are today, more than twice as likely as White children to live in poverty (NCES, 1997).
- In 1995, 42% of African American and 39% of Hispanic children lived in families classified as being below the national poverty level (NCES, 1997). A majority of these children resided in large urban school districts that have been primary targets of school reform in the 1990s. Many of these districts, such as Los Angeles, Chicago, and Boston, have shown some achievement gains, but in general, millions of minority children living in impoverished families still fall well below national averages on standardized tests.
- A disproportionate number of minority students constitute the 12% of American students participating in special education programs (NCES, 2001).

High school dropout rates in urban school districts such as Chicago are nearly 50%. Many thousands of urban adolescents join street gangs and participate in criminal activity ("By the Numbers," 1998). Many more thousands of dropouts have no jobs or jobs at minimal wages in perhaps the fast-food industry (Hill & Celio, 1998).

Many social researchers claim that a new *social underclass* developed during the 1990s and this underclass is separate from the traditional definition of *lower class* (Jencks & Peterson, 1991). Sociologists such as Wilson (1997) claim that many millions of Americans lack the job and social skills to ever function successfully (to hold a job) in society. This division of the traditional lower class into an underclass further illustrates the drift of American society into the "haves" and "have-nots" clearly visible today in both urban and rural America.

The primary importance of the rapid growth of an *economic underclass* to schools is that a significant percentage of those in this category are students (Jencks & Phillips, 1998). This is especially cogent because underclass families provide children very few financial, emotional, and educational resources. Lower income families always have struggled to provide resources to their children that would allow them to successfully compete against peers from higher income families. Today, however, the numbers have swelled, and now millions of underclass families are unable to provide adequately for their children (Mayer, 1997). Most troublesome is the fact that this condition exists at a time when major efforts are being made to reduce all forms of social welfare—even those that provide bare essentials such as food and clothing. In the inner cities, an intricate mix of economic and social issues affects the condition of the family. Wilson (1997), for example, concludes that many urban males avoid marriage and family responsibilities for both social and economic reasons.

Accompanying an increase in the number of children living in poverty and in single-parent households have been changes in the ways that Americans parent their children. Some recent studies highlight the popular media claim that average American parents talk or interact with their child only 17 waking hours per week. Add to this the influence of television watching, Internet browsing, organized activities (many school sponsored), and peer group clustering outside the home (e.g., at shopping malls), and it becomes readily apparent that traditional family activities are becoming rare. Consequently, many children do not learn how to be productive family members or members of any functional social group. Just as American society is bifurcated along social and economic lines, so is it divided on the basis of parenting. Americans born after 1970 fall into one of two groups: those who grew up with a father and those who did not. Many in the former group bene-fited from psychological, social, educational, and moral assistance provided by a male par-ent; most in the latter group had to depend entirely on a female parent who often worked outside the home. The decline of patrimony is due largely to the devaluation of nuclear family life. Those who have studied this problem conclude that the depreciation of fatherhood is a ticking social time bomb. For example, children from fatherless homes have been found to be both less productive in school and responsible for a high percentage of criminal behavior (Blankenhorn, 1995).

Few contemporary families fit the image of the traditional American family—one that consists of a working father and a stay-at-home mother and two or three children. As a result, many children do not eat family meals, attend church activities, visit relatives, and engage in family recreation. The Norman Rockwell family portrait represented the value of what Americans thought the family *should* be like. Family structure is important because it has a profound influence on preparing children to learn, supporting their learning activities, and providing a moral compass for social behavior. It also influences what public schools are able to do.

For much of the last half of the 20th century, for example, educators were asked to assume many of the traditional responsibilities previously held by the family and church. Sex education, alcohol and drug education, character education, health education, and preschool education are just a few examples of evolving responsibilities that take teachers and administrators away from teaching the basic subjects that form the base for current high-stakes testing programs mandated by nearly every state.

Educational achievement also is affected by the extent to which children have their needs met within the family unit. Some social psychologists have noted that parenting practices have changed subtly over the past few decades. Some families are generally clas-sified as *child centered*, meaning that their resources are focused on the needs of children. Most middle-class American families are in this group. Many other families, however, are viewed as being *adult centered*. In this category, priority is given to using available resources to satisfy adult needs. Parents in these typically lower class or underclass families have great difficulty just coping with day-to-day necessities (e.g., food, rent, and clothing). Children in these families are commonly pushed to the rear; they are not provided structure, behavioral expectations, health care, and skills needed to be successful in school (Jencks & Phillips, 1998). Often these families are dysfunctional, producing physically and emotionally abused children (Stratton, 1995).

Although educators have long recognized the nexus between poverty and achievement, they have been less cognizant of research that links educational achievement to parenting style and even peer group values (Steinberg, 1996). Some studies, for instance, indicate that children, regardless of ethnic or economic or family background, parented in either an *authoritative* or *responsive* style, typically do much better in school than children raised in either an *autocratic* or *laissez-faire* parenting mode (Steinberg). In other words, these studies conclude that positive parenting can often overcome some of the debilities of poverty and discrimination.

CHANGES IN SCHOOLS

Contrary to popular thought, there have been many changes in public education during the last half of the 20th century. Most, however, have been the products of fated interactions between schools and society rather than the products of purposeful planning. Consider the following examples:

♦ *Altered political environments.* Politics arguably has been a part of public education since the inception of this institution; the process has been intensified significantly in the last 50 years. As a result, school administrators are often caught in the crossfire of competing interests. The unionization of teachers and other employees provides an excellent example; a superintendent is expected to represent the interests of taxpayers and the school board while maintaining positive relationships with employees.

♦ *Intervention of the courts.* Litigation has become a common means for resolving serious conflict in education. Consequently, the role of the courts in setting policy has become greater. Decisions involving taxation, district spending, student discipline, and personnel administration exemplify the manner in which the nation's legal system has played a prominent role in shaping current policy and regulations. A significant legal related issue has been school safety. Incidents of in-school shootings and violence have brought daily police presence to many schools. A near national obsession with security has created in many schools an almost lockdown environment with locked doors, security badges, and metal detectors.

♦ *Scientific developments.* Since the early 1980s, schools have had to spend immense sums of money for technology. The infusion of the computer into instructional environments has had a dramatic effect on the teaching-learning process.

Alterations such as these reshape the institutional context for school administration. Thus, the practitioner needs to understand both the nature of this institution and how its structure continues to evolve.

The Unique Position of Public Education

The local school district is one of the very few remaining political institutions unprotected from direct citizen influence. For example, angry taxpayers can usually voice their discontent directly to board members, and their grievances are more likely to generate attention and action. This condition is especially noteworthy in multicultural settings where two conditions contribute to conflict and political interventions:

1. Citizens often vehemently disagree with each other over the role of school prayer, sex education, teaching of reading, bilingual programs, and how much public money is to be spent supporting public education (Spring, 1998).
2. Board members often are elected because of support from racial, ethnic, or political groups. Accordingly, they are politically responsive to the agendas of these groups (Kowalski, 1999).

In many states, a school-related referendum is the only opportunity citizens have to participate directly in tax decisions. Theoretically, decisions in the public economy are to be made by representatives of the community who are expected to make decisions in the best interests of all who are affected (Fowler, 2000). But unlike decisions made by Congress, state legislatures, or even large-city councils, those promulgated by school boards are usually subjected to the personal interests of stakeholders. This is because school board members typically represent smaller constituencies. It is also because the percentage of households having school-age children in many communities, both suburban and rural, is less than 30% (Stratton, 1995, p. 18). Nonparent taxpayers not only are prone to vote against proposed tax increases, but they are also becoming increasingly active in trying to influence school board members and fellow citizens on fiscal and related policy matters. About the only districts in which most taxpayers remain parents are those in the inner cities. In these settings, inadequate resources are often associated with opposition to higher taxes from large property owners and low voter participation in school referenda.

Even though local school boards have become increasingly vulnerable to political interventions, this concept of local government appears secure (Flinchbaugh, 1993); their legitimate function has changed very little since 1920. Some role modifications, however, appear likely to happen in the first decades of the 21st century. Increasing levels of cultural diversity and increased political interventions are prompting a reconsideration of primary responsibilities. For example, school board members may be more effective devoting their time and energy to functions such as visioning and planning. As representatives of the community, they are probably in the best position to bring different factions together to reach consensus about the purposes of public education. Focusing more on policy and less on the day-to-day operations, however, will require most board members to spend less time with fiscal management and parental concerns. In this vein, local boards will function more as policy boards. By capitalizing on their access to participative democracy, they could be the glue that unifies and holds together diverse communities (Danzberger, Kirst, & Usdan, 1992). The evolution of local boards from political to policy entities heightens the need for accurate and timely communication between the school and its wider environment.

Condition of Public Schools

The most apparent changes that have occurred recently in schools relate to people (students, employees) and programs (curricula, scope of extracurricular activities). Students are not only far more diverse than they were just 30 years ago, their educational needs have been revised by America's transition to an information age. Although today's student will live and work in an ever-changing world, their educational experiences often do not reflect this fact. For example, too many schools still place far more emphasis on rote learning than they do on teaching children to access and use information to solve problems. Enrollment in America's elementary and secondary schools is expected to increase well into the 21st century. In 1995, there were 36.8 million public school children and in 2000 some 47 million (NCES, 2001). The U.S. Department of Education projects that by 2007 that number will swell to over 50 million. The previous peak level of school enrollment was in 1971 when 51.5 million children attended America's schools (NCES, 1997). Already, early in the 21st century nearly 40% of students belong to minority groups. If current forecasts are correct, a large number of these approximately 18 million minority children will not live in homes where English is the primary language (Stratton, 1995). Perhaps as many as 60% of Hispanic children do not speak English. Many urban and suburban districts (e.g., Seattle, San Francisco) already report that as many as 40 to 50 different languages are spoken by their students and parents.

Statistics about minority enrollments are important for at least three reasons. First, there is a high correlation between students dropping out of school and their abilities to speak English (NCES, 1997). Second, the issue of bilingual education has become another political football for educators; the recent referendum prohibiting bilingual instruction in California and the subsequent reaction by many educators exemplifies the tensions created by this issue. Third, administrators in multicultural districts may have to adjust their practices in order to communicate with their various publics. This not only means communicating in several languages, but it also entails adjusting to cultural differences associated with communication.

Immigrant Students

The number of immigrant students has been accelerating for more than a decade. Students from Hispanic countries, Asia, and the Middle East constitute a growing percentage of urban schools. Some of these students adapt well to American schooling, whereas others do not. For example, immigrant students from countries where their school was interrupted or spasmodic may encounter academic problems. Many Mexican American students suffer great difficulties with English language acquisition, accentuated by living in poverty environments. Immigrant students needing personalized assistance in both content knowledge and language development often do not receive those services in the schools they attend (Ruiz-de-Velasco, 2000).

The number of high school graduates is expected to increase between 2000 and 2110. In 2000 the U.S. Census Bureau reported 81.6% of Americans below the age of 25 possessed a high school diploma or certificate. These statistics include a continuance of present dropout rates that run nearly 50% in many urban school districts such as Chicago, Cleveland, and Los Angeles. Recent statistics released by the U.S. Department of Education show that the percentage of African American students graduating from high school has reached the same level of White students—84% (Gerald & Hussar, 1997). These statistics, however, do not reveal the extent to which students are being prepared adequately for work or for entering higher education.

In the very near future, high schools in many urban areas may be overcrowded due to increased enrollments, more stringent graduation requirements, curricular revisions, and higher levels of individualized instruction. Unfortunately, many urban high schools are located in outdated buildings, and with the exception of technology-based subjects, their curricula have changed very little in the past 50 years. Thus, if these schools are to succeed, they will have to increase taxpayer costs—often dramatically—in order to build new facilities and provide smaller class sizes ("By the Numbers," 1998).

Evolving Purposes

Even though a majority of children live and attend schools in an ever-increasing urbanized America, most school districts are still small in enrollment and located in nonurban environments. More than 70% of the nation's 14,800 districts enroll less than 3,000 students. More than 4,500 districts have fewer than 500 students (NCES, 2001). It is ironic that an urban nation has an educational system that in many respects is still organized to serve a rural society. Summer vacations and a 5-hour school day are both vestiges of an agrarian society in which children worked on the summer harvest and did chores before and after school.

A little discussed 21st-century challenge facing America's public education is how to restructure schools to make them more reflective of community life in a technological, urban society. The literature in the late 20th century abounds with reform initiatives, many promising to improve the image of schools. Few, however, have advocated a totally new paradigm of public education. Instead of concentrating on meaningful restructuring of existing institutions, many critics have promoted options that essentially bypass public schools (Tyack & Cuban, 1995). The advocacy for charter schools, for example, is rooted in the belief that competition will force public schools to improve without massive infusions of new resources.

Especially in the 1980s, state legislatures responded to demands for reform by promulgating intensification mandates. This was often done without much thought about the systemic consequences for the educational system or students. Many high schools, for instance, now have semester schedules in which 70 to 80% of scheduled sections are in core subjects such as mathematics, English, and science. Electives such as music, art, and home economics have been pushed to the background so that university-bound students can take advanced placement classes (Glass, 1994). In many high schools, large numbers of students are taking four or five units of science and mathematics. It is not unusual to find high schools with underutilized elective subject classrooms and overcrowded core subject classrooms.

In the 21st century, the gap between rich and poor may also be described as a gap between those Americans with and those Americans without access to technology. This is why the technology issue is critical to schools serving children from low-income families. In a world dominated by technology, greater value may be placed on technology-related skills than on diplomas and degrees.

Whether or not the public schools fully enter the technology world depends largely on adequate funding from taxpayers, the private sector, or other governmental sources. Many districts are already charging students technology fees, trying to obtain technology equipment through school–corporate partnerships, and lobbying for additional technology funds. Many schools are currently faced with the hard choice of reducing programs, increasing class sizes, or deferring facility maintenance to free up money to buy technology equipment. Only about half of the nation's schools can boast of having a computer for every four students. Even fewer schools can say that all of its teachers are computer literate and integrate technology in their teaching every day.

Unfortunately, public schools in the future will be either technology-rich or technology-poor. Technology-rich schools will offer students distinct advantages that will be manifested in higher standardized test scores, access to the best colleges and universities, and higher income in adulthood. Students in the technology-poor schools, by contrast, will struggle to be competitive (Trotter, 2002).

Intensification mandates and the utilization of technology are but two forces creating uncertainty about public education and instability within schools. Most experts agree that the challenges presented by these conditions are more likely to be resolved locally. This is why decentralization has become so popular. Meaningful restructuring of schools should be anchored in some reasonable consensus about purpose, and such consensus is more likely to be achieved within local communities. In this context, school administrators are expected to engage the broad community in fundamental discussions about the purposes of education and means for achieving those purposes. Both communication and the exchange of information are essential.

ADDRESSING THE RELATIONSHIP BETWEEN SOCIETY AND SCHOOLS

The restructuring of public education should be based on both the needs of society and the potentialities of schools. This contention is largely responsible for a shift in thinking about school reform—a shift from centralized, coercive change models to decentralized, cultural models. More precisely, current reform efforts are focusing more directly on improving schools one at a time. This strategy is predicated on the belief that cooperation between community and school creates the most positive environment for achieving lasting changes, especially in foundational areas such as values and beliefs. In this context, school public relations is an essential tool for rebuilding bridges to the community.

Using Public Opinion

General data about societal change are essential but insufficient to effective practice. The modern administrator also needs to consistently monitor public thinking in the community. Writers such as Mathews (1996) have concluded that schools suffer because they have drifted far away from their publics. For example, far too many administrators do not personalize their contacts with parents; in far too many districts, decisions about community and student needs are made by a relatively small number of high-ranking school officials. Regrettably, only a handful of districts engage in the formal process of public opinion, and some of these do so only when faced with a direct need for public support (e.g., referenda on school construction or other tax increases).

It is unlikely that administrators can mount a successful public relations program connecting the schools with community groups unless they know:

◆ The public's level of knowledge about the district
◆ The public's attitudes toward the district's effectiveness
◆ The public's needs and wants

Because communities vary substantially, administrators cannot assume that national or even state data are correct for their districts and schools. Nor can they be confident that data collected 5 or 6 years ago remain accurate. In most communities, public opinions are fluid and are influenced by evolving political, economic, and social issues. Finally, public opinion cannot be adequately assessed through casual contacts or informal polling. This is true for at least four reasons:

1. Communities are divided between parent taxpayers and nonparent taxpayers. The latter constitute a majority in virtually all districts—in some districts, nonparents may constitute 80% of the taxpayers. Although many districts do a reasonably good job of providing information to parents, most do very little to communicate with nonparents. Nonparents are most likely to have limited accurate information and to view the schools as being nonbeneficial to them. Just asking parents about an issue may result in a very distorted picture of reality.

2. Most communication between the school and patrons is one-sided. That is, school officials disseminate selected information but make no attempt to gather or receive information. Thus, many patrons are not accustomed to communicating with school officials, and they may be more guarded and less than candid in casual conversations than in formal surveys.

3. Informal approaches tend to be sporadic; public opinion should be collected systematically at reasonable time intervals to ensure accuracy.

4. Most communities are culturally diverse. Values and opinions may differ significantly from one group to another. Informal approaches tend to ignore certain groups.

Potential problems such as these indicate that public opinion should be studied formally, periodically, and inclusively (Glass, 1997). Chapter 13 in this book is devoted to collecting and analyzing data for this purpose.

SUMMARY

The fracturing of the American family has resulted in two distinct political positions on public education. One contention is that schools must do more. That is, schools should furnish many of the services heretofore provided by the family. The reasoning underlying this position is that children will not reach their academic potential unless they are reasonably prepared to learn. Coming to school hungry or being abused at home places a child at serious risk of not being successful in school. The concept of full-service schools (schools that are prepared to meet all the needs of the child, including medical, dental, social, and nutritional assistance) exemplify this position.

By contrast, there are others, such as the religious right and fiscal conservatives, who envision reform as entailing higher expectations, higher standards, and a return to teaching the basics. These individuals oppose an expanded role for public education, either because they fear that moral or religious instruction will be part of this expanded mission or because they view the expanded mission as just another ploy to allocate more money to public schools. They also believe that more government intervention is counterproductive to refocusing responsibilities on local communities, families, and individuals.

These two very different positions exemplify the difficulty of trying to change education through centralized mandates. The most reasonable opportunity to reconcile competing values and beliefs exists at the community level. Thus, administrators need to rekindle a close relationship between schools and their neighborhoods; they need to facilitate rather than dictate; and they need to be respectful of public opinion.

CASE STUDY	Unforeseen Community Unrest

The Smithfield School District is growing rapidly and is located about 20 miles from the farthest suburb of a large midwestern city. Smithfield is the county seat of Washington County, which is mostly rural with rich corn fields and swine farms. A commonly heard joke in Smithfield is that the county has 10 times as many pigs as people.

In the past 10 years, many new families have moved to Smithfield from the metropolitan area. Many of these families have built new homes, and others have bought the large Victorian houses lining several wide streets shaded by 100-year-old oak trees. Almost all the newcomers are white-collar professionals who commute to high-technology workplaces in the far suburbs. They have chosen Smithfield because of the desire to live in a *real* community with a Main Street, courthouse, and 25-cent overtime parking tickets. More than several of the newcomers have commented that Smithfield is close to being Mayberry, USA.

The Smithfield School District comprises three elementary schools, a middle school, and a high school, with one of the best vocational-agricultural programs in the state. All of the schools were built in the 1950s and 1960s, and very little remodeling has occurred. Historically, about 25% of Smithfield high school graduates have gone on to college or university. Most of the graduates not going on to postsecondary education remained in Smithfield to work in several nearby factories, on farms, or in nearby towns. Prior to the influx of outsiders, the population of Smithfield had been steady for three or four generations.

In the past several years, the children of the new families have been so numerous that each of the buildings has become seriously overcrowded. Last year the district employed a consulting firm to do a demographic study, which found the district to be on the verge of an even larger influx of new students. The board of education in turn employed an architect to determine the costs of building a new elementary school and putting additions on all the existing schools. A bond referendum was held for $30 million several months ago and failed by a margin of 2 to 1.

A self-appointed volunteer committee of newcomer parents had spearheaded community efforts to pass the referendum. The board of education, a minority composed of native Smithfield residents, was not overly active in speaking to community groups, having coffee sessions, or distributing campaign materials. One board member opposed and actually voted against the referendum. His excuse was that it simply was too much money for many senior citizens living on fixed incomes to pay. Tax rates in Smithfield are very high because only 20% of the assessed evaluation is commercial; about two-thirds of the district budget revenues are raised from property taxes on homes. Only about 20% of the district's revenues come from state aid. The dissenting board member was quoted in the local newspaper as not questioning the need for the new school space, but he just couldn't see how the local citizens could pay for it.

The board, however, was shocked at the size of the "no" vote, since there had been no real sign that so many people would vote against the referendum. This was especially true since the referendum committee had distributed thousands of pieces of literature, held dozens of coffee sessions, and conducted an extensive telephone campaign. Furthermore, there had been no organized opposition.

At the first board meeting following the referendum defeat the board decided to ask consultants from the College of Education of a nearby state university to conduct a public opinion poll followed by a series of focus groups. The purpose of the studies was to discover what went wrong. Issues to be considered included: Did the aggressive behavior of the newcomers in trying to get new and technologically updated schools antagonize the old-time Smithfield residents? Were there just too many Smithfield residents who could not afford to have their property taxes go up anymore? Is there a division between traditional and emerging values in Smithfield, between the old-time residents and the professional white-collar newcomers? Are there signs of a division of values in the community? What effect is this division having on the school district? What should the school district do? Should it wait a couple of years until the number of newcomer votes exceed that of the Smithfield natives?

About 3 months later the consultants reported the findings of the public opinion poll and focus groups. The overall findings were that all segments of the community in general actually supported the school district. However, many nonparents complained they knew nothing about the building needs of the district nor did they even know how well students were doing in the present buildings. A large number of parents residing all their lives in Smithfield questioned the need of increasing tax rates to build space for computer technology. A focus group session with local business people was dominated with questions and comments about how the cost of the contemplated buildings was arrived at by the architects. Another focus group session with senior citizens brought forth a collective opinion that taxes were too high and should be raised only with very good justification. They did not feel the district and the board had provided a strong justification for the referendum.

QUESTIONS AND SUGGESTED ACTIVITIES

CASE STUDY

1. If you were the superintendent of schools in Smithfield, what actions would you have recommended to the board of education prior to the election?
2. If you were the superintendent of schools in Smithfield, what actions would you recommend to the board of education after the referendum defeat?
3. If you were one of the Smithfield board members, what information would you feel you needed before voting to have another referendum?
4. What information should be communicated to district parent groups about the failed referendum?
5. To what extent are changing demographics causing political strife in the district?
6. What might be the focus of a community information campaign sponsored by the district in upcoming months?

7. What types of community involvement activities might result in parents and nonparents being supportive at the polls in future referenda?

CHAPTER

8. Do public schools differ from other governmental agencies with respect to dealing with patrons? If so, how?
9. What factors have contributed to the decline of the traditional American family?
10. How may students be affected by not living in a traditional family?
11. What is the concept of a full-service school? What is the underlying reason for creating such schools?
12. What conditions have contributed to an increasing level of cultural diversity in many districts?
13. To what extent does cultural diversity affect communication needs in a school district?
14. To what extent do parents and other taxpayers communicate with administrators in your school district? What basis do you have for your answer?
15. Is it possible for public schools to compensate for social and economic problems faced by many students? Why or why not?
16. Does your district have a well-developed system of keeping in touch with the community?
17. Has your district developed a strategy of intervention for children who are at risk of academic failure?
18. How well does your district work and collaborate with social agencies, political entities, and the private sector? How might this collaboration be improved?
19. What are the differences between centralized and decentralized approaches to governance? Which is more congruous with the intention of having close relationships between school and community?

SUGGESTED READINGS

Blankenhorn, D. (1995). *Fatherless America: Confronting our most urgent social problem*. New York: Harper.

Blau, J. (1992). *The visible poor: Homelessness in the United States*. New York: Oxford Press.

Danzberger, J. P. (Ed.). (1986). *School boards: Strengthening grass roots*. Washington, DC: Institute for Educational Leadership. New York: Crown Publishers.

Etzioni, A. (1993). *The spirit of community: Rights, responsibilities, and the communitarian agenda*. New York: Crown.

Hill, P., & Celio, M. (1998). *Fixing urban schools*. Washington, DC: Brookings Institution Press.

Jencks, C., & Phillips, M. (Eds.). (1998). *The black-white test score gap*. Washington, DC: Brookings Institution Press.

Mathews, D. (1996). *Is there a public for public schools?* Dayton, OH: Kettering Foundation Press.

Mayer, S. E. (1997). *What money can't buy: Family income and children's life chances*. Cambridge: Harvard University Press.

National Center for Education Statistics (NCES). (1996). *Learning about education through statistics*. Washington, DC: U.S. Department of Education.

National Center for Education Statistics (NCES). (1998). *Students' reports of school crime: 1989 and 1995*. Washington, DC: U.S. Department of Education.

Sergiovanni, T. J. (1994). *Building community in schools*. San Francisco: Jossey-Bass.

Smith, T. L. (Ed.). (1997). *The condition of education: 1997*. Washington, DC: U.S. Department of Education.

Starratt, R. J. (1996). *Transforming educational administration: Meaning, community, and excellence*. New York: McGraw-Hill.

Steinberg, L. (1996). *Beyond the classroom: Why school reform has failed and what parents need to do*. New York: Simon & Schuster.

Tyack, D., & Cuban, L. (1995). *Tinkering toward utopia: A century of public school reform*. Cambridge: Harvard University Press.

Wilson, W. J. (1997). *When work disappears: The world of the new urban poor*. New York: Alfred Knopf.

Zweigenhaft, R. L., & Domhoff, G. W. (1998). *Diversity in the power elite: Have women and minorities reached the top?* New Haven: Yale University Press.

REFERENCES

Becker, G. S. (1993). *Human capital: A theoretical and empirical analysis with special reference to education*. Chicago: University of Chicago Press.

Blankenhorn, D. (1995). *Fatherless America: Confronting our most urgent social problem*. New York: Harper.

Blau, J. (1992). *The visible poor: Homelessness in the United States*. New York: Oxford Press.

By the numbers: The urban picture (Special issue, The urban challenge: Quality counts). (1998). *Education Week, 17*(7), 6–9.

Danzberger, J. P., Kirst, M. W., & Usdan, M. D. (1992). *Governing public schools: New times, new requirements*. Washington, DC: Institute for Educational Leadership.

Flinchbaugh, R. (1993). *The 21st century board of education*. Lancaster: Technomic Press.

Fowler, F. (2000). *Policy studies for educational leaders*. Upper Saddle River, NJ: Prentice Hall.

Gerald, D. E., & Hussar, W. J. (1997). *Projections of education statistics to 2007*. Washington, DC: U.S. Department of Education.

Glass, T. E. (1994). Lost in space: Assessing the adequacy of facilities. *School Business Affairs, 60*(3), 13–21.

Glass, T. E. (1997). Using school district public opinion surveys to gauge and obtain public support. *The School Community Journal, 7*(1), 101–106.

Hill, P., & Celio, M. (1998). *Fixing urban schools*. Washington, DC: Brookings Institution Press.

Jencks, C., & Peterson, P. E. (Eds.). (1991). *The urban underclass*. Washington, DC: Brookings Institution Press.

Jencks, C., & Phillips, M. (1998). Black-white test score gap: Introduction. In C. Jencks & M. Phillips (Eds.), *The black-white test score gap* (pp. 1–54). Washington, DC: Brookings Institution Press.

Kowalski, T. J. (1999). *The school superintendent: Theory, practice and cases*. Upper Saddle River, NJ: Prentice Hall.

Mathews, D. (1996). *Is there a public for public schools?* Dayton, OH: Kettering Foundation Press.

Mayer, S. E. (1997). *What money can't buy: Family income and children's life chances*. Cambridge: Harvard University Press.

National Center for Education Statistics (NCES). (1997). *The social context of education*. Washington, DC: U.S. Department of Education.

National Center for Education Statistics (NCES). (2001). *Overview of public elementary and secondary schools and districts: School year 1999–2000*. Washington, DC: U.S. Department of Education.

Ruiz-de-Velasco, J. (2000). *Overlooked and underserved: Immigrant students in U.S. secondary schools*. Washington, DC: Urban Institute.

Sergiovanni, T. J. (1994). *Building community in schools*. San Francisco: Jossey-Bass.

Spring, J. (1998). *Conflict of interests: The politics of American education* (3rd ed.). Boston: McGraw-Hill.

Steinberg, L. (1996). *Beyond the classroom: Why school reform has failed and what parents need to do*. New York: Simon & Schuster.

Stratton, J. (1995). *How students have changed: A call to action for our children's future*. Arlington, VA: American Association of School Administrators.

Trotter, A. (2002). Electronic learning goes to school (Special issue). *Education Week, 18*.

Tyack, D., & Cuban, L. (1995). *Tinkering toward utopia: A century of public school reform*. Cambridge: Harvard University Press.

Wilson, W. J. (1997). *When work disappears: The world of the new urban poor*. New York: Alfred Knopf.

3

Public Opinions and Political Contexts

Edward P. St. John
Margaret M. Clements

Increasingly, senior school administrators are finding that they confront two different sets of beliefs about schools when they enter the public forum. The opinions about education held by most educators are increasingly divergent from the opinions about education held by the citizens in their communities, including parents (Ridenour & St. John, in press). During the 1990s, there was a shift in public opinion, altering the old consensus about the value of public education. Indeed, during most of the 20th century, there was a high level of congruence between the beliefs of most citizens about the value of a common public education and the beliefs of most educators. Most teachers were attracted to their profession out of its social orientation (Smart, 1989) and there was a broad consensus about the value of public education. However, with the emergence of major initiatives for charter schools and other school-choice schemes in the past two decades, the old value of a common public system of schooling may no longer be a goal of the general public. Although taxpayers appear to be shifting toward a position of limited support for public schools, educators expect unqualified support.

The fact that education surfaced as a major policy issue in the 1990s adds to the complexity of contending with this division in beliefs about education. In the last presidential election, education was one of the major campaign issues. Further, public opinions on school improvement and school choice have become central in the election of candidates for national and state offices along with school board representatives. Thus, education became an even more political issue than it was in the 1990s. In this context, educational leaders need to think openly and critically about new ways of facilitating a discourse about educational policy issues.

This chapter examines the interrelationship between public opinion and the policy context for educational improvement and reform. First, it reviews trends in public opinions about education policy issues and compares them to educators' opinions about similar issues. Then, it examines how the context for education policy decisions has changed over the past few decades. Next, it considers different ways of viewing the interrelationship between public opinion and policy decisions within school districts and school buildings. Finally, it concludes with a case study about how an urban school district has contended with a new set of state and local policy initiatives. All these issues help to place public relations in the context of current political conditions.

PUBLIC OPINIONS

There have been recent changes in the ways both the public and educators view policy issues in education. Indeed, the perspectives of the two groups on critical policy issues are increasingly divergent, whereas their views on the purposes of education remain consonant. Thus, recent shifts in attitudes accentuate differences in points of view held by educators and the general public.

The General Public

Emphasizing the value of education for individuals over its value for society as a whole, a new conservative perspective on education, is manifested in two issues: the school-choice and testing movements. However, the issue of using public education funds for privately perceived gains due to individual choice is complex. The public often has competing, if not seemingly contradictory, views pertaining to key reform issues. Public attitudes toward education have been routinely collected and published by the Gallup/Kappan polls since 1969. Trends in public attitudes about school choice, the goals of education, and national testing are reviewed here.

School Choice. Since 1993, the Gallup organization has consistently included survey questions pertaining to public attitudes about giving parents the opportunity to use public funds to support private schools. The majority of the public has consistently opposed this idea. Nationally, support for choice grew between 1993 and 1996 (Rose, Gallup, & Elam, 1997). Yet, support for public funding of school choice declined from 50% of the public in 1990 to 34% in 2001 (Rose & Gallup, 2001). However, this type of question does not fully capture public attitudes about school choice because it does not make explicit the form that public financial support would take. Given the history of providing direct public subsidies to schools, many respondents would assume this question would include both direct subsidies for private schools, as a means of financing school choice, and subsidies of students. Since several states already provide direct subsidies to private schools, this would be a logical assumption.

When a more explicit question was asked about tuition subsidies—one that directly addressed the funding approach commonly referred to as vouchers—44% of the general public favored this option. This support level was moderately higher than the support level recorded for the more general public subsidy question (44% compared to 34%). More public school parents favored the option of vouchers than opposed it in the 2001 poll (Rose & Gallup, 2001). Thus, parents of school children are now the major proponents of vouchers. In an earlier poll, more African Americans also supported the choice movement (62% favored vouchers and 34% opposed) (Rose et al., 1997).

The support for tuition subsidies was linked to a concern about accountability. Most respondents (82% in 2001) favored holding church-related schools that accept government tuition accountable in the way public schools are accountable (Rose & Gallup, 2001, p. 45). Thus, whereas tuition subsidies—or vouchers—seem to be a widely accepted alternative, the general public would expect increased accountability for these funds. The public support for tuition subsidies as a form of financing school choice is far from being a mandate. However, most parents of school-age children and most African Americans favor the option.

Public Goals and Public Education. Responses to questions about imposing public standards on private schools illuminate underlying beliefs about the purpose of education. The 2001 Gallup/Kappan poll indicated that most of the public (72%) believed that the United States should focus on reforming the existing system rather than funding an alternative system (Rose & Gallup, 1997). Similarly, 71% of those included in the 1996 poll responded favorably on this question (Rose et al., 1997). Of the quarter (25%) who favored replacing the public system with a private system in the 1996 Gallup/Kappan poll, about a third (31%) cited their reasoning as being based on a belief that "private is better" and means "better quality" (Elam, Rose, & Gallup, 1996, p. 43).

To be sure, the issue of change is complex and conflicted. Despite the continuing support for the choice movement, the public supported accountability more strongly than it supported school choice. A majority (55%) favored increased use of standard-ized tests in 2001 (Rose & Gallup, 2001). Most adults favored holding schools account-able (75%) and giving states increased authority over spending (77%). Most (80%) believed that minority children had the same educational opportunities as Whites (Rose & Gallup, 2001).

Earlier polls identified racial integration as a social objective shared by the majority. In 1996, most of the public (83%) believed that racial integration was a desirable goal for pub-lic education, whereas only a small percentage (13%) believed that it was not. Most peo-ple (61%) furthermore believed that integration has improved schooling for African Americans. The population in general was evenly split (45%, yes; 44%, no) as to whether desegregation has improved education for Whites. This is contrasted to a Gallup/Kappan poll conducted in 1971 indicating that only 23% of Whites thought education was improved by integration (Elam et al., 1996). Clearly, the public school system was viewed as the main forum for racial integration. However, the latest polls have not reported on attitudes about integration (e.g., Rose & Gallup, 2001). Ironically, the public schools are now more segregated than they were in the early 1950s and efforts to desegregate schools have essentially ended (Fossey, in press).

These trends indicate there is no broad consensus about the current policies in Wash-ington. Indeed, there is solid public support for standards and accountability. However, issues of social justice seem to be fading as a public concern.

Teachers

In the 1990s, the Gallup organization and Phi Delta Kappa polled teachers about their atti-tudes toward public schools. Findings about school choice and testing are especially cogent to this chapter.

School Choice.   The Gallup/Kappan poll reports a strong difference between how teach-ers and the public viewed the impact of current trends to increase public use of funding for private schooling. Although the public believed that moving to private schooling would enhance performance for high-achieving students, most teachers believed that achieve-ment among these students would remain about the same. Also more than double the percent of teachers (25%) than the public (11%) believed that academic achievement for students who remained in the public school system would get worse if a large proportion of students moved to private schools (Langdon, 1997).

National Tests and National Standards.   There was almost an inverse relationship between public attitudes and teacher attitudes toward achievement testing. Teachers were twice as likely to believe that achievement testing was overemphasized, and the public was twice as likely to believe that achievement testing was underemphasized (Langdon, 1997).

In general, teachers expressed concern over potential misuse of the data collected from national achievement tests as well as resulting changes to the curriculum. In 1997, about twice as many teachers (70%) as general citizens (36%) indicated that teachers should have more authority in deciding the public school curriculum (Langdon, 1997).

In conclusion, educators and the public disagreed substantially about the two issues that dominate press coverage of education: achievement tests and school choice. These areas of disagreement illustrate the conflicted political context for education. It is also clear from case study research that parents and teachers in public schools continue to hold radically different views of school choice and reform methods (Ridenour & St. John, in press).

POLITICAL CONTEXTS

To build an understanding of the significance of these dominant public views of policy issues in education, it is also important to consider how the political context for education changed in recent decades. During most of the 20th century, there was broad public support for expanding educational opportunity, first by building schools and school systems, then for enhancing those systems to provide equitable opportunity for students with diverse backgrounds and diverse learning needs. Throughout this progressive period, the notion of expanding educational opportunity was considered integral to the political consensus among diverse publics in support of social and economic development. Those who supported economic development generally supported educational investment because it provided labor for industry. Those who supported social goals valued educational investment because it provided a means for upward mobility. The broad political contexts, in which public opinion was forged, shifted over time, but the balance was maintained, at least until the 1990s.

Themes Underlying Public Support of Schools

Throughout the century of progressive school development, the consensus between supporters of economic and social goals has held together. Even Catholic voters remained part of a broad consensus because they were willing to make a choice—those who wanted to send their children to religious schools paid tuition, whereas those who wanted to send their children to common public schools did so. However, a shift in public opinion, and especially the emergence of a majority favoring tuition vouchers, represents a major change in political contexts. The old political consensus around the support of public education was constructed around four themes related to local community control, comprehensive education, equal opportunity, and educational excellence. A broad consensus among the public and educators emerged around each of these issues in the 20th century.

Foundation Theme 1: Local community involvement and control is essential to the general public's support of education.

From the colonial period forward, local communities created and operated schools. Even before the common school movement started in the mid-19th century, communities created taxes to support schools (Marsden, 1994). With the emergence of common schools, these older schools were organized into local districts. In spite of the development of a nearly national curriculum over the last 100 years, the value of local community control remains central for those who continue to support public schools. After more than a century of incremental centralization, the core belief that the primary locus of control resides with parents and the community continues to exert an influence on policy decisions in school districts across the country. This continues to be a foundational belief about public education in spite of shifting public attitudes about educational issues. Consider the following description of a recent event in El Paso, Texas: "The community organizing efforts among the Alliance Schools in El Paso helped to establish the constituency that took decisive action to stop administrators from firing a principal and closing a school that the community considered particularly successful. When almost 500 parents, community members, and teachers filed into a board meeting, board members quickly reinstated the principal and shelved the plans to close the school" (Hatch, 1998, p. 17).

The school site remains the basic unit of educational enterprise, and the foundation for public support rests upon the bedrock of local collaboration among educators, parents, and community members. These linkages help explain why the general public consistently rates their own schools better than they rate schools nationally. When this public support for local schools is disturbed, schools and school systems become conflicted. Conversely public support for education can probably be strengthened through public relations strategies that promote local collaboration.

Foundation Theme 2: By providing comprehensive education, public schools broadened their base of public support.

A second theme underlying the public school consensus in the early 20th century was an education public policy focusing on building comprehensive schools. Around 1920, states began to play a stronger role in the financing of local schools. This support was coupled with increasing levels of control that became visible in areas such as extended school years and longer school days. For example, state requirements that schools provide more comprehensive high school opportunities led to the consolidation of districts through the middle part of the 20th century; the number of school districts declined nationally from 127,649 in 1932 to 15,690 in 1983 (Burrup, Brimley, & Garfield, 1988). However, the number of districts has declined by less than 10% in the past decade (the National Education Association, 1998, reports 14,461 districts in the United States).

The idea that the role of public schools is to provide a comprehensive education for all students has become part of the common public school ideal. Indeed, the comprehensive mission of schools—to meet the learning needs of all students—remains a core belief among public school advocates. Most advocates of public schools, however, stop short of endorsing full market-oriented, school-choice models because they fear that the most needy students would remain in public schools whereas most others would opt for alternative forms of education. More precisely, private schools would skim off the wealthier and higher ability students (e.g., Kozol, 1991). In the context of the current political environment, experts question the future of the "comprehensive ideal" (Wraga, 1992).

It is the comprehensive ideal, the belief that schools can meet the learning needs of all students, that is perhaps most challenged by the new emphasis on school choice. The ability to provide a comprehensive array of services in school systems has been linked to consolidation, especially to the creation of districts and schools of sufficient size to provide choices within school buildings. The new challenges raise questions about how to provide educational choice—within comprehensive public schools and systems or through other means.

Foundation Theme 3:   The goal of equal educational opportunity provides a rationale for meeting the learning needs of students from diverse communities.

The emphasis on equalizing educational opportunity emerged in the 1960s as an extension of the historical goal of expanding the opportunity for an adequate education. In states, litigants in state school-finance cases argued that state systems had great inequities across school districts. Since the passage of the Elementary and Secondary Education Act (ESEA) of 1965, the federal government has played a substantial role in equalizing opportunity. It has supported compensatory education for students with educational and financial need under Title I, as well as support for special education. Federal programs supplemented the capacity of schools to meet the needs of all students. Federal programs also mandated that parents be involved in school-site governance of Title I starting in 1965. Over time, federal requirements for parent involvement have been strengthened through requirements that parents approve individual educational plans.

The courts also have had a substantial influence on the equal opportunity goal. Starting with *Serano v. Priest,* school advocates litigated for increased adequacy and equity of funding among districts in a given state. More recent litigation has raised questions about the adequacy of state funding in Kentucky and Ohio. Periodic legal challenges serve to remind educational policy makers about the difficulty of balancing diverse public interests in the ongoing development of state education systems.

Litigation over school desegregation has also influenced movement toward equalizing learning opportunities for all students. More specifically, it has further added to the comprehensive nature of public schools by establishing the expectation that schools meet the learning needs of all students. Interestingly, desegregation plans that included magnet schools provide early experiments with school choice (Willie, 1991). Through the 1970s, the expanded role of government in public education did not erode the old consensus. However, efficiency also began to emerge as a policy issue. Steadily rising costs for public education spawned cries for accountability since many educators made no attempt to link increases in fiscal support with improvement in outcomes.

Unrest about the costs of government began to emerge in the mid-1970s. In 1976, Jimmy Carter was elected president on a platform of controlling government spending. He ushered in zero-based budgeting, which increased emphasis on conducting cost-benefit analyses of educational programs. At the same time, he supported the creation of the United States Department of Education. The strategy for the Education Consolidation and Improvement Act, which consolidated federal programs and gave block grants to school districts, was formulated in this period of transition (Turnbull, 1981).

The movement toward federal block grants stimulated the return of decisions about the direction of education programs back to state and local communities, where decisions about what to fund can more appropriately be made. However, a new wave of reduction in services was also ushered in during this period, raising questions about whose needs are being met in the educational system. The anti-affirmative action movement, now evident in many parts of the country, raises further questions about the distribution of resources within schools and school districts. Thus, although educational opportunity remains central to educational policy, the mechanisms used to support equal opportunity have become more controversial within local communities.

Foundation Theme 4:   Parent involvement remains both an aim of public policy and an essential core element of local support of schools.

For the past few decades, the dominant conception of parent involvement has been a hierarchical model developed by Epstein (1988). As refined (Epstein & Dauber, 1991), this model includes:

1. Basic obligations of parents (for health and safety, as well as positive home conditions)
2. Basic obligations of schools (communications with parents about schooling and student progress)
3. Involvement at schools (as volunteers)
4. Involvement at home (in learning activities at home and in school)
5. Involvement in decision making as child advocates and in participatory roles

This conception of parent involvement is highly compatible with the notion that schools control the agenda and parent involvement meets the interest of schools. However, in the new context of growing public concern about school quality and choice, this conception does not capture the need to involve parents in deeper and more fundamental ways. In recent research on family involvement in restructuring schools, a new form of family involvement appears to be emerging: "When parents are welcomed into restructuring, their experience becomes an integral part of the process. They also begin to take personal ownership for the efforts they make to change their schools. And as schools begin to change, to become more welcoming and involving places for parents as well as children, they also become schools of choice, places where parents choose to enroll their children" (St. John, Griffith, & Allen-Haynes, 1997, p. 71).

Thus, the process of involving parents in local discourses about educational improvement in essence engages them in a genuine dialog with educators about critical educational issues. This interaction potentially changes the political context for policy development. The success of this strategy depends on how parents are treated. Will they be treated as political pawns or as partners in restructuring?

The Shaky Foundations of Public Support for Education.

With the emergence of excellence as a new theme in educational policy, the older foundations of public support for education are now uncertain. The review of public opinion confirms that the older goals of public education—including support for local schools and equal opportunity—remain as important to the general public as they do to educators. However, the new goal of excellence ushered in a new set of public policy goals, including growing support for national testing and school choice. Public support for these new goals has created a deeply conflicted policy context, with new divisions between the values of the general public and the educators.

Emergent Themes in a Conflicted Political Context

In the 1996 presidential election, education was perhaps the most widely debated issue. President Clinton argued for national tests, school choice (limited to public schools), and increasing emphasis on educational quality; Senator Robert Dole made similar arguments, but was less supportive of public schools than Clinton (e.g., Dole was an advocate of vouchers). In the 2000 election, the American public elected a president who favors vouchers for private schools. President Bush, however, also has promoted legislation that increases the emphasis of standardized testing. Perhaps most noteworthy, a monumental Supreme Court decision rendered in June of 2002 has opened the door for states to pass laws permitting vouchers (Walsh, 2002). Below, emergent policy themes are examined.

Emerging Theme 1: The excellence movement ushered in a renewed commitment to quality improvement in public education.

The excellence movement in education was a by-product of political maneuvers by Secretary of Education Terrell Bell. As President Reagan's first secretary of education, he fended off the administration's efforts to eliminate the recently established Department of Education. He defined a new federal role in providing educational leadership (Bell, 1982) and initiated a study group that published *A Nation at Risk*. This report focused public attention on the growing populations of students who were at risk of dropping out of school.

In the aftermath of reports criticizing the effectiveness of public schools, most citizens accepted the argument that the quality of these institutions had declined. Thus, doubts about education grew steadily after 1983. By the end of that decade, a new generation of conservative educational leaders had totally shifted the debates about the government's role in education. Finn (1990), for example, argued that the focus of public policy should shift from equalizing inputs (money to education) to improving outcomes, especially student achievement. There is little doubt that the public is now primarily concerned about quality, and consequently the focus of educational policy has shifted to new indices, especially test scores. Recent polls indicate public support of standards and standardized testing remains high (Rose & Gallup, 2001).

Emerging Theme 2: Achievement tests are generally accepted by taxpayers as a mechanism for accountability in education.

In the past two decades, new developments in the use of standardized achievement tests have influenced public attitudes about education (First, 1992). These developments include:

1. In the early 1980s, the U.S. Department of Education developed "wall charts" to compare states' scores on the Scholastic Aptitude Test (SAT) and other indicators.
2. Over the next decade, the Department of Education improved and expanded the National Assessment of Educational Progress (NAEP) as a means of comparing achievement across states.

3. Most states developed formal "report card" processes to report on achievement of school districts and schools.
4. School districts have used test scores as a means of tracking and monitoring educational achievement in schools. In many districts, the local press routinely reports test scores.

In this environment, the public has been oriented toward using test scores as a means of comparing schools. All too frequently, test score data have been used to emphasize problems with schools rather than strengths of school systems. For instance, the press usually ignores research findings that indicate American schools maintain their competitive position internationally (Atkin & Black, 1997; Mislevy, 1995; Wadsworth, 1998). Negative public perceptions of the quality of public education are complicated by two related developments:

1. Testing and curriculum tend to be tightly linked. As a consequence of the national testing movement, there is a clear movement toward a national curriculum (Stedman & Riddle, 1992).
2. The comparison of test scores across school districts usually leads to focusing public attention on the education problems of inner-city schools.

Criticisms of schools in the popular press draw attention to achievement scores in inner-city schools, which in turn cause administrators in inner-city schools to tighten their control over curriculum. The proclivity to respond to concern about test scores by controlling curriculum is enhanced by textbook companies that seek to link achievement solely with school-based experiences. This has influenced a standardization of curriculum that limits the ability of schools to respond to the learning needs in diverse ways. Ironically, the movement toward a national system of testing has constrained the capacity of schools to respond to the interests of their local communities, especially in urban schools (Miron & St. John, in press). The number of curricular choices within many schools has dwindled, as the national standards for curricular content has expanded.

Emerging Theme 3: Comprehensive school restructuring has emerged as a widely accepted means of improving problem schools.

Negative perceptions of public education, and especially of inner-city schools, have generated myriad restructuring methodologies that focus on making fundamental changes. The goal of many of these methods is to improve education in schools that serve students who are at risk of failure because of their family and social circumstances. The test-driven reform movement has not served these children well, nor the schools that serve them. Three methods have been systematically pilot tested in urban settings across the country:

1. Comer's School Development Process (Comer, Haynes, Joyner, & Ben-Avie, 1996)—whose pilot tested originally in the New Haven, Connecticut, schools and expanded to urban systems in Detroit, New Orleans, and other cities—combines systematic curriculum reform with community development methods.
2. Slavin's Success for All (Slavin & Madden, 1989)—pilot tested originally in Baltimore and expanded to urban centers across the United States—has a well-developed process of intervening to improve reading achievement.

3. Levin's Accelerated Schools Project (Finnan, St. John, McCarthy, & Solvacek 1996; Hopfenberg, Levin, & Associates, 1993)—pilot tested in the San Francisco Bay area and expanded to more than 1,000 schools nationally—provides a systematic process focusing on using inquiry to address challenges confronting school communities.

In 1998, these and other restructuring methods were approved for use in a new federal program that infuses millions of dollars into inner-city schools. Each program includes an emphasis on involving parents in the school restructuring process, suggesting that there will be a sustained push to require parental involvement in systematic, comprehensive school improvement efforts. Attempts to reform inner-city schools reinforce the importance of local commitment and community involvement in education improvement, and these are values that historically have been integral to public schools.

Although independent research on the effects of comprehensive school reform has been limited, there is some evidence that it could facilitate improvement in urban schools (St. John, et al., in press). Comprehensive reforms are associated with reductions in retention and referral to special education, as well as enabling more children to pass standardized tests. Thus, they could keep more children in the educational mainstream and improve achievement. However, not all comprehensive reforms work equally well in all settings. Schools should carefully study reform options before choosing a comprehensive reform or a reading reform model (St. John, Loescher, & Bardzell, in press).

Emerging Theme 4:   School choice is gaining public acceptance as a means of financing education.

The most fundamental shift in public attitudes about schools has been in the domain of school choice. Historically, the concept of neighborhood schools dominated policies about school attendance. This approach was consonant with deep local commitment to schools. However, three forces have converged to influence growing public support for more open choice schemes:

1. The concept of vouchers, introduced in the 1960s by conservative economist Friedman (1962), has gained increasing support as an alternative approach to the public financing of education.
2. As a result of experiments with magnet schools in desegregation processes, some liberal desegregation advocates began to argue for increasing the emphasis placed on choice (George & Farrell, 1990; Willie, 1991).
3. Union advocates began to rethink their beliefs about school choice and to argue for a more limited model of public school choice (e.g., charters).

As a result of these developments, there has been increasing experimentation with new approaches to school choice in the 1990s. Two forms of voucher experiments have received extensive press coverage.

First, many states have legislation enabling districts to start charter schools, which are open-enrollment schools that are exempt from most district and state regulations. In some states, the legislation pertains only to public schools. However, in some other states, private schools can apply for charters (and thus receive state support). To date, only the

Cleveland and Milwaukee voucher experiments have extended public funds to include tuition subsidies for private school attendance (Witte, 1998). Indeed, the whole concept of charters blurs the distinction between public and private schools.

Second, in several cities, private donors have come together in support of private voucher schemes (St. John & Ridenour, 2001). These programs provide scholarships to meet some of the cost of attending private schools for children from low-income families. Several of the recent programs—in New York, Washington, Dayton, and San Antonio— have had experimental designs, including both treatment groups (scholarship recipients) and control group (nonrecipients). Advocates for these programs argue that they will inform public policy about the impact of school choice on student achievement.

There is substantial evidence that vouchers are associated with modest test score gains (Metcalf et al., 1998; Peterson, 1998; Witte, 1998). However, vouchers add to the stress of school reform. Senior administrators can adapt their plans, but principals usually contend with serious constraints (St. John & Ridenour, in press). The tight alignment between curriculum and standards makes it difficult for public schools to adapt. Thus, private schools receiving voucher students have not been held accountable in the same way as public schools.

There are reasons to question further whether changing the place where students attend will improve their achievement test scores and their parents' satisfaction with schools. It is possible that the issue is deeper and more complex than where students attend, or if they attend a public or private school. In fact, an authentic consonance between parent interests, school strategies, and learning needs of children may be necessary for schools to maintain parent and community support. Although research on these new choice experiments may eventually provide information that will address these questions, the new contested terrain of local education policy and school improvement often requires immediate action.

POLITICAL CONTEXTS AND PUBLIC OPINION

How should educators view the emerging political context for public schools? Educators increasingly need to reflect on their communication with parents and other groups about educational issues. In past decades, when there was a broader consensus about the goals of public education, it was less necessary to engage in such reflection. Today, educators who want to facilitate and lead local efforts to improve schools must recognize the various views held by diverse constituents. This new relationship between educators and the public can be viewed in three ways (St. John et al., 1997).

An Instrumental View

When school policies are set at the district and state levels, then schools are being treated instrumentally. Instrumental action has been defined as being implementation oriented, as having little relationship to strategic choices about goals and actions (Habermas, 1984, 1987). In school districts with tight control, educators feel as though they are being treated instrumentally, as though they have little influence over the policies that shape their roles as teachers (St. John et al., 1997). To the extent that the new political context exerts pressures on schools to implement standard curriculum, teachers and principals may feel a loss of power. That is, they may see themselves as instruments of externally constructed policies.

How do parents perceive the effects of these tightly regulated school contexts? Very frequently, they feel alienated: they show up to receive report cards—if they show up at all (St. John et al., 1997). In tightly regulated schools, parents and other community members often resort to agitation to address their interests (Miron, 1996), much like the example in El Paso described previously. In this view, collective political action constitutes an alternative for community groups to contend with schools that are highly regulated by government agencies and their managers.

When there was a broader consensus about educational policy, teachers and administrators simply assumed they knew what was best for students, schools, and districts. But as more policy issues were contested and as parents became more active in expressing their values and beliefs about the goals for education and their goals for their children, educators discovered that they could neither dictate decisions nor take parental support for granted.

A Strategic View

One of the central aims of the excellence movement is to build a decision capacity within schools, through the development of school-site plans formulated by school-site councils. When these processes take hold, when they are used to engage educators and parents in a conversation about the direction of the school, then the loci of strategic action shifts, at least in part, from central offices to the schools. The process of setting strategic goals and moving toward those goals can be characterized as strategic action (Habermas, 1984, 1987).

To the extent that schools develop and pursue their own goals, they increase their chances of becoming more distinctive. The strategic decision process allows parents to influence decisions in schools and to take actions that influence schools in ways they think are best for their children (St. John et al., 1997). This type of environment can be more compatible with the new choice environment advocated by many reformers. However, this idealized strategic environment can be difficult to actualize, especially given the divergent visions of educators and parents. One of the limitations of the strategic model as it applies to education is that it assumes a high degree of goal compatibility between schools and district offices, schools and educators, and schools and families.

Since the initial passage of The Elementary and Secondary Education Act (ESEA) in the mid-1960s, there has been a growing government mandate for parental involvement. Yet parents often feel excluded from decision processes, even when there are mechanisms that support their involvement (Igo, 1997; St. John et al., 1997). Therefore, the strategic planning processes—including the local site-based planning now required for schools in many states—do not seem to have substantially improved this situation.

A Communicative View

Communicative action focuses on building understanding rather than on achieving goals per se (Habermas, 1984, 1987). In one study of restructuring schools, the following characteristics were associated with a communicative approach to educational leadership:

1. Public testing of personal hypotheses about the causes of problems
2. Wrestling internally with the morally problematic aspect of educational practice (that is, critical reflection)
3. Helping and encouraging the development of others (St. John et al., 1997, pp. 10–11)

When these concepts are applied to the current discourse between schools and their various publics, one discovers that a radically different leadership attitude is needed. First, it is difficult for leaders who believe in control to be open about their framing assumptions, their personal hypotheses about the causes of problems. However, when dealing with parents and educators, critical reflection is necessary to generate and sustain open discussions. Candid, two-way communication is foundational to school reform, especially the exchange of ideals that could radically alter the organization of public schools.

These exchanges between educators and parents need to get beneath the surface of claims and counterclaims about the goals of education. Educators need to seek an understanding of why parents are advocating for new directions, just as parents need to understand the educational and social values that underlie the arguments of educators. When both groups have a chance to explore their points of view, a new common understanding can emerge.

Second, the notion that educators should wrestle internally with the morally problematic aspects of educational practice is now widely advocated (Foster, 1986; Miron, 1996), but infrequently practiced when difficult issues are being debated. In the current conflict between liberal and conservative ideologies about education, the problematic aspects of the espoused positions seldom get fully addressed. Claims are frequently made about the reasons for opposing or resisting any particular policy initiative. For example, if one believes that vouchers would skim the best students out of public schools, then it could be difficult to hear the voices of disillusioned parents who have little hope for their children in schools as they are currently constructed. Alternately, school-choice advocates need to wrestle with the problems associated with their claims that it would cost less to finance vouchers, as the advocates of California's voucher initiative discovered. Underfunding education—spreading fewer dollars across more students (which would result if vouchers really did go to students in private schools and total public spending on education was reduced)—could create even worse circumstances for children in at-risk situations than the present system. In other words, when administrators and other educators wrestle internally with the moral aspect of the positions they hold, it is easier for them to listen to others.

Finally, the notion that educational leaders should be supportive of the professional development of teachers has long been recognized in the education literature (Bull & Buechler, 1996). However, it is frequently difficult for educators and other professionals to act in ways that are consistent with the espoused value of empowering other professionals (Argyris, 1993; Argyris, Putnam, & Smith, 1985). Further, this argument is not frequently extended to include parents since it relates to their involvement in schools. In research on communicative action in schools, it is becoming apparent that educational leaders need to use open discourse as a means of encouraging teachers and parents to state and publicly test their views (St. John et al., 1997).

Questions about how learning communities can create more open discourses about education remain critical, however. There have been recent calls for open public forums on the purposes of education (Carr, 1995; Rose & Rapp, 1997; Sokoloff, 1997). Also, parent groups seem very concerned about their own involvement in school decisions (Igo, 1997; Storer, Licklider, & Cychosz, 1996). If these new public forums constrain their topics to public schools, without opening the dialogue to broader questions about private school choice, then a growing percentage of taxpayers may feel alienated. Whether educators will enter into open dialogue about the critical issues that divide them from the general public—the measurement of outcomes and the opening of school choice—remains a vital question.

Educational leaders may need to create forums where diverse and divergent views can be examined and evaluated in ways that not only support the development and improvement of educational systems, but also provide a forum for creating a local agenda for educational improvement. The real moral challenge, viewed from a postconventional frame (Habermas, 1991), is to build an understanding within local communities about why existing patterns have emerged in the first place. The most complex questions pertain to ways of reformulating policy when local public attitudes are divergent from the plans developed by educational systems.

SUMMARY

When trends in the opinions held by the public are examined and contrasted to the views commonly held by educators, several incongruencies become apparent. These new areas of disagreement are complicated by a rapidly changing policy context. First, the general public seems increasingly supportive of using tuition subsidies for open choice about public and private schools, whereas educators are less supportive of extending choice schemes to private schools (Ridenour & St. John, in press). However, even though more of the public now supports than opposes tuition subsidies for students attending private schools, there is not a clear public mandate to move in this new direction. Indeed, less than half of the population supports this strategy in the latest poll even though a slightly larger percentage favored this option than opposed it. Further, the majority of public opinion also supports integration in schools eligible to receive public subsidies, an attitude that would seem to extend to schools that accept tuition vouchers. In contrast, educators support more limited choice schemes that extend the opportunity to families to choose among public schools. Thus, there is contested terrain that could complicate the efforts of educational leaders to build support for their educational plans.

Second, achievement tests and their use in the policy arena have emerged as an area of disagreement between educators, parents, and the public (Ridenour & St. John, in press). The majority of the public would like to see more testing. In contrast, educators are more concerned about the uses of test information in the public forum. Indeed, many experts have expressed concerns that the public does not understand how to interpret test scores, thus they are used to compare schools with respect to effectiveness or they are used to make comparisons with other countries. Further, educators are much less convinced that the new testing movement is actually helping schools to improve.

The policy context is also contested. States and the federal government are increasingly focusing their reform efforts on restructuring and choice schemes, as well as on refining their approaches to testing student achievement. All these reform efforts complicate local school planning and policy development because they conflict with the attitudes held by educators in public school systems. Indeed, the current policy context reflects public attitudes more than it reflects educators' attitudes, and many educators hold beliefs that are in conflict with the policies that now govern public education. After nearly two decades of public investment in new approaches to testing, educators remain unconvinced of their value. Therefore, there is reason to question how the new initiatives to increase choice and restructure schools will be viewed by educators and whether they will embrace these new initiatives as opportunities for innovation or continue to resist them after they have been legislated.

There is also an embedded conflict between school choice and the methods being used for school accountability. The emphasis on testing and standards constrains change in public schools, inhibiting adaptation to choice schemes (Ridenour & St. John, in press; St. John & Ridenour, in press). Public schools are often caught in two contradictory forces, one forcing student-centered changes, the other inhibiting these changes.

The new policy context presents a challenging situation for administrators who are concerned about public relations in education. In this new policy environment, public relations will involve more than disseminating information about the goals established through district planning processes. Schools need better information about the expectations of parents and taxpayers so they can communicate with these groups about opportunities that exist within schools. It may also involve creating new forums within school communities to discuss the new challenges facing education.

CASE STUDY[1]	Charter Schools in The City

In 1997, The State passed legislation that created two levels of approval for new charter schools. A process was established that enabled local school boards to approve charters; at the same time, groups in communities seeking to start charter schools could appeal directly to The State for charters. In The City, the school board initiated a process for reviewing and approving charters in the winter of 1998. However, the approval process became intermingled with other educational issues.

---

[1]"The City" and "The State" are used to disguise the setting of this case study.

A CHANGING CONTEXT

The City was one of the cities in The State with consistently low achievement test scores. During the prior year, the superintendent had worked with a team of professors at the University of The City, teachers and principals from selected schools, representatives of the teachers' union, and representatives of parent groups on the design of a school improvement process. Representatives of Comer's School Development Project at Yale were actively involved in the design of the project. A forum of educators had been created to address challenging educational issues.

However, there was strong community support for new school-choice initiatives in The City. In January 1998, a Privately Funded Scholarship Program (PFSP) was announced. The PFSP provided scholarships for children from low-income families who sought to attend private schools and out-of-district public schools. It was anticipated that about 1,000 scholarships would be awarded for fall 1998. This would include 675 scholarships for public school students choosing private schools or attending out-of-district public schools, along with 675 students in a control group (nonrecipients included in a study of the program). The remaining scholarships would be awarded to students already enrolled in private schools. The City public schools had lost enrollment over the prior 2 years as a result of a more aggressive grant program in Catholic schools. Thus, the introduction of a new private program posed a further threat to enrollment.

In addition, The City public schools formed a new desegregation strategy approved by the U.S. Department of Justice in 1997–1998. The new plan created three choice zones for families, with a choice of public schools in each zone. The new system replaced a desegregation strategy that emphasized forced busing.

Thus, there were preconditions in The City that seemed to favor introducing charter schools. However, the teachers' union was not supportive of charters that would substantially change working conditions or limit teaching slots for union members.

DEVELOPING A CHARTER STRATEGY

The superintendent worked with three groups to bring proposals to the board for approval. His decision to work with local groups was influenced by his reflections on the political context. He had thought critically about the new policy environment that was emerging. Although he had once been opposed to school choice, he rethought his position based on recent political developments (interview cited in St. John & Ridenour, 2001). In addition, there was a local private scholarship initiative under way that increased the need for public schools to compete to keep their students.

First, the superintendent worked with the Edison Project to secure approval for converting up to five local elementary schools into Edison charter schools. His plan was to convert some of the lower achieving public schools to Edison Project schools. The Edison Project incorporated the structure of Success for All in reading and is widely regarded as an effective new school program. Run by a private corporation, the Edison Project was controversial. Representatives of the teachers' union criticized it in the local press. However, the Edison Project proposed to work with the local union and employ union teachers.

Second, the Alliance for Education, a local group of involved citizens, developed a charter proposal to create a new charter school. It proposed to use Levin's Accelerated Schools model as a basis for a new school, built from the bottom up. It would start with kindergarten through third grade, then add a new class of students each year. The Alliance chose the Accelerated Schools Project after a careful review of alternative restructuring processes. The proposal, which had been discussed widely among community groups, also had favorable local press. However, since the Alliance planned to open employment opportunities to both union and nonunion teachers, it ran the risk of alienating the union. Superintendent Williams met with the Alliance and provided support for its proposal.

Finally, the Concerned Christian Businessmen, a local civic group, developed a proposal that it brought to the board. The proposal did not receive the same press as the other proposals because it was developed in a shorter time frame. It also received a general endorsement from the superintendent.

INCREMENTAL DECISIONS

At their March meeting when The City School Board met to review proposals, the Edison Project schools and Christian Businessmen's proposal received an initial endorsement, but the Alliance proposal did not. Both of these groups began contract negotiations with the school board. After reflecting on the situation, the leaders of the Alliance decided to take its proposal to the state for approval and received a favorable response in its initial inquiries. However, there was criticism of the school board in the local press.

Subsequent to the news release, the local teachers' union announced it did not approve the Edison Project. Then the school board reversed its earlier position, denying approval of the proposal for the three Edison charter schools. The Edison Project's initial response was to say it would continue to plan to open a school. However, within a month of the board's decision to not endorse the Edison Project charter schools, it announced it would pull out of The City.

Throughout the spring of 1998, there was extensive local press on both the charter school proposals and the PFSP project. The number of applications from public school students for PFSP scholarships was substantially lower than anticipated. The program revised its design, reducing some of the experimental control embedded in the program, as a means of encouraging more families to apply. However, there was a larger than expected number of applications from low-income students who were already enrolled in private schools. Further, the program continued to get favorable press in both The City and The State capitol.

QUESTIONS AND SUGGESTED ACTIVITIES

CASE STUDY

1. How do state and local policy developments described in The City case relate to national trends in public opinion?
2. How do the actions of the teachers' union in The City reflect the opinions of teachers in national polls?
3. How are recent changes in the national policy context reflected in The City case?
4. How did The City superintendent adapt his strategies based on the new political context?

5. Was a public forum created in The City to discuss the conflicting notions of educational improvement?

6. How were school-restructuring methodologies (the School Development Process, Success for All, and Accelerated Schools) reflected in the district's school improvement process and the charter schools' initiatives?

7. How did the public respond to the new scholarship program? How strong an interest was there in the new choice program among low-income families in The City?

8. Were parents involved in the planning processes for school restructuring? For charter schools?

9. How are the themes that underlie the support of public education evident in the case?

10. How are the emerging themes of the new policy context evident in the case?

11. Whose interests are represented in the changes that seem to have occurred in The City?

12. How might a forum be created to encourage discussion about the underlying issues in The City?

CHAPTER

13. How do the opinions of educators and taxpayers compare and contrast?

14. How are the opinions about education policy held by parents reflected in the emerging political context?

15. How do changes over time in public policy for education relate to the opinions about education held by taxpayers?

16. How does the popular reform concept of school-based management relate to the instrumental, strategic, and communicative views discussed in this chapter?

17. What are some of the tensions between the values of educational excellence and educational equality?

SUGGESTED READINGS

Carr, B. (1995). Communication failure can threaten progress. *Journal of Educational Relations, 16*(4), 18–22.

Comer, J. P., Haynes, N. M., Joyner, E. T., & Ben-Avie, M. (Eds.). (1996). *Rallying the whole village: The Comer process for reforming schools.* New York: Teachers College Press.

First, P. F. (1992). *Educational policy for school administrators.* Boston: Allyn & Bacon.

Howe, H., II. (1996). The continuing question: Will public schools make it in America? *The School Administrator, 53*(5), 14–17.

Miron, L. F., & St. John, E. P. (Eds.). (in press). *Reinterpreting urban school reform: A critical-empirical review.* Albany, NY: SUNY Press.

Sokoloff, H. (1997). Convening the community: Why schools must invite the public to join the dialogue on public education. *The American School Board Journal, 184*(11), 25–27.

REFERENCES

Argyris, C. (1993). *Knowledge for action: A guide to overcoming barriers to organizational change.* San Francisco: Jossey-Bass.

Argyris, C., Putnam, R., & Smith, D. (1985). *Action science: Methods and skills for research and intervention*. San Francisco: Jossey-Bass.

Atkin, J. M., & Black, P. (1997). Policy perils of international comparisons. *Phi Delta Kappan, 79*(1), 22–28.

Bell, T. H. (1982, November). The federal role in education. *Harvard Educational Review, 52*(4), 375–380.

Bull, B., & Buechler, M. (1996). *Learning together: Professional development for better schools*. Bloomington, IN: Indiana Education Policy Center.

Burrup, P. E., Brimley, J. V., & Garfield, R. R. (1988). *Financing education in a climate of change*. Newton, MA: Allyn & Bacon.

Carr, B. (1995). Communication failure can threaten progress. *Journal of Educational Relations, 16*(4), 18–22.

Comer, J. P., Haynes, N. M., Joyner, E. T., & Ben-Avie, M. (Eds.). (1996). *Rallying the whole village: The Comer process for reforming schools*. New York: Teachers College Press.

Elam, S. M., Rose, L. C., & Gallup, A. M. (1996). The 28th Annual Phi Delta Kappa/Gallup poll of the public's attitudes toward the public schools. *Phi Delta Kappan, 78*(1), 41–59.

Epstein, J. L. (1988). How do we improve programs of parent involvement? *Educational Horizons, 91*(3), 58–59.

Epstein, J. L., & Dauber, S. L. (1991). School programs and teacher practices of parent involvement in inner-city elementary schools. *The Elementary School Journal, 91*(3), 289–305.

Finn, C. E. (1990). The biggest reform of all. *Phi Delta Kappan, 72*(1), 584–592.

Finnan, C., St. John, E. P., McCarthy, J., & Slovacek S. P., (Eds.). (1996). *Accelerated schools in action: Lessons from the field*. Thousand Oaks, CA: Corwin Press.

First, P. F. (1992). *Educational policy for school administrators*. Boston: Allyn & Bacon.

Fossey, R. (in press). School desegregation is over in inner cities: What do we do now? In L. F. Miron & E. P. St. John (Eds.), *Reinterpreting urban school reform: A critical-empirical review*. Albany, NY: SUNY Press.

Foster, W. (1986). *Paradigms and promises: New approaches to educational administration*. Buffalo, NY: Prometheus Books.

Friedman, M. L. (1962). *Capitalism and freedom*. Chicago: University of Chicago Press.

George, C., & Farrell, W. C. (1990). School choice and African-American students: A legislative view. *Journal of Negro Education, 59*(4), 521–525.

Habermas, J. (1984). *The theory of communicative action: Volume one, reason and the rationalization of society*. Boston: Beacon Press.

Habermas, J. (1987). *The theory of communicative action: Volume two, lifeworld and system: A critique of functionalist reason*. Boston: Beacon Press.

Habermas, J. (1991). *Moral consciousness and communicative action*. Cambridge, MA: MIT Press.

Hatch, T. (1998). How community action contributes to achievement. *Educational Leadership, 55*(8), 16–19.

Hopfenberg, W. S., Levin, H. M., & Associates. (1993). *Accelerated schools resource guide*. San Francisco: Jossey-Bass.

Igo, S. (1997). Continuing a commitment. *Phi Delta Kappan, 78*(10), 771–773.

Kozol, J. (1991). *Savage inequalities*. New York: Harper.

Langdon, C. A. (1997). The fourth Phi Delta Kappa poll of teachers' attitudes toward the public schools. *Phi Delta Kappan, 79*(3), 212–220.

Marsden, G. M. (1994). *The soul of the American university*. New York: Oxford University Press.

Metcalf, K. K., Boone, W. J., Stage, F. K., Chilton, T. L., Muller, P., & Tait, P. (1998). *A comparative evaluation of the Cleveland Scholarship and Tuition Program: Year One, 1996–97*. Bloomington, IN: The Junior Achievement Evaluation Project, Indiana University.

Miron, L. F. (1996). *The social construction of urban schooling: Situating the crisis*. Cresskill, NJ: Hampton Press.

Miron, L. F., & St. John, E. P. (Eds.). (in press). *Reinterpreting urban school reform: Have urban schools failed or has the reform movement failed urban schools?* Albany, NY: SUNY Press.

Mislevy, R. J. (1995). What can we learn from international assessments? *Educational Evaluation and Policy Analysis, 17*(4), 419–437.

National Education Association. (1998, March). American education statistics. . . . At a glance [Online data file, pp. 1–4]. Retrieved from http://www.nea.org/society/estat98.pdf, 1–4.

Peterson, P. E. (1998). School choice: A report card. In P. Peterson, P. E. Hassel, & B. C. Hassel (Eds.), *Learning from school choice* (pp. 3–32). Washington, DC: The Brookings Institution.

Ridenour, C. S., & St. John, E. P. (in press). Private scholarships and school choice: Innovations or class reproduction? In L. F. Miron & E. P. St. John (Eds.), *Reinterpreting urban school reform: Have urban schools failed, or has the reform movement failed urban schools?* Albany, NY: SUNY Press.

Rose, L., & Gallup, A. M. (2001). The 33rd Annual Phi Delta Kappan/Gallup poll of the public attitudes toward public schools. *Phi Delta Kappan, 83*(1), 41–58.

Rose, L. C., Gallup, A. M., & Elam, S. M. (1997). The 29th annual Phi Delta Kappan/Gallup poll of the public's attitudes toward the public schools. *Phi Delta Kappan, 79*(1), 41–56.

Rose, L. C., & Rapp, D. (1997). The future of the public schools: A public discussion. *Phi Delta Kappan, 78*(10), 765–768.

Slavin, R. E., & Madden, N. A. (1989). What works for students at risk: A research synthesis. *Educational Leadership, 46*(5), 4–13.

Smart, J. C. (1989). Life history influences on Holland vocational type development. *Journal of Vocational Behavior, 29,* 216–225.

Sokoloff, H. (1997). Convening the community: Why schools must invite the public to join the dialogue on public education. *The American School Board Journal, 184*(11), 25–27.

St. John, E. P., Griffith, A. I., & Allen-Haynes, L. (1997). *Families in schools: A chorus of voices in restructuring.* Portsmouth, NH: Heinemann.

St. John, E. P., Loescher, S. A., & Bardzell, J. S. (in press). Improving early reading in grades 1–5: A resource guide for programs that work. Thousand Oaks, CA: Corwin Press.

St. John, E. P., Manset-Williamson, G., Chung, C. G., Simmons, A. B., Loescher, S. A., Hossler, C. A., et al. (in press). Research-based reading reforms: The impact of state-funded interventions on educational outcomes in urban elementary schools. In L. F. Miron & E. P. St. John (Eds.), *Reinterpreting urban school reform: Have urban schools failed or has the reform movement failed urban schools?* Albany, NY: SUNY Press.

St. John, E. P., & Ridenour, C. S. (2001). Market forces and the influence of private scholarship on planning in urban school systems. *The Urban Review, 33,* 269–290.

St. John, E. P., & Ridenour, C. S. (in press). School leadership in a market setting: The influence of private scholarship on educational leadership in urban schools. *Leadership and Policy in Schools.*

Stedman, J. B., & Riddle, W. C. (1992). Report for Congress. *National educational goals for federal policy issues: Action by the 102d Congress.* Washington, DC: Congressional Research Service.

Storer, J. H., Licklider, B., & Cychosz, C. M. (1996). Perceptions of educators and parents—Where they disagree causes conflict. *Journal of Educational Relations, 17*(4), 2–5.

Turnbull, B. J. (1981). Issues for a new administration: The federal role in education. *American Journal of Education, 89*(4), 396–427.

Wadsworth, D. (1998). Prevailing perceptions of public schools. *The American School Board Journal, 185*(5), 41–42.

Walsh, M. (2002). Charting the new landscape of school choice: Justices settle case, nettle policy debate. *Education Week, 21*(42), 1, 18–21.

Willie, C. V. (1991). Controlled choice: An alternative desegregation plan for minorities who feel betrayed. *Education and Urban Society, 23*(2), 200–207.

Witte, J. F. (1998). The Milwaukee voucher experiment. *Educational Evaluation and Policy Analysis, 20,* 229–252.

Wraga, W. G. (1992). School choice and the comprehensive ideal. *Journal of Curriculum and Supervision, 8*(1), 28–42.

4

Legal and Ethical Aspects of Public Education

Joseph R. McKinney

Court decisions over the past four decades have set in motion social changes that fundamentally alter the relationship between public schools and the communities they serve. Supreme Court decisions concerning school desegregation, the role of religion and the schools, the rights and freedoms of teachers and students, sexual harassment, race discrimination, gender discrimination, the rights of individuals with disabilities, and the teaching of values had important and lasting ramifications for the larger society. The increased role of the courts in education has drawn much comment from legal and education scholars. In *School Days, Rule Days*, Kirp and Jensen (1986) refer to the substantial involvement of the judiciary in shaping school affairs as the "legalization" of education. In *Law and The Shaping of Public Education*, Tyack, James, and Benevat (1987) document the dramatic increase in litigation and the heavy reliance on the courts in shaping American educational policy since World War II. Yudolf, Kirp, Levin, and Moran (2002) outline the continuing enormous influence the law has on public education.

The field of school-community relations, which is a subcategory of public relations, dates back to the 1920s and is guided and formed today by the law both in policy making and practice. The relationship between the law and public relations is clearer in light of modern definitions of both community relations and public relations. Bagin and Gallagher (2001) define educational-community relations as two-way communication between a school and its publics. West (1985) explains that the province of educational public relations consists of "the essential blending of two elements: communications and human relations" (p. 45).

Who is involved in blending communication and human relations in the context of school-community relations? The literature of school-community relations is replete with references to communication between educational organizations and internal and external constituencies or publics (Bagin & Gallagher, 2001; West, 1985). The *internal public* generally consists of school board members, school administrators, teachers, all other school employees, and students. *External publics* variously include parents, nonparents, volunteers, parent-teacher groups, the media, the business community, community groups, special-interest groups, politicians, and to a certain extent, collective bargaining units. Schools interact with these publics in different forms and activities, and the law accordingly touches on individual school-community relations activities. Schools overlooking the significance of the legal aspects of school-community relations not only face the risk of financial liability for running afoul of the law, but also stumble in failing to educate and lead their many publics in understanding the importance of safeguarding America's democratic values and individual constitutional rights.

VARIETY AND VOLUME OF LITIGATION AFFECTING SCHOOL-COMMUNITY RELATIONS

Studies available to date on litigation rates in education indicate the extent and pervasiveness of the impact of the law on school-community relations. Most studies are based on analyzing reported (published) judicial decisions. The general conclusion that emerges is that the total amount of education-related litigation greatly increased from the 1960s to the mid-1970s, then decreased modestly from 1977 to 1987—mainly because of a decrease in new school desegregation filings. But litigation rates remain today at historically high levels (Alexander & Alexander, 2001; Zirkel, 1997). Imber and Thompson (1991) estimated, on the basis of their study, that in any single year one lawsuit is filed against a school in the United States for every 3,500 students attending public school. The litigation rates in many categories of school law, including those particularly affecting school-community relations, have significantly increased in recent years. These include such suits as those related to the rights of individuals with disabilities, negligence, and equity in funding. Other areas of school law with rising litigation rates affecting school-community relations are search and seizure suits, church-state cases filed in federal courts, challenges to the curriculum, and suits by outsiders.

Empirical studies of education-related litigation do not begin to fully capture the legal ramifications associated with school-community relations (or any other educational practice). Most studies are based on actual lawsuits filed against school districts and do not consider threatened or potential lawsuits. Another complicating factor is that many legal challenges are brought pursuant to extrajudicial or alternative dispute procedures. These alternative forums to court proceedings include local and state grievance procedures (often personnel related), administrative procedures, and challenges brought directly to a local school board. Of course, schools must comply with a complex body of federal and state statutes and regulations as well. The picture of the volume and variety of litigation related to school-community relations is not complete without taking these factors into account.

DESEGREGATION AND THE SCHOOLS

The Supreme Court decision in *Brown v. Board of Education* (1954) stands as the most important case ever in terms of judicial impact on school-community relations. In *Brown*, the court ruled the separate-but-equal doctrine unconstitutional but established no remedy for desegregating the public schools. In *Brown II* (1955), the Supreme Court fashioned an ambiguous remedy when it declared that school desegregation would proceed with all deliberate speed. The Court left to the local schools and communities the responsibility of desegregation. Almost every facet of school operations touching on school-community relations was covered by the *Brown II* decision: "problems related to administration, arising from the physical condition of the school plant, the school transportation system, personnel, revision of school districts and attendance areas" (p. 295). The resistance to school desegregation is well documented elsewhere, and a recitation of its long history is not necessary or possible here. As Alexander and Alexander (2001) explain, "over a generation after *Brown*, judicial decisions are still required to settle social and legal issues emanating from the circumstances surrounding desegregation" (p. 506). Desegregation cases exemplify the interplay of communities, schools, and the law. Where progress in school desegregation has been made since *Brown*, it has been achieved only as a result of open two-way communication between schools, their many publics, and the courts.

LIABILITY TORTS

A school district's greatest exposure to lawsuits in the context of school-community relations lies in the category of tort law. In attempting to build and maintain effective relationships with its many publics, a school must find ways to generate community participation. Increasing the flow of information among internal and external publics and involving the community in the educational enterprise through increased participation in school and school-related community functions carries many benefits, but it also carries increased legal risks.

In an action based in tort against a school district, the injured party seeks a judgment holding the school district and/or a school employee responsible for the consequence of a wrongdoing. By allowing compensation for injuries sustained by individuals in school, tort law requires schools to take appropriate steps to provide for a safe and orderly environment. Tort law imposes liability on schools for injury or harm to individuals using the school, including students, parents, and outsiders injured at school. There are three major categories of tort law: (a) negligence; (b) intentional torts, including defamation; and (c) strict liability. The categories of negligence and intentional torts are relevant to school-community relations.

Negligence

The most prevalent tort action involving schools and school personnel is negligence. Negligence may be defined as conduct falling below an established standard fixed and imposed upon the parties by the law, common or statutory, that results in injury (Keeton, Dobbs, Keeton, & Owen, 1984, p. 288). Negligence encompasses all human behavior. The commonly employed test used by the courts to determine negligence is grounded in the nature of a formula created by the courts, which have created a hypothetical person who "has never existed on land or sea: the reasonable man of ordinary prudence" (p. 174). The "reasonable" person conducts himself or herself in an ideal manner; he or she is a community standard. Although the reasonable person operates as a community model, his or her conduct varies appropriately with the circumstances under which he or she acts. In a negligence lawsuit the question becomes, would the reasonable person have been expected to foresee, and as a result, to have been able to take action to prevent the injury that occurred? An affirmative answer to the question suggests that the defendant in a negligence action was negligent.

There are four elements in a cause of action for negligence:

1. There must be duty of care between the plaintiff and the defendant.
2. There must be breach of the duty of care by the defendant.
3. The defendant's breach of duty must have been the proximate cause of the resultant injury to the plaintiff.
4. The plaintiff must have suffered actual loss or damage as a result of the injury. (For liability to be proven, all four elements must be shown by the plaintiff.)

An effective school-community relations program encourages the use of school facilities and school visits by citizens. Making the school available for community use builds support for school personnel and programs. In a more global sense it allows the school to function as a social institution serving the public interest (Bagin & Gallagher, 2001).

School personnel have a duty to maintain school buildings and grounds and equipment in proper condition. A school corporation will be held liable to an injured person if it knew or should have known of an unreasonably dangerous or hazardous condition at the school and failed to take steps to eliminate the danger. Courts impose a high standard for the proper maintenance of school facilities and equipment, and concomitantly the judiciary has looked favorably on schools that have developed preventive maintenance programs that provide for regular facility and equipment inspection.

Within the general framework of negligence tort liability as discussed here, most states have developed special liability rules concerning owners and possessors of property and buildings and their duty toward occupiers of the property (premises liability). Individuals who enter upon the property of another are legally classified according to the level of duty owed them as trespassers, licensees, or invitees. A *trespasser* is an individual who enters upon the property of another without a privilege to do so or without consent from the possessor. A *licensee* is a person who enters upon the property of another with permission (express or implied). An *invitee* is defined as an individual who is invited (express or implied) to enter and remain on the premises of another for a particular reason. Invitees include individuals on premises as members of the public for purposes for which the property is held open to the public (American Law Institute, 1986).

Traditionally, most individuals entering a school who are not students, parents, or employees are considered to be licensees. Licensees include community groups and organizations using the school facility for meeting purposes. A school district owes a licensee only a duty to be warned of concealed dangerous conditions of which the school district has actual knowledge. A school district owes a greater degree of care to an invitee than it does to a licensee. School districts that open the doors to their facilities to external groups and individuals run the risk of creating invitees out of groups traditionally characterized as licensees. A school district owes an invitee a duty to exercise reasonable care for his or her safety and to take reasonable steps, including regular inspection of the premises, to make sure the premises are safe for the invitee. This heightened duty to invitees means in practical terms that school districts must, among other things, be vigilant in mopping and drying slippery floors, in removing dangerous snow and ice from entrances and sidewalks, in adequately lighting halls and parking lots, and in providing or increasing security measures when attacks on school invitees are foreseeable. These precautions are generally met when school is in session, but they become problematic when a school not in session allows community groups to use its facilities as part of a school-community relations program.

What constitutes due care and adequate supervision depends largely on the circumstances surrounding an injury. The traditional standard of care and supervision applicable in most situations is the level of care and supervision an ordinary prudent person would exercise under the circumstances. However, when on the job supervising students, school personnel are held to a higher standard of care and supervision than is the ordinary, reasonably prudent person. In general, school district liability for injuries sustained to individuals other than students will be decided within the framework of the general and special (premises liability) tort liability framework.

Adequate Supervision and Violence in the Schools.   The amount of crime committed in the nation's schools is a major concern to the entire school community. Students ages 12 through 18 were victims of about 880,000 nonfatal violent crimes (serious violent crime and simple assault) at school in 1999 (National Center for Education Statistics, 2001). School authorities have a legal obligation to maintain safe and violence-free environments. The duty to provide adequate supervision and security extends to parents and citizens invited to school. School officials should go on the offensive and take proper precautionary action if assaults on school personnel, students, and members of the community using the school are reasonably foreseeable. These safety measures might include warning the public, beefing up on-campus security, increasing crowd control at sporting events, keeping all but the front door to the school locked, installing metal detectors (in the worst situations), and establishing mentoring programs. The legal reasoning applied in school violence cases appears to be grounded in whether or not a school could reasonably have foreseen the violence and prevented the injury under all the circumstances of the case.

Many school districts attempt to get nonparents involved in the schools through volunteer programs. Schools often invite senior citizens to read to students, eat lunch with students, and volunteer in the library. A school district that utilizes volunteers for activities exposes itself to liability for the tortuous acts of volunteers. Schools may want to consider personal background checks on volunteers engaged in long-term programs. Many school districts are adopting policies that address behavioral expectations for volunteers. In a New Jersey case, a volunteer instructor during a school-board-sponsored swimming program sexually molested an 8-year-old student in a swimming pool. The parents of the child sued the school district. The court adopted the "deliberate indifference" standard to evaluate the action of the school board and the swimming program coordinator to screen volunteers. The court ruled in favor of the school because the board had developed and followed their official policy of screening volunteers (*C.P. v. Piscataway Tp. Bd. of Educ.*, 1996).

A 1998 case illustrates a school's duty to maintain a safe environment. A student's mother brought an action against a school district and school official, arising from the death of her son who was attacked and stabbed in a classroom. The mother contended that despite previous student violence at the school, nothing had been done to implement security or safeguards at Dartmouth High School beyond hanging a "No Trespassing" sign near the front door. The court agreed and found the school district (town of Dartmouth) was not immune from a negligence suit where it had neither adopted nor implemented any security policy, procedure, or safeguards (*Brum v. Town of Dartmouth and Others*, 1998).

Defenses Against Negligence.   Several defenses against liability are available to educators. The most common defenses are contributory negligence, assumption of the risk, and governmental immunity (Alexander & Alexander, 2001). In order to prove contributory negligence, a school district must demonstrate that the plaintiff (the party filing the suit) failed to exercise reasonable care for his or her own safety and that that failure contributed to the plaintiff's own injury. Contributory negligence is a potent defense for educators because, if shown, the defense totally excuses a school district from liability. Because of the harshness of the "complete bar to recovery" rule of contributory negligence, the majority of states have adopted the defense of comparative negligence, which permits damages to be apportioned according to the assessed degrees of fault of all parties. However, in some states where comparative negligence has replaced contributory negligence, the comparative fault provisions do not apply to tort claims brought against government entities, including school districts.

Another defense available to schools is the defense of assumption of the risk. It involves a plaintiff's consent or voluntary acceptance (express or implied) of a specific risk or danger of which the plaintiff has actual knowledge. Assumption of the risk operates to relieve a school district of liability even if the school district has created the risk of danger. The doctrine of assumption of the risk has been frequently and successfully raised in the sports-injury arena. In a number of cases against school districts where damages were requested for injuries that were allegedly sustained by spectators and other members of the community as a result of actions by players or other spectators at sporting events sponsored by schools, recovery has been denied on the basis of assumption of the risk. School districts have successfully used the defense of assumption of the risk in circumstances where spectators were struck by batted or thrown baseballs, struck by football players executing plays, knocked down by children (also spectators) engaged in horseplay, and struck by a tennis ball while watching a match (Korpela, 1971).

Prior to the 1970s, litigation against public schools and most government entities was limited or entirely prohibited by the doctrine of immunity. Governmental immunity in America is based largely on English common law, exemplified by the ancient maxim that "the king can do no wrong." The prevailing doctrine in the United States has been that both the state and federal government are immune for torts committed by their officers and employees unless the government consents to such liability. The doctrine of sovereign immunity was traditionally extended to school districts in most states for injuries to individuals that were caused by the negligent acts of governmental employees. Governmental immunity for school districts in tort actions still exists under common law, even though judicial actions have partially eroded the vitality of this doctrine in most states (McCarthy & Cambron-McCabe, 1998).

In many states where governmental immunity does not protect school districts from tort liability, state legislatures have passed legislation that limits the amount of damages an injured party may recover as compensation for losses as a result of governmental negligence. Many states also allow school districts to purchase liability insurance that covers the school district and its employees from being held personally liable for damage awards. Moreover, several states have passed statutes (tort claim acts) that must be complied with as a prerequisite to recovery by anyone claiming an injury as a result of governmental negligence.

Protection of educators against personal liability varies among the states. Traditionally, states have made a distinction, for tort liability purposes, between whether the educator was performing a ministerial function or discretionary function. States permit immunity for torts committed while performing discretionary acts but hold school personnel responsible for the ministerial actions. *Discretionary actions* involve the exercise of professional judgment, formulation of school policy, setting of goals, and planning. *Ministerial activities* involve compliance with mandates of legal authority not requiring the exercise of judgment.

As a last resort, to protect against financial ruin, schools can purchase adequate insurance coverage. Drake and Roe (2003) suggest that school districts purchase all-risk property insurance, comprehensive liability insurance, and errors and omissions liability insurance for teachers, administrators, and school board members.

Defamation

The tort that most directly touches on all aspects of school-community relations is defamation. The law of defamation, like school-community relations, is centered on communication. *Defamation* consists of the twin torts of libel and slander. *Slander* is spoken defamation, and *libel* is written defamation. *Defamation* is an injury or invasion of a person's interest in his or her good reputation, name, and character by a false and defamatory communication concerning the person (American Law Institute, 1986).

In seeking to keep the community informed about their programs, needs, and problems, schools use various communication tools. Since school-community relations is properly viewed as a two-way communication process, citizens are encouraged to discuss school issues and even criticize school policy where appropriate. All these interactions between the school and the community open the door to misinformation, propaganda, and false statements.

Cases involving alleged defamatory communication among parents, students, citizens, and school authorities concerning school matters have been the subject of defamation suits. But proving a defamation action is quite difficult. Effective defenses are available to school personnel who become defendants in defamation actions. Of course, a defamatory statement that is true is not actionable in a defamation suit.

Defenses Against Defamation. An absolute privilege completely excuses a defamatory statement. It is usually accorded speech made in legislative, judicial, or executive proceedings. Such statements are protected if made in the performance of legitimate public duties (American Law Institute, 1986). Statements made by school board members and superintendents in the course of evaluating school personnel or investigations into wrongdoing are often protected by an absolute privilege. (They are certainly protected by a qualified privilege.)

A *conditional* or *qualified privilege* excuses defamatory speech made in good faith and without malice. School personnel have used it extensively as a defense. The qualified privilege arises from common law and is pertinent to communications between parties sharing an interest or duty, including school personnel. The judiciary has noted the public's interest in education and has extended the qualified privilege to teachers engaged in evaluating students and to school administrators communicating information about teacher performance. Parents also have available the defense of qualified privilege when communicating about teacher performance and other matters directly bearing on the welfare of their children at school.

The Supreme Court in *New York Times, Inc. v. Sullivan* (1964) ruled that the First Amendment requires that a "public official" who files a defamation suit against critics (for example, individuals or the press) of his or her "official conduct" must show that the defamatory statements were made with "actual malice" and that the defendant(s) made the statements with knowledge of their falsity or with reckless disregard of whether they were true or false. The courts have been divided on the issue of whether school administrators and teachers who have been defamed are public officials within the meaning of *Sullivan*.

The judicial trend has been toward not considering administrators and teachers as public officials. However, school board members, superintendents, and principals have been considered public figures (Alexander & Alexander, 2001). When viewed as private citizens, teachers need only to prove that defamatory statements made against them are untruthful.

In disseminating information about the school to the community through the mass media, the *Sullivan* (1964) rules concerning defamatory communication are applicable. After *Sullivan*, defamation liability is extremely difficult to prove against the media when the defamatory communication concerns a public figure or official. This in no way obviates a school from practicing honest, well-researched journalism, however.

CONSTITUTIONAL TORTS

Many of the school-community relations issues facing contemporary educators touch on some aspect of constitutional law. Issues related to school discipline, freedom of speech, religion, assembly, and the press; voting rights; and invasion of privacy, due process, and equal protection rights are some of the more frequent and important constitutionally protected rights that come into play in school-community relations. School districts that interfere with the federal constitutional rights of individuals may be liable to the party injured in an action known as a *constitutional tort*. Constitutional torts protect and secure individual rights under the U.S. Constitution from being interfered with by the state. Schools have witnessed dramatic increases in the number of constitutional tort actions brought against them. The legal authority for maintaining a constitutional tort against a school district is found in the Civil Rights Act of 1871, which was codified in the federal laws as Title 42 of the United States Code shortly after the Civil War. Congress intended that awards under the Civil Rights Act of 1871 would deter the deprivation of the constitutional rights of newly freed Black citizens.

The most prevalent statute under Title 42 used by plaintiffs to bring constitutional tort actions against school districts is 42 U.S.C.S. § 1983. Section 1983 provides in part:

> Every person who, under color of any statute, ordinance, regulation, custom or usage, of any state or Territory . . . subjects or causes to be subjected any citizen of the United States or other person within the jurisdiction thereof to the deprivation of any rights, privileges, or immunities secured by the Constitution and laws shall be liable to the party injured in an action at law. (42 U.S.C. § 1983, 2002)

In *Monell v. Department of Social Services of New York* (1978), the Supreme Court held that Section 1983 suits could be brought against government units like school boards. However, the Court held that governmental bodies cannot be held liable under Section 1983 on a respondent superior theory whereby employers are liable for the acts of their employees. Therefore, school districts are liable under Section 1983 for a constitutional wrong committed by an employee only when the actions represent well-established custom or official policy of the school district.

In *Wood v. Strickland* (1975), a case involving student discipline, the Supreme Court held that individuals, including school board members, could be held liable for committing constitutional torts. Before *Wood v. Strickland*, school employees had been completely immune from Section 1983 actions. However, in *Wood*, the Supreme Court granted school employees a "good faith immunity." The Court said that a school board member or school employee loses the immunity and may be liable for damages under Section 1983 if "he knew or reasonably should have known that the action he took within his sphere of official responsibility would violate the constitutional rights of the students affected" (*Wood*, p. 322). In *Harlow v. Fitzgerald* (1982), the Court explained that as long as a school employee's action does not "violate clearly established statutory or constitutional rights of which a reasonable person would have known" (p. 818), he or she will not be held liable under Section 1983.

The number of student-initiated Section 1983 lawsuits against schools and school personnel have dramatically increased during the past 10 years (Alexander & Alexander, 2001). Many of the cases involve charges of sexual misconduct, peer-to-peer sexual harassment, enforcement of "zero tolerance" policies, and student-to-student violence that is not prevented by school officials.

Political Speech

Teachers and other school employees play a central role in a school-community relations program. Bagin and Gallagher (2001) maintain that a strong external communication program is impossible without the support and participation of school employees. Positive employee relations depend on a school's recognizing human needs in order to build a community spirit among school employees. High morale among employees is associated with a strong school-community plan. Teachers should feel free to express themselves on matters related to the welfare of the school. However, school employees cannot be expected to always agree with school leaders or school policy. Sometimes what a teacher believes to be constructive criticism is viewed by school administrators as insubordinate behavior.

Prior to the 1960s, public employment, including the employment of teachers, was considered a privilege rather than a right. Accordingly, teachers were expected to limit and give away their First Amendment rights to their employers. However, during the 1960s, with the public's attention focused on individual rights, the courts determined that the "privilege doctrine" was inappropriate, and the relationship between teachers and school boards began to change (Alexander & Alexander, 2001). The U.S. Supreme Court in *Pickering v. Board of Education of Township High School District 205* (1968) established the legal principle that public school teachers have the First Amendment right of freedom of expression. In *Pickering*, a school board terminated the employment of a teacher for writing a letter to a local newspaper that was published, criticizing the school superintendent and school board for spending school funds on athletic programs and neglecting to inform the district taxpayers of their decisions. The Supreme Court applied a "balance of interests" test in determining that the teacher's letter did not disrupt the orderly educational process. The Court struck the balance in favor of the teacher, recognizing the right of teachers as citizens to express their views on matters of public concern. However, a teacher's right of speech and expression is not of unlimited scope. If a teacher's comments seriously damage the relationship between employer and employee or are deliberately or recklessly false or seriously impede the educational mission of the school, then the exercise of such speech may be grounds for dismissal. However, the burden of proving any of these matters rests with the school district.

Where an educator's First Amendment right is at issue, the judiciary uses a three-step analysis. The court must first determine if the teacher's speech is constitutionally protected. Here the court determines whether the statements made by the teacher, taken as a whole, are on a matter of public concern. Second, a court must ascertain whether the school board's dismissal was motivated by the teacher's exercise of his or her First Amendment rights. Third, the school district must be given an opportunity to demonstrate that it would have taken the same action in the absence of the teacher's constitutionally protected conduct. A federal district court used the three-step analysis to determine that a school district's policy prohibiting criticism from staff members other than to the person being criticized, the principal, the superintendent, or at a school board meeting to be unconstitutional. As written, the policy would have prohibited speech that numerous courts had already determined was protected. The court found that the policy failed to narrowly define *criticism*, and Webster's dictionary definition included activity that the school admittedly did not seek to prohibit; therefore, the policy did not provide employees with fair warning as to what could and could not be said (*Westbrook v. Teton County School District*, 1996).

Right of Privacy: The Teacher

Increased community participation and public interest education results in a better understanding of community concerns and values. Although this is most often positive in building the future of public schools, it can also cause legal problems for school districts. Certainly, schools belong to the community, but the concept of community ownership does not imply that the community can unilaterally impose its values and morality on the schools and their employees at the expense of individual constitutional rights. However, the courts recognize the role of community values and attitudes in the context of teacher employment.

Although the U.S. Constitution does not expressly mention privacy, the Supreme Court has interpreted the Constitution to include a fundamental right of privacy. A teacher's conduct outside the classroom may be the basis for cancellation of a contract or disciplinary action. The problem in cases involving protection of personal privacy is to arrive at a balance among the privacy interests of the teacher, community morals, and the school's interest in maintaining an appropriate educational environment. Teachers have been discharged from public school employment for matters arising in their private lives that conflict with community sentiment.

Most states have tenure laws that variously set forth grounds for terminating a teacher's employment. One ground for dismissal that often leads to conflict between privacy rights and community values is commonly referred to as *immorality*. In an often-cited case involving allegations of teacher immorality, the Pennsylvania Supreme Court defined *immorality* as "not essentially confined to a deviation from sex morality; it may be such a course of conduct as offends the morals of the community and is a bad example to the youth whose ideals a teacher is supposed to foster and to evaluate" (*Horosko v. Mount Pleasant Township School District*, 1939, p. 868).

In 1974, on the basis of widespread allegations of abuse and misuse of student records, Congress enacted the Family Educational Rights and Privacy Act (FERPA), commonly referred to as the Buckley Amendment. The handling of student records by school officials was criticized on several grounds, including the release of information to third parties such as police, news media, social service agencies, and vendors without the consent of parents, failure to provide parents with access to records, and maintenance of inaccurate records. In response, Congress passed legislation that provided substantive and procedural safeguards for the privacy rights of students and their parents. FERPA grants parents, and students upon attaining 18 years of age, a legal right of access to student records. Within a reasonable period of time from their request, parents must be allowed to inspect and review (and make copies of at their own expense) all records directly related to their child. In no event may the school stall for more than 45 days from the parent's initial request for records. With respect to inaccurate records, FERPA provides parents with an avenue to amend records, and if not satisfied, parents may request an impartial hearing on the issue. Parents may also file complaints concerning violations of FERPA with the Department of Education. Schools found not in compliance with FERPA face the ultimate sanction of losing federal aid.

FERPA mandates that most data contained in student records are kept confidential. Personally identifiable information contained in school records may be released only with written consent from the student's parents. The most common exception to the rules regarding confidentiality is that the student records may be made available to school officials, including teachers within the school district where the child attends school, who have legitimate educational interest in the student. Schools must keep a record of individuals and agencies that are given access to the records of a student. Under FERPA, public schools may release general information to the public, including a student's name, address, telephone listing, date and place of birth, major field of study, participation in activities and sports, dates of attendance, and degrees and awards received.

In addition to the privacy rights protected by FERPA, the Individuals with Disabilities Education Act (IDEA) contains specific confidentiality requirements covering the records of students with disabilities. Moreover, most states have enacted legislation according confidentiality rights in records containing personal information kept by state agencies, including public schools. In some instances, state privacy statutes grant more privacy rights to students than does FERPA.

The U.S. Supreme Court recently weighed in on a FERPA issue. The Court determined that the practice of students grading other students' papers does not violate FERPA. The Court emphasized it was answering the narrow question of whether peer grading violates FERPA (*Owasso v. Falvo*, 2002).

Religion, Community, and Public Schools

The relationship between religion and the public schools is an extremely important, delicate, and controversial issue in the context of school-community relations. Wide-ranging issues of community concern such as prayer, Bible reading, distribution of religious materials, student-initiated devotional meetings on school property, and the use of school facilities by religious groups are among the thorniest church-state separation issues confronting a school-community relations undermined and/or dominated by issues related to the role of religion in the public schools.

The First Amendment of the U.S. Constitution provides that "Congress shall make no law respecting an establishment of religion or prohibiting the free exercise thereof." The majority of church-state cases in the public education setting arise under this establishment clause. In most church-state cases since 1970, the Supreme Court has applied a three-part test derived from the Court's ruling in *Lemon v. Kurtzman* (1971). Although the so-called *Lemon* test has been severely criticized by many of the current Supreme Court justices, the Court has not eliminated the test from establishment-clause adjudication. The tripartite test developed in *Lemon* is as follows: first, the governmental action or statute must have a secular purpose; second, its primary effect must neither advance nor inhibit religion; finally, the governmental action must avoid excessive governmental entanglement with religion.

In two landmark Supreme Court decisions in the early 1960s, the Court struck down school-sponsored Bible reading and daily prayers. These decisions were controversial and unpopular with the general public. Supported by popular opinion, almost half of the states enacted legislation permitting some form of prayer (silent meditation or voluntary prayer, for example) in the public schools. In *Wallace v. Jaffree* (1985), the Court found an Alabama statute calling for a daily 1-minute period of silence for meditation or prayer to violate the First Amendment. However, the Court suggested that a statute authorizing a moment of silence for meditation or prayer during the school day might pass constitutional muster if the state legislature's intent in passing the law was not motivated by a religious purpose. In 1997, the Eleventh Circuit Court of Appeals said that public schools may begin each day with a state-mandated moment of silence (*Brown v. Gwinnett*, 1997). However, the Supreme Court held that a school district's policy of permitting an invocation over the loud speaker before football games, by an individual elected by the student body, violated the Establishment Clause (*Santa Fe Ind. Sch. Dist. v. Doe*, 2000).

One school-sponsored activity involving the entire community—graduation exercises— has turned into a hotbed of legal activity. In fact, a national debate over prayers at graduation ceremonies erupted after the Supreme Court, in *Lee v. Weisman* (1992), struck down school-arranged clergy-led benedictions and invocations at graduation ceremonies. The prayers contested in *Lee* were designated nondenominational and given by a local rabbi who was invited by the school principal. The Court found the active participation of school authorities in organizing the prayer, students' susceptibility to peer pressure, and the importance of graduation ceremonies to students (coercive pressure to attend) coalesced to create a violation of the Establishment Clause. However, the Court left unresolved the constitutionality of student-organized and student-led prayers at graduation. Indeed, in 1993, the Supreme Court let stand a Texas high school policy that permitted student-initiated invocations and benedictions at graduation ceremonies (*Jones v. Clear Creek Independent School District*, 1993). In addition, the Eleventh Circuit held that a school district's policy of permitting a graduating student, elected by classmates, to deliver an unrestricted message of her choice at the beginning and/or closing of the graduation ceremonies was not facially in violation of the Establishment Clause (*Adler v. Duval Co. Sch. Bd.*, 2001).

Students, community groups, and organizations often request the use of school facilities for religious purposes. Requests by students and community groups for the use of school facilities for meetings and other activities have been distinguished and related differently by the judiciary. In 1990, the Supreme Court upheld the constitutionality of the Equal Access Act (passed by Congress in 1984), which permits student-initiated religious groups to meet on school premises during noninstructional time. If a public high school has at least one noncurriculum-related student group, then *Board of Education of Westside Com-*

munity Schools v. Mergens (1990) holds that a school must recognize a wide array of groups, regardless of the philosophical, political, or religious content of their members' speech.

In *Lamb's Chapel v. Center Moriches School District* (1993), the Supreme Court held that a school board's refusal to permit a church access to school facilities, after hours, to show a film series on family and childrearing issues was unconstitutional. A close analysis of the case reveals that the Court ruled narrowly on the issue of public access to school facilities for religious purposes.

The Supreme Court upheld the right of an outside adult-led group that sought to actively preach and provide religious instruction to elementary school students to meet on school grounds immediately after the school day. The Court affirmed the right of the religious club to be on school grounds on the same basis as any other club or activity (*Good News Club v. Molford Central Sch. Dist.*, 2001).

One other volatile church-state separation issue involves the distribution of religious literature by students on school property. Beginning in the late 1980s, most courts have held that students have a free-speech right to distribute religious materials on school property. Schools maintain the right to set reasonable rules regarding the time, place, and manner of distribution of religious literature on school premises (*Harless v. Darr*, 1996; *Peck v. Upshur County Bd. of Educ.*, 1998).

COMMUNITY VALUES AND THE CURRICULUM

One paradox of an effective school-community relations program is that increased community involvement in school affairs does not always result in agreement on school programs or school purposes. The tension between community values and attitudes and the goals and mission of the public schools is particularly felt in curricular decisions. Tyler (1949), known as the father of curriculum making, identified three major sources of the curriculum: society, learners, and knowledge. Curriculum makers must consider information, beliefs, and values from each source. Parents and interest groups aligned with myriad causes attempt to influence curriculum, experiences, and information provided in public schools. The influence and efforts of special-interest groups and organizations cannot be underestimated. According to the Office for Intellectual Freedom, there were close to 5,000 challenges to materials in schools or school libraries between 1990 and 2000. Approximately 1,140 challenges were made to "sexually explicit" material and 1,013 to material considered to use "offensive language" (Office for Intellectual Freedom, 2002).

The Seventh Circuit upheld a school board in a case where parents attempted to prevent the elementary school from using the *Impressions* reading series as the main supplemental reading program in grades K–5. Parents contended that the reading series violated the First Amendment by promoting wizards and witches and other creatures with supernatural powers, thus indoctrinating children in anti-Christian values. The court reiterated that schools have broad discretion in curriculum matters, and courts should interfere only where constitutional values are directly implicated. The court rejected the notion that stories with witches, goblins, and Halloween violated the Establishment Clause, holding instead that Halloween is an American tradition and is a purely secular affair (*Fleischfresser v. Directors of School Dist. 200*, 1994).

One particular educational approach known as *outcome-based education* (OBE) has been at the center of censorship controversy during the 1990s. Zlatos (1993) reported, "All across America, the battle lines are drawn over OBE. From Pennsylvania to Washington, from Iowa to Oregon, hundreds of angry parents have jammed public hearings, and thousands of opponents have taken to the streets" (p. 12). What is OBE? Although no single definition exists, at its core, OBE stands for the proposition that all students can learn. Zlatos summarized the many variations of OBE: "Its approach, in short, is to define clearly what students are to learn (the desired outcomes), measure their progress based on actual achievement, meet their needs through various teaching strategies, and give them enough time to help to meet their potential" (p. 13).

Twenty-four states have enacted some form of OBE as part of broader assessment and accountability reform programs. The most common approach to OBE is to develop sets of core outcome goals for specific academic areas, for such areas as self-esteem, and to measure student progress locally. Critics of OBE claim that its costs are unknown and that the outcomes cannot be measured. Religious groups claim that OBE promotes values and morals inconsistent with their religious beliefs.

Courts have granted local school leaders broad discretion to determine matters related to the school curriculum. However, the discretion granted to school authorities is not absolute; the courts also consider the constitutional rights of students, teachers, and parents. Most state legislatures have granted primary responsibility for public school education to local school boards, which generally have considerable power in regulating the instructional program. Local school authorities have broad powers concerning curriculum, textbooks, and other educational matters. But the Supreme Court made it clear in *Board of Education, Island Trees Union Free School District No. 26 v. Pica* (1982) that books may not be removed from a school library by school officials if they are motivated by an intent to suppress or deny access to ideas with which they disagree. In *Board of Education, Island Trees Union Free School District No. 26 v. Pica*, the Court maintained that school boards could remove books from a school library if motivated by the "pervasive vulgarity of the book," its "educational unsuitability," its "bad taste" or "irrelevance," or because of age and grade inappropriateness. Alexander and Alexander (2001) warn that the direction of the courts in the 1990s on issues related to the curriculum "appear to place less emphasis on a broadly conceived standard that secures the expansion of knowledge preventing the 'casting of a pall of orthodoxy' and allows more flexibility in allowing curriculum decisions to be made on the basis of local school board judgment and possibly, local political pressure" (p. 289).

COPYRIGHT ISSUES

Every school-community relations program disseminates information about the school to the community through print, audio, and visual media activities as well as through performances and school displays. Every school district uses and produces copyrighted work and must be aware of copyright law. The purpose of copyright law is to protect the ownership and use of original works of authorship. Copyright provides the creator of an original work control over many activities, including the right to reproduce, distribute, display, perform, adapt, and translate the work (17 U.S.C. § 101 *et seq.*).

Congress passed the Copyright Act of 1976, substantially amending the Copyright Act of 1909 that made copyright law a matter of federal law. Federal copyright protection attaches upon any original work of ownership, fixed in any tangible form of expression. Registration of the copyright with the U.S. Copyright Offices is not a condition of a valid copyright. However, registration is a prerequisite to filling a copyright infringement action. The copyright law extends to such items as literary works, computer programs, multimedia works and lyrics, dramatic works, graphic and sculptural works, sound recordings, and audiovisual works. Significantly, copyright does not cover ideas, procedures, and concepts (17 U.S.C. § 101, 102).

The 1976 copyright law places some limitations on the exclusive rights enjoyed by copyright owners. Section 107 of the act sets forth the "fair use" doctrine, which is particularly relevant to educators. This doctrine states in pertinent part that "the fair use of a copyrighted work, including such use . . . by reproduction for purposes such as: criticism, comment, new reporting, teaching (including multiple copies for classroom use) scholarship or research is not an infringement of copyright" (17 U.S.C. § 107). Further guidelines for educators regarding reproducing multiple copies of copyrighted work for educational purposes (and cited by courts) are found in the Classroom Guidelines of the Fair Use doctrine (H.R. 94–1476), 94th Cong., 2d sess. 66, 1976). These guidelines represent part of the legislative history of the 1976 act, but are not considered part of the law. They permit educators to make multiple copies (not to exceed in any event more than one copy per pupil in a course) for classroom use of discussion, provided that the copying meets the tests of brevity and spontaneity and the cumulative effect test and that all copies contain a notice of copyright. It is clear that the copying of anthologies containing substantial portions of copyrighted books or articles without the permission of the copyright owner even for educational purposes violates the fair use doctrine (*Basic Books Inc. v. Kinko's Graphics Corp.*, 1991).

Computer software is given protection under the copyright laws. The owner of a copy of a computer program may make copies of the program only when the new copy is created as an essential step in using the program in conjunction with a machine or when the new copy is for archival purposes only. All archival copies of the program must be destroyed when the program is no longer used (17 U.S.C. § 117, 2002). It is clearly illegal for a school to load a copy of a program on one machine and "boot" that copy into the fixed memory of its microcomputers. The state of the law in the area of computer software is complex and rapidly evolving. Schools districts are well advised to inform teachers and students of the changing law regarding the use of copyrighted software.

The Internet has become a major instructional tool in schools all across America. The Internet and the World Wide Web have generated an array of new copyright issues. A number of bills have been introduced into Congress to address copyright issues in cyberspace. Many of these laws would rewrite current copyright law and practice related to the Internet. Daniel (1998) has summarized copyright law as it impacts Internet use by schools, and he suggests that the following provisions should be included in acceptable use policies:

1. Students may use computing facilities for educational purposes only. Acceptable use of the Internet refers to activities that support teaching and learning.

2. Students must observe standard copyright restrictions, which are the same for printed materials.
3. Students may not send or receive copyrighted material without permission.
4. The unauthorized installation, use, storage, or distribution of copyrighted software or materials on a school district computer is prohibited.

ETHICS AND SCHOOL-COMMUNITY RELATIONS

The set of nonlegal rules—those outside the legal systems that guide human relationships—is known as *ethics*. What is generally called the ethics of a profession is actually the consensus of expert opinions to the human responsibilities and obligations involved in a profession. References to ethics suggest that the term relates to moral action, human character, and a sense of duty; that it pertains to what is fair, equitable, good, and professionally right, conforming to professional standards of conduct.

During the past 20 years, American educators have shown a growing interest in, and a genuine concern for, ethical and moral issues related to educational theory and practice. Textbooks on ethical leadership in school administration, the inclusion of ethics courses in educational administration preparation programs, and a proliferation of scholarly articles devoted to exploring the ethics of school leadership are evidence of a heightened awareness of the importance of ethical issues in education (Kimbrough, 1985; Rebore, 2001; Strike, Haller, & Soltis, 1988). Indeed, Crowson (1989) suggested that educators face ethical issues on a daily basis: "To a large degree all [educational] administrative decisions are rooted in moral codes and cultural values, thus all decisions have an ethical component" (p. 418). Pratt and Shin (1997) point out the importance of reputation management or credibility enhancement as the key element in generating public support.

Many of the legal issues discussed here raise recurring ethical issues in the context of school-community relations. Incident-specific issues related to teacher dismissal, values inoculation, freedom of the press, student discipline, the Internet, parental rights, copyright infringement, student and teacher privacy rights, teacher and student free-speech rights, compliance with federal and state laws and regulations, and teacher evaluation pose ethical choices in individual cases (Moore, 1999). Beyond these incident-specific legal issues, policy, and governance matters concerning school choice, allocation of resources, school-based management, teacher preparation, class size, school consolidation, and student assessment practices present ethical dilemmas in the context of school-community relations.

Many education scholars argue that incident-specific issues must be examined as taking place in a much broader ethical context. McInerny (1997–1998) argues that ethics must be taught as more than one course or unit; ethics must be integrated throughout the curriculum. Starratt (1991) contends that the educational program "is supposed to serve moral purposes (the nurturing of the human, social and intellectual growth of the youngsters)" (p. 187). As a consequence, "[t]he administrator who assumes that the educational environment, the organization, the system, the institutional arrangements (the curriculum, the daily and weekly schedule, the assessment and discipline and placement and promotion policies) enjoy a value neutrality, or worse already embody the desirable ethical standards, is ethically naïve, if not culpable" (p. 187). Reitzug (1994) summarizes the importance of recognizing and understanding the ethical issues faced by educators:

> Surfacing and addressing ethical issues daily practice is perhaps the most crucial task in which administrators engage. The specific ethical issues that are analyzed and the way in which they are resolved will mold the culture and character of the school; define the school's purpose and the measures of effectiveness it considers crucial; and determine whether the school is a static entity or transformational and empowering community. (p. 37)

If the engine driving a school is purpose and defining its empowering capabilities is fueled by that school's ability to address ethical issues on a daily basis, then it is incumbent upon educators operating within the school-community relations milieu to be familiar with the ethical precepts theory and the practice relevant to education.

Code of Ethics

The search for the meaning and the practice of ethics in any profession generally begins with an examination of the profession's code of ethics. An ethics code is a set of standards and guidelines aimed at promoting the ideals of social responsibility within the context of a profession. From the standpoint of school-community relations, it is important to note that most of the professional mass-communications organizations have established ethical codes. Compliance with these codes is generally voluntary. The Public Relations Society of America (PRSA), the National School Public Relations Association (NSPRA), the Society of Professional Journalists (SPF), the American Society of Newspaper Editors (ASNE), and the International Association of Business Communications (IABC) have laid down ethical principles for communication professionals to follow. In fact, an issue of the journal *Public Relations Review* was devoted to public relations ethics, and several articles called for creating a universal ethics to cover the entire public relations professional community (Hiebert, 1993).

The National Education Association (NEA) adopted a code in 1929, and since then there have been many amendments to that code. The basic standards of the NEA code are meant to apply to all educators. The National Association of Secondary School Principals (NASSP) adopted a statement of ethics in 1973 for all educational administrators. The NASSP Code of Ethics specifically addresses the relationship between school administration and school-community relations. The code states, "The administrator acknowledges that the schools belong to the public they serve for the purpose of providing educational opportunities to all. However, the administrator assumes responsibility in providing professional leadership in the school and community" (*NASSP Bulletin*, 1988).

The NASSP ethics code sets forth 10 principles that make it incumbent upon the educational administrator to:

1. Makes the well-being of students the fundamental value in all decision making and actions.
2. Fulfills professional responsibilities with honesty and integrity.
3. Supports the principle of due process and protects the civil and human rights of all individuals.

4. Obeys local, state, and national laws.
5. Implements the governing board of education's policies and administrative rules and regulations.
6. Pursues appropriate measures to correct those laws, policies, and regulations that are not consistent with sound educational goals.
7. Avoid using positions for personal gain through political, social, religious, economic, or other influence.
8. Accepts academic degrees or professional certification only from duly accredited institutions.
9. Maintains the standards and seeks to improve the effectiveness of the profession through research and continuing professional development.
10. Honors all contracts until fulfillment, release, or dissolution mutually agreed upon by all parties to contract.

The National School Public Relations Association (NSPRA), which comprises school district public relations directors, school administrators, and others interested in improving public understanding of public schools, was founded in 1935. In 1981, NSPRA adopted a code of ethics for its members.

NSPRA Code of Ethics

The National School Public Relations Association shall have an ethics code for members, as follows:

1. Be guided constantly by pursuit of the public interest through truth, accuracy, good taste, and fairness; follow good judgment in releasing information; not intentionally disseminate misinformation or confidential data; avoid actions, which lessen personal, professional, or organizational reputation.
2. Give primary loyalty to employing organization, insisting on the right to give advisory counsel in accordance with sound public relations ideas and practices; cooperate with other groups while avoiding conflicts with primary responsibilities; object to untenable policies or activities.
3. Be aware of personal influence, avoiding promises or granting of unprofessional advantage to others; refrain from accepting special considerations for influences on organizational decisions, avoid unauthorized use of organizational facilities, resources, or professional services for personal gain or for promotion of the candidacy of aspirants to elected offices; forego derogatory acts or utterances against other professionals.
4. Recognize that effectiveness is dependent upon integrity and regard for ideals of the profession; not misrepresent professional qualifications; give credit for ideas and words borrowed from others; cooperate with professional colleagues to uphold and enforce this Code.

The NASSP and NSPRA codes of ethics are useful, as a beginning point, in reflecting on ethical issues in education because they represent the professions' shared values. However, codes of ethics are of little help in actual decision making because educational judgment involves more than simply following preestablished rules. Martinson (1997–1998) contends that professionals who are truly interested in acting in an ethical manner must incorporate an ethically grounded theoretical construct into their decision-making process. Ethical decisions are contextually bound and are made only after independent and reflective thought. Stories by and about individuals making ethical decisions document the multiplicity of experience in a way that shows the inadequacy of applying a static code of ethics. Questions like, "What do our relationships ask of us?" or "Who controls us and how shall we govern ourselves?" or "Who benefits by these arrangements?" (Starratt, 1991, pp. 189, 199) cannot be answered by codes of ethics.

Administrative Ethics

Kowalski (2003) suggests that administrative ethics can be divided into three categories:

1. Nonroutine issues of morality and personal practice. This category includes ethical choices administrators confront on an irregular basis, where one choice may result in personal pleasure or personal (as opposed to professional) gain. Examples falling into this category include misuse of funds, sexual indiscretion, and certain conflicts of interest.
2. Nonroutine issues of professional practice. This category includes ethical choices administrators confront on an irregular basis that deal with professional matters. Examples falling into this category include nepotism, yielding to influential constituents in order to avoid trouble, and terminating teachers (for example, those who need the salary provided by teaching and try hard but are ineffective teachers).
3. Daily issues of administrative practice. This category includes the application of power (for example, the imposition of one person's will upon another), the shaping of people and organizations, the determination of "correct" values, the justification of power usage, and the justification of choices exercised (p. 368).

Greenfield (1993) identifies four main sources of values relevant to guiding educators involved in school-community relations: (a) society's standards of good conduct; (b) the education profession's rules of conduct; (c) the school's or school district's standards (found in school board policy and state and federal laws); and (d) the community attitudes and standards. The question immediately arises: Which set or source of values should guide school personnel involved in resolving ethical issues related to school-community relations?

Starratt (1991) proposes a model or framework within which one may ground ethical judgments in the school environment. This framework recognizes the intersection between school-community relations, social responsibility, and ethics. Starratt incorporates three perspectives into this framework for identifying, evaluating, and making ethical decisions: the ethic of critique, the ethic of justice, and the ethic of caring. The *ethic of critique* is focused on confronting "the moral issues involved when schools disproportionately benefit some groups in society and final others" (p. 190). Central to this ethic is an examination of the structural (managerial) issues involved in educational leadership, such as bias in the workplace. School personnel viewing the world through the lens of the ethic of critique reflect upon and explore such constructs as bureaucratic leadership, power, and domination. Questions raised by the ethic of critique seem especially useful when considering the school administrator's relationship with internal publics.

The *ethic of justice* is concerned with values such as individual rights, the common good, and democratic participation in school governance. Starratt points out that, in educational institutions where consideration of the ethic of justice takes place, "specific ethical learning activities are structured within curricular and extracurricular programs to encourage discussion of individual choices as well as discussions of school community choice" (p. 193). The ethic of justice requires an examination of the tension between the claims of the individual and community needs. Starratt observes that "the claims of the institution serve both the common good and the rights of individuals in the school. . . . [D]iscussions about the curriculum, about appropriate textbooks, about a visiting speaker's program and the like will need to be carried on . . . for the moral questions they raise about public life in the community" (p. 194).

The *ethic of caring* emphasizes human connection and relationships. The ethic of caring provides a perspective of dealing with both a school's internal and external constituencies. Most centrally, the ethic of caring is "grounded in the belief that the intent of human relationships should be held sacred and that the school as an organization should hold the good of human beings within it as sacred. This ethic reaches beyond concerns with efficiency" (Starratt, 1991, p. 195). The ethic of caring examines the motives and reasons attendant on the administration of a school. The ethic of caring draws attention to stereotyping and language that interferes with honest two-way communication. The elements of a positive school culture are found in the ethic of caring, which is reflected in a school-community relations program where school officials stress empathy and concern and caring for others, value cooperation over competition, and emphasize participative forms of decision making.

Starratt's theoretical concept avoids being centered on the most prevalent ethical system in the public relations' field, which is known as situational ethics (Leeper, 1996). Martinson (1997–1998) points out that situational ethics has been called "the new morality," and it is premised on the belief that no law or principle is absolute. From this viewpoint, almost any action may be justified because any principle or law can be deemed moral depending upon the circumstances of the action.

Attention to diversity has moved Reitzug (1994) to challenge educators to become more sensitive to the ethical issues of diversity. He asserts:

> . . . sensitivity to diversity recognizes *cultural differences* due to race, ethnicity, gender, and class, as well as *opinion differences* due to varying beliefs concerning educational practice. Evidence of sensitivity to diversity is found in practices such as multicultural curricula, and shared decision-making interventions such as site-based management. (p. 1)

Ethics and Cultural Diversity

Today, school-community relations are played out in an increasingly pluralistic society, and educators should be acutely aware of ethical issues arising out of cultural diversity. Rebore (2001) contends that there are three dimensions of pluralism. The first dimension focuses on the conditionality of values, pointing out that values differ from culture to culture. These values must be examined from a vantage point that appreciates diversity. The second dimension revolves around the notion that conflict is unavoidable and what constitutes the "good life" is diverse and varied according to different generations and cultures. The third dimension of pluralism centers on how conflict can be resolved. Conflict resolution is most often achieved when the parties to the conflict can focus on their shared values.

Educational leaders have a moral responsibility to communicate with all segments of a diverse community. Shingles and Lopez-Reyna (2002) maintain:

> . . . often members of the dominant culture, in an effort to ensure a nonbiased approach to people from other cultures, attempt to stress so-called color-blindness, or an inability to recognize a cultural difference. . . . In most cases, treating everyone the same means treating everyone as if they were members of the dominant cultural group. Problems arise from the fact that not everyone is the same and that engaging everyone from a single cultural perspective will place some cultural groups at a district disadvantage. (p. 6)

In other words, treating everyone the same does not necessarily translate into treating everyone fairly.

Glazer (1997) maintains that schools must honor and respect the need to show all students their group's distinctive contributions to American life. However, Glazer argues that schools must not dwell on a negative view of American history, especially the country's alleged failure to achieve full educational opportunities for all minorities. He believes that such an emphasis on American failures would lead only to disunity and separation. Instead, he believes that schools should emphasize the underlying democratic values that unite the country.

Ethics and the Educative Role of School-Community Relations

The interplay between ethics and school-community relations is most directly located in the educative function of the public school. Education for life must be the ultimate mission of any school-community relations program. Bellah, Madsen, Sullivan, Swindler, and Tipton (1992) deliver a clarion call for schools to transform their districts, towns, and cities into learning communities. They explain that Americans must begin to view schools less as part of the "infrastructure for competition and more as an invaluable resource in the search for the common good" (p. 175).

This is the kind of school-community relations plan that John Dewey sought when he urged schools to assume the role of educating the public not only to the needs of the school but to the needs of the community as well (McKinney & Place, 1992). Dewey stated: "The schools are not doing, and cannot do, what the people want until there is more unity, more definiteness, in the community's consciousness of its own needs; but it is the business of the school to forward this conception, to help the people to a clearer and more systematic idea of what the underlying needs of modern life are, and of how they are really to be supplied" (1901/1940, p. 37).

Leeper (1996) suggests that public relations always seeks to establish a sense of community. Schools that have a strong community focus are always acting in their own best interest. Garrison (1998) writes, "the key to freedom and the good life lies in recognizing the needs of others as well as our own, and in working together to build more inclusive, better communicating, democratic communities" (p. 26).

The ethical challenges to school-community relations today is to create and use the culture of the school in ways that will involve the schools' pluralistic constituencies in a common effort to build a just and caring school and community.

SUMMARY

The field of school-community relations is shaped by the law, both in policy making and in everyday educational practice. Four major sources of law (constitutional, case, statutory, and administrative law) directly impact the many aspects of school-community relations. Schools interact with internal and external publics in different forms and through various activities, and the law accordingly touches on individual school-community relations programs in ways that reflect those differences. Schools that ignore the significance of the legal dimensions of school-community relations do so at their own peril.

Educators face ethical issues on a daily basis in regard to their school-community relations program. Issues related to free speech, parental rights, values inculcation, the Internet, teacher evaluation, allocation of resources, and school consolidation pose ethical dilemmas in the context of school-community relations. The ways in which ethical issues are analyzed, presented to the public, and resolved greatly impacts the relationship between schools and their communities. Perhaps the greatest challenge today for schools in the context of school-community relations is to recognize the many ethical issues that arise out of an increasingly pluralistic society. The extent to which these complex ethical issues are resolved will define whether the school will be successful in creating a sense of community among all its pluralistic constituents.

| CASE STUDY | The Superintendent Learns About Community Values |

Mary Wright was excited as she drove to the first school board meeting of her second year as superintendent of the Gallup Community Schools (GCS). Gallup, with a population of 100,000, is an aging industrial community in the Midwest, and Wright had enjoyed a first-year "honeymoon" with the school board and surrounding community as she attempted to learn about the schools and the community and concentrated on not rocking the boat. But now she was determined to address a litany of educational concerns that she felt had been previously ignored by the school district.

In hiring her, the school board had conducted what they considered to be a complete background search. Wright had been pleased that the school board had not discovered that she had recently filed for bankruptcy and, as a result, had been virtually penniless when she first came to Gallup. She was also glad that the board had not discovered that she had been seeing a psychiatrist for the past 3 years after suffering from psychological fatigue. Although members of the GCS school board had asked her previous employer (members of the Blueline school board) if Wright had any medical or other "in-the-closet" problems that might interfere with her performance as superintendent, the Blueline board had not informed GCS about Wright's financial or psychological problems even though the Blueline school board was familiar with them.

On the basis of information that she and her school-community relations director, Tom Sample, had gathered, Wright was now prepared to make the annual "state-of-the-GCS address." In that address at this first school board meeting of the year, Wright announced the following initiatives:

1. Because of the growing AIDS epidemic and an increase in local teenage pregnancies, GCS would explore offering a sex education program (beginning in kindergarten).
2. Because of school disturbances motivated by racial and ethnic animosities, GCS would immediately introduce courses on promoting understanding and tolerance among students from different racial and ethnic backgrounds (a multicultural program beginning in ninth grade).
3. In an effort to curb gang activity and prevent school dropout, GCS would immediately implement a community-oriented program to be cosponsored by the schools, law enforcement agencies, and the Gallup prosecuting attorney's office. GCS counselors, principals, and deans would target students with extensive disciplinary problems for mandatory conferences involving parents, school personnel, the police, and a representative from the prosecuting attorney's office. The team of educators, police officers, and attorneys would advise students and parents of the ramifications of getting in trouble and dropping out of school.
4. Having obtained a waiver for three GCS elementary schools (as a pilot program) from state-mandated testing, GCS would now implement an alternative assessment (AA) program at those schools covered by the waiver, with a view toward developing a districtwide AA program in the elementary schools.

The day after the meeting, Wright encountered a wave of criticism of her proposal's new programs. Reverend Robert Wunder, minister at King's Garden Church, appeared on television and called Mary Wright an "antifamily nut." He demanded that the school board not approve the sex education program. Reverend Wunder claimed that sex education interferes with parental rights and violates his congregates' (and their school-age children) freedom of religion. Next, Wright received a phone call from the president of the local chamber of commerce, Buck Speakes, who said that any attempt to introduce multicultural education into the school curriculum would be challenged by his group and other community groups already concerned about declining test scores because of a "watered down" curriculum. Speakes also stated that he feared multicultural education would lead to a further "disuniting" of the community.

Three days later, Wright received a letter from the local chapter of the American Civil Liberties Union (ACLU), which claimed that her plan to work cooperatively with the police and the prosecuting attorney's office would lead to serious violations of students' privacy rights. The ACLU was prepared to challenge the program in court.

By the end of the week, Wright was feeling the political heat from her school board presentation. She picked up the morning newspaper, only to find a letter to the editor from Bea Line, a GCS elementary principal criticizing Wright's position on sex education as radical and unnecessary. Line also wrote that she had located and sent local community leaders copies of an article written by Wright and published in a scholarly research journal. The article advocated condom distribution in public high schools.

After a short weekend, Wright returned to her office to be confronted by two school board members and several influential members of the community. They were particularly upset about the sex education program, claiming it was offensive to local values, and they were incensed over the AA program. One citizen remarked that the AA program "sounded a bit like outcome-based education, and Gallup won't stand for that."

Wright contacted Tom Sample, who seemed to be the only person she could trust in Gallup. In fact, one evening over drinks, she had told Sample about the bankruptcy proceedings. Now she asked him to prepare and distribute a quick but slick-looking response to the criticism of the AA program. She told him to deny that AA had any parallels with outcome-based education. Sample was perplexed because just a month earlier Wright had sent him a summary report of AA objectives, a report replete with positive references to outcome-based education.

QUESTIONS AND SUGGESTED ACTIVITIES

CASE STUDY

1. What ethical and legal issues are raised in the case study? What ethical perspectives would you employ in the case study to make decisions? In your opinion, which legal challenges to Wright's proposals for new programs are most likely to succeed? To fail?

2. The case study lends itself to role-playing. Form a group and assign (or choose) characters. Try to empathize with the character you are playing. What points of view are not compatible? What are the alternatives to filing a lawsuit for the character opposed to Wright's view? What should Tom Sample do about writing a response regarding outcome-based education for the press?

3. Are there legal or ethical limits concerning a school board's authority to remove books and other materials from the curriculum? Is there any legal or ethical difference between removing books from the regular school curriculum and removing books and other materials from the school library? Would the removal of religiously oriented books from the school library violate the First Amendment? If a book is offensive to a minority student, should it be removed from the curriculum or the school library?

CHAPTER

4. What interests do the courts balance in cases involving a teacher dismissal?

5. Define *defamation* and explain the difference between absolute and conditional or qualified immunity as it relates to school-community relations.

6. Should all outsiders to a school be considered trespassers? Licensees? Explain your answers from a legal and a school-community relations point of view.

7. Is there any place for religion in the school curriculum? If parents object to textbooks or course offerings on religious grounds, should schools exempt their children from using the textbooks or from taking the courses? What legal and ethical considerations are relevant to your decision making?

SUGGESTED READINGS

Baker, L. (1993). *The credibility factor: Putting ethics to work in public relations*. Homewood, IL: Business One Irwin.

Champion, W. T. (1993). *Sports law in a nutshell*. St. Paul, MN: West Publishing.

Cubb, I. E., & Moe, T. M. (1990). *Politics, markets, and America's schools*. Washington, DC: Brookings Institution.

Dayton, J. (1998). Free speech, the Internet, and educational institutions: An analysis of *Reno v. ACLU*. *Education Law Reporter, 123*, 997–1011.

Dewey, J. (1966). *Democracy and education*. New York: Macmillan.

Etzioni, A. (1996). *The new golden rule: Community and morality in a democratic society*. New York: Basic Books.

Fletcher, G. (1996). *Basic concepts of legal thought*. New York: Oxford University Press.

Foster, W. (1986). *Paradigms and promises: New approaches to educational administration*. Buffalo, NY: Prometheus.

Gardner, C. (1995). *Justice and Christian ethics*. New York: Cambridge University Press.

Giroux, H. A. (1988). *Schooling and the struggle for public life*. Minneapolis: University of Minnesota Press.

Goodlad, J. I. (1984). *A place called school*. New York: McGraw-Hill.

Grossman, H. G. (1998). *Achieving educational equity*. Springfield, IL: Charles Thomas Publisher Ltd.

Harvey, C. (1997). Liberal indoctrination and the problem of community. *Synthese, 111*, 115–130.

Hogan, J. C. (1985). *The schools, the courts, and the public interest* (2nd ed.). Lexington, MA: Lexington Brooks.

MacIntyre, A. (1984). *After virtue*. Notre Dame, IN: University of Notre Dame Press.

McCarthy, C. (1990). *Race and the curriculum*. London: Falmer Press.

Noddings, N. (1984). *Caring: A feminine approach to ethics and moral education*. Berkeley: University of California Press.

Orfield, G., & Monfort, E. (1988). *Radical change and desegregation in large school districts*. Alexandria, VA: National School Boards Association.

Redman, G. (1999). *A casebook for exploring diversity in K–12 classrooms*. Upper Saddle River, NJ: Merrill/Prentice Hall.

Shapiro, J., & Stefkovich, J. (2001). *Ethical leadership and decision making in education*. Mahwah, NJ: Lawrence Erlbaum Associates.

Smolla, R. V. (1991). *Law of defamation*. New York: Clark Boardman.

Sommerville, D., & McDonald, S. (2002). *Developing school and community partnerships to meet the needs of students with challenging behaviors*. Arlington, VA: CASE.

U.S. Commission on Civil Rights. (1999). *Schools and religion*. Washington, DC: Author.

Weston, A. (1997). *A practical companion to ethics*. New York: Oxford University Press.

REFERENCES

Adler v. Duval Co. Sch. Bd., 250 F.3d 1330 (11th Cir. 2001).

Alexander, K., & Alexander, D. (2001). *American public school law* (5th ed.). Belmont, CA: West-Wadsworth Publishing.

American Law Institute. (1986). *Restatement of torts, second edition*. St. Paul, MN: American Law Institute Publishers.

Bagin, D., & Gallagher, D. (2001). *The school and community relations* (7th ed.). Boston: Allyn & Bacon.

Basic Books Inc. v. Kinko's Graphics Corp., 754 F. Supp. 1522 (S. D. N. Y. 1991).

Bellah, R. N., Madsen, R., Sullivan, W. M., Swindler, A., & Tipton, S. M. (1992). *The good society.* New York: Vintage Books.

Board of Education, Island Trees Union Free School District No. 26 v. Pica, 457 U.S. 853 (1982).

Board of Education of Westside Community Schools v. Mergens, 496 U.S. 226 (1990).

Brown v. Board of Education, 447 U.S. 483 (1954).

Brown v. Board of Education (Brown II), 349 U.S. 294 (1955).

Brown v. Gwinnet, 112 F.3d. 1464 (11th Cir. 1997).

Brum v. Town of Dartmouth and Others, 690 N.E.2d 844 (Mass. Ct. App. 1998).

C.P. v. Piscataway Tp. Bd. of Educ., 681 A2d 105 (N.J. Super A.D. 1996).

Crowson, R. (1989). Managerial ethics in educational administration: The rational choice approach. *Urban Education, 23*(4), 412–485.

Daniel, P. (1998). Copyright law, fair use and the Internet: Information for administrators and other educational officials. *Education Law Reporter, 122,* 899–911.

Dewey, J. (1940). The people and the schools. In J. Ratner (Ed.), *Education today.* New York: G.P. Putnam's Sons. (Reprinted from *The elementary school teacher,* 1901.)

Drake, T. L., & Roe, W. (2003). *The principalship* (6th ed.). Old Tappan, NJ: Pearson Publishing Co.

Fleischfresser v. Directors of School Dist. 200, 15 F.3d 680 (7th Cir. 1994).

Garrison, J. (1998). The paradox of indoctrination, pluralistic selves and liberal communitarianism. *Educational Foundations, 12,* 17–27.

Glazer, N. (1997). *We are all multiculturalists now.* Cambridge, MA: Harvard University Press.

Good News Club v. Molford Central Sch. Dist., 121 S. Ct. 2093 (2001).

Greenfield, W. O. (1993). Articulating values and ethics in administrator preparation. In C. S. Capper (Ed.), *Educational administration in a pluralistic society* (pp. 267–287). Albany: State University of New York Press.

Harless v. Darr, 937 F. Supp. 1351 (S.D. Ind. 1996).

Harlow v. Fitzgerald, 457 U.S. 800 (1982).

Harris v. Joint School District, 41 F.3d, 447 (9th Cir. 1994).

Hiebert, R. (1993). Public relations review (Vol. 19, No. 1). Greenwhich, CT: JAT Press.

Horosko v. Mount Pleasant Township School District, 6 A.2d 866 (1939).

Imber, M., & Thompson, G. (1991). Developing a typology of litigation in education and determining the frequency of each category. *Educational Administration Quarterly, 27*(2), 225–244.

Jones v. Clear Creek Independent School District, 930 F.2d 416, cert. denied, 113 S. Ct. 2750 (1993).

Keeton, P., Dobbs, D., Keeton, R., & Owen, D. (1984). *Prosser and Keeton on the law of torts* (5th ed.). St. Paul, MN: West Publishing.

Kimbrough, R. B. (1985). *Ethics: A current study for educational leaders.* Arlington, VA: American Association of School Administrators.

Kirp, D, & Jensen, N. (1986). *School days, rule days.* Philadelphia, PA: Falmer.

Korpela, A. E. (1971). *American law review* (Vol. 35). San Francisco: Lawyers Co-operative Publishing.

Kowalski, T. J. (2003). *Contemporary school administration: An introduction* (2nd ed.). Boston: Allyn & Bacon.

Lamb's Chapel v. Center Moriches School District, 113 S. Ct. 2141 (1993).

Lee v. Weisman, 112 S. Ct. 2649 (1992).

Leeper, K. A. (1996). Public relations ethics and communitarianism: A preliminary investigation. *Public Relations Review, 22,* 133–151.

Lemon v. Kurtzman, 43 U.S. 602 (1971).

Martinson, D. L. (1997–1998). Public relations practitioners must not confuse consideration of the situation with "situational ethics." *Public Relations Quarterly, 42,* 39–44.

McCarthy, M., & Cambron-McCabe, N. (1998). *Public school law* (4th ed.). Needham Heights, MA: Allyn & Bacon.

McInerny, P. M. (1997–1998). Ethics throughout the curriculum. *Public Relations Quarterly, 42,* 44–47.

McKinney, J. R., & Place, A. W. (1992). John Dewey and school-community relations. *Journal of Research for School Executives, 2,* 3–36.

Monell v. Department of Social Services of New York, 436 U.S. 658 (1978).

Moore, R. L. (1999). *Mass communication law and ethics.* Mahwah, NJ: Lawrence Erlbaum Associates.

NASSP Bulletin. (1988). Statement of ethics. *NASSP Bulletin, 72*(512), 95.

National Center for Education Statistics. (2001). *Indicators of school crime and safety.* Washington, DC: Author.

New York Times, Inc. v. Sullivan, 476 U.S. 254 (1964).

Office for Intellectual Freedom, American Library Association. (2002). *The 100 most frequently challenged books of 1990–2000.* Retrieved June 12, 2002, from http://www.ala.org/bbooks/bbwdatabase.html.

Owasso v. Falvo, 534 U.S. 426, 122 S. Ct., 934, 151 L. Ed. 2d 896 (2002).

Peck v. Upshur County Board of Education, 155 F.3d 274 (1998).

Pickering v. Board of Education of Township High School District 205, 391 U.S. 563 (1968).

Pratt, C., & Shin, T. (1997). Ethical implications of corporate communications. In C. Caywood (Ed.), *The handbook of strategic public relations & integrated communications.* New York: McGraw-Hill.

Rebore, R. (2001). *The ethics of educational leadership.* Upper Saddle River, NJ: Merrill/Prentice Hall.

Reitzug, U. C. (1994). Diversity, power and influence: Multiple perspectives on the ethics of school leadership. *Journal of School Leadership,* 197–222.

Santa Fe Ind. Sch. Dist. v. Doe, 530 U.S. 290 (2000).

Shingles, B., & Lopez-Reyna, L. (2002). *Cultural sensitivity in the implementation of discipline policies and practices.* Arlington, VA: CASE.

Starratt, R. J. (1991). Building an ethical school: A theory for practice in educational leadership. *Educational Administration Quarterly, 27*(2), 185 –202.

Strike, K., Haller, M., & Soltis, J. (1988). *Ethics of school administration.* New York: Teachers College Press.

Tyack, D., James, T., & Benovat, A. (1987). *Law and the shaping of public education.* Madison: University of Wisconsin Press.

Tyler, R. (1949). *Basic principles of curriculum and instruction.* Chicago: University of Chicago Press.

Wallace v. Jaffree, 472 U.S. 38 (1985).

West, P. (1985). *Educational public relations.* Beverly Hills, CA: Sage.

Westbrook v. Teton County School District, 918 F. Supp. 1475 (D. Wy. 1996).

Wood v. Strickland, 420 U.S. 308 (1975).

Yudolf, M., Kirp, D., Levin, B., & Moran, R. (2002). *Educational policy and the law* (4th ed.). Belmont, CA: Wadsworth Group/Thomas Learning.

Zirkel, P. A. (1997). "The explosion" in education litigation: An update. *Education Law Reporter, 114,* 341–350.

Zlatos, B. (1993). Outcome-based outrage. *Executive Educator, 15*(9), 12–20.

5

Public Relations in a Communication Context
Listening, Nonverbal, and Conflict-Resolution Skills

Angela Spaulding
Mary John O'Hair

No substitution exists for personal communication. New information technology such as electronic mail (e-mail), video-conferencing, cellular phones, and interactive television may be thought to reduce the need for personal communication in schools. In reality, the need for school professionals to personally share information, persuade and guide actions within a community, and develop partnerships with business, government, and community service organizations has never been greater. Through effective communication, educators have the opportunity to guide the actions of others—whether it's the media, community service organizations, or business—in the best interest of children.

Through effective communication, educators can provide the public with accurate information rather than allowing, by impassivity, those who are less informed to interpret educational news. Through effective communication, educators can confront inaccurate and unfavorable reports and explain or qualify difficult-to-understand or distorted content. In addition, effective communication helps reduce negative educational reports by keeping the public fully informed and actively participating in school governance. As a result of active participation, effective communication impacts the school's organizational culture and climate, developing a trust between schools and the media, business, and community members that leads to new working relationships. Only in an atmosphere of cooperation and collegiality will healthy, productive partnerships be developed to address the needs of America's youth and enhance student learning and productivity.

As American society moves into a highly technological and informational age, helping educators communicate to diverse groups of students and their parents becomes increasingly important. A school that communicates effectively will be able to establish effective intervention and public relations programs that result in precrisis management. One of the most important lessons we can learn about American society is the fact that there is no "culture of one." Over the past decade, demographic changes have greatly affected notions of who is "majority" and who is "minority." "According to the 2000 Census, no racial or ethnic group in California forms a majority" (California Department of Education, 2002).

Ours is a homogeneous society, infused with many diverse cultures, each with its own collection of experiences, beliefs, values, attitudes and notions of what is important. Many students live in cultural environments that are quite different from those of the school and the mainstream community. Only by reaching across the lines of ethnicity and multicultural differences can school systems hope to reach the at-risk and troubled students. One way to accomplish this is through an acculturation process involving the successful implementation of a cultural awareness program that is capable of reaching across the communication barriers that currently exist in our schools and communities. "Knowledge entails developing a nonstereotyping, flexible understanding of cultural, social, and family dynamics of diverse groups, along with a comprehension of the critical sociopolitical, historical, and economic contexts in which people from diverse multicultural groups are embedded" (Sanchez, 1995).

To establish better lines of communication and understanding as well as foster more effective community involvement in the educational process, some businesses and school systems have begun implementing mentoring programs. Studies by Blake-Beard and McGowan (2001) found that mentoring could indeed span the gulf created by race, class, age, and gender differences. The Financial Women's Association (FWA) High School Mentoring Program linked low-income minority youth in an urban New York high school with professional businesspeople and discovered that mentor relationships worked best when the mentor was sensitive to the protégé's family and cultural background (Blake-Beard & McGowen, 2001).

Effective communication is the foundation upon which effective public relations is built. Communication holds the key to unlocking hidden suspicions and fears in our educational system and to encouraging constructive dialogue on important issues. Unless a concerted effort is made through effective communication, gaps between educators and school communities will continue to grow.

How important is this home-school connection? Research reveals that school programs that communicate well with parents and communities have students who outperform those in schools who do not communicate well (Warner, 1997); benefits include "better attendance, improved behavior, a higher quality of education, and a safe, disciplined learning environment" (p. 4). For example, Sussex Technical High School in Georgetown, Delaware, attributes its success with parental involvement to a major communication initiative. Before the first day of school, ninth-grade students and their parents are sent their class schedule to review. An open house is scheduled so parents and students can visit the school and "walk through" the class schedule. On Back-to-School Night, parents attend a 3-hour program allowing them to interact with teachers. In addition, the school offers newsletters, award programs, conferences, planning and assessment meetings, and a variety of other activities for parents (Warner, 1997). From a public relations standpoint, the communication taking place at Sussex brings students, teachers, parents, and administrators together so that they can solve problems, share ideas, plan activities, and support one another.

Principals in restructured schools view communication skills as the skills most needed for success as schools move from a traditional, isolated stance to one fostering shared vision and collegiality (Fullan, 1991; O'Hair & Reitzug, 1997). Thurston, Clift, and Schacht (1993), emphasizing the development of an educator's abilities to reflect and communicate, stated that "Communication will be crucial in establishing a schoolwide commitment to a mission and in sharing the decision-making process" (p. 262). Communication is the key to establishing trust, promoting collaboration, and managing conflict.

Unfortunately, communication skills are an often neglected part of an educator's formal and informal education. Generally when one thinks of communication skills, the first image that comes to mind is that of speaking. Unless accused of poor listening or of being unobservant, educators tend to downplay the importance of listening and nonverbal communication. However, when a crisis exists, listening and observation skills may be more important than verbal skills, especially when an educator is trying to bridge the cultural gaps in any given classroom. "Although there has been a greater recognition of the need for training in multicultural competence across professions, many programs still conceptualize this training as more of an 'add-on'; that is, programs require only one or two courses for their particular professional specialty" (Sanchez, 1995).

Although speaking and writing can always improve, the communication skills needing the greatest attention from school principals include information sharing, seeking feedback, listening, nonverbal awareness, and conflict resolution (McNulty & O'Hair, 1998). A study of 17 New York educators found the following communication skills to be vital for effective school change: reducing conflict, enhancing collaboration in interpersonal and group situations, and gathering feedback (Miles, 1993). Without adequately developed communication skills, school life and school public relations are simply incomplete and ineffective. This chapter examines a foundation for successful school communications consisting of three core communication competencies:

Competency 1: Listening effectively

Competency 2: Defining and decoding nonverbal communication

Competency 3: Understanding and managing conflict

COMPETENCY 1: LISTENING EFFECTIVELY

Research studies have shown that about 75% of the interactions in a school building are one-on-one meetings (Dolan, 1996). These meetings involve students, faculty, parents, secretaries, and administrators in classrooms, in hallways, during lunch, during class changes, and before and after school. To avoid miscommunication, a great deal of effort must be devoted to listening. In order to improve listening skills, one must first understand the barriers that impede the ability to listen.

Barriers to Effective Listening

What barriers affect the ability to listen? Golen (1990) identified a number of common listening barriers; they are presented in test form in Table 5–1.

Every "yes" answer indicates a barrier to listening abilities. Educators should take a serious inventory of their listening skills; otherwise, improvement is not possible.

Improving Listening Skills

As discussed earlier, successful school communication requires an understanding of the importance of effective listening and an understanding of the barriers to effective listening. Figure 5–1, a visual image of a listening process referred to as the strategic listening process, can be used to improve listening skills (O'Hair, 1998b). Key components of this process are shown.

Understanding and Committing to the Listening Process

"Listening" comprises three elements: what is heard, what is understood, and what is remembered. Listening includes hearing, or receiving aural stimuli from the environment; connecting or processing the stimuli into meaningful messages; and storing messages for immediate or delayed retrieval. Listening occurs at different levels, depending on the message. For example, a simple request, such as "close the door" or "turn off the lights," generally requires basic processing and rarely the more complex task of reflective thinking. However, reflective listening requires the listener to understand the sender's personality, culture, and environment. As schools become increasingly diverse, reflective listening becomes more difficult and more necessary. Although the teaching force remains predominately White and female, the student population is becoming more diverse in terms of

TABLE 5–1

Top-Ranked Barriers to Effective Listening

Listening Barrier	Yes	No
Do you listen primarily for details or facts?		
Do you become distracted by peripheral noises like those from room office equipment, telephones, or other conversations?		
Do you daydream or become preoccupied with something else?		
Do you think of another topic or follow some thought prompted by what the speaker has said?		
Do you find that you have no interest in the speaker's subject?		
Do you concentrate on the speaker's mannerisms or delivery rather than on the message?		
Do you become impatient with the speaker?		
Do you disagree or argue outwardly or inwardly with the speaker?		
Do you try to outline everything mentally?		
Do you fake attention to the speaker?		
Do you jump to conclusions before the speaker has finished?		
Do you become emotional or excited when the speaker's views differ from yours?		
Do you cease to listen if the subject is complex or difficult?		
Do you allow your biases and prejudices to interfere with your thinking while listening?		
Do you pay attention only to the speaker's words rather than to the speaker's feelings?		
Do you avoid eye contact while listening?		

Continued

TABLE 5–1
Continued

Listening Barrier	Yes	No
Do you fail to put yourself in the speaker's shoes or to empathize?		
Do you refuse to relate to and benefit from the speaker's ideas?		
Do you refuse to give feedback?		
Do you refuse to paraphrase to clarify a point?		
Do you overreact to certain language, such as slang or profanity?		
Do you not listen because it takes too much time?		
Do you not read the speaker's nonverbal cues?		
	Total =	Total =

Source: From "A Factor Analysis of Barriers to Effective Listening," by S. Golen, 1990, *Journal of Business Communication*, *27*, pp. 25–36. Copyright 1990 by S. Golen. Adapted with permission.

race, class, language, and gender-role socialization patterns (Grant & Secada, 1990; Murdock, Hoque, Michael, White, & Pecotte, 1995).

Some listeners tune out during a meeting because of disagreement with the messages being communicated. However, listening, even under protest, is informative and crucial to school success. New ideas and concepts may be sparked at any given time, even under protest. Successful educators are committed to the listening process and rarely tune out conversations.

Listening Between the Words

Effective listening requires more than hearing words. In his 1988 campaign, President George Bush seized on the slogan: "Read my lips. No new taxes." The impact of the message was supported by his paralanguage or the *way* he said those six words. Later, when he broke his promise, this statement caused Bush and his advisers much embarrassment. Perhaps his critics and voters in general would not have remembered so vividly the original message if his paralanguage had not been so compelling.

Effective listeners must do more than merely read lips—or hear words. Effective listeners listen for deeper meanings. Listeners can miss 100% of the "feeling content" of spoken messages by not listening *between* and *beyond* the words. To understand deeper meanings in oral communication, educators must listen for the paralanguage elements of speech. Paralanguage refers to *how* something is said rather than *what* is said. More specifically,

FIGURE 5–1

The Strategic Listening Process
Source: O'Hair (1998b)

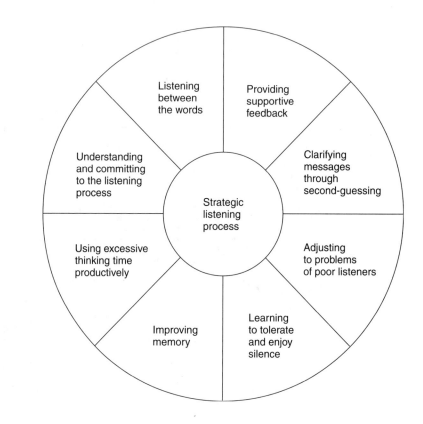

paralanguage involves aspects of verbal communication that are unrelated to the words used. For example, after a teacher has worked for weeks on a PTA program, his principal stops by his classroom and congratulates him on a job well done. However, the teacher notes that the principal's voice lacks enthusiasm and excitement, and he begins to question the principal's sincerity; he wonders what his principal really thought about the PTA program. Tone and loudness are two of the more obvious elements of paralanguage, but there are others which are more difficult to discern.

Improving Memory

Memory is crucial to the listening process because memory increases listening comprehension. After examining the purely informational level of listening, the majority of oral communication is ignored, misunderstood, or quickly forgotten. It makes little sense to hear, attend to, comprehend, and then fail to remember oral communication.

Memory is often thought of as "storage." The memory can store great amounts of information and is often examined through the temporal classifications of short- and long-term memory. Short-term memory (STM) involves pattern recognition by transfer from sensory storage to the form of memory described by memory researchers as "attention." Unfortunately, STM consists of a very brief unit of information, usually about 15 seconds, unless the unit is rehearsed, which allows for an extension of up to 60 seconds. Generally, the term *memory* commonly refers to long-term memory. However, long-term memory is rarely activated until at least 60 seconds after the presentation of a stimulus. Actual entry into long-term memory may depend on both rehearsal and organizational schemes. In other words, long-term memory requires a linkage between the new stimulus and the old information previously stored in memory. The storing and retrieval of information that is unconnected and meaningless is extremely difficult.

Teaching individuals to develop visual images in listening situations results in a significant increase in comprehension and memory for both children and adults. The visual images produced while listening to a conference speaker or while watching a video can provide the framework for organizing and remembering key information.

Providing Supportive Feedback

Conversation with individuals who do not provide feedback—that is, give no nods of the head or utter "uh-huhs"—is extremely uncomfortable. Under normal conversational conditions, it is extremely difficult to carry on a conversation with someone who is unresponsive. Without feedback, the sender does not know if the receiver is in agreement or disagreement with the message, is bored and ready to terminate the conversation, or is daydreaming and not properly hearing the message. Feedback is essential for strategic communication to occur.

Good listeners provide appropriate supportive feedback by:

◆ Demonstrating interest in what the speaker says
◆ Maintaining appropriate eye contact
◆ Smiling and showing animation
◆ Nodding occasionally in agreement
◆ Leaning toward the speaker to demonstrate an attitude of interest and confidentiality
◆ Using verbal reinforcers like "I see" and "yes"
◆ Phrasing interpretations of the speaker's comments to verify understanding
◆ Consciously timing their verbal and nonverbal feedback to assist rather than hinder the speaker

If listening is gaining meaning from situations involving the spoken word, then feedback is crucial in gaining meaning. Feedback helps the continuity of conversations, which in turn provides verbal and nonverbal cues that help inform and guide the individual to understand others' motivations, fears, and goals. Without feedback, listeners are deprived of this fundamental information.

Clarifying Messages Through Second-Guessing

It is common, while strategically listening, to be skeptical of the initial interpretation of the message received from a speaker. This skepticism is referred to as "second-guessing," or seeking the "truth" in a message. The theory of second-guessing expands the role of cognition in communication to help clarify the hearer's understanding of the truth behind the message. Second-guessing is a mental process through which listeners attempt to make better sense of what they believe to be a "biased" message. By reviewing and analyzing additional information pertinent to the original biased message, listeners gain a clearer picture of the true state of affairs rather than a slanted and prejudiced view from only the sender of the message (Hewes & Graham, 1989).

Second-guessing is used only when a perceived need for accuracy in information exists. For example, a principal's superintendent tells her that the shared governance report that she has worked on for the last several weeks is "interesting and informative." The principal is not sure what the superintendent means by "interesting and informative." Does she mean literally "interesting and informative" or does she mean "not exactly what I wanted but I know that you worked hard"? Rather than take the comment at face value, the principal may have reason to doubt the message. At this point, she may decide that her superintendent's feelings about the project are not important and she really does not need complete accuracy of the message; thus she accepts the initial interpretation and stops analyzing the message further. However, if message accuracy is important to her, she might begin to second-guess. After second-guessing, she might request clarification from her superintendent to determine the superintendent's true feelings.

Second-guessing as a listening strategy can help redefine and clarify messages and can guide the listener to respond appropriately. The second-guessing process involves exploring alternative interpretations, prioritizing interpretations, and selecting the best interpretation. The reinterpretations are assumed to be closer to the truth than the initial face-value interpretation of the message, though it is still possible that upon reflection in the reinterpretation phase an individual will return to the original interpretation.

Using Excess Thinking Time Productively

Most people do not realize the amount of excess thinking time that is available during listening. Speech speed is much slower than thought speed (approximately 90 to 200 words per minute versus 1,000 to 1,500 words per minute). The arduous speaker uses only a fraction of the listener's thought capacity. Thus, listeners have a great amount of "free time" while listening. The difference between good and poor listeners is that good listeners use excess thinking time to concentrate on the message while poor listeners indulge in negative listening behaviors such as daydreaming. Few individuals can daydream without losing a great part of the speaker's message.

Effective listeners use excess thinking time to:

◆ Outline mentally the speaker's message
◆ Identify the speaker's purpose and determine how the speaker's points support that purpose
◆ Organize listening by constantly summarizing previous points and identifying main points with key words or phrases
◆ Evaluate the soundness of the speaker's logic
◆ Paraphrase

- ◆ Verify and integrate information presented with past knowledge and experience
- ◆ Maintain eye contact in order to observe and interpret the speaker's nonverbal signals
- ◆ Formulate questions to ask at appropriate moments in order to verify the accuracy of their understanding
- ◆ Provide encouraging verbal and nonverbal feedback

Without constantly processing information received, listeners may experience daydreaming.

Learning to Tolerate and Enjoy Silence

How do you feel about silence? If there is a lull in conversation, do you immediately begin talking to fill the void? Unfortunately, many people feel uncomfortable with silence. Silence provides opportunity to reflect. It brings people face to face with themselves and often forces them to deal with issues they might otherwise avoid. Silence is essential to self-communication, which is vital to personal growth. Consider the following personal suggestions for learning to tolerate and even enjoy silence: (a) turn off the car stereo when driving to and from work; (b) plan to spend some quiet time at home, free from TV, radio, or computer distractions; (c) when in conversation, encourage others to fully develop their ideas; (d) plan to have a silent day in which reflecting and listening replace talking; and, (e) think of someone whose words were previously ignored and make special time to "lend them an ear." Learning to tolerate and enjoy silence is an essential preparation for meaningful communication.

Adjusting to Poor Listeners

Poor listeners have a habit of interrupting speakers. To prevent this, verbally request that all interruptions or comments be held until the speaker has completed his or her communication. Interruptions prevent speakers from thoroughly developing and explaining key points and ideas. If interruptions occur, the speaker should return to the topic to adequately complete the discussion. Repetition is advantageous when communicating with poor listeners.

COMPETENCY 2: DEFINING AND DECODING NONVERBAL COMMUNICATION

Improving listening behavior is a difficult and time-consuming task. Careful attention to overcoming listening barriers and eliminating the silent enemy, a negative attitude toward listening, helps educators improve communication within their school context. However, improving listening behavior alone will not provide educators with complete communication competence. Understanding the nonverbal message is equally important in that task.

Nonverbal communications are those behaviors that convey meaning without the use of language. It includes any behavior that does not use words. The manner in which principals use their voices, faces, and bodies—or even how they arrange their offices—communicates meaning to their publics. Nonverbal behaviors can even unintentionally convey information. For example, feelings of dislike or disapproval may be expressed although there is no conscious attempt to do so.

As the school community becomes increasingly diverse, understanding nonverbal communication becomes vital for educators. Everything from lifestyles to products to technologies to the media is becoming more heterogeneous. This increased diversity produces complexity, which in turn, means that schools need more and more data and know-how to function effectively. Awareness of nonverbal communication can help educators access essential information.

The verbal communication process is, by and large, controllable and intentional, but nonverbal behavior is often difficult to manage and control. Communication scholars consider nonverbal communication to be a double-edged sword (O'Hair, Friedrich, & Shaver, 1998). If used effectively, it can enhance one's ability to communicate with others. It can also damage one's ability to act constructively.

This section of the chapter examines nonverbal communication research over the past 30 years and focuses on those areas that are relevant to improving public relations through effective school communication. Major functions of nonverbal communication and synthesizing these functions into the framework of visual receiving skills are discussed.

Major Functions of Nonverbal Communication

Nonverbal communication serves a number of functions in a school context. Argyle (1988) identifies four functions of nonverbal behavior. The first is to *express emotions*. Emotional expression is as important in school settings as it is in personal encounters. When school members communicate excitement through their voices and gestures, it is possible to get a sense of their commitment to what they are saying. In addition, educators can have an idea of how school members feel about their duties and responsibilities by how they sit or by their facial expressions. Without nonverbal behavior, the understanding of emotions would be difficult, and schools would have less knowledge of how others feel and respond to educational issues.

The second function of nonverbal communication is to *convey interpersonal attitudes*. Expressing opinions through nonverbal communication reveals interpersonal attitudes. When a parent enters the school office, a perceptive principal can often tell how the parent feels about the visit. If she says "Hello" without much expression in her voice and without looking directly at anyone, she may simply be going through the motions expected of all humans. If, however, she smiles, turns, and looks directly at the principal, she is perceived to be genuine in her greeting.

The third function of nonverbal communication is to *present one's personality to others*; this is sometimes labeled the process of impression formation and management (Burgoon, Buller, & Woodall, 1989). Without tone of voice, gestures, facial expressions, and so forth, humans appear and sound mechanical and uncaring. As communicators, educators can obtain an accurate sense of what others are trying to transmit by knowing their personality. For example, nonverbal behavior can provide a rich source of information about a person's character, disposition, and temperament. An awareness of another's personality characteristics allows principals to make and confirm predictions about school members' actions, plans, and behaviors. This makes communicating easier. For instance, a parent who talks loudly and positions himself directly in the principal's face could be perceived as aggressive and pushy. In contrast, parents who avoid eye contact, talk softly, and use few gestures may be perceived as shy and reluctant to confront others on issues. Without understanding culture, race, and gender expectations, it is difficult to accurately interpret nonverbal cues that convey another person's personality.

The fourth function of nonverbal communication is to *accompany verbal communication*. Nonverbal behavior can *reinforce* what is said verbally (smiling while stating satisfaction for a project); it can help *regulate* verbal behavior (breaking eye contact to signal that a conversation is over); it can *complement* oral communication (talking very slowly and deliberately to make an important point); it can *substitute* for verbal behavior (nodding, winking, or gesturing approval); and it can even *contradict* verbal language (stating pleasure at meeting someone without establishing eye contact) (O'Hair & Ropo, 1994). When verbal and nonverbal messages contradict, the receiver of the message relies on nonverbal behaviors. Educators should carefully monitor nonverbal behaviors to ensure that they reinforce rather than contradict verbal messages.

Framework of Visual Communication

A *framework of visual communication skills* describes the essential components of nonverbal communication in business and educational settings (O'Hair, 1998a). The framework has five major components: facial expression, eye and visual behavior, gesture and body movement, space, and dress. Each component is described and discussed in relation to nonverbal communication in educational settings in Figure 5–2.

Facial Expression. One of the most expressive channels of nonverbal communication is the face. Although only a few words are available to describe them (for example, frown, smile, sneer), there are, in fact, more than 1,000 different facial expressions (Ekman, Friesen, & Ellsworth, 1972). The challenge is to interpret these various expressions and to decode their messages. They are the most reliable signal for determining an individual's emotional state. A principal who pays close attention to facial expressions is likely to accurately judge an individual's true feelings.

Facial expressions also provide feedback as to how communication is being understood. For example, a teacher may *state* that she understands a particular assignment but *look* confused. A principal who is aware of facial expressions and uses feedback appropriately is alerted immediately to a potential problem. Facial expressions are beneficial in determining the real motivations and intentions of others. Often individuals try to change their facial expressions to deliberately mislead others about how they feel. Although facial expressions are important for principals to observe and analyze, this information alone is

FIGURE 5–2
Framework of Visual
Communication Skills
Source: O'Hair (1998a)

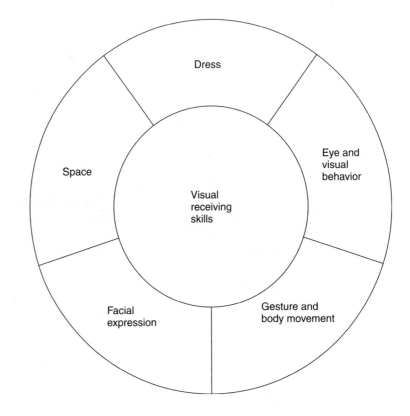

probably not enough to establish a high degree of accuracy concerning another's emotional state. According to the framework of visual communication skills, other nonverbal clues are needed.

Eye and Visual Behavior.   The eyes provide rich information. Because humans are becoming more and more visually oriented, the movement of the eyes and how they are focused on other people and objects provides a great deal of knowledge and insight.

   Eye gaze indicates that one person is looking directly at another individual's face, particularly the eyes. *Eye contact* refers to mutual and simultaneous eye gaze between two people; that is, both people are looking directly into each other's eyes (Harper, Wiens, & Matarazzo, 1978; O'Hair & Ropo, 1994). With eye gaze, one person is searching for information about another. With eye contact, both individuals are committed to the communication process (O'Hair et al., 1998). Research on nonverbal communication through the eyes alerts educational leaders to the need to consider cultural, social, and gender differences and provides clues to communication avoidance.

   Cultural, Social, and Gender Differences.   Cultural differences in eye gaze and eye contact are well documented. The eyes are important in regulating the flow of communication among people. For example, when one person greets another, a certain sequence is generally followed: gaze, smile, eyebrow lift, quick head nod (Eibl-Eibesfeldt, 1972).

This behavior may seem to be one of those things known through common sense until educators realize that all parents, staff, and community members do not share the same nonverbal behaviors. The most distinguishing feature in the cross-cultural use of eye contact is the focus of the listener's eyes (Burgoon et al., 1989). Anglos are socialized to gaze directly at the speaker's face when they are listening; Native Americans and African Americans often refuse to look directly into the eyes of any authority figure. In their culture, direct eye gaze with an authority figure is considered rude and inappropriate. Japanese Americans avoid eye contact when listening by focusing on the speaker's neck. Educators may damage professional relationships by being unaware and insensitive to cultural differences.

A summary of research findings reveals other factors involving eye behavior and nonverbal communication:

- People tend to "match" the gaze duration of their conversational partner.
- Speech rate is higher when the speaker looks at the listener.
- Eye gaze increases when communicating positive information and decreases when communicating negative information.
- Smiling causes a decrease in eye gaze.
- In groups, there is a tendency to look more while speaking and look less while listening. (The opposite is true when only two people are talking.)
- People who gaze longer are better liked.
- Increased gazing causes favorable impressions when positive information is communicated and unfavorable impressions when negative information is revealed.
- Compared with high-status people, people with lower status (less power) look more when listening than when speaking.
- Females gaze more than males.
- Females are looked at more than males.
- Females are more uncomfortable when they are unable to see their conversational partner.

An awareness of cultural, social, and gender differences may prove helpful in understanding visual behavior and improving communication.

Communication Avoidance.   Visual behavior is a good indicator of communication avoidance. It is important for educators to understand that certain meanings are to be found in both intentional and unintentional avoidance. In addition, educators must remember that there are several reasons why an individual may avoid eye contact. First, the individual may be unwilling to communicate. An individual may feel unprepared to answer a question, may be busy thinking about something else, or may even be unhappy with someone and, as a result, avoid eye contact. Emotional arousal may also reduce eye contact. As mentioned earlier, the face is an excellent source of clues for determining the emotional state of an individual. The eyes can provide that type of information as well. Sometimes adults avoid eye gaze to cover up emotional arousal such as despair, depression, and even stress. For example, consider the nonverbal behavior of a parent who feels embarrassed. The parent will probably divert his or her eyes to objects rather than look directly at people. This is an effort to recover lost self-esteem (O'Hair & Ropo, 1994). Once the parent recovers, normal eye behavior will resume. A principal's awareness of nonverbal communication will allow the parent time to regain self-esteem and return willingly to the conversation. Understanding eye and visual behavior is important in understanding people and building the trust needed to develop productive relationships between educators and the public.

Gesture and Body Movement.   Gestures and body movement, sometimes referred to as "kinetics," are another aspect of nonverbal communication. Individuals use gestures to complement what they say verbally. Communication problems occur whenever a person's gestures suggest a different meaning than the verbal message. As mentioned earlier, it is important for educators to remember that whenever a contradiction exists between the verbal and nonverbal message, listeners believe and accept more readily the nonverbal message (Burgoon et al., 1989).

Emblems and posture are two types of body gestures. Emblems refer to gestures that take the place of words. All cultures have emblems. Some are universal in meaning, others are not. Postures refer to the positions of the body. For example, postures include the crossing of legs, folding of arms, slouching, and sitting on one's knees. Cultural awareness of nonverbal emblems and posture is a necessity.

Space.   Often school leaders and the public respond and react differently to space. Space may be examined from two differing viewpoints: personal space and environmental space.

Personal Space.   Proxemics, or the distance that exists between communicators, is referred to as "personal space." School leaders must consider two aspects of personal space: first, the distance measured in feet and inches, and second, the perceived distance measured only by how comfortable people feel about the spatial distance between them and their communicating partners (O'Hair & Ropo, 1994). People differ according to their tolerance for personal space; some individuals prefer very close communicating distances, and others require further distances. Hall (1973) developed a system of determining personal space preferences. Four zones in which all communication takes place consist of the intimate, the personal, the social, and the public. The intimate zone (skin contact to 18 inches) is not often observed in educational settings. It is usually reserved for family or other close persons. The personal zone (18 inches to 4 feet) is reserved for interactions that are personal or private. The social zone (4 to 12 feet) is used a great deal in educational committee meetings or small-group problem-solving sessions. The public zone (12 feet and beyond) is used in educational orientation sessions or assembly programs. If administrators violate the rules of personal space as dictated by these zones, others may be offended or repulsed. Entering the intimate zone with a casual acquaintance can be misleading and troublesome. However, if administrators choose to interact at distances that are greater than what the situation requires, they may be perceived as cold and aloof.

The culture, age, and gender of individuals may also affect personal space preferences. For example, many cultures display differences in spacing and touching distances. In general, adhering to the norms of the situation, culture, and degree of acquaintance is the best advice for educators in using personal space appropriately.

Environmental Space.   This space refers to how individuals perceive, construct, and manipulate physical space in educational settings. Environmental space is important because people are influenced by what they see. Office arrangement, reception areas, decorations, wall hangings, colors, plants, and furniture are what school visitors see first when entering the building. Not only are first impressions of school personnel important to keep in mind when developing a school's professional image, but first impressions of the building, classrooms, cafeteria, and principal's office are important to consider as well.

The effective use of environmental space offers schools the "power of suggestion" in that administrators can express to their school community through space arrangement that they are student centered, professional, personable, effective, and accessible. For example, principals can communicate professionalism and accessibility through their office arrangement. The best office arrangement is one that puts the least distance and fewest barriers between communicators. The objective is to produce walkways, functional sitting areas, and relaxed meeting space. Making effective use of environmental space is a constant challenge for educators.

Dress.   What others wear and their general appearance communicate a great deal about the wearer and the school organization. It has been found that human relationships are established, reconfirmed, or denied within the first 4 minutes of contact (Zunin & Zunin, 1972). Dress has much to do with the early stereotyping and misconceptions. Acceptable dress may reduce inaccurate perceptions and improve first impressions. What is "acceptable" may vary based on the community, climate, geographical location, and fashion trends.

Accurately decoding the nonverbal communication of others and being aware of one's own nonverbal behavior can help educators project a positive, caring image to the public. Providing the human touch in school public relations involves understanding the personalities, emotions, and feelings of others. Awareness of nonverbal communication provides educators with an in-depth analysis of human behavior often otherwise overlooked.

COMPETENCY 3: UNDERSTANDING AND MANAGING CONFLICT

No longer does the old flying-by-the-seat-of-the-pants approach to conflict work, if it ever truly did. Now, more than ever, schools must proactively plan for conflict because conflict is an undeniable and inescapable reality in any organization. Although many people fear and even avoid conflict, it is, if handled appropriately, an extremely valuable and productive public relations tool. Whereas conflict is inevitable, positive and productive growth from conflict is not. In order for conflict to have a positive effect, it must be directed, guided, and supported. To gain the most positive results, administrators must recognize those elements of conflict that contribute to unproductive organizational and individual behavior. Second, they must understand the types of conflict that occur so that they can structure communications appropriately.

Conflict Contaminants

Conflict contaminants are occurrences or happenings that have a detrimental effect on the school climate. Several authors (e.g., Harvey & Drolet, 1994; Roberts, 1982) refer to these contaminants as pollutants that clog and choke an organizational climate. Although they are not inherent in the conflict itself, they provide the conditions in which negative conflict grows and thrives. The following are some of the contaminants that commonly affect schools.

1. *Negativism*—People get into more harmful types of conflict in environments where negativity abounds. Negative environments also have a higher incidence of conflict (Harvey & Drolet, 1994). This is true because feelings of doom and gloom are nurtured.
2. *Unrealistic expectations*—When unrealistic expectations are placed on employees and students, negative and unproductive conflict are likely. For example, unproductive conflict occurs when teachers or students are asked to achieve projects or goals within unrealistic timelines or guidelines.
3. *Poor communication skills*—Without effective communication skills, individuals and schools leave themselves vulnerable to rumors, misinformation, and missed information. These products also contaminate the communication process.
4. *Personal stressors*—Personal stressors may include health problems, financial difficulties, poor organizational abilities, and poor interrelationship skills. People having difficulties in these areas are more likely than others to engage in unproductive types of conflict (Harvey & Drolet, 1994).
5. *Lack of support and trust*—Individuals in schools need to feel supported and trusted. These feelings enhance creativity, communication, and personal and organizational growth and development. When these qualities are missing, the probability of negative conflict increases.
6. *Preference protection*—Preference protection is exemplified by the "my way or the highway" syndrome. Individuals need to spend more time thinking about where they are going and less time arguing about how they are going to get there. Tunnel vision occurs when individuals or organizations feel that their preferred way is the only way. This disposition not only creates negative conflict, but it also inhibits organizational creativity and growth.
7. *Savior syndrome*—Some individuals try to fix everyone's problems. They constantly engage in harmful conflict. "When you try to solve someone else's problems, you do two perilous things. First, you rob the other person of the opportunity to grow. . . . Second, you increase the chances that you will become an actor in the conflict yourself (Harvey & Drolet, 1994, pp. 75–76). A strong administrator encourages others to own up to their problems; they act as a consultant, not a savior.
8. *Jumping to conclusions*—Some individuals jump to conclusions before getting all the information necessary to make an effective decision. In such situations, conflict is almost certain because not all the facts have been considered. Jumping to conclusions often escalates the original problem and creates additional problems.

Conflict Types

Harvey and Drolet (1994) identified five types of conflict. Their categorization is useful because it breaks conflict into definable and understandable categories. If administrators cannot define conflict, they cannot manage it.

Value Conflict.   Value conflicts involve individual values, beliefs, or convictions, making them the most difficult to resolve. Values are more than simple preferences. As Harvey and Drolet (1994) explain, "value conflicts, often involve convictions held on faith, independent of evidence or logic" (p. 80). These convictions are likely to be deep-seated beliefs that have been individually tested over time.

Tangible Conflict.   Tangible conflict can also be referred to as resource conflict because it occurs over measurable resources. Measurable resources may include time, money, supplies, parking spaces, classroom space and location, personnel, benefits, and technology. Tangible conflicts in schools have steadily escalated because resources have declined and special-interest groups have become more influential. Tangible conflict, however, is one of the easier types of conflict to resolve if resources are available or can be creatively gained. If ignored, tangible conflicts can spawn secondary conflict. For example, two teachers having a conflict over sharing classroom space (a tangible conflict) grow to dislike each other.

Interpersonal Conflict.   Interpersonal conflict results when an individual has strong feelings of dislike about another individual. Most interpersonal conflicts occur as a result of another type of conflict. Although interpersonal conflicts are common in schools, they are resolved very infrequently. Next to value conflicts, interpersonal conflicts are the most difficult type of conflict to resolve (Harvey & Drolet, 1994).

Territorial Conflicts.   Territorial conflicts occur as the result of territorial invasions, or as the result of someone expecting another to expand his or her present territory (or responsibility). Consider the elementary teacher who, for the first time in his 15-year career, is asked to share his classroom with another teacher. He feels the room is his private property. Conflict is generated by a territorial invasion. Or, consider a biology teacher who has been told by her principal that her teaching load will increase to include a health class. Resistance produces conflict based on territorial expansion.

Perceptual Conflicts.   Conflicts frequently contain a small core of truly incompatible goals, surrounded by a thick layer of misperceptions of the adversary's motives and goals. People in conflict frequently form distorted images of one another. These distorted images cause people to jump to conclusions about the motives and goals of others. Conflicting parties often have mirror-image perceptions of one another—each attributes the same virtues to themselves and vices to their adversaries (Meyer, 1987). For example, when both sides believe that they are doing beneficial things for students, they see their adversaries doing detrimental things. Perceptual conflict may occur between teachers and parents. Parents may have a perception of a teacher that is created from the comments and opinions of their child. Most perceptual conflicts occur because individuals fail to get the facts. Perceptual conflicts are easier to resolve if they do not grow into another type of conflict.

Conflict-Resolution Strategies

Handled ineffectively or ignored, conflict can lead to dysfunctional behavior. Managed effectively, conflict can be beneficial, enhancing individual and group growth and development. The following conflict-resolution strategies provide alternatives for effective management. Fourteen diverse strategies for conflict resolution are presented below to assist you in promoting effective resolution of conflict (Ball, 1989; Filley, 1975; Harvey & Drolet, 1994; Huse, 1975; Meyer, 1987).

1. *Expanding or developing resources*—Scarcity of materials, time, territory, personnel, information, or influence may produce conflict (Ball, 1989). This problem may be resolved by expanding existing resources or by developing new resources. For example, the conflict between two teachers fighting over limited instructional materials may be alleviated by buying more materials.
2. *Compromise*—Compromise is a settlement in which each individual gives up part of what he or she wants in order to resolve the issue. Compromise is most effective when parties believe they are making reasonably equal concessions.
3. *Group dynamics intervention*—Group dynamics interventions include actions such as multicultural awareness, cooperative learning approaches, team building, personality inventories, trust building, and questioning strategies. They help individuals and organizations better understand each other. For example, placing conflicting groups together allows the parties to get better acquainted. Misperceptions may be clarified, goal compatibility may be identified, and conflicts may be resolved.
4. *Outside intervention*—Sometimes tensions and suspicions between conflicting groups are so high that direct communication is impossible. In such cases, outside intervention may be needed. Outside intervention consists of a third party entering a conflict situation to assist resolution. It can occur formally (e.g., negotiator, arbitrator, or intervenor) or informally (offering friendly advice).
5. *Interdependence analysis*—According to Harvey and Drolet (1994), "When individuals and organizations understand that their interests are independent and that they need each other for future success, a basis exists for resolving conflict" (p. 88). This is the "I need you and you need me so lets work out something we can both live with" resolution strategy.
6. *Organizational structural alteration*—Organizational structural alteration is a conflict-resolution strategy whereby structural changes are made in the organization. In a school setting, the structural alteration may include changing a teacher's job responsibilities, changing the physical space of a school or a classroom, creating a new organizational chart, terminating or reassigning a teacher, or changing a student's class schedule. There is a potential downside to this approach. The symptoms of the conflict may be relieved without rectifying the underlying problem.

7. *Seeking additional information*—Too often, conflict occurs because of the lack of information or the use of misinformation. Seeking additional information is an important resolution strategy because it allows us to gain a deeper understanding of the conflict and helps us clarify misunderstandings.

8. *Constant communication*—A constant communication channel helps to prevent unproductive conflict. For example, many teachers attempt to communicate with parents through classroom newsletters, conferences, and telephone calls. These teachers know that the more aware parents are of what is going on in the classroom, the less trouble they have with conflict based on misperception.

9. *Direct order*—A direct order is one of the most common types of strategies used today. However, because it requires little or no participation by the conflicting parties, most parties lack the commitment to resolve the conflict or prevent future conflict. Harvey and Drolet (1994) suggest using a direct order when a resolution is needed immediately and when authority is acceptable to the parties involved.

10. *Role clarification*—Many times, conflict will occur because people are unclear about their own roles or the roles of others in their organization. An effective role clarification process includes having each individual define his or her own role responsibilities and expectations, and having each individual define the role responsibilities and expectations for others in their organization. When completed, the results are compared. Often, points of conflict (different perceptions or expectations about roles and responsibilities) emerge. This permits roles to be redefined or clarified to prevent further conflict.

11. *Appealing to a higher value*—This strategy appeals to values, beliefs, or goals that are deemed more important than the immediate conflict. Teachers often make the statement, "We are all in this for the sake of the students." This is a value or belief statement that overarches most conflict in schools. A teacher may agree to do something he or she would rather not "for the good of the students." Organizations and their leaders have been known to create or expose a common threat as a strategy for building group cohesiveness and cooperation. Social, economic, and educational barriers are often dropped as people help each other cope with a common enemy. The struggle creates a cohesive and cooperative spirit, effusing people with the value of uniting behind a common enemy.

12. *Avoidance*—Avoidance is probably the most overused resolution strategy. Although helpful in dealing with some conflict, it can actually exacerbate a problem. Most problems do not resolve themselves.

13. *Democratic vote*—A democratic vote is a "majority wins" strategy for resolving conflict. A verbal vote can be taken to determine how many individuals are for or against an issue. The group with the most votes wins. The negative side of using this strategy is that it creates winners and losers. Whenever possible, win-win resolutions to conflict are preferable.

14. *Initiating conciliatory gestures*—Sometimes conflict is so intense that communication comes to an impasse. At such times, conciliatory gestures—a soft answer, a warm smile, or a concession—by one party may elicit reciprocal conciliatory acts by the other party (Meyer, 1987; Osgood, 1962, 1980). Conciliation begins when one side announces its desire to reduce tension and describes the conciliatory act

prior to performing it. After the act is completed, the adversary is asked to reciprocate in an equal manner. This then elicits public pressure on the adversary to participate in the conciliatory process. The intent of conciliation is to edge both conflicting parties toward greater cooperation and less tension, and eventually conflict resolution. Repeated conciliatory acts breed greater trust and cooperation.

Matching Conflict Types With Appropriate Resolution Strategies

One of the most difficult aspects of managing conflict is to match the conflict type with the most appropriate resolution strategy. Table 5–2 demonstrates the relationship between the conflict types and resolution strategies. Keep in mind that all conflict-resolution strategies are situational, modifiable, and combinable. Therefore, educators must carefully reflect on their choices before selecting a conflict-resolution strategy. Reflection is important because it permits the simulation of possible outcomes based on the understanding of the context in which the conflict occurred.

Understanding the causal situations surrounding conflict guides administrators in selecting conflict-resolution strategies that coincide with the context of the problem. Although Table 5–2 will facilitate matching appropriate conflict-resolution strategies to conflict types, the following questions should also be considered:

1. What is the source of the conflict? What additional conflicts are likely to arise as a result of this conflict?
2. Do the conflicting groups or individuals have the necessary communication or problem-solving skills to work through their differences?
3. Do potential losses outweigh possible gains?
4. Who stands to gain—one party or all parties?
5. How much time is available for resolving the conflict?
6. Is the issue major or minor?
7. Is additional research or information needed?
8. Are tempers too hot for a productive resolution?
9. Will a temporary solution suffice for the present?
10. What communication failures are at the base of the conflict?

Establishing meaningful lines of communication between the surrounding community and any given educational institutions is dependent upon the successful development of conflict-resolution systems. Conflict in the home translates into conflict in the classroom. Only by working in unison and acknowledging the constant barrage of social differences can community and school leaders hope to reach the culturally disadvantaged and ethnically challenged students in our educational systems. Only by training educators in the vast new technological advantages of the 21st century can we hope to make education more feasible for the next generation of students. Conflict is born of differences; mutual respect is the product of understanding these differences and making the appropriate changes in technique and style. Recent studies in the causes of conflict and social behavior management have produced some invaluable conflict-management resources.

TABLE 5–2

Matching Resolution Strategies With Conflicts

Conflict-Resolution Strategy	Value Conflict	Resource Conflict	Interpersonal Conflict	Territorial Conflict	Perceptual Conflict
Expanding and developing resources		++		++	
Compromise	+	+		+	
Group dynamics intervention		+	++	+	+
Outside intervention			+	++	+
Interdependence analysis	++		+	+	+
Organizational structural alteration		++	+	+	
Seeking additional information	+		+		++
Constant communication			+		++
Direct order	+	+	++	+	
Role clarification			+	++	+
Appealing to a higher value	++	+	+	+	
Avoidance	+		+		
Democratic vote	++	+			
Initiating conciliatory gestures	+	+	++	+	

+ Strategy match for the conflict type
++ Preferred strategy match for the conflict type
Source: From *Building Teams, Building People,* by T. Harvey and B. Drolet, 1994, PA: Technomic. Copyright 1994 by Technomic Publishing Company, Inc. Adapted with permission.

The Thomas-Kilmann Conflict Mode Instrument (TKI) has been the leader in conflict resolution assessment (Thomas & Kilmann, 2002). This instrument is a catalyst in learning how our conflict-handling styles affect personal and group dynamics. Many of the multicultural barriers in society and in our schools can be better understood and eliminated once we realize that "conflict-handling behaviors are neither good nor bad. Rather, conflict resolution is simply a matter of expanding skill sets and choosing the most effective group of behaviors for a particular situation." The TKI inventory provides invaluable data about conflict-handling style and the five distinct modes of dealing with ethnic, gender, and multicultural difficulties: competing, avoiding, compromising, collaborating, and accommodating.

- ◆ *Competing:* High assertiveness and low cooperativeness. The goal is to "win."
- ◆ *Avoiding:* Low assertiveness and low cooperativeness. The goal is to "delay."
- ◆ *Compromising:* Moderate assertiveness and moderate cooperativeness. The goal is to "find a middle ground."
- ◆ *Collaborating:* High assertiveness and high cooperativeness. The goal is to "find a win-win situation."
- ◆ *Accommodating:* Low assertiveness and high cooperativeness. The goal is to "yield."

Administrators and community leaders alike acknowledge the merits of the TKI model. Many require that their employees attend TKI workshops that specialize in effectively developing better communication and conflict-management skills. Learning to understand and accept one's own cultural biases and misgivings enables a person to begin facing the challenges of an ever-changing multicultural society.

SUMMARY

This chapter discussed public relations in a communication context. Developing effective communication skills, whether from an individual or organizational perspective, is not easy. The three competencies addressed in this chapter—listening, nonverbal, and conflict-resolution skills—are essential to developing successful relationships with peers, students, administrators, and the community.

| CASE STUDY | Greenhill School District: A Context of Ineffective Communication and Conflict |

The Greenhill School District is a large, inner-city district located in what is known as the "slums" of a large industrial city. As required by a new state mandate, the Greenhill School District had initiated a competency-testing program for graduating seniors. According to the mandate, students are required to score to the 70th percentile on the test in order to participate in graduation ceremonies and to receive their certificate of graduation. Upon completion of the competency tests in Greenhill High School, it was discovered that one-fourth of the seniors had failed to reach the minimum passing percentile. Parents of the failing students were notified by letter and were informed that their child would need to attend summer school for remedial instruction. Following summer school, the students would be given an opportunity to retake the competency test.

Two days following the notification of test results, the school was inundated with complaint calls from parents whose students had failed the test. Finally, the school's administrative staff, who rarely heard from parents in the past, declined to take calls and sent home a memo restating the school's position: Students who failed the competency test would not be graduating, regardless of the number of calls made to complain.

Memos were the usual way of communicating with parents of the Greenhill School District, and memos had earlier been sent home with students to explain the competency test. Interpersonal contact between parents and school staff was extremely rare. Parents never came to the school and were never invited, unless it was to attend a sporting event. According to the administrative staff, it was useless to try to involve parents in school events and issues because parents lacked the knowledge to make useful contributions, were too busy just trying to keep food on the table and their children off the streets, and/or were indifferent and uncaring as to what went on at school.

Four days after the test results had been mailed, the superintendent of the Greenhill School District received a call from B. J. Halihan, attorney at law. Halihan stated that he represented a newly formed parent group called "Parents for Fair Educational Opportunities." According to Halihan, the parents who had formed this group had students at Greenhill High School who had failed the graduation competency test, but a large number of other parents who were sympathetic to the cause had also joined with the group. The parent group was attempting legal action against the district for educational negligence. In addition, parents were making issue of the lack of communication from the school staff concerning the academic welfare of their children. Most parents stated that they had been unaware of the new competency test requirement.

A preliminary meeting was set up between the parent group and the school's administrative staff. In attendance was a representative from the state educational agency. During the hearing Halihan, as lawyer for the parent group, quizzed the school's administrative staff on the accuracy and appropriateness of the competency test and the effectiveness of the district's teachers. He also criticized school communications stating that parents were not made aware of the competency test until 2 days prior to the testing. Furthermore, according to Halihan, if memos were indeed sent out, the memos had not made it home to parents. He further criticized the school for not providing the type of assistance that students needed in order to pass the test. In his argument, Halihan was quick to point out that many of the students who had failed the graduation competency test had successfully passed all of their classes throughout the school year. He questioned the type of instruction provided by teachers, the type of curriculum used by the district, and the lack of or shortage of resource support provided by the school. In particular, Halihan mentioned the lack of equipment in the science and math labs; the shortage of desks, textbooks, and classroom space; poor lighting in the majority of classrooms; leaking roofs; and the out-dated library.

The administrative staff was unprepared to deal with the accusations of the parent group. No record of the original memo sent to parents explaining the graduation competency test could be found. In the end, the school requested and was granted permission from the state educational agency to provide the failing students with tutorial assistance for 3 weeks in order to prepare the students to retake the test before the graduation deadline. Students who still did not pass the test would have to take a summer school session before taking the test again. Although not completely satisfied, the parent group agreed with the decision.

Whereas the hearing failed to provide evidence of educational negligence, the state agency did feel that the high school had serious problems that needed immediate attention. The state agency ruled that in order to maintain its accreditation, the school was to develop and implement a plan that addressed all of the issues that the parent group had identified. The plan was to be developed with parental and community input. The agency further recommended a communication audit to determine the types, amounts, and implications of communication at Greenhill. It was the feeling of the agency that Greenhill lacked appropriate communication channels. According to the state agency, this lack of communication had resulted in a poisoned relationship between the school personnel and parents.

QUESTIONS AND SUGGESTED ACTIVITIES

CASE STUDY

1. It is now time to begin work on Greenhill's improvement plan. Describe your thoughts and concerns as you begin working on the plan. What concepts can you apply from this chapter to help you? Where should you begin?
2. Create a detailed school improvement plan, one that will incorporate the input of the school staff, parents, community, students, and the state agency.
3. What kinds of conflict contaminants were evident in the case study? What types of conflict did the contaminants lead to?
4. After answering question 3, list and describe several resolution strategies for dealing with the conflict in this case study.

CHAPTER

5. As a listener, what first impressions do you make? Ask for feedback from a colleague and a few close friends to help you with your self-analysis.
6. On the basis of the results of your self-analysis, describe areas for improving your listening skills. Use key concepts of the strategic listening process to help you identify your listening strengths and weaknesses.
7. Walk the halls of your school, paying particular attention to various classroom arrangements. What nonverbal characteristics create a climate conducive for learning, and what nonverbal characteristics detract from a favorable climate?
8. Evaluate your success at implementing the framework of visual communication skills covered in this chapter. Select two or three areas in which improvement is needed and develop an action plan.
9. Consider two recent conflict situations in which you were involved. Describe the context for each situation, the contributing factors, and the strategies you used (or wish you had used) for conflict resolution.

SUGGESTED READINGS

Daly, J. A., & Wieman, J. M. (1994). *Strategic interpersonal communication*. Hillsdale, NJ: Erlbaum.

Dolan, K. (1996). *Communication: A practical guide to school and community relations*. New York: Wadsworth.

Doyle, D., & Pimental, S. (1997). *Raising the standard: An eight-step action guide for schools and communities*. Thousand Oaks, CA: Corwin Press.

Glickman, C. D. (1993). *Renewing America's schools: A guide for school-based action*. San Francisco: Jossey-Bass.

Hamilton, C., & Parker, C. (1993). *Communication for results* (4th ed.). Belmont, CA: Wadsworth.

Hocher, J., & Wilmot, W. (1995). *Interpersonal conflict* (4th ed.). Madison, WI: Brown & Benchmark.

McIntyre, D. J., & O'Hair, M. J. (1996). *The reflective roles of the classroom teacher*. Belmont, CA: Wadsworth.

O'Hair, D., Friedrich, G., & Shaver, L. (1998). *Strategic communication in business and the professions* (3rd ed.). Boston: Houghton Mifflin.

O'Hair, D., Friedrich, G., Wiemann, J., & Wiemann, M. (1997). *Competent communication* (2nd ed.). New York: St. Martin's Press.

O'Hair, M. J., & Odell, S. J. (1995). *Educating teachers for leadership and change*. Newbury Park, CA: Corwin Press.

Warner, C. (1997). *Everybody's house: The schoolhouse*. Thousand Oaks, CA: Corwin Press.

Wilson, G. (1996). *Groups in context: Leadership and participation in small groups*. New York: McGraw-Hill.

REFERENCES

Argyle, M. (1988). *Bodily communication* (2nd ed.). London: Methuen.

Ball, S. (1989). Micro-politics versus management: Towards a sociology of school organization. In S. Walker & L. Barton (Eds.), *Politics and the processes of schooling* (pp. 218–241). Philadelphia: Open University Press.

Blake-Beard, S., & McGowan, E. (2001, February). The magic of mentoring. *HGSE News*, Harvard Graduate School of Education.

Burgoon, J. K., Buller, D. B., & Woodall, W. G. (1989). *Nonverbal communication: The unspoken dialogue*. New York: Harper & Row.

California Department of Education. (2002). *Diversity: Issues and responses. Cultural diversity, multicultural issues in education—Race, language, and culture*. Quotes from the 2000 U.S. Census Bureau. Retrieved April 30, 2002, from http://www.cde.ca.gov/iasa/diversity.html.

Dolan, K. (1996). *Communication: A practical guide to school and community relations*. New York: Wadsworth.

Eibl-Eibesfeldt, I. (1972). Similarities and differences between cultures in expressive movements. In R. A. Hinde (Ed.), *Nonverbal communication* (pp. 297–314). Cambridge, England: Cambridge University Press.

Ekman, P., Friesen, W. V., & Ellsworth, P. (1972). *Emotion in the human face: Guidelines for research and an integration of the findings*. New York: Pergamon.

Filley, A. (1975). *Interpersonal conflict resolution*. Glenview, IL: Scott Foresman.

Fullan, M. G. (1991). *The new meaning of educational change*. New York: Teachers College Press.

Golen, S. (1990). A factor analysis of barriers to effective listening. *Journal of Business Communication, 27*, 25–36.

Grant, C. A., & Secada, W. G. (1990). Preparing teachers for diversity. In W. R. Houston (Ed.), *Handbook of research on teacher education* (pp. 402–422). Upper Saddle River, NJ: Merrill/Prentice Hall.

Hall, E. T. (1973). *The hidden dimension*. Garden City, NY: Anchor.

Harper, R. G., Wiens, A. N., & Matarazzo, J. D. (1978). *Nonverbal communication: The state of the art*. New York: Wiley.

Harvey, T., & Drolet, B. (1994). *Building teams, building people: Expanding the fifth resource*. Lancaster, PA: Technomic.

Hewes, D. E., & Graham, M. L. (1989). Second-guessing theory: Review and extension. In J. A. Anderson (Ed.), *Communication yearbook 12* (pp. 213–248). Newbury Park, CA: Sage.

Huse, E. (1975). *Organizational development and change*. New York: West.

McNulty, R., & O'Hair, M. J. (1998). *Crucial elements of communication to address when initiating change*. Paper presented at the annual meeting of the Association for Supervision and Curriculum Development, San Antonio.

Meyer, D. G. (1987). *Social psychology*. New York: McGraw-Hill.

Miles, M. B. (1993). Forty years of change in schools: Some personal reflections. *Educational Administration Quarterly, 29*(2), 213–248.

Murdock, S. H., Hoque, M. N., Michael, M., White, S., & Pecotte, B. (1995). *Texas challenged: Implications of population change for public service demand in Texas*. College Station: The Center for Demographic and Socioeconomic Research and Education, Texas A&M University.

O'Hair, D., Friedrich, G., & Shaver, L. (1998). *Strategic communication in business and the professions* (3rd ed.). Boston: Houghton Mifflin.

O'Hair, M. J. (1998a). *The framework of visual communication skills*. Unpublished manuscript, University of Oklahoma.

O'Hair, M. J. (1998b). *The strategic listening process*. Unpublished manuscript, University of Oklahoma.

O'Hair, M. J., & Reitzug, U. C. (1997). Restructuring schools for democracy: Principals' perspectives. *Journal of School Leadership, 7*(3), 266–286.

O'Hair, M. J., & Ropo, E. (1994). Unspoken messages: Understanding diversity in education requires emphasis on nonverbal communication. *Teacher Education Quarterly, 21*(3), 91–112.

Osgood, C. E. (1962). *An alternative to war or surrender*. Urbana: University of Illinois Press.

Osgood, C. E. (1980). *GRIT: A strategy for survival in mankind's nuclear age?* Paper presented at the Pugwash conference on New Directions in Disarmament, Racine, Wisconsin.

Roberts, M. (1982). *Managing conflict from the inside out*. San Diego, CA: Learning Concepts.

Sanchez, W. (1995). Working with diverse learners and school staff in a multicultural society. *ERIC Digest*, ERIC Clearinghouse on Counseling and Student Services. Retrieved April 30, 2002, from http://www.ed.gov/databases/ERIC Digests.com.

Thomas, K. W., & Kilmann, R. H. (2002). *Thomas-Kilmann conflict mode instrument (TKI)*. Retrieved April 30, 2002, from http://www.careerlifeskills.com.

Thurston, P., Clift, R., & Schacht, M. (1993). Preparing leaders for change-oriented schools. *Phi Delta Kappan, 75*, 259–265.

Warner, C. (1997). *Everybody's house: The schoolhouse*. Newbury Park, CA: Corwin Press.

Zunin, L., & Zunin, N. (1972). *Contact—The first four minutes*. New York: Ballantine Books.

6

The Social Dimensions
of Public Relations

Patti L. Chance

Lars Björk

School administrators today work in a much different environment than they have in the past. Societal demands and expectations, when combined with increasing issues of litigation, evolving social and political venues, and massive demographic shifts, make the job of school superintendent or building principal one of the most difficult in the country. It does not matter whether one is a CEO of a great city school or a small rural one; the expectations from internal and external publics are tremendous.

School administrators, once trained to be effective managers, must now be leaders who are able to affect the culture of the community while providing moral direction to the school (Senge, 1990; Sergiovanni, 1992). They must serve with expertise and success in the dual worlds of management and leadership. Such a task is not an easy one, but it is being accomplished by countless administrators throughout the country.

Contemporary administrators also need a multitude of skills that enable them to work with a variety of stakeholders in multiple venues. In effect, they are consistent and constant purveyors of public relations. Whereas many districts may be able to hire a public relations director, for the vast majority of them that task falls not to a well-trained expert and specialist, but rather to the superintendent and principals. Even in districts where public relations experts are employed, the function should be the concern of every district employee.

This chapter explores the social dimensions of public relations. All communications—school to community, community to school, and internal communications within the school—affect the public's perceptions of schools; this fact becomes even more evident as districts and schools are viewed as social institutions. This chapter also provides a framework for understanding public relations in terms of the dynamics of open social systems that exist within a larger cultural context. Both internal communication and information exchanges between the school and community have the potential of shaping the public image of schools and effecting change. Social systems theory is used to explain the complex, symbiotic relationships between schools and the communities in which they operate.

Social systems theory also helps explain the communication dynamics of organizations, which is fundamental to all public relations efforts. Three interrelated concepts relevant to the social dimensions of public relations are addressed in the chapter:

- ◆ systems thinking as a conceptual framework for understanding public relations within the context of organizational dynamics;
- ◆ the role of leadership in building and communicating a shared school-community vision; and
- ◆ schools as communities that reflect the diversity of American culture and the leader's role in working with multiple stakeholders.

SYSTEMS THINKING

During previous decades, schools were viewed as providing a unique service to society and as a consequence they were infrequently challenged and provided adequate public resources (Tyack & Hansot, 1982). In this stable environment, conventional inward-looking management practices were built on notions of corporate values of efficiency, scientific management, hierarchical organizational structures, apolitical perspectives, and professionalism (Björk, 2001; Rowan & Miskel, 1999). During the past several decades, however, changing demographic trends (Reyes, Wagstaff, & Fusarelli, 1999); increasing political involvement of interest groups and an expanding role of the courts in shaping education policy (Björk & Lindle, 2001); fluctuating economic conditions; and contested values have altered the landscape of American education. Educators are being forced to look outward and develop a better understanding of the dynamic relationship between society and schools (Björk & Keedy, 2001a). In addition, it has become necessary for school leaders to develop "very different ways of thinking about the purposes of their work, and the skills and knowledge that go with these purposes" (Elmore, 2000, p. 35).

Changing school contexts pressed school leaders to increase political acuity (Björk & Keedy, 2001a; Carter & Cunningham, 1997); share decision making (Ogawa, Crowson, & Goldring, 1999); adopt distributed, instructional, and moral leadership practices (Björk, 1993; Sergiovanni, 1992; Spillane, Halverson, & Diamond, 1999; Starratt, 1996); know about school cultures and professional communities (Firestone & Louis, 1999); and interact with the political community (Björk & Keedy, 2001b). Thus, conventional ways of doing administration shifted from management and control by the few to leadership and consultation by the many.

The Concept of System

Systems theory emerged as a reaction to the unrealistic assumption that organizations and human behavior could be separated from external environmental forces (Hoy & Miskel, 2001). Classical organizational theories tend to be one-dimensional, view organizations as static, and embrace simplistic assumptions about organizational relationships. Systems theories, however, tend to be multidimensional, include complex assumptions about organizational relationships, and view organizations as continuously changing in pursuit of equilibrium with their external environment. The systems perspective advances the notion that organizations are dependent on their environment for survival. Thus, viewing them as closed systems is both artificial and limiting. It also suggests that it is equally unrealistic to view them as completely open because they would be overwhelmed by inputs that would diminish their functional capacity.

Darwin's notion of natural selection is often used to illustrate the idea that organizations, like organisms, are compelled to adapt to changes in their external environment or face extinction. Although this example may be better suited to private-sector organizations that are compelled to struggle for survival rather than public ones, which have rarely faced competition, recent reform concepts, such as charter schools and vouchers, are beginning to alter this condition. However, the idea that organizations need to be responsive to their respective clients is a universally important concept. A common liability among schools and other government agencies has been the tendency to screen out or ignore information from their external environments that could improve their performance. School boards, shared governance, and site-based management reflect attempts to ensure public accountability and enhance the responsiveness of schools to community and parent demands.

Parsons (1967) underscored the importance of organizations maintaining connection with the community. In his discussion of a general theory of formal organizations, he acknowledged that no organization can exist in isolation and that they are interdependent with the larger social system from which they derive legitimacy, meaning, and support. The ecology of organizations is characterized as a symbiotic relationship in which organizations and society derive mutual benefits. With regard to public schools, this relationship is unambiguous: Society provides resources to schools in exchange for their producing numerate and literate citizens. The inability of schools to meet these expectations can jeopardize continuing public support.

Systems are composed of interdependent parts that engage in ongoing relationships. These characteristics can be observed in a single school having graded classes, counselors, administrators, and office staffs; a district composed of many schools; or a district that is part of a state education system. Two basic concepts define a system. First, the notion of *complex causality* helps guard against adopting simplistic cause and effect relationships that can lead to inappropriate administrative decisions. Events are often influenced by multiple factors, and understanding complexity may lead to more appropriate decisions. Second, the notion of *subsystems* suggests that an organization is composed of interdependent parts that must work in concert for it to survive and adapt. Thus units within a school, district, or state education system are interdependent and as such should align with corresponding units at different levels in the system.

Systems theories of organizations have two distinct strands: (a) the notion of cybernetics advanced by Wiener (1948) and (b) general systems theory advanced by Bertalanffy (1951). Although management and social systems theories have been influenced by different social science traditions and have distinct analytical approaches, they share a number of important assumptions. Cybernetic and social systems theorists concur that because external organizational environments are often turbulent, unpredictable, and in a constant state of change, codifying events can help administrators understand complex relationships and make decisions that ensure organizational survival.

Wiener (1948), known as the father of cybernetics, employed a wide array of techniques to understand organizational complexity and environmental uncertainty. His work was directed toward improving organizational efficiency and decision-making processes and was focused on improving organizational efficiency (Shafritz & Ott, 2001). These efforts contributed to development of systems analysis tools such as Planning, Evaluation, Review Technique (PERT), Zero Based Budgeting Systems (ZBGS), Planning, Programming, Budgeting Systems (PPBS), and more recently Total Quality Management (TQM) approaches. These paradigms rely on computer-based management information systems to identify problems, select optimum solutions, and adjust organizational activities.

Although the emergence of cybernetics and systems analysis techniques held considerable promise for understanding organizational dynamics, social scientists were troubled by the dominance of technology in understanding social process. Social systems perspectives were grounded in the seminal work of Mayo (1933), Roethlisberger and Dickson (1939), and Follett (1940). Biologist Bertalanffy (1951), considered the founder of general systems theory, discussed the importance of viewing a living organism as part of its larger, natural environment. He saw organisms as being interdependent with other organisms and posited that any change in their environment or in any other organism with which it was interdependent would force it to adjust to survive. The notion of mutual interdependence contributed to formulating an approach to analyzing organizations as interdependent parts of the larger social system. Sociologists, anthropologists, political scientists, social

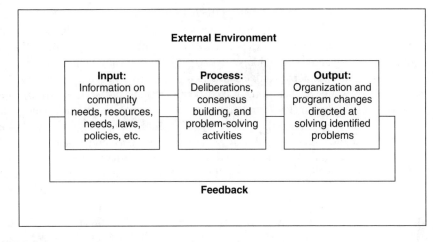

FIGURE 6–1
General Systems Model

psychologists, and scholars studying complex organizations assimilated this concept. They also made clear that in an orthodox sense, systems theory is not a theory because it does not attempt to explain phenomena (Katz & Kahn, 1966). Rather, it is a heuristic theory that is limited to describing and categorizing events in an effort to understand complex relationships between organizations and their environments.

Bertalanffy (1951) proposed a general systems model that had four basic components: inputs, processes, outputs, and feedback. Figure 6–1 illustrates how the general systems model can be applied in a school or district school setting. The nature of the systems process involves:

1. environmental *inputs* that identify demands and needs of the community, state policies, court decisions, resources, knowledge, goals, and shared societal values;
2. organizational *processes* that identify and convene internal and external experts to deliberate on the issue, build consensus, and determine actions needed to resolve the problem at hand;
3. *outputs* resulting from processes that change how an organization does work or the product delivered to meet the demand; and
4. formative and summative *feedback* that provides information to those in the organization.

Formative feedback occurs as a normal part of program implementation that is directed toward improving operations. Summative feedback is evaluative in nature and examines the impact of the program in relation to its intended purposes at the end of a specified period of time (e.g., student performance on standardized tests at the end of the school year). Information transferred through feedback loops becomes new input into system deliberations. During the last half of the 20th century, notions derived from systems dynamics influenced the work of political and social scientists interested in better understanding the relationship between organizations and environments, institutional behavior, and organizational learning.

Easton (1965) described the political system as a subsystem of the larger social order. He referred to his conceptualization of these interactions between the political system and the larger environment as political systems analysis. Subsequently, political and social scientists rationalized that schools are part of the political subsystem because board members are elected and make authoritative decisions regarding the allocation of resources (Campbell, Flemming, Newell, & Bennion, 1987). Their actions are legitimated by the larger community (Thompson, 1967) and persist in society as a means through which schools and society can adapt to change (Easton, 1965). Wirt and Kirst (2001) as well as Tyack and Hansot (1982) applied Easton's political analysis approach to understanding the relationship between education organizations and society. They persuasively argued that because school boards mediate inputs (demands and supports) from the external environment and convert them into appropriate outputs (action, program, or policy), schools are part of the political subsystem.

Campbell et al. (1987) extended the work of Easton (1965) and Wirt and Kirst (2001) in developing an open-systems view of school administration. This perspective provided a more definitive framework on how systems thinking can be used to increase the effectiveness and efficiency of schools as organizations. Recently, Björk and Keedy (2001b) found that the relationship between school boards and superintendents often influence these processes, suggesting that school leaders are also part of the political process, not merely administrative functionaries. These findings make a compelling argument for the utility of systems thinking in understanding complex political relationships between communities, school boards, and district superintendents.

Getzel and Guba (1957) drew upon systems thinking in discussing the relational nature of social systems in organizations. They noted that internal social systems have two classes of phenomena that are independent yet interactive and influence the behavior of organizational members: (a) the institutional (nomothetic) and (b) the individual (idiographic) dimensions. The institutional dimension represents the organization's ascribed roles and expectations that are embedded in formal structures and cultures. The individual dimension encompasses idiosyncratic personality and need-dispositions that motivate individuals. Social behavior of individuals in organizations emanate from interplay between institutional expectations and individual need-dispositions.

In school organizations, formal offices and positions represent the nomothetic dimension. These formal positions are accompanied by role expectations that are typically defined in written job descriptions as well as group norms. Individuals (idiographic dimension) who hold these offices and positions have their own personalities and need-dispositions that also influence how they carry out their duties. The mechanism through which the needs of the organization and individuals are accommodated or balanced is the work group. The dynamic interaction among individuals that compose work groups, the culture and climate of the organization, and individual personalities contribute to balancing institutional and individual needs and influence social behavior. Continuous monitoring provides feedback that helps school administrators ascertain the degree to which institutional and individual needs are met and whether an appropriate balance between the two is achieved within the work group. Understanding the relational nature of social systems can provide opportunities to influence goal achievement and staff satisfaction within the social system.

Argyris (1982) also acknowledged the relational nature of institutions and their environments and provided a normative prescription for enhancing organizational learning.

He observed that although people in modern industrial societies learn from their individual actions, they are often unaware of dissonance between their theories of action and organizational contexts. He argued that significant changes in role behavior can be achieved through learning processes that focus on detecting and correcting errors; integrating knowledge, action, and reflection; as well as synthesizing independent learning accrued over time.

Argyris and Schön (1974) characterized adaptive behavior produced by identifying and correcting errors, or troubleshooting, as single-loop learning. Single-loop learning is described as initial feedback in the systems process and is suited to stable conditions, high levels of control, and a rational system of organizing. In these circumstances, fundamental operating assumptions are neither examined nor altered to achieve a change in behavior. Double-loop learning, however, is useful in complex situations in which basic assumptions governing behavior and action are examined to determine whether they are contributing to the problem. Argyris and Schön posit that through the integration of reiterative cycles of reflective inquiry and action, root causes of problems can be uncovered, organizational performance improved, and equilibrium with its external environment achieved. Although the notion of organizational learning holds promise, Argyris (1982) also recognized that most people in modern societies are acculturated and predisposed by theories of action commonly referred to as accepted ways of doing things. Recognition that theories of action inhibit fundamental organizational change challenged the field to reconceptualize the notion of leadership in learning organizations.

Senge's (1990) pioneering analysis of learning organizations is an insightful attempt at using systems thinking and knowledge to create learning organizations and acknowledges that institutionalizing change takes time. He drew upon the notion that organizations are interconnected systems (Katz & Kahn, 1966; Weick, 1976) and notions derived from systems dynamics in conceptualizing and redefining the work of organizational members as nonlinear interrelationships and processes rather than conventional, cause and effect linear processes. Thus, Senge's (1990) reality is composed of circles of causality in which actions change the future state of affairs of the organization. He calls systems thinking the fifth discipline because it is the conceptual foundation for other disciplines including personal mastery, mental models, building a shared vision, and team learning. Taken as a whole, they contribute to a shift from seeing parts to seeing wholes; from viewing individuals as reactors to viewing individuals as active participants in organizational life; from seeing change as a snapshot in time to seeing change as a process; and from dwelling on the present to creating the future. Senge contends that creating and sustaining organizations where individuals are responsible for their learning is highly dependent on the nature of leadership, and characterizes visionary leaders as designers, stewards, and teachers who help guide ongoing processes of questioning, testing assumptions, and learning. These leadership activities are intended to continuously expand the capacity of individuals to understand the complexity of their organization, clarify its purposes, and share mental models. Senge's (1990) concept of organizational learning offers organizations opportunities to anticipate and correct difficulties before they become problems. Over the past decade empirical research has moved Senge's compelling theoretical description of schools as learning organizations from a hopeful literature into the realm of possibility (Leithwood, Jantzi, & Steinbach, 1998; Louis & Kruse, 1998).

Chaos theory offers a number of useful perspectives that can augment social systems thinking. It emerged out of wide-ranging interdisciplinary research in physics, chemistry, mathematics, meteorology, medicine, economics, and epidemiology that use terms including *nonlinear dynamics*, *dynamical systems theory* or *dynamical systems methods* in referring to phenomena (Griffiths, Hart, & Blair, 1991). This body of work explores the relationship between order and disorder in an attempt to understand the nature of complex systems in which nonlinear problems are examined holistically.

Over the past several decades, two branches of chaos theory have emerged (Hayles, 1990). The first branch posits that chaos in a system facilitates rather than inhibits self-organization (Prigogine & Stengers, 1984). Those who hold to the "order out of chaos" perspective tend to focus on issues of being and becoming and are often criticized by the scientific community as being more philosophically oriented than empirically grounded. The second branch argues that chaos is not a system out of order and events are not random but are governed by deeply encoded structures called strange attractors (Gleick, 1987; Lorenz, 1963; Mandelbrot, 1983). The "strange attractor" group tends to focus on problems of practical interest and emphasizes the ability of chaotic systems to generate new information to help in self-renewal.

Griffiths and colleagues (1991) analyzed characteristics of chaos theory and identified several concepts that can be applied to the field of educational administration. The *butterfly effect* heightens awareness that seemingly unrelated small events produce large consequences. Thus, school administrators are cautioned to pay attention to seemingly innocuous incidents as they can grow into major problems. The impact of *random shocks* to a stable system is often small and as a consequence, the system will regain equilibrium quickly. If the system is nonlinear, a small random shock can alter the system and inhibit it from returning to its original state. *Strange attractors* refer to a hidden element around which events revolve. Changes in the characteristics of the strange attractor can signal changes in the system's behavior and help predict where it will be in the future. Therefore, school administrators should be aware of changes in recurring education or organizational themes because they may signal a change in the school system.

Recursive symmetries suggest that structural forms are replicated across different levels and alert school administrators to look for and align organizational functions across levels to enhance efficiency. *Feedback mechanisms* reflect a fundamental principle of systems thinking: output is fed back into the system as new input that causes it to change. Thus, school administrators can use school performance data (e.g., disaggregated student test scores) to enhance teaching and learning for all students. Chaos theory underscores the notion that turbulent and unpredictable environments are pervasive. It also acknowledges that systems have the capacity to reorganize and adapt to changing circumstances.

Wheatley (1996) characterized organizations as open, dynamic systems in which chaos and order are complementary elements in the ongoing self-renewal process. She believes that organizations must be understood holistically as well as relationally within the larger environment. Terms including *interdependence* and *interconnectivity* imply that relationships contribute to defining and redefining structures, work, and meaning over time. She persuasively argues that schools are living systems that possess the same capacity to adapt and survive that is common to all life, and that these circumstances call for different ways of leading. Wheatley contends that leaders of dynamic social systems can neither predict nor control events, as is assumed by classical management theories. As a consequence they must develop skills that complement organizational learning, change, and innovation. Leadership in self-regulating, learning organizations is not of the few but of the many. Thus, emphasis is placed on the quality of relationships, broad participation, and building staff capacity for innovation and continuous change. The flow of information is enhanced by ever-widening circles of exchange. The simultaneous flow of information across multiple and diverse levels in the organization also contributes to self-referent behavior, sense making, and clarity of purpose.

During the last several decades, the American public has persistently demanded that schools reform conventional practices to better align their work with changing demographic, social, economic, political, and technological realities of society, as detailed in Chapter 2. Although some school administrators are threatened by these events, others recognize them as change opportunities. Systems thinking provides a framework for understanding the relational nature of schools and society. Using systems theories, educational leaders may better identify conflict among subsystems, assess the nature of problems, deliberate on their causes, build consensus for solutions, evaluate the relative effectiveness of corrective measures, change basic assumptions of schools and practice to improve organizational effectiveness, and achieve greater congruence with society (Hoy & Miskel, 2001).

Systems thinking is essential for education leaders' understanding of public relations and the role it plays in change processes. The Public Relations Society of America (2002) offered the following comment about the role of public relations.

> Public relations helps our complex, pluralistic society to reach decisions and function more effectively by contributing to mutual understanding among groups and institutions. It serves to bring private and public policies into harmony.

Thus, at the heart of public relations is the mediation of the complex flow of information between the school and its diverse stakeholders as well as among its various internal subsystems. Systems thinking helps education leaders see public relations as a continual, systematic process, rather than as a single activity.

Developing a Shared School-Community Vision

One of the most viable methods that school administrators can use in working with a multitude of external and internal publics is creating a collaborative school-community vision. Much of what is commonly thought of as public relations deals with a school's formal communication with its external environment, such as news releases, newsletters, business partnerships, and meetings. However, systems thinking helps us understand that such communications are only one part of a much more complex web of information flow. Because schools should be open systems, the flow of information into and out of the school environment should be constant. Schools as open systems seek to maintain equilibrium with community culture and values. Indeed, the school is not separate from community culture: it influences as well as responds to changes in it. Vision development is a way to provide a strong focus and sense of purpose for both the school and the community. A shared school-community vision acts as a platform for facilitating school improvement and guiding education reform that complements, rather than clashes with, community values.

The concept of vision is not new, although it is often confused with a school's mission. In simplest terms, a school mission is what people do in schools, whereas a school vision represents where people want their school to be in the future. Visions are, without exception, future oriented in wording and concept. The importance of a vision has perhaps always been recognized, but has gained greater prominence through much of the educational reform efforts and leadership research of the past few years.

A vision has been variously described as "the development, transmission, and implementation of a desirable future" (Manasse, 1985, p. 150) or as a "journey from the known to the unknown . . . creating a montage of facts, hopes, dreams . . . and opportunities" (Hickman & Silva, 1984, p. 151). At the core of all vision definitions is that a vision shapes an organization or an institution as it moves toward a better future (Chance, 1992; Rutherford, 1985; Shieve & Shoenheit, 1987). The transformation of vision from a concept to action is the result of leadership.

Sergiovanni (1996) suggested that the role of the principal is vital in the vision process because "most of us are not accustomed to thinking in terms of vision" (p. 84). Carter and Cunningham (1997), in their work on the school superintendent, indicated that "the superintendent must lead the schools in developing a clear vision of curriculum, instruction, and student achievement connections" (p. 189). They expanded on the importance of the role of the superintendent by concluding that "successful superintendents recognize that the power of a clear vision . . . can be more effective than the power of authority" (p. 189).

Nanus (1992) noted that "vision attracts commitment and energizes people . . . vision establishes a standard of excellence . . . vision bridges the present and future" (pp. 16–17). Certainly, research and leadership literature points to the need for an organizational vision. But how does this vision develop? Does it emanate from the leader, who dictates his or her vision in the form of an edict to subordinates and stakeholders in the organization? Vision that is imposed on an organization is often doomed to ultimate failure. The sense of disequilibrium created by such an act either leads to outright rejection of the vision or results in a type of creative insubordination.

Any approach to developing a vision should adopt a philosophy of inclusiveness that results in a collaborative stakeholder effort. In an educational setting, involving both those in the community and those in the school district is imperative. The creation of a shared school-community vision may be one of the most important public relations activities in which a school administrator participates. A vision developed collaboratively opens lines of communication; it provides for constructive involvement of a widely representative group of the school's stakeholders and constituents; and it charts a path for the school district to strive for into the future.

How is a collaborative school-community vision built? It does not happen spontaneously or serendipitously. Vision building is a planned event, requiring strong leadership committed to building coalitions among all school stakeholders and community partners. Chance (1992) developed a process for vision development, which has been successful in school districts and communities, that invites participation and collaboration. The most significant result of shared vision building is the tremendous community support that it generates for the school district and the educational process. Through school-community vision building, everyone comes together in mutual agreement about the direction in which the school district should be moving. The feeling of goodwill between those in the school district and those in the community extends to issues such as school bond elections, curriculum design, school discipline, and parent-teacher conversations.

The first component of the five-step vision development process is for school district leaders to *identify and develop their personal educational visions*. Involved leaders include, but are not limited to, the superintendent, other central office personnel, site administrators, board members, and lead teachers. This initial step provides an opportunity for reflection as those involved recognize their personal values and beliefs and examine their professional careers. After self-reflection, school leaders think about the school district's strengths and weaknesses. They also examine the district's relationship with the external environment and reflect on how all the various interpersonal components of the district (social system) work together. Finally, they discuss with one another their concepts of an ideal school and identify the types of learning-related activities that would take place in these school environments. At this point, participants do not write the vision statement; the initial step simply focuses on reflection and sharing. During this first stage leaders bond, making them more prepared to provide direction for other stakeholders at subsequent stages.

Step two of the vision process results in the *development of an overall collaborative school-community vision*. A variety of individuals who represent the diversity of the school district and its community are invited to participate. Community leaders, parents, nonparents, teachers, staff members, board members, district administrators, and students may be included. Depending on the size of the school district, the total number of participants can be as high as 300.

The development of the organizational vision involves a multitiered effort that gradually moves from numerous small groups composed of 5 to 7 members to one large, democratically selected group of 10 to 15. Members of the small groups representing the diversity of the school and community respond to questions related to school district strengths and weaknesses, community support, community concerns, and the focus of the school district for the future. A consensus-building process is used that allows group members to come to agreement on a group response. Representatives from each group are elected to move forward to form new groups with members from other groups. Consensus is again reached in these newly formed groups. The process continues in a similar manner until a final group of 10 to 15 members, representing initial stakeholder groups, is formed. At this point, a school vision is finalized.

During this second phase, short- and long-term goals are also developed. This stage of visioning is complex and multifaceted, and it is important to allow ample time for the process to work. Too often administrators and others rush through this step, and this results in serious problems.

The process at this step represents a tremendous public relations opportunity, allowing people to work together in a positive way. Seldom do stakeholders representing a variety of viewpoints discuss the future direction of the school district. Sharing ideas, concerns, and beliefs can unify school and community forces, resulting in a greater sense of stakeholder collaboration and cooperation.

The third step involves *communicating the vision and the newly developed short- and long-term goals to internal and external publics*. Effectively communicating the vision is a public relations function. Generally, a vision is best communicated by metaphorical statements, symbols, or models. Pronouncements representative of the vision such as "Where Dreams Grow," "Excellence and Equity," and "Striving for Excellence" provide both impetus and direction for an organization.

Communicating the vision, however, is not an end unto itself. A vision without action is useless. Action is represented by the short- and long-term goals established through the vision process. These short- and long-term goals constitute step four, *actualizing the vision*. In addition to the goals, strategies and evaluation procedures are developed. Without monitoring and evaluation, administrators are unable to ascertain progress toward goal achievement. Vision-monitoring teams should be established at each school.

An annual vision audit helps school officials to remain focused on the district's vision and to document and communicate what the district has accomplished. Some of the persons who were involved in shaping the vision can be vision ambassadors—individuals who help communicate progress for the broader community. Often these individuals have a sense of ownership in the vision.

The final step in this five-step process is *sustaining the vision*. Administrators can be easily distracted after a vision statement is adopted. For example, something new comes along and diffuses the impetus toward goal attainment. That is why the last step, a continual focus on the school district's vision, is important. Before a new program is adopted, one question must be answered: Does it help the district achieve its vision? That question should guide all decisions. There must be an ongoing opportunity by school leaders to reflect on and analyze the direction of the school district. Finally, a visionary culture embedded in the organization's social system should be established because organizations with a visionary culture "display a remarkable resiliency, an ability to bounce back from adversity" (Collins & Porras, 1994, p. 4). When disequilibrium strikes a school district social system, it will recover quickly if a visionary culture keeps everyone focused on what is to be accomplished.

The process of developing and pursuing a collaborative school-community vision is a potent public relations force for school administrators. It opens lines of communication across all ethnic, social, political, and economic barriers, and it provides for a positive imaging of the school to all educational and community stakeholders. The use of internal and external vision ambassadors, for example, assists in institutionalizing the vision so that all subsequent decisions and programs are evaluated on their relevance to the vision.

Developing Community Among Diverse Stakeholders

School administrators work with numerous stakeholders in both individual and group settings. More often than not, they work with groups in order to accomplish district or school goals. To accomplish an organizational vision and to maintain equilibrium within a social system while facilitating change, an administrator needs to build collaborative teams. Collaborative teams, when properly developed, result in a level of expanded self-esteem for all educational stakeholders while building a strong degree of cooperation among various group members (Maeroff, 1993).

Building collaboration among stakeholders involves bringing together people from diverse backgrounds and bridging multicultural borders. In discussing multicultural aspects of public relations, Banks (2000) proposed that public relations is cultural because it "communicates across cultural borders" and "it is a cultural practice itself" (p. 29). Moreover, Banks pointed out that cultural boundaries are determined by a group's cohesive and homogeneous understanding of particular practices. Thus, even though a school's stakeholders may represent various cultures as defined by race, ethnicity, religion, gender, and so on, these groups may come together as one culture bound by their common understanding and lived experience of the school community.

Such collaboration and cultural blending are what school-community vision building is all about. The school leader who successfully builds collaboration among stakeholders is one who is knowledgeable about group dynamics and skilled in facilitating communication among diverse populations.

This section introduces some fundamental concepts related to group dynamics and a leader's role in facilitating communication among group members in order to lead stakeholders toward a common vision. This is an essential, but often overlooked, function of public relations and a key to understanding the social dimensions of public relations.

Groups formed to accomplish a school-related task should be diverse. This characteristic creates a strong support foundation for educational decisions (in the same manner the vision process does). A variegated group may be more difficult to work with, but its members will often have more useful aggregate knowledge and skills to accomplish the group's agenda. The effective development of work groups may be easier to accomplish if one remembers that groups evolve through a series of developmental stages. According to group theorists, groups develop in a sequential, highly predictable manner. Groups, like social systems, have characteristics similar to living organisms. They come into being, evolve, change, and mature as a result of experience, opportunities, and knowledge.

The development and the functioning of each group also must be viewed in light of sociological differences. Each group member's gender, ethnicity, age, socioeconomic status, educational background, and beliefs and values contribute to successful functioning or failure of each group. Additionally, considerations related to the school organization, the ruralness or urbanness of the community, personal and community aspirations, and the school administrator's ability to establish group parameters and expectations of performance affect the group's development and success.

When working with stakeholders, school leaders should be cognizant of the multi-cultural dimensions of the community. Although each member of a group may represent a unique cultural aspect of the community, cohesive work groups eventually form their own cultural identity. *Culture* refers to the values, beliefs, norms, and ways of thinking of a group of people (Owens, 1995). Banks (2000) proposed that "a culture is as large or small as the group whose ways of constructing meaning about any salient practice are cohesively and homogeneously defined. It is the saliency of a particular practice that determines the cultural boundary of concern to the public relations communications" (p. 12).

Thus, the intent of bringing together stakeholder groups should be to develop mutual agreement about important educational issues, practices, or decisions that will be supported by all stakeholders in the community. In essence, school leaders utilize stakeholder groups in an effort to seek common values that bind, rather than divide.

One of the most important skills for a school administrator is knowledge of group developmental theories. For the purpose of this chapter, only one of them is discussed. This theory identifies five distinct stages of group development: forming, storming, norming, performing, and adjourning (Tuckman & Jensen, 1977). All five stages are best utilized by a school administrator as they relate to the group's task and changes in interpersonal relationships.

The first stage, *forming*, is associated with the creation of a new group and the feeling of discomfort that can result from such a situation. This initial period of caution, apprehension, and uneasiness is followed by a period of storming. *Storming*, the second stage, is best understood as a time when the group members begin to focus on their individual perceptions of the task and when they vie for influence and power. Conflict can come in several forms and, in the extreme, can destroy group productivity before the group reaches stage three.

The third stage is aptly called *norming*. This stage occurs when explicit and implicit norms are established. A sense of order is evidenced at this third stage, allowing for movement to the fourth stage, *performing*. At the performing stage, work begins to be accomplished; the group's focus is on the task at hand. Group membership and individuals' roles are well defined, and group norms are entrenched. Productivity is high, and there is an increased sense of camaraderie among group members.

The final stage, *adjourning*, takes place after the group has accomplished its task. Too often groups continue to meet, but their work is aimless because there is nothing more to be done. If new tasks are not assigned, the group's function is complete and the group should be disbanded. A group without a purpose or task is both ineffective and inefficient.

Community involvement in task forces and work groups helps school districts promote educational concepts. Stakeholders who participate in such activities become savvy consumers of educational priorities and needs. Consequently, work groups should be viewed as vehicles for school improvement and effective public relations. Taken from this perspective, an administrator's role is to facilitate a group so that it maintains a positive focus and achieves, in terms of social systems theory, equilibrium.

In designing groups, school leaders should keep in mind that a group will be effective only if each member perceives his/her association with the group as satisfying personal needs. Furthermore, leaders should consider diversity in group membership. The initial involvement of a diverse population whose members represent various interests creates a stronger foundation for organizational support of decisions or recommendations made by the group. The size of the group should also be considered. The larger the team, the more difficult it will be to maintain focus and facilitate communication. The task to be accomplished may affect the size of the group. Complex activities may require greater numbers of people to be involved, and this large group may need to break into smaller subgroups to accomplish specific tasks.

After a group's initial formation, the leader should anticipate conflicts that may arise as the group enters the storming stage. It should be remembered that the variety of perspectives, knowledge, and experiences that individual members bring to the group serve to enhance productivity and improve the quality of desired outcomes, but it is inevitable that disagreements will arise due to these differences. A leader should prepare for this by seeking the assistance of all group members in setting ground rules that facilitate task completion. Ground rules should include agreement on attendance, promptness, participation, agendas, and group behavioral expectations. The explicit rules will facilitate the group's development of implicit norms, which characterizes a group's movement into the third stage.

The following are some implicit norms indicative of effective and productive group behavior:

- People are listened to and recognized.
- Members criticize ideas but not individuals.
- Objectivity and honesty are valued by the team.

A leader can facilitate the development of positive norms, which promote a group's effectiveness, through modeling desired communication strategies and interpersonal behaviors. If team coordination and facilitation is delegated to group members, the leader should provide training and direction to these individuals.

With the parameters outlined above firmly established, the group should be ready to enter the performing stage. At this point, the group's task should be clarified and expected outcomes delineated. Questions to be considered at this stage might include:

- What is the problem to be studied?
- What standards or criteria must be applied to the problem?
- What are the group's boundaries or limitations, especially related to time, money, and information to be provided?
- What is the authority of the group? Will the group make recommendations to administration or will the group make final decisions that will be implemented? (Scholtes, 1988)

Not all groups work as well as expected. Often that is because the group is unable to move past the storming stage. It may also be related to the roles that individual group members choose. Roles are often a reflection of personality, the group task, and the level of commitment by an individual to the task at hand. Obviously, there are roles that facilitate group performance just as there are roles that hinder group productivity. A school administrator should foster the roles that assist with group output while discouraging roles that are negative.

Some of the group's roles that the school administrator should support include:

- *Encourager*—praises and supports others
- *Summarizer*—brings the group's ideas into focus
- *Elaborator*—builds on the ideas of others
- *Harmonizer*—mediates disagreements and seeks common ground
- *Procedural expert*—understands rules and policies of the organization
- *Energizer*—motivates and moves the group forward

Roles to discourage include:

- *Blocker*—disagrees for the sake of disagreement
- *Aggressor*—attacks group members, not their ideas
- *Dominator*—tries to control and manipulate the group
- *Withdrawer*—fails to participate and blames the group for this failure
- *Recognition seeker*—wants to talk of himself or herself and be the center of attention
- *Special-interest pleader*—has a personal agenda for the group

A leader can choose from many methods to facilitate the development of group roles that assist in the completion of group tasks. Obviously, one of the most important things school leaders must do is be prepared for each and every meeting with the group. The strategy of using questions that keep the group's focus on productive behavior is perhaps one of the best approaches a school administrator may choose.

Questions fall into several categories and can be asked in several different ways. They may be front-end loaded, where the individual's name is spoken first. Questions may be nebulous and not asked to any one individual. They can be rear-end loaded, where the question is asked and then a person's name is called. Each approach to the question has both weaknesses and strengths. Questions fall into several categories, but the following represent those most often used.

◆ *Factual questions*—seek needed information
◆ *Leading questions*—gather opinions and move people toward a particular conclusion
◆ *Alternative questions*—most often elicit a "yes" or "no" response, with follow-up questions as necessary
◆ *Ambiguous questions*—can be interpreted in several ways and provoke critical thinking
◆ *Provocative questions*—are designed to create an emotional response from the group

The types of questions used depend upon both the situation and the particular need at a given time. Group focus, intensity, and productivity help determine the types of questions to be asked.

As one works with groups, conflict becomes inevitable. It certainly takes place at the storming stage, but may also happen at the productive or performing stage. Although this chapter is not intended to discuss conflict resolution in detail, a brief mention of it is needed here (see Chapter 5 for in-depth coverage). Conflict happens within all social systems and among all people. It is important for the administrator to be able to determine if conflict is constructive or destructive. Constructive conflict offers an opportunity for group and system growth. It most often reflects differences in goals, methods, values, and group or organizational focus. Destructive conflict, however, is often the result of pettiness, jealousy, inordinate power struggles, and individual or group immaturity. Destructive conflict can destroy any group or social system.

As administrators work with the multitude of social systems that compose their professional world, they must not allow conflict to destroy a focus on vision. If conflict is not successfully resolved or managed, the organization may cease to be productive. A school administrator's ability to listen, conceptualize, interpret, react or respond, and synthesize are only a few of the skills necessary to end a conflict within the school setting. A sense of timing and a capacity to communicate effectively may be an administrator's best tools for resolving conflict.

In order to successfully carry out the goals and objectives of the school district or school site, the administrator must be able to work with a variety of individuals representing diverse beliefs and values. Much of this work takes place in groups. Therefore, knowledge of group developmental theories and how groups function is crucial. The ability to diagnose and successfully resolve conflict becomes an important tool in the school administrator's repertory. Group-related facilitation skills that ensure group and organizational productivity are vital to guarantee long-term success. Thus, an administrator's group leadership skills are needed assets for effective public relations.

Evolving Systems: Community Development in Cyberspace?

This chapter has presented public relations in terms of understanding the dynamics of the school as a social system and in terms of building community among diverse stakeholders. Systems theories describe organizations as dynamic systems involving constant interactions among the formal and informal systems within the organization as well as exchanges (feedback and input) between the organization and systems outside the organization. Individuals and groups communicate both through formal structures, such as department or grade-level meetings, and informal structures, such as a conversation after school in the faculty workroom. In addition, a school organization receives information from the outside environment, as feedback or input, and produces output that is exported to the outside environment.

As new information technologies (specifically the Internet) become commonplace, the lines of information access are increasing and becoming more complex. Building community in cyberspace is an aspect of public relations that educational leaders must seriously consider. To what extent can cyberspace communication promote the development of school culture, where stakeholders share common values, beliefs, and ways of thinking? Computer-based information technologies, like other communication venues, can either promote or impede community building.

Advantages of computer-based information technology include greater access and interconnectivity among a variety of stakeholders instantaneously and without actually occupying the same space. Through Web pages, schools can provide information that is more easily updated and less costly than print media and can even offer interactive opportunities through electronic chat rooms, electronic surveys, threaded discussions, e-mail, and the like. However, stakeholders most likely to utilize information-based technologies are those who are computer literate and who have ready access to the technology. It is probable that certain segments of a school's community will be left out of electronic communication, thus widening a gap that already exists between various subcultures, particularly related to socioeconomic and age factors. However, Chance and Lee (2001) noted that change is ubiquitous to technology development, resulting in apparent spontaneous metamorphoses of systems. They further observed that technology allows for customization, a defining characteristic of the information age. Thus, there is a potential for information technology to play an increasing role in defining future educational cultures by allowing more involvement from a diverse array of stakeholders and by creating greater capacity to respond to individual needs of stakeholders.

Whereas information technology is a reality of modern life that is, in effect, transforming ways of conducting personal and professional business, it has yet to fully redefine our shared cultural experiences. Cultural boundaries defined by common construction of meaning and purpose require full participation and interaction among all stakeholders. Banks (2000) proposed that building community requires dialogue that promotes mutual disclosure, validation of others' viewpoints, and authentic desire for shared endeavors. Thus, whereas new technologies offer invaluable vehicles for disseminating and receiving information, they do not offer a panacea for community building and developing a shared school-community vision to guide educational decision making. The fundamental building blocks of public relations will continue to be personal communications that foster trust among stakeholders who share a common cultural bond surrounding educational issues.

SUMMARY

Systems theories provide a conceptual framework for understanding public relations in educational settings. Public relations is a fundamental responsibility of education leadership. School administrators work in a highly complex system with a multitude of expectations from a variety of stakeholders. School leaders are accountable to a variety of publics and must balance the needs of various cultures within a pluralistic society. Thus, they must be system thinkers. Understanding systems theories will aid school leaders in communicating, decision making, and problem solving for a complex organization.

Although educational leaders are public servants, they are also change agents. A clear, concise vision for the future, with well-established organizational goals and strategies to achieve them, is the most effective tool for organizational change and improvement. When everyone supports the direction of the organization, coalitions are built among a variety of stakeholders. The creation of a collaborative productive work environment focused on the future is the result of groups of people working together to achieve something greater than their individual needs and wants. The development of such a collaborative milieu among all the various internal and external publics requires educational leaders who are able to facilitate various work groups and who exhibit an appreciation for the contributions of diverse members of the community. Ultimately, systems theories teach us that public relations is a systematic process for bringing together various groups and institutions for a common goal.

| CASE STUDY | The Dynamics of District-Level Systemic Reform |

Moore County School District is a moderately growing, high-wealth district because golf resorts and retirees have raised the per capita income level to seventh out of 100 counties in the state. Although it is one of the wealthiest districts in the state, it also has one of the lowest tax rates. Out of 117 school districts, it ranks as one of the highest in receiving state funds and one of the lowest in receiving local support. Overall, it ranked 69th in the state with a per pupil expenditure of approximately $6,200. However, outside its two major municipalities, it is very rural and less affluent and has one of the fastest growing Hispanic populations in the state. The Moore County School District has about 11,000 students of which 64% are White, 32% are African American, and 4% are Hispanic. Income levels of families vary widely across the county. Districtwide, 37% of students qualify for free and reduced lunches, but that ranges from school to school, from as low as 14% to as high as 80%.

Superintendent Pat Denny is the fourth superintendent in Moore County during the past 50 years. Two superintendents who preceded him had long tenures in office, with one serving for 35 years and the other 12 years. The only "outsider" hired, other than the current superintendent, lasted 18 months.

When Denny arrived in Moore County in 1999, he learned that the County Commission and the Board of Education adopted a local accountability agreement in 1996–1997. The Moore County Commission, a politically and financially conservative body, wanted some way to assess the appropriateness of school district requests for funding. The local accountability agreement stated that the four core criteria for comparing the success of Moore

County Schools in educating children to other counties in the state would include SAT scores, dropout rate, proficiency level of students as a district, and the State Accountability status that classifies schools as having expected exemplary growth or as being a low-performance school. The agreement also established a five-year averaging model.

During the first 5-year period, Moore County's ranking out of the state's 117 districts went from 47th to 53rd, and then to 44th. Superintendent Russo was hired by the Moore County Board of Education at the end of the second year of this 5-year period. He raised expectations for students, implemented a data-driven assessment system for schools, began annual performance reviews of administrators, and placed an emphasis on increasing academic performance of all students. During the last 2 years of the 5-year period the district improved its ranking, moving to 27th and then to 22nd. The most recent estimates place Moore County ranking around 15th in the state. Moore County presently is considered a high-performing, large district ranking in the top 10% of the state's schools. Although the district's efforts to improve learning for all students not only met board and county commission expectations and strengthened community support for schools, Superintendent Denny understood that continued progress, particularly for students who performed less well academically, could not be achieved without systemic reform.

Denny believed that having greater program discretion, financial flexibility, shared governance and decision making at the school level, and forging partnerships with other education systems would lay a foundation for better serving all students. Denny and John Dempsey, president of Sandhills Community College, informally talked about ways they could collaborate to expand educational opportunities for Moore County high school students. Both the Moore County Board of Education and the Board of Trustees of Sandhills Community College endorsed the notion of collaboration and asked that they explore how the two education systems create partnerships. As a consequence, they developed "Strategic Moment for Moore County," a 12-point white paper outlining possible collaboration in technology and several other joint program ventures. As these programs were being developed, they discovered that state regulations governing public education and community colleges inhibited innovation. For example, state regulations prohibited any student less than 16 years old from taking classes at a community college. In the natural course of events, the question was raised as to whether or not the state could grant waivers to increase flexibility of community colleges and school systems in pursuing creative education programs. Subsequent meetings with staff at the Office of Charter Schools and the Public Policy Forum failed to answer questions or generate support for their ideas.

The two administrators approached their state legislative delegation, including two Democratic senators and a Republican member of the House, and posed the question of pursuing deregulation to gain greater program and operating flexibility. In a remarkable act of solidarity, all three agreed that the notion of increasing flexibility for the district was worthwhile and encouraged them to proceed. During the next month and a half they looked at several possible approaches to increase flexibility, including drafting a legislative bill. There were a number of different drafts that were shared with selected stakeholders. The first two drafts referred to a "charter school district" initiative. In addition, the Democratic senator drafted a Senate Blank Bill as a way of putting that legislation "on the table" for consideration during the legislative session. This Blank Bill allowed Moore County to move forward with drafting legislation. Drafts of the proposed bill were shared with many people including members of the state legislative delegation, a member of the state board of education who lives in Moore County, and a representative of the state education association that acts on behalf of about 30% of the teachers in Moore County.

The superintendent reviewed and adopted a number of recommendations that shaped the language of the bill including removing the term *Charter School District* from the title. The term provoked considerable negative reactions across the state and generated political opposition to the initiative. In addition, language establishing a process by which the Moore County Board of Education could petition the state superintendent of education for consideration and approval of any waivers for deregulation. Essentially, the language allowed the state superintendent to approve a request for waiver, pass it on to the state board of education for consideration, and if no action were taken within 60 days the request would automatically be approved. Third, the district would receive "lump sum" funding. Consequently, the name was changed from "Charter School District" to "First in America," which reflected the former governor's "First in America" project that was still in place and the two key points remained the core of the proposed legislation in subsequent drafts.

Throughout the spring, as language of the bill evolved, the superintendent continued to solicit input from various sources and correct rumors and misinterpretation of the intent of the initiative. The state education association openly voiced opposition to the proposed legislation and planning process. The senior Democratic senator who advised school district officials during the previous several months called Superintendent Denny and told him that he could not support the bill unless there was greater school and community support for the initiative. In addition, he advised the superintendent that he was referring the bill to the Education Oversight Committee, a move that would allow consideration during the "short" legislative session.

Board members who encouraged the initiative also supported it by approving the proposed project during its April meeting with a 7 to 1 vote. Many board members were instrumental in this systemic reform effort and remained supportive and involved in the process. During April, as information about the project was being shared with district staff, it was evident that many people were not familiar with or opposed to the charter district concept and had negative reactions to it. Local newspapers reported on reactions to certain aspects of the initiative that fueled continued controversy and rumors. Over a period of a week, a well-orchestrated campaign flooded both state senators' offices with hundreds of e-mails and telephone calls against this piece of legislation. Throughout this period, the Moore County Board of Education remained steadfast in its support of the superintendent and supported continuation of the planning and development process.

In an effort to correct misinformation being circulated and to maintain an open process, Superintendent Denny visited every school in the district during the last 5 weeks of the second semester, explained the school improvement initiative, and asked for feedback. More than 72% of voting staff indicated a desire to move forward with the project. A similar series of community town meetings on the topic were held in each of the district's three regions. These meetings attracted members of the business community as well as representatives from the chamber of commerce, Kiwanis, and Rotary clubs. Informal votes taken at these meetings generated an 80% positive vote to continue the planning and development effort.

Strong support for the project in the schools and community convinced the superintendent to establish a yearlong planning process designed along the lines of the process proposed in the draft legislation. He created a district Planning and Framework Team to guide the process. Their task was to organize a large-scale planning effort that ensured deliberations would be conducted in an open and inclusive environment in which schools and community citizens could establish clear understanding of expectations for schools and provide direction for accomplishing future goals. Invitations to participate in the planning process were published in the local newspaper and on the local radio station, and an open invitation to participate was personally extended by Superintendent Denny at community meetings. No community member was denied the opportunity to serve on this team. In addition, he asked for a teacher representative from each school, invited representation from support staff, and included 11 of the district's 22 principals. It was a large-scale effort, the intent of which was to involve as many people in the planning process as possible.

The initial meeting of the Planning and Framework Team convened approximately 120 individuals including teachers, support staff members, community citizens, state representatives, and state and national experts. Two meetings were held in the fall—one in September and one in November. The first one helped set the stage for the yearlong planning process. The November meeting began the process of delineating tasks. Eleven teams and subteams were established in specific areas including technology; high school model, learning environment, and school and class size; school and instructional time; curriculum, testing, and accountability; exceptional needs children and preschool programs; human resources; parental and community engagement; governance issues; and funding. Each team was appointed based on expressed interest and stakeholder group including parents, community members, staff members, teachers, and principals. Individuals who chaired or cochaired the teams were district staff and were ensured they would be given the time to commit to the effort. The Planning and Framework Team, acting as a body of the whole, charged each group with the task of using the intervening $3\frac{1}{2}$ months to prepare feedback and recommendations to the group as to how they may improve the system.

On March 18, the Planning and Framework Team convened a meeting during which all the teams and subteams made preliminary reports, discussed findings, and formulated future plans. An analysis of these preliminary recommendations indicated that the vast majority of the recommendations did not need enabling legislation or waivers from the state. The district had the authority to move forward and implement these reforms. It was decided that before the next meeting planned for April 19, teacher representatives would be asked to share the 64 recommendations with colleagues at their respective schools. During this intervening period, Superintendent Denny conducted another round of regional community meetings to share recommendations. Over 600 concerns and questions were generated and answered in writing by the Planning and Framework Team. The objective of the April 19 meeting was to vote on each of the recommendations and to decide whether the district should continue to examine its viability or eliminate it from future work. The superintendent reiterated that a vote to continue discussion was not a final vote to adopt any of the proposed recommendations. It was only a vote as to whether or not the Planning and Framework Team should continue considering its relative merits.

During the April 19 meeting, six to eight teacher representatives indicated they felt very uncomfortable about voting on these recommendations insofar as they had received written answers to their questions only several days prior to the meeting and had little opportunity to poll sentiments of their colleagues. In keeping with the spirit of the planning process, Superintendent Russo gave teacher representatives an opportunity to caucus and discuss the issue to ensure everyone felt comfortable before moving forward. They spent over half an hour caucusing, came back with a number of recommendations, including that a meeting be called by the principal at each school dedicated to discussing concerns and questions about the 64 "First in America" recommendations. The teacher representatives would review each recommendation and then the school faculty would vote on each. A composite school vote would be compiled for each recommendation that would obligate the representative to vote in accordance with the wishes of their respective schools. It was also agreed that a vote of 50% plus one vote constituted consensus to move forward on any recommendation. Voting would be by secret ballot; however, composite data by recommendation and by school would be available to anyone, thus ensuring an open process. In addition, a series of regional community meetings were planned. Using the same process, a community sentiment for each recommendation was recorded that guided voting by their representatives. Furthermore, it was agreed to convene the Planning and Framework Team on May 21 to finally vote on each of the 64 recommendations. Members of the Planning and Framework Team who were unable to attend the May 21 meeting were mailed copies of the recommendations with Scantron ballots.

An examination of voting pattern provides considerable insight into school and community responses to the comprehensive planning process and the complexity of school and community relations. When teacher representatives polled their colleagues in their respective schools to ascertain how they should vote in the May 21 meeting, they found considerable variation in support for proposed recommendations. Two schools rejected all recommendations and four others approved less than 10. Most schools fell somewhere in between, with two voting "yes" on nearly all of them. Superintendent Russo said, "That's a dramatic statement for schools relative to their overall nonsupport of this initiative." A final count of school-based teacher voting indicated that they approved only 27 of the 64 recommendations for moving forward for further planning and development. Some recommendations that teachers did not support included host academies (schools within schools), smaller school size, smaller class size, expanded opportunities for elementary education, more guidance counselors, alternative schedules, choice within district schools, year-round schools, 11-month contracts that would increase their salaries and provide opportunities for staff development, technology training for teachers, collaboration with Sandhills Community College for academic programs and staff development, and school funding. In addition, governance recommendations creating parent councils, staff leadership teams, and increased decision-making authority in each school did not pass. It is evident that teachers did not support major systemic reforms in schools.

Members of the Planning and Framework Team were evenly divided between school and community representatives. The team included other staff members, principals, noninstructional support staff, as well as teacher and community representatives. On May 21 a meeting was convened to vote on the recommendations. Of the original 103 members who participated as members of the Planning and Framework Team throughout the year, 89 attended the meeting or returned a Scantron ballot. Approximately 17 individuals that were originally part of the process were considered "interested parties"; however, they did not have voting privileges. A tally of their vote indicates that 56 out of the 64 recommendations received consensus (50% plus one) and were advanced to the next planning and development stage.

The initial question raised by Superintendent Denny as to how to give schools greater flexibility to innovate was posed to the Moore County Board of Education. Rather than inhibiting change, they joined with Denny in engaging the local community and school staff in defining the role of schools in the community and how they could increase opportunities for all children and enhance their academic performance. The comprehensive community planning process was highly successful; however, teachers, those most directly responsible for school improvement, were reluctant to change.

QUESTIONS AND SUGGESTED ACTIVITIES

CASE STUDY

1. What external and internal factors (inputs) motivated the superintendent to pursue increasing flexibility for the district and schools?
2. Assess the superintendent's strategy to involve school and community citizens in a comprehensive district planning and development effort. Compare his process with the shared community vision development process described in the chapter.
3. What risks did the superintendent take when he contacted the Moore County state senators and representative and discussed how the district could gain greater flexibility through deregulation and waivers?
4. What were the outcomes (outputs) of the district planning process?
5. Analyze the voting patterns (feedback) from teachers, staff, and community members of the May 21 meeting.
6. Discuss what teachers, administrators, and staff and community members learned from the comprehensive planning process and whether their respective assumptions about teaching, learning, and governance changed.
7. Based on an analysis of votes taken at regional community meetings as well as the May 21 meeting, what strategies would you recommend the superintendent adopt to move the planning and development process forward to the next stage?
8. Discuss how the external and internal dynamics influenced the district and school reform initiatives.
9. Discuss how steadfast support of the board of education may have positively influenced community support and continuation of the planning process.

CHAPTER

10. What are the major elements of general systems theory?
11. What are common characteristics across systems approaches developed in the social sciences and used in the field of educational administration?
12. How can these components contribute to understanding relations between the school organization and its environment and among elements?

13. Why is educational vision important? Which is the more important element of vision development, process or product? Why?
14. Explain the relationship between facilitating group processes and public relations.

SUGGESTED READINGS

Ambrose, D. (1998). Creative organizational vision building through collaborative, visual-metaphorical thought. *Journal of Creative Behavior, 32*(4), 229–243.

Brandt, R. (1998). Listen first. *Educational Leadership, 55*(8), 25–30.

Decker, L. E. (2001). Allies in education. *Principal Leadership, 2*(1), 42–46.

Nichols-Solomon, R. (2000). Conquering the fear of flying. *Phi Delta Kappan, 82*(1), 19–21.

Ogawa, R. T., & Bossert, S. T. (1995). Leadership as an organizational quality. *Educational Administration Quarterly, 31*(2), 224–243.

Schein, E. H. (1996). Culture: The missing concept in organization studies. *Administrative Science Quarterly, 41*(2), 229–240.

Scoolis, J. (1998). What is vision and how do you get one? *Thrust for Educational Leadership, 28*(2), 20–21, 36.

Stern, R. N., & Barley, S. R. (1996). Organizations and social systems: Organization theory's neglected mandate. *Administrative Science Quarterly, 41*(1), 146–162.

REFERENCES

Argyris, C. (1982). *Reasoning, learning and action.* San Francisco: Jossey-Bass.

Argyris, C., & Schön, D. A. (1974). *Organizational learning: A theory of action perspective.* Reading, MA: Addison-Wesley.

Banks, S. P. (2000). *Multicultural public relations: A social-interpersonal approach* (2nd ed.). Ames: Iowa State University Press.

Bertalanffy, L. von. (1951). General systems theory: A new approach to unity of science. *Human Biology, 23,* 303–361.

Björk, L. (1993). Effective schools—effective superintendents: The emerging instructional leadership role. *Journal of School Leadership, 3*(3), 246–259.

Björk, L. (2001). The role of the central office in decentralization. In T. Kowalski (Ed.), *21st century challenges educational administration* (pp. 286–319). Lanham, MD: Scarecrow Press.

Björk, L., & Keedy, J. (2001a). Changing social context of education in the United States: Social justice and the superintendency. *Journal of In-Service Education, 27*(3), 405–427.

Björk, L., & Keedy, J. (2001b). Politics and the superintendency in the USA: Restructuring in-service education. *Journal of In-Service Education, 27*(2), 275–302.

Björk, L., & Lindle, J. C. (2001). Superintendents and interest groups. *Educational Policy, 15*(1), 76–91.

Campbell, R., Flemming, T., Newell, L., & Bennion, J. (1987). *A history of thought and practice in educational administration.* New York: Teachers College Press.

Carter, G. R., & Cunningham, W. G. (1997). *The American school superintendent: Leading in an age of pressure.* San Francisco: Jossey-Bass.

Chance, E. W. (1992). *Visionary leadership in schools: Successful strategies for developing and implementing an educational vision.* Springfield, IL: Charles C. Thomas.

Chance, P. L., & Lee, K. (2001). Exploring technology, change, and chaos theory: Moving educational leadership preparation programs into the new millennium. In T. J. Kowalski & G. Perreault (Eds.), *21st century challenges for school administrators* (pp. 189–202). Lanham, MD: Scarecrow Press.

Collins, J. C., & Porras, J. I. (1994). *Built to last: Successful habits of visionary companies.* New York: Harper & Row.

Easton, D. (1965). *A systems analysis of political life.* New York: Wiley.

Elmore, R. (2000). *Building a new structure for school leadership.* Washington, DC: The Albert Shaker Institute.

Firestone, W., & Louis, K. (1999). School cultures. In J. Murphy & K. Louis (Eds.), *Handbook of research on educational administration* (2nd ed., pp. 297–336). San Francisco: Jossey-Bass.

Follett, M. P. (1940). In H. C. Metcalf & L. Urwick (Eds.), *Dynamic administration: The collected papers of Mary Parker Follett.* New York: Harper & Row.

Getzel, J., & Guba, E. (1957). Social behavior and the administrative process. *School Review, 65,* 423–441.

Gleick, J. (1987). *Chaos: Making a new science.* New York: Penguin Books.

Griffiths, D., Hart, A., & Blair, B. (1991). Still another approach to administration: Chaos theory. *Educational Administration Quarterly, 27*(3), 430–451.

Hayles, N. (1990). *Chaos bound: Orderly disorder in contemporary literature and science.* Ithaca, NY: Cornell University Press.

Hickman, C. P., & Silva, M. (1984). *Creating excellence: Managing corporate culture, strategy and change in a new age.* New York: New American Library.

Hoy, W., & Miskel, C. (2001). *Educational administration: Theory, research and practice* (6th ed.). New York: McGraw-Hill.

Katz, D., & Kahn, R. (1966). *The social psychology of organizations.* New York: Wiley.

Leithwood, K., Jantzi, D., & Steinbach, R. (1998). Leadership and other conditions which poster organizational learning in schools. In K. Leithwood & K. S. Louis (Eds.), *Organizational learning in schools* (pp. 67–90). Lisse, Netherlands: Swets and Zeitlinger.

Lorenz, E. (1963). Deterministic non-periodic flow. *Journal of Atmospheric Sciences, 20,* 16–19.

Louis, K., & Kruse, S. (1998). Creating community in reform: Images of organizational learning in inner-city schools. In K. Leithwood and K. S. Louis (Eds.), *Organizational learning in schools* (pp. 17–45). Lisse, Netherlands: Swets and Zeitlinger.

Maeroff, G. I. (1993). Building teams to rebuild schools. *Phi Delta Kappan, 74*(7), 512–519.

Manasse, A. L. (1985). Vision and leadership: Paying attention to intention. *Peabody Journal of Education, 63*(1), 150–173.

Mandelbrot, B. (1983). *Fractal geometry of nature.* New York: W. H. Freeman.

Mayo, E. (1933). *The human problems of an industrial civilization.* New York: Viking Press.

Nanus, B. (1992). *Visionary leadership.* San Francisco: Jossey-Bass.

Ogawa, R. T., Crowson, R. L., & Goldring, E. B. (1999). Enduring dilemmas of school organization. In J. Murphy & K. Louis (Eds.), *Handbook of research on educational administration* (2nd ed., pp. 277–295). San Francisco: Jossey-Bass.

Owens, R. G. (1995). *Organizational behavior in education.* (5th ed.). Boston: Allyn & Bacon.

Parsons, T. (1967). *Sociological theory and modern society.* New York: Free Press.

Prigogine, I., & Stengers, I. (1984). *Order out of chaos: Man's new dialogue with nature.* New York: Bantam.

Public Relations Society of America. (2002). *About public relations.* Retrieved June 25, 2002, from http://www.prsa.org/Resources/Profession/index.asp?ident=prof1.

Reyes, P., Wagstaff, L., & Fusarelli, L. (1999). Delta forces: The changing fabric of American society and education. In J. Murphy & K. Louis (Eds.), *Handbook of research on educational administration* (2nd ed., pp. 183–201). San Francisco: Jossey-Bass.

Roethlisberger, F., & Dickson, W. (1939). *Management and the worker.* Cambridge, MA: Harvard University Press.

Rowan, B., & Miskel, C. (1999). Institutional theory and the study of educational organizations. In J. Murphy & K. Louis (Eds.), *Handbook of research on educational administration* (2nd ed., pp. 359–383). San Francisco: Jossey-Bass.

Rutherford, W. L. (1985). School principals as effective leaders. *Phi Delta Kappan, 67*(1), 31–34.

Scholtes, P. R. (1988). *The team handbook: How to use teams to improve quality.* Madison, WI: Joiner Associates.

Senge, P. (1990). *The fifth discipline: Mastering the five practices of the learning organization.* New York: Doubleday.

Sergiovanni, T. J. (1992). *Moral leadership: Getting to the heart of school improvement.* San Francisco: Jossey-Bass.

Sergiovanni, T. J. (1996). *Leadership for the schoolhouse: How is it different? Why is it important?* San Francisco: Jossey-Bass.

Shafritz, J., & Ott, J. (2001). *Classics of organizational theory* (5th ed.). Fort Worth, TX: Harcourt College Publishers.

Shieve, L. T., & Shoenheit, M. B. (1987). Vision and the work of educational leaders. In L. T. Shieve & M. B. Shoenhiet (Eds.), *Leadership: Examining the elusive* (pp. 93–104). Washington, DC: Association for Supervision and Curriculum Development.

Spillane, J., Halverson, P., & Diamond, J. (1999). *Distributed leadership: Toward a theory of school leadership practice.* Paper presented at the annual meeting of the American Educational Research Association, Montreal.

Starratt, R. (1996). *Transforming educational administration: Meaning, community, and excellence.* New York: McGraw-Hill.

Thompson, J. (1967). *Organizations in action.* New York: McGraw-Hill.

Tuckman, B. W., & Jensen, M. A. C. (1977). Stages of small group development revisited. *Groups and Organizational Studies, 2*(4), 419–427.

Tyack, D. B., & Hansot, E. (1982). *Managers of virtue: Public school leadership in America.* New York: Basic Books.

Weick, K. (1976). Educational organizations as loosely coupled systems. *Administrative Science Quarterly, 21,* 1–19.

Wheatley, M. (1996). *Leadership and the new science: Discovering order in a chaotic world.* San Francisco: Berrett-Koehler.

Wiener, N. (1948). *Cybernetics.* Cambridge, MA: MIT Press.

Wirt, F., & Kirst, M. (2001). *The political dynamics of American education.* Berkeley, CA: McCutchan.

7

Effective Programming at the District Level

Arthur Stellar

Theodore J. Kowalski

School public relations should begin with the recognition that "Education is Politics."

Shor & Pari, 1999

School safety was a hot topic for the Oklahoma City Public Schools district; it even became the focus of a bond-issue campaign. The administrative staff planned and executed a public relations strategy. All the right things were brought into play: citizen input, speakers' bureaus, media publicity, and opinion-leader (individuals who shape public opinion in the local community) support. After 20 years without winning a bond issue, the school community was confident of victory this time. However, a critical piece of the public relations strategy—provisions for anticipating problems—was missing.

The first rule a public relations officer should honor is "What *can* happen, often *does* happen." In the case of Oklahoma City, the planners knew teacher negotiations were under way, but they never considered a possible nexus between this process and the bond referendum. Weeks before the citywide vote, negotiations with the teachers' union hit a snag. Unexpectedly, union officials declared public opposition to the bond initiative. Suddenly the issue of teacher salaries and the referendum became inextricably linked. The board members, however, were unwilling to approve salary increases (for which they believed funds were not available) to gain the union's endorsement. More than 10,000 votes were cast in the referendum, the highest number in the history of the school district; the bond issue failed by fewer than 200 votes.

This true case exemplifies why school district officials should be prepared to do more than simply treat public relations as the dissemination of information. In the real world, the ability to handle *unplanned* events often determines success. Public relations literature focuses largely on rational plans and theoretical constructs, frequently ignoring the controversies, vendettas, nastiness, crises, and other totally unexpected situations that can attenuate even the most effective plans. Public relations guru Edward Bernays compared planning with drama, "a drama that hasn't happened yet, in which every step of the drama, every appearance of every actor, every scene is outlined . . . yet, all are subject to change" (Davis, 1986, p. 29). This does not negate the need for program planning; rather, it points out the need for administrators to be flexible so that they are able to lead the organization through transitions.

This chapter offers suggestions about orchestrating one's drama with researched detail, planning, and foresight. Just as important, this chapter presents ideas on how to plan for the unexpected in local district administration. Both ingredients are essential to producing a public relations program capable of developing the attitudes, perceptions, actions, information, and results important to an educational institution.

IT STARTS AT THE TOP

One of the more essential skills for today's superintendents is the ability to communicate—personally as well as organizationally. "A superintendent sets the tone, the style, and the philosophy of a school system's organizational approach to communication. Superintendents need to have public-relations expertise at their fingertips, and, without apology, they must commit resources to managing community relations or public affairs" (Bohen, 1998, p. 219).

Promoting and modeling open two-way communication is often difficult for superintendents. Many of them have been socialized to believe that the media are the enemy and that community involvement simply spawns additional conflict. For some, dispositions toward dealing with media are rooted in personal experiences. Those who have served as superintendents can relate to the emotions associated with reading the morning paper, as described by an administrator in a recent book (Johnston et al., 2002):

> During particularly tumultuous time of contentious labor negotiations and dealing with a new board member whose agenda was my "head on a platter," it dawned on me how tense I was each morning when I walked down the driveway to pick up the daily newspaper. My stomach and my shoulders would knot up, and I would hold my breath as I slipped the rubber band off the paper and scanned the headlines while returning to the house. I always hoped the headlines said nothing controversial or negative about me or anyone else in my school district. I realized I also hoped that no one else in public education was being beaten up either. (p. 21)

Apprehensions about creating an open district climate, however, are lessened by the realities of modern practice. Seasoned superintendents realize that schools are unlikely to be restructured unless the educators and taxpayers collaborate to build a vision and plan for positive change. Eight superintendents who jointly reflected and analyzed their practitioner experiences developed a list of lessons they had learned about this difficult assignment. Those most cogent to community relations included (Johnston et al., 2002, p. 30):

- ◆ Rely on multiple forms of input to draw conclusions about a community.
- ◆ Study the history and culture of a school district before trying to change it.
- ◆ Participate in community organizations and inspire others to do community service.
- ◆ Develop a network of key supporters in the community who can be resources in both positive and negative situations.
- ◆ Seek participation from community groups, even from those with differing perspectives.
- ◆ Develop and use a media relations plan.
- ◆ Give the district a human face in the community by being part of the community.

In the case of district-level public relations, good programs start at the top. These programs are encouraged and nurtured by superintendents who understand that positive community relations, democratic administration, and shared governance are politically advantageous and morally correct.

CHANGING TIMES

Twenty years ago, a school public relations program that included a good newsletter, six positive stories in the local newspaper, a strong PTA, and consistent bond levy promotions was likely to be judged effective. But communities have changed, and so have the standards for good practice. Families a century ago obtained information from sources close to home: church, school, and neighbors. Today, information is readily available from multiple sources, not the least of which are the print and electronic media. Equally momentous has been the increasing tendency of the general public to question and criticize public institutions and those who operate them.

Contrary to popular thought, however, intense criticism of public education is not a recent phenomenon. Approximately a decade before the well-known report A *Nation at Risk* was published in 1983, Unruh and Willier (1974) wrote that public criticism "has placed educational institutions on the defensive, perhaps because it has come from so many sources and in so many unexpected ways" (p. 150). Noting that schools like other organizations were not perfect, they argued that "what's right with the schools is far greater than what's wrong" (p. 150). Their insights are equally relevant today. Too much attention is given to problems and deficiencies, many of which are beyond the control of educators, and too little attention is given to productivity and success.

Both technology and the drive for school reform create unprecedented opportunities for local school district officials to provide more balanced coverage of schools. Technology facilitates improved communication so that superintendents and other administrators can engage in two-way communication in and outside of the organization. Such information exchanges through Web pages, e-mail, and cable television broadcasts serve both professional and political purposes; they help ensure that schools respond to changing needs and wants and they help ensure that taxpayers are better informed about schools (Kowalski, 1999). School reform also contributes to a political environment favorable to educating the public. Reporters, for example, remain interested in education stories, and continued attention from state legislatures sustains open and candid discussions about schools. Technology and school reform, however, enable rather than guarantee success. Superintendents are more likely to capitalize on these opportunities when they accept the broad definition of public relations articulated in this book and proceed to develop a comprehensive district public relations plan.

AN ORGANIZATIONAL PERSPECTIVE

Organizational format and extent of planning are two key variables defining district public relations programs. Organizational format pertains to control and responsibility; planning level pertains to the extent to which the program has been purposefully designed. The option ranges for these characteristics are illustrated in Figure 7–1.

There are three basic organizational concepts that can be used to determine how public relations services will be administered and implemented.

1. *Centralization*—This organizational structure requires superintendents or other district administrators (e.g., public relations director) to control and perform all or most public relations responsibilities. One of the perceived advantages is technical efficiency. By restricting public relations functions to one or two central office personnel possessing the necessary knowledge and expertise, advocates hope to achieve several economically based objectives. The more common are: (a) reducing staff development costs (fewer employees need to be prepared to engage in public relations functions); (b) reducing supervision costs (fewer employees require supervision to perform public relations functions); (c) reducing duplication costs (the same

FIGURE 7–1

Range of Organizational Alternatives
for a District Public Relations Program

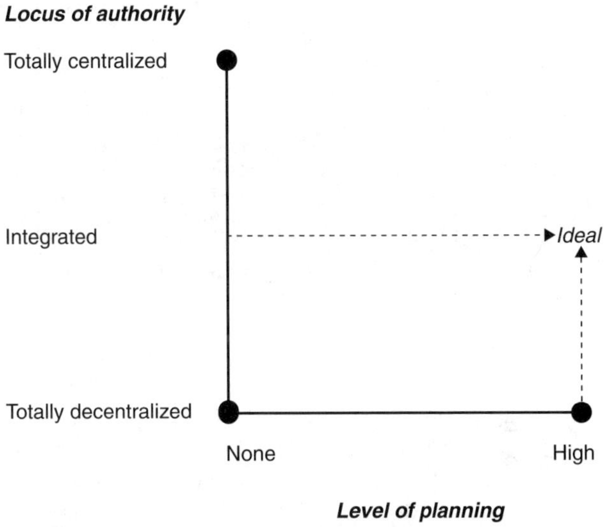

functions do not have to be performed at each school); (d) reducing errors (activities are highly controlled by standards and implemented by just one or two employees). Centralization also may reflect an attitude that principals have neither the time nor the expertise to engage in this function. This organizational arrangement, however, usually errs on the side of too much control. Because only one or two persons conduct the program, communication may suffer. Neither internal nor external aspects of public relations are likely to function effectively in district environments where the flow of communication is restricted (Kowalski, 1999).

2. *Decentralization*—This organizational structure delegates authority to school principals and their staffs to control and perform virtually all or most of the responsibilities. Decentralization is supported primarily by the contention that community relations efforts are best executed on a school-by-school basis, especially in districts where culture, social conditions, and economic conditions vary markedly from one school to the next. Underlying this concept is the premise that principals and school faculties have a greater understanding of parents and other taxpayers than do district-level personnel; consequently, school-based administrators are likely to be more effective communicating with the school's broader community.

Total decentralization, nonetheless, can result in disorder and the approach ignores the reality that certain issues are best addressed on a districtwide basis. As examples, building goodwill for the passage of a bond referendum or redrawing district attendance boundaries are decisions that potentially affect all district residents. Having individual principals communicate independently with the public on these matters could produce conflicting information and competing perspectives. In addition, the quantity and quality of communication provided to the public may vary substantially simply because the principals are not equally prepared for or committed to the task.

3. *Integration*—This organizational structure divides control and role responsibilities between district and school administrators. Integrated approaches are designed to meld the best features of centralization and decentralization. With this hybrid structure, public relations planning occurs at both the district and school levels; school plans are developed as extensions of the district plan. Therefore, the nature of specific functions determines how public relations responsibilities are divided between district or school officials. The integrated approach symbolically reinforces the belief that all administrators have a responsibility to engage in public relations. In addition, this approach can maximize the use of human resources. Dividing responsibilities, however, can spawn conflict—a potential problem that requires management.

Public relations programs also may be described with respect to the level of planning that underlies the function. Planned programs are considered ideal practice because contemporary administrators are expected to be both leaders and managers. Leading entails taking the organization to planned levels of achievement, an activity that requires vision and goals. Operating with a written plan clearly provides a distinct advantage for district and school administrators because stated public relations goals are assessed and evaluated. Such activities determine whether a school district is moving in the desired direction. In reality, however, many district programs have simply evolved from past practice and tradition; administrators react to evolving conditions rather than attempting to provide leadership and management to fulfill a shared vision. The absence of planning may result in a total indifference toward public relations or in situations where administrators basically address public relations through trial and error.

Although all types of public relations programs have been successful in isolated situations, there are general preferences for organizational format and planning. In general, integrated programs tend to be more effective than either highly centralized or highly decentralized programs. The fact that planning is preferable to not planning is even more evident.

CREATING A SCHOOL DISTRICT PLAN

Topor (1992) noted that public relations plans should strongly resemble a mosaic communicating a dynamic and powerful message to viewers. It should focus on the big picture, ensure a balance between individual elements, and include smaller pieces, each with its own marketing value. Whether it is the district's mission statement, an employee newsletter, an awards ceremony, a superintendent's speech, or a conversation, each element contains intrinsic power and contributes to the whole. Topor wrote, "As with tesserae within a mosaic, the power of each piece is not fully revealed unless it is arranged (marketing strategy) as part of a grander, more comprehensive plan (a marketing plan)!" (p. 46).

A district public relations plan is influenced by variables such as enrollment, social composition, tradition, and philosophy. Since these factors are not constant across all local districts, no single plan is universally effective. Following is an outline of the components of a plan developed by a large local school district with approximately 50,000 students. Public relations activities in this school system are coordinated by a central administrative unit called the Communications Department.

♦ *Organizational chart*—details the division of responsibilities within the Communication Department and between the department and other district divisions (including individual schools).

♦ *Mission statement*—identifies functions of the Public Information Program encompassing media relations, dissemination of information, release of public information, internal communication, parental involvement, business partnerships, use of public facilities, community partnerships, television broadcasts, and community use of facilities; defines responsibilities in relation to assessing attitudes, news media relations, coverage of board meetings, news releases, community organizations, advisory groups, partnerships, coalitions and task forces, and the district's educational foundation.

♦ *Vision statement*—provides a picture of the desired future; lists general and specific program goals that provide a basis for performance, assessment, and program evaluation.

♦ *Communications calendar*—details tasks and deadlines for the school year.

♦ *Summary of relevant laws and policies*—provides information about laws and policies that affect aspects of public relations. Basically, these aspects involve communicating with employees, students, and the general public. Examples include policies for allowing the public to use school buildings or policies concerning media relations.

♦ *Distribution of policy*—details information about procedures for disseminating information about policy and includes a summary of procedures for developing and altering policy.

♦ *Publications/Web site*—includes a list of district publications and other information that is accessible via the district's Web page.

♦ *Information services*—provides a list of information services provided by the district. Examples include procedures for contacting the superintendent and making inquiries to the board of education, and a list of district divisions generating and maintaining data.

♦ *Parent information*—lists information such as parenting classes, the family resource library, the parent helpline, and referral services available to district residents.

♦ *Television and video production*—contains descriptions of television and video production services and details the duties of the Communication Department in relation to these services.

♦ *News media/special events*—includes information and procedures for dealing with the media. Examples of content include contact information for media representatives, instructions for preparing press releases, guidelines for dealing with media representatives, and policy, rules, and suggestions for dealing with the media during a crisis situation.

♦ *Volunteer and partnership programs*—provides a summary of existing programs and pertinent data that can be used to publicize the programs or answer questions about them.

Several attributes of the plan are especially relevant:

♦ It provides program goals for public relations.
♦ It transmits information about communication norms.
♦ It is written in language suited for both employees and community members.
♦ It provides a basic framework that principals can use to develop more detailed school public relations plans.

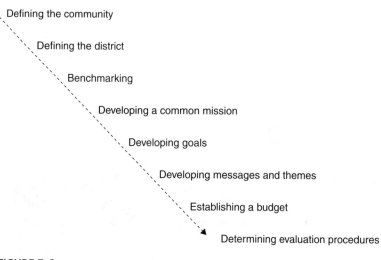

FIGURE 7–2
Key Functions in Developing a District Public Relations Plan

Public relations planning may include many functions. They range from data analysis to goal setting to establishing a communications office and employing a program director. Those discussed in this chapter are shown in Figure 7–2.

Defining the Community

Discussing collaboration between schools and communities, Kirst and Kelley (1995) emphasized the importance of administrators conducting a needs assessment. According to them, this process enables school officials to accurately understand community demographics, including "racial composition, cultural and language diversity, poverty levels, and indicators of risk factors for children" (p. 37). Given the political nature of public institutions, superintendents often discover that it is also important to identify patron *wants*. The procedure of determining community dispositions (both needs and wants) is referred to as *defining research*.

Much of the information for defining research can be extracted from existing databases maintained by the school district or other agencies (e.g., state statistical reports). For example, principals may have already completed surveys of students and parents, and local businesses or the chamber of commerce may have studies that include education-related components. Some data, however, must be collected through surveys or other assessment procedures (see Chapters 10 and 13 for a more in-depth discussion of data collection and analysis). The following are information sources a school district employed to conduct defining research:

◆ A demographic review of the community conducted by school officials that included income, age, race, gender, location, occupation, hobbies, interests, lifestyle, and connection to the organization

- ◆ Results from an opinion poll conducted with parents
- ◆ Data collected in conjunction with a bond referenda that reveals voter preferences with respect to tax increases
- ◆ Public reactions to critical decisions made by the school board in the past 3 years
- ◆ Demographic data extracted from state and county statistical reports (e.g., population projections)
- ◆ Opinions expressed by focus groups consisting of community leaders

The defining process has become more essential in the current political environment where the responsibility for school reform has been relegated largely to district and school officials. Authors who have questioned why public schools have not improved significantly despite decades of governmental interventions (e.g., Kantor & Brenzel, 1993; Yancy & Saporito, 1995) have commonly concluded that a lack of understanding about the idiosyncrasies of local communities and even neighborhoods is primarily responsible. These observers maintain that improvement in student performance is unlikely if administrators rely on generic strategies that often have only limited relevance for their students. Put another way, they believe that meaningful reform is impossible unless education leaders understand and address the changes that have occurred and are occurring in the community being served.

Defining the Organization

Effective public relations plans also require accurate information about the school district. Hence, defining research should be extended to include this entity, and the process for doing that is nearly identical to the one used for the community. Here, however, emphasis is placed on determining district strengths and weaknesses and on interpreting these attributes in relation to needs and desired program initiatives.

As with community data, much of the information for defining the organization may already exist. The following are examples of resources used by a school district:

- ◆ Accreditation reports
- ◆ Annual reports for the state department of education (e.g., free lunch data)
- ◆ Student records (e.g., grade reports, standardized test scores)
- ◆ Staff surveys (of opinions, perceptions, and attitudes)
- ◆ Student surveys (relating to curricular and extracurricular needs and interests)
- ◆ Surveys of higher education officials (e.g., admission expectations)
- ◆ Follow-up studies of graduates
- ◆ Program evaluation outcomes (e.g., state and regional accrediting reports)
- ◆ Staffing reports (identifying ratios, needs)
- ◆ School facility feasibility studies
- ◆ Student discipline records

Because administrators may find it difficult to be objective in defining the district, a validation process, such as using consultants or an external review panel, often is employed.

Benchmarking

In addition to gaining a full understanding of the community and the district, administrators should study highly successful educational institutions. The purpose is to identify conditions most associated with goal attainment so that these conditions could possibly be replicated and even improved. The process of identifying these characteristics is called *benchmarking*. Fortune 500 corporations such as AT&T, Du Pont, Ford Motor, Motorola, and Xerox have used benchmarking as a standard management tool.

Most administrators in other districts are willing to share their knowledge and skills, including the detailed plans and strategies they have developed for school improvement. Such information can be accessed more quickly and economically than in the past. Consider the following ways that this information could be transmitted:

- ◆ Telephone interviews
- ◆ Site visits
- ◆ Attendance at national conferences where this information is discussed
- ◆ Web page data
- ◆ Plans, reports, or other documents that can be faxed, e-mailed, or sent via regular mail
- ◆ Videotapes

The purpose of benchmarking is not to replicate unthinkingly programs or standards developed elsewhere; contextual variables unique to a district often attenuate such action. Being totally dismissive of successes in other districts, however, may be an even greater error. The keys to effective benchmarking are to interface the successful practices of other districts with the actual conditions that exist in your district and to make necessary adaptations based on that evaluation.

Refining the Mission

When the research component is completed, the planners can move to reshape the district's mission as appropriate. The terms *vision* and *mission* are frequently used synonymously, but doing so is a mistake. A vision represents a picture of what the district can and should become, and it is influenced by philosophical dispositions (e.g., values and beliefs). A mission statement provides a brief but concise statement of an organization's purpose. As an example, a school district's mission is to provide educational services as prescribed by state laws and policies and local school board mandates. The district's vision provides an image of what the district should look like as an organization at some point in the future. Often an organization's actual mission broadens or changes incrementally, but administrators fail to adjust the statement accordingly.

Topor (1992) observed that a good public relations program must be nurtured. He wrote, "[As] with many things in life, [public relations] needs to have its roots in fertile soil to succeed. The 'nutrients' that feed marketing should grow out of the institution itself" (p. 18). A good public relations program is grounded in a shared vision (e.g., a picture of the future that is widely supported by district employees and residents), an accurate mission, and specific goals that outline how the vision is to be achieved. As an example, districts should have public relations mission statements that detail the purposes of this function; possible functions were outlined in Chapter 1. Many planning scholars (e.g., Fullan, 1999; Kirst & Kelley, 1995) believe that meaningful reform becomes less likely if a school district's vision is not shared by a majority of the employees and taxpayers and when its mission does not accurately reflect purposes supported by them.

Developing Goals

Goals are extensions of the mission, and they should be written from both short-term and long-term (spanning more than 2 years) perspectives. Bond issues and levy campaigns, for example, should be planned long before they are announced to the public. Most important, goals should be flexible—that is, they should be mutable. Largely because administrators must be ready to deal with the unexpected, continuously gathering information, both inside and outside of the organization (referred to as environmental scanning in strategic planning), is necessary. This action allows administrators to adjust specific goals as conditions warrant. For instance, a goal to improve school facilities by a specified date may have to be altered if state laws governing the financing of capital outlay are later changed.

Ideally, school public relations plans are extensions of the district plan. Whereas district goals provide long-range targets, school plans ought to provide more specific short-term objectives. The nexus between the district and individual school plans is predicated on the objective of balancing centralization and decentralization. That is, the arrangement allows the district to pursue broad objectives while permitting individual schools the flexibility to utilize its resources to address specific needs. The two levels of planning are also connected at the evaluation stage; assessment and evaluation of school plans are conducted first and these data are then used to complete the same tasks in relation to the district plan.

An organization's mission and goals are the grout holding the mosaic together; they are the bridges connecting internal and external themes. Mission and goals become central to all communication efforts; they accommodate cohesion and balance. From placing district and school logos side by side at an awards program to working with the news media in a fashion that balances school district and individual school interests, the mission and goals provide the administrator with a framework for practice.

Developing Messages and Themes

Once the mission and goals are written, administrators are in a position to craft the organization's messages and themes. These elements of the public relations plan serve two critical purposes: (a) they help garner support for the organization, and (b) they help people understand the directions in which the organization is moving. Good themes are usually concise, rhythmic, memorable, and easy to understand. Themes used by schools include such ringing phrases as "Quest for Quality," "Getting Better for Kids," "Public Education: A Sound Investment in America," and "Champions of Learning" (Bagin, Ferguson, & Marx, 1985, p. 112). More so than the mission statement, messages and themes are cultural. That is, they express symbolically the values and beliefs of the organization; they are an overt expression of organizational culture and philosophy.

Themes and messages can be very powerful, as evidenced by case studies of successful businesses (Deal & Kennedy, 1982). To be effective, though, they should be predicated on reality. Consider, for example, administrators who decided on the theme "Established Excellence" when, in fact, test scores in their district had been declining for 15 years. False claims are likely to be challenged, and if they are proved false, the school district suffers. Thus, themes and messages should be positive, honest, and truly reflective of the district's vision, mission, and goals.

Establishing a Budget

No public relations office can function effectively without an adequate budget. When budgets are slim and teachers' salaries are frozen, the public relations staff is often an easy target, criticized as "fluff" and described as something the district can live without. The budget of any division of a school district has both direct and symbolic importance; that is, the amount of money dictates program scope and conveys a message to employees and the community about the importance placed on this function.

Often, school officials make the mistake of believing that a public relations program is fiscally neutral—that it can be implemented with little or no cost by simply having employees do a little more. This assumption is rarely if ever true. Modern public relations as defined in this book is a comprehensive program requiring both human and material resources. If designed and managed appropriately, however, a program could produce a favorable cost-benefit ratio. For example, effective use of communication and information may facilitate the quality of administrative decisions—an outcome that could reduce expenditures associated with correcting mistakes or collecting the same data repeatedly.

Determining an Evaluation Procedure

All programs in a school district should be subjected to periodic evaluation. As noted earlier, program evaluation should be both summative and formative; it should serve to determine the extent to which the mission and goals have been achieved and should provide insights for future program improvement. Chapter 15 provides an in-depth discussion of this topic.

APPLICATIONS AND STRATEGIES

Even the best of plans can falter if they are not implemented properly. For this reason, thought must be given to how the public relations plan will be implemented. These considerations extend beyond organizational design and include fundamental questions about communication channels, priorities, responsibilities, and standard procedures associated with a school district public relations plan.

Employing a Public Relations Specialist

One of the most critical decisions made by the chief executive officer of an educational organization relates to employing a public relations administrator. What type of person is needed? Do the responsibilities justify a full-time position? Additionally, the superintendent must consider responsibilities and working conditions for this person. Life in an information age dictates that, compared with conditions just a decade ago, qualifications for this position should be more stringent, and the position should have higher stature in the organization.

Qualifications.   When public relations is defined and applied as a broad construct, the job requirements of a chief public relations officer obviously are more extensive. The person assuming this position must be a planner, an analyst, a communication expert, a manager, and even an evaluator. Because the public relations director is involved in so many fundamental activities, he or she is an integral part of the administrative team. Studies of practitioners (e.g., Zoch, Patterson, & Olson, 1997) indicate that overall responsibilities of school public relations directors typically fall into two broad categories: managers and technicians. In the recent past, it was common for educational institutions to relegate public relations responsibilities to a full-time English teacher or an administrator who appeared to have a knack for communicating. Both the present context of schools and communities and the refinement of the public relations profession (more specifically, the infusion of sociological, psychological, and economic theory) suggest that perpetuating such past practices is not advisable. Ideally, candidates for this position should have academic preparation and experience in both administration and public relations (or communication).

Stature.   The district's director of public relations should be an integral part of the administrative team. Preferably, this individual should have easy and open access to the superintendent; having the director report directly to the superintendent is the best way to achieve this objective. Having to go through an intermediary (e.g., an assistant superintendent) or excluding the individual from key administrative meetings may prevent timely communication regarding potentially controversial situations. For example, when a school district is contemplating closing a school, announcing test scores, or changing a school board policy, the public relations specialist should provide input regarding how and when these issues should be communicated to employees and the public.

Creating a Public Relations Division

In creating a public relations division, superintendents often give considerable thought to naming this entity. Quoting Edward Bernays, Davis (1986) wrote, "Words are as fragile as lace or a soap bubble. The words and their meanings get kicked around . . . so today the words 'public relations' are so muddy in meaning that to some they do mean press agentry or flackery" (p. 14). Consequently, many superintendents and school board members avoid using the words *public relations*. More common titles have been "Division of Communication Services," "Community Relations Division," and "Division of School-Community Relations." The scope of responsibilities assigned to the division is more important than title. As long as the division's mission, articulated in the district's plan, reflects the broad concept of public relations, the title is not critical.

Once the division has been named, other key questions must be answered. They include the following:

- Where should the division's office be located?
- How many employees will be assigned to the division and what roles will they have?
- What material resources are necessary to support the division?
- How will the division interface with individual school principals?

As noted earlier, answers to resource-related questions have practical and symbolic significance.

Determining Scope of Communication

Planned actions in the area of communication are central to implementing a district public relations program. For example, relying on one-way formal channels or viewing public relations solely as an external process can attenuate effective planning. Administrators should consider how they would communicate with employees and students as well as with parents and other taxpayers. Individuals within the organization are expected to know, firsthand, what is really occurring. In the case of education, individuals and groups tend to offer their opinions frequently and freely even when their input is not requested. Consider that every person coming in contact with an organization will tell an average of 22 people about it, and a little over 10% of them will tell even more people. Remember that these messages are both good and bad (Levinson, 1989).

Rather than building positive internal communications, educators are at times their own worst enemies. Davis (1986) wrote:

> School boards argue among themselves, and with the community, and many times with the superintendent they hired. Teachers argue with administrators and the school board. Administrators unionize and talk tough and lob verbal hand grenades back at teacher union invectives. We argue about back-to-basics versus relevant education, about class size and working conditions and fringe benefits, about who is to blame for declining test scores, about accountability and productivity, and about vandalism and violence. We castigate each other over declining enrollments, closing schools, desegregation, politics, bureaucracies, finances, community advisory committees and plenty of other things. (p. 16)

There are at least four reasons why internal communication is an important element of a public relations program:

1. An organization is more likely to fulfill its mission if district personnel know the organization's mission and goals.
2. District personnel possess information that can make organizations more effective; this potential asset is wasted when communication is not flowing in all directions.
3. When employees are involved in key decisions, they are more apt to develop a sense of ownership.
4. A school district simply functions more effectively when information is shared. (Bagin et al., 1985)

Internal communication is most effective when it is honest and open. In addition, the superintendent and other higher level administrators must have contact with district employees on a regular basis.

External communication is equally important. Historically, educational organizations have been prone to "*not* thinking, planning, executing, and evaluating services from an *external* point of view" (Topor, 1992, p. 21). External communication entails far more than just sending newsletters and pamphlets to targeted publics. Collecting information about needs and wants, for instance, requires two-way external communication. Advisory committees, shared governance councils, and ad hoc groups offer channels for gaining community input.

When past and present conceptualizations of educational public relations are compared, one finds that the two most glaring communication differences are a dedication of energy and resources to the open exchange of information within the organization, and a two-way communication with the wider communities served by the schools. Both have become essential elements of administrative behavior in an information age.

Working With the Media

Public perceptions are shaped by the news media, although many persons associated with public education believe this influence is generally unfair. Significant numbers of educators can resonate with these statements by David Berliner and Bruce Biddle (Maeroff, 1998, p. 30):

> In our opinion, on educational issues, the press—
>
> ◆ Is biased and covers the negative side of news stories much more diligently than the positive side.
> ◆ Presents too simplistic and incomplete a view of the educational problems and issues that they are reporting.
> ◆ Is more critical of the schools in its editorial policies than it is complimentary.
> ◆ Has editorial policies that are biased against public schools, against school change, and in particular, against the schools that serve the poor.
> ◆ Displays a lack of understanding of statistics and social science research, without which reporters cannot properly interpret the huge amount of data that the educational system produces.
> ◆ Shows an ignorance of the role of poverty as a root cause of many of the difficulties in our schools.

Maeroff (1998), who has been both educator and news media member, offers a more balanced opinion. He writes:

> Education and the media are locked in a symbiotic relationship that—like a bad marriage—leaves both parties feeling uncomfortable and, often, less than satisfied. . . . Disgruntled educators might say that the relationship is one-sided and they could just as readily forgo it. . . . But the public would be poorer for the loss. Admittedly, coverage of education is not all it might be. The public, however, deserves to be well-informed about education. . . . The onus for improving the quality of education coverage usually is placed on the media, but this narrow view overlooks the responsibilities of the education establishment and of the public. If what happens in the media is to improve, then the media cannot act alone to make it happen. The education establishment must show more respect for the public's right to know and a greater understanding of the media's role as an intermediary between the world of education and the public. . . . education should do

all it can to explain complexities to the media and to facilitate articles that show understanding and insightfulness. (pp. 221–223)

Educators should expect the truth, often delivered with candor, from the news media. Maeroff further cautions educators that "the media cannot, should not, and, one might hope, never will be a public relations vehicle for education. If that were to happen, the media would lose their credibility and the puffery would not be worth the newsprint or videotape on which it appeared" (p. 224).

In the end, like it or not, dealing with the media is central to effective school district administration. In this vein, Ordovensky and Marx (1993) offer the following advice:

When you decided to get involved in education you also committed yourself to working with the news media. The media are a part of each educator's professional life for several reasons. Here are just two: People want to know how well schools are teaching students. People want to know how their tax dollars are being invested. In short, our schools deal with two things very clear to people, their children and their tax dollars. (p. 1)

A community's perceptions about its schools are greatly influenced by the media; many people rely solely on radio, television, and the newspapers to access information about schools. Consequently, local districts should have a prescribed media relations plan. Such a document is typically a component of the district's public relations plan. An excellent way to work with the news media is to use a planned and integrated approach to communication—one in which a district public relations specialist establishes and monitors a decentralized media liaison program and properly educates school-level personnel to participate in it (Meek, 1999).

A media liaison is a school employee who acts as publicity chair for that school. He or she prepares news releases; promotes media attention for programs, events, and honors; and assists the principal in informing the community about what is happening at the school. The same functions, on behalf of any departmental office in the central administration, can be performed by designated people in those departments. (p. 56)

The topic of working with the media is covered in detail in Chapter 11.

Effectively Planning Public Meetings

A school board meeting is the easiest and most effective communication tool available to district administrators. Yet, the outcomes of these meetings have often been negative. For example, some are seemingly out of control, lasting 5 or 6 hours and dominated by bickering and pessimism. These sessions often suggest chaos and managerial ineffectiveness. At best, such unruly meetings occur because school officials overlook the fact that they are "on stage."

All open meetings sponsored by the school district affect organizational image and, therefore, should have a public relations purpose. They should be treated as opportunities to balance criticism, concerns, and problems with positive information that showcases successful programs, model students, and outstanding employees. In the case of school board meetings, for example, some agenda items should be dedicated to providing information about specific achievements.

Procedures and personal behavior also are important elements of public meetings. At the district level, the superintendent sets the tone for normative behavior. If he or she engages in open, honest, and appropriate communication, other employees will be influenced by this behavior. However, incomplete, inaccurate, or grammatically incorrect messages from the top executive indicate that communication is relatively unimportant.

Encouraging Citizen Participation

Over the past three or four decades, there has been a growing recognition that schools do not function well when they are isolated from their communities (Kowalski, 2000). Accordingly, one of the goals of public relations programming should be to involve as many district residents as possible in the process. This task is made both more necessary and more difficult because many taxpayers do not have direct contact with their schools through children, grandchildren, or employment. As a result, their opinions about schools are usually based on secondhand or thirdhand information sources.

Among the ideas that can be used to enhance citizen participation are the following:

- Parent–teacher associations
- Open houses
- Parent–teacher conferences
- Special events (e.g., plays, musicals, and award ceremonies)
- Electronic newsletters or bulletin boards
- Periodic coffees or teas with administrators
- Focus groups
- School partnership programs (e.g., with businesses, parents, or other public agencies)
- Advisory groups (e.g., on extracurricular programs or fundraising)
- School councils

Public participation also can be increased by having key district communicators network with each other; this interaction allows them to coordinate their information exchanges so that they are able to expand their contacts (Pawlas, 1995).

Preparing for the Unexpected

Dealing with unexpected crisis or controversy further tests the quality of the public relations program. Controversy, like crisis, can result in unpleasant situations requiring administrative action. Consider teacher pickets, lawsuits, vendettas, or parental displeasure with a science curriculum.

The impact of controversy was easily seen in a situation that involved budget cuts and the closing of a high school in an urban district. Parents and other community members who opposed these decisions tended to create their own facts. They speculated as to why this particular high school was targeted, and their stories ranged from creative to absurd. Soon their anger was directed toward the district's top administrators. Rumors spread about the superintendent and eventually they prompted a grand jury investigation. The superintendent's telephone and travel records were subpoenaed. Although the grand jury found no merit to the accusations, the superintendent and other officials had to expend a great deal of energy to deal with the controversy. This situation demonstrates that controversy can be unpredictable and a catalyst for new problems.

Anytime educators propose change, they are likely to face opposition; therefore, communication related to the proposed change is a critical issue. The relationship between change and communication was noted by Ledell and Arnsparger (1993) when they wrote, "Educators who propose substantive change in public schools have an obligation to engage and inform the public. They also have an obligation to protect schools from being manipulated by special interest groups who seek to misinform the general public or advance a narrow agenda" (p. 35). Because school leaders make tough, public decisions, their integrity, professionalism, and decision-making skills are always subject to challenge.

In preparing to manage controversy, the following steps may prove useful:

◆ Recognize that controversy will exist. Philosophical, economic, political, and social differences within districts make such strife virtually inevitable.
◆ Recognize that when controversy erupts, the media will cover it—even if the conflict entails personal attacks.
◆ Collect the facts because an appropriate response requires accurate information.
◆ Share the facts both through district communication and media outlets.
◆ Act fairly, honestly, and legally even when others create emotionally explosive situations because they do not.

Although controversies and unexpected happenings inevitably occur, administrators can anticipate them and plan measured responses. Conners (2000) advocates making the "Bleiker Lifepreserver" part of the school district's communications plan. To do this, she recommends that school administrators reflect on these points:

◆ Don't sell the solutions, sell the problem. Is it serious? What would happen if you did nothing?
◆ Keep the school's or district's mission in mind. Are you the right agency to tackle the problem?
◆ Who is directly affected by the problem? Who may have reason to try to derail or stop your efforts and why?
◆ Educate and communicate about the problem.
◆ Review past and current efforts to address the issue. Were you responsible before? Did you listen to all sides of the issue? Did you demonstrate that you cared? Did you fail in your responsibility? If so, state it, and make recommendations on how you can change it or address it. (p. 6)

SUMMARY

District administrators are spending more time on public relations than ever before. This is largely true for two reasons: choices available to parents are increasing, and more and more taxpayers are becoming reluctant to support spending increases for schools. Faced with an uncertain future, superintendents are encouraged to embrace the broader definition of public relations articulated in this book and to develop, implement, and evaluate a comprehensive plan for delivering these services. Unfortunately, many administrators err in using an inside-outside approach to building community relationships. This means that their communication foci continue to be the dissemination of information, albeit through improved products such as videotapes and Web pages (Carroll & Carroll, 2001).

Every facet of a district public relations program is affected by communication and community relations. Planning, establishing a public relations division, and even structuring public meetings depends on the superintendent and other administrators having an accurate assessment of community needs, wants, values, and biases.

Although communication services can be highly centralized or decentralized, a hybrid approach relying on intricate planning is recommended. The development of a district plan including broad goals precedes and informs the development of individual school plans. One or more specialists employed at the district level serve to coordinate services and educate employees to be productive participants.

CASE STUDY	High Hopes Gone Sour

A little more than 3 years ago, when Tom Clancy arrived in Lawrence, he was hailed as the superintendent who was going to radically improve the local public schools. Many taxpayers, however, have concluded that the expectation has not yet been fulfilled. Although patrons readily agree that the school system has not deteriorated under his leadership, most are quick to point out that he has failed to produce meaningful improvements. Dr. Clancy fully realizes that the survival clock is ticking because his contract is up for renewal in another year.

A small, working-class midwestern city, Lawrence has faced many of the problems plaguing urban areas, including intense criticism of its public schools. The city's political elites, individuals who possess tremendous power, have frequently made the schools their scapegoats by suggesting that most of the city's problems are rooted in education. When the economy experienced a downturn and jobs were lost, for example, the schools were blamed for not properly preparing graduates. When juvenile crime increased, poor school discipline was blamed. This was the context in which Clancy was employed. The school board members described him as a dynamic change agent who would rebuild an excellent school system.

The belief that schools were at the center of the community's problem was the main reason why Dr. Clancy's predecessor, Dr. Rebecca West, had left. She was the first and only female to serve as the head of the Lawrence school system and she had been hired by a five-member board that included three women. Two of the female board members, however, were defeated in the next election. Dr. West's relationship with the board deteriorated after the election and she began to be criticized openly by her detractors. Letters to the newspaper printed on the editorial page often portrayed her as "an academic who is too soft on discipline." The letters also criticized her reform program, suggesting that most administrators and teachers had never really supported her ideas.

Dr. Clancy pursued the job in Lawrence knowing the last two superintendents had had a combined tenure of only 4 years. An experienced administrator, he thought he knew all the risks. His apprehensions were reduced by the fact that the mayor and the entire school board supported his selection. He successfully negotiated a 5-year contract and accepted the position.

Superintendent Clancy had barely placed the family pictures on his new desk when he realized that he had underestimated the complexity of Lawrence and the intensity of conflict in the school district. Unlike his previous superintendent assignments, he found himself inundated with paperwork that confined him to his office. For instance, every purchase over $500—and there were many—required his personal review and signature. He had also discovered other discomforting facts:

◆ He was the only "outsider" on the administrative team. All the others were lifelong residents of Lawrence and graduates of the local high schools.
◆ There were dozens and dozens of committees functioning in the district. No decision of any consequence was made without a roomful of people being present. Consequently, politics were almost always the driving force for school decisions.
◆ No administrative staff member had been fired, disciplined, or reprimanded for years. When principals or central office personnel got into trouble or did not complete their work satisfactorily, they were simply moved to another assignment.
◆ The school board members were engaged in micromanaging; most got involved in day-to-day administrative decisions.
◆ The employee unions were very powerful. They had lucrative contracts and exerted considerable influence in school board elections.
◆ There was no organized method for communicating with staff or the public. For example, administrators often ignored telephone calls and letters from patrons.
◆ The climate of the organization was closed; that is, administrators and board members tried to prevent community interventions in their decisions and activities.

After 2 months on the job, Dr. Clancy had shared his concerns about the school district with several other superintendents. They basically advised him to become more active in public relations. More specifically, they encouraged him to get out into the schools and community and meet directly with teachers and patrons. They believed that the closed political climate of the district made him vulnerable to becoming yet another scapegoat for a variety of deficiencies. He decided to follow their advice.

To accommodate public relations activities, Dr. Clancy relegated much of his routine work to an assistant superintendent, Bill Evans, a longtime employee with 38 years of experience in the district. This allowed him to spend more time out of his office. He joined local organizations to broaden his contact with the public, and he accepted every invitation to speak before community groups. Although he wanted to make himself more accessible to employees and to the general public, his primary purpose was to gain information. Unfortunately, many individuals were either reluctant to talk to him or they only offered negative comments. For example, employees just wanted to complain about other employees; parents often suggested that they were unhappy with teachers but did not want to elaborate, fearing that there would be repercussions for their children.

After his first year in Lawrence, Dr. Clancy's goal of devoting more time to public relations experienced a setback. Evans, the assistant who had assumed many of the routine management responsibilities, had decided to retire. The board president immediately exerted pressure on Clancy to promote a principal, Gene Glenn, to the vacated position. Initially, the superintendent resisted, indicating that he wanted to conduct an open search that included external candidates. Eventually, the superintendent was persuaded to reach a compromise. He would agree to promote Glenn in exchange for the board president's promise to support two recommendations: the creation of a new administrative position—director of public information services—and a reorganization of the administrative staff. The superintendent realized that the board president's support meant that approval of his recommendations would be a mere formality.

Betty Simmons, a lifelong Lawrence resident and high school journalism teacher, was selected to be the director of public information services. The board praised Dr. Clancy for his selection and the media reported favorably on the decision. The reorganization of staff, by contrast, proved to be highly controversial. Clancy had hoped to realign positions and to remove four unproductive administrators who had been shuffled from one position to another over the last 10 years. His recommendations, however, were tabled by the school board. The board president advised Dr. Clancy that he had not anticipated the removal of administrators when he agreed to support a reorganization plan. The four administrators adversely affected by the superintendent's plan launched a concerted effort to dissuade board members from supporting it. After 6 months of haggling, the board reluctantly approved a modified plan that eliminated only one individual—an elementary assistant principal who was scheduled to retire at the end of the current school year. After the matter was finally decided, reporters criticized the superintendent for having engaged in a "senseless game of musical chairs that only intensified employee dissatisfaction and public confidence."

The setback with the administrative realignment plan made Dr. Clancy more vulnerable politically. In just over 2 years in the district, he was being criticized openly by detractors. In addition, his decision to promote Glenn to assistant superintendent was proving to be disastrous. Glenn was disloyal to the superintendent and often expressed independent viewpoints to the board president who remained his close friend. Instead of being a positive force for creating a more open climate, Glenn turned out to be a potent barrier to change. He became a role model for the bureaucrats who openly resisted reforms promoted by recent superintendents. For example, when Superintendent Clancy recommended a $15,000 appropriation for creating a district public relations plan, Glenn actively encouraged board members to reject the idea. He even went further to suggest that the newly created position of director of public information services was unnecessary. Glenn took this position despite clear evidence that Simmons had vastly improved the district's newsletter, improved relationships with the media, and established the district's first Web page.

QUESTIONS AND SUGGESTED ACTIVITIES

CASE STUDY

1. For years, the school district has been blamed for many of the city's problems. To what extent is the district's closed climate (i.e., reluctance to interact with external forces) a contributing factor to the district being made a scapegoat?
2. Should Dr. Clancy have created the position of director of public information services before having developed a district public relations plan? Why or why not?
3. What options might Clancy have pursued instead of agreeing to promote Glenn in order to create the position of director of public information services?

4. Assess the reluctance of parents to talk to the superintendent.
5. Dr. Clancy attempted to increase public relations activities in two ways: creating a new position in public information services and personally spending more time outside of his office. What additional actions should he have considered?
6. Based on the information presented in the case study, was Dr. Clancy sufficiently prepared to create the new position of director of public information services?
7. How can the superintendent counteract the statements made by Glenn that neither a public relations plan nor the position held by Simmons is necessary?

CHAPTER

8. A hybrid approach to planning public relations, one that balances centralization and decentralization, is recommended in this chapter. In such an approach, what is the ideal relationship between the district and individual school plans?
9. What is benchmarking? Why is this concept relevant to public relations?
10. What steps can administrators take to ensure that public meetings serve as a public relations asset?
11. Why is the superintendent's communication behavior symbolically important with respect to public relations?
12. What are the attributes of a good district public relations plan?
13. What is defining research? What role does it play in public relations planning?
14. What are some activities a superintendent could initiate to improve communication between district personnel and community members?

SUGGESTED READINGS

Armistead, L. (2000). Public relations: Harness your school's power. *High School Magazine, 7*(6), 24–27.
Arnett, J. S. (1999). From public enragement to engagement. *School Administrator, 56*(8), 24–27.
Bete, T. (1998). Eight great community relations ideas. *School Planning and Management, 37*(5), 49–57.
Bushman, J., & Boris, V. (1998). Listening to the public. *American School Board Journal, 185*(12), 27–29.
Carroll, S. R., & Carroll, D. (2000). *EdMarketing: How smart schools get and keep community support.* Bloomington, IN: National Educational Service.
Deasy, J. E. (2000). Moving from oversight to insight: One community's journey with its superintendent. *Phi Delta Kappan, 82*(1), 13–15.
Enderle, J. (2000). Three school districts honored for their community relations efforts. *School Planning & Management, 39*(5), 26, 28–31.
Kaplan, G. R. (1992). *Images of education: The mass media's version of America's schools.* Arlington, VA: National School Public Relations Association.
Soholt, S. (1998). Public engagement: Lessons from the front. *Educational Leadership, 56*(2), 22-23.
Uline, C. L. (1998). Town meeting and community engagement. *Journal of School Leadership, 8*(6), 533–557.
Van Meter, E. J. (1993). Setting new priorities: Enhancing the school–community relations program. *NASSP Bulletin, 77*(554), 22–27.
Wanat, C. L., & Bowles, B. D. (1993). School–community relations: A process paradigm. *Community Education Journal, 20*(2), 3–7.

REFERENCES

Bagin, D., Ferguson, D., & Marx, G. (1985). *Public relations for administrators*. Arlington, VA: American Association of School Administrators.

Bohen, D. B. (1998). Communication: Illusions and realities. In R. R. Spillane & P. Regnier (Eds.), The superintendent of the future: Strategy and action for achieving academic excellence (pp. 219–236). Gathersburg, MD: Aspen Publishers.

Carroll, S. R., & Carroll, D. (2001). Outside-inside marketing. *School Administrator, 58*(7), 32–34.

Conners, G. (2000). *Good news: How to get the best possible media coverage for your school*. Thousand Oaks, CA: Corwin Press.

Davis, B. R. (1986). *School public relations: The complete book*. Arlington, VA: National School Public Relations Association.

Deal, T. E., & Kennedy, A. A. (1982). *Corporate cultures: The rites and rituals of corporate life*. Reading, MA: Addison-Wesley.

Fullan, M. (1999). *Change forces: The sequel*. Philadelphia: Falmer.

Johnston, G., Gross, G., Townsend, R., Lynch, P., Novotney, P., Roberts, B., et al. (2002). *A view inside public education: Eight at the top*. Lanham, MD: The Scarecrow Press.

Kantor, H., & Brenzel, B. (1993). Urban education and the truly disadvantaged: The historical roots of the contemporary crisis, 1945–1990. In M. Katz (Ed.), *The underclass debate: Views from history* (pp. 366–402). Princeton, NJ: Princeton University Press.

Kirst, M. W., & Kelley, C. (1995). Collaboration to improve education and children's services: Politics and policy making. In L. Rigsby, M. Reynolds, & M. Wang (Eds.), *School–community connections: Exploring issues for research and practice* (pp. 21–44). San Francisco: Jossey-Bass.

Kowalski, T. J. (1999). *The school superintendent: Theory, practice, and cases*. Upper Saddle River, NJ: Merrill/Prentice Hall.

Kowalski, T. J. (2000). *Public relations in our schools* (2nd ed.). Upper Saddle River, NJ: Merrill/Prentice Hall.

Ledell, M., & Arnsparger, A. (1993). *How to deal with community criticism*. Denver, CO: Education Commission of the States.

Levinson, J. (1989). *Guerrilla marketing*. Boston: Houghton Mifflin.

Maeroff, G. (1998). *Imaging education: The media and schools in America*. New York: Teachers College Press.

Meek, A. (1999). *Communicating with the public: A guide for school leaders*. Alexandria, VA: Association for Supervision and Curriculum Development.

Ordovensky, P., & Marx, G. (1993). *Working with the news media*. Arlington, VA: American Association of School Administrators.

Pawlas, G. E. (1995). *The administrator's guide to school–community relations*. Princeton Junction, NJ: Eye on Education.

Shor, I., & Pari, C. (1999). *Education is politics*. Portsmouth, NH: Boyston/Cook.

Topor, R. (1992). No more navel gazing! Mountain View, CA: Topor & Associates.

Unruh, A., & Willier, R. A. (1974). *Public relations for schools*. Belmont, CA: Lear Siegler/Fearon.

Yancy, W. L., & Saporito, S. J. (1995). Ecological embeddedness of educational processes and outcomes. In L. Rigsby, M. Reynolds, & M. Wang (Eds.), *School–community connections: Exploring issues for research and practice* (pp. 193–228). San Francisco: Jossey-Bass.

Zoch, L. M., Patterson, B., & Olson, D. L. (1997). The status of the school public relations practitioner: A statewide exploration. *Public Relations Review, 23*(4), 361–375.

8

Effective Programming at the School Level

George Perreault

Richard K. Murray

Few people would deny the importance of good human relations, nor would they wittingly shun any practice that helped to achieve such goodwill. As a movement in industry and education, human relations has been, to many, a kind of salvation for the worker who had heretofore toiled under rigid scientific-management principles. As a way of relating to one another in the home, at work, and in the marketplace, human relations is not only sensible but also a step toward inviting harmony into one's existence. Good human relationships engender respect, cooperation, and collaboration and are essential to organizational efforts such as site-based management and total quality management. But good human relationships do not happen in and of themselves; they must be planned and implemented with careful deliberation. This kind of planning in any organizational context requires an effective public relations (PR) program that, if viewed analytically, incorporates the best in human relations and communication practices (West, 1985).

ESTABLISHING THE NEED FOR A SCHOOL-LEVEL PR PROGRAM

Prior to the 1990s, boards of education had not opted for PR programs in their districts. Looking upon them as a form of gimmickry best left to big corporations that wanted to attract potential product users, many boards and their superintendents considered PR programs as luxuries rather than as necessities. Even today, many people view PR as being synonymous with verbs like *cover up, obfuscate, misrepresent,* and *lie* (Martinson, 1995). In addition, the benefits derived from a PR program often go unnoticed until a crisis occurs within a school system, whereas the additional and continuous expense it represents to already overburdened taxpayers is immediately apparent.

Although many educational reforms initiated in the 1980s were predicted on decentralization, most school districts either ignored PR or retained a centralized approach to PR. Centralization entails a PR director, functioning as a member of the superintendent's staff, orchestrating the program from the central office. In this approach, individual schools follow, rather than lead.

Creating Awareness

Unfortunately, totally centralized PR programs often err on the side of too much control, and as a result, they often overlook or underestimate the potential contributions of individual schools. Conversely, total decentralization can result in chaos; that is, each school goes in its own direction, and the superintendent has little or no control over the PR process or outcomes. Ideally, a PR program is both centralized and decentralized. The PR director (or other central office administrator responsible for the program) and principals work as partners, and there are both a districtwide plan and individual school plans. The former provides goals and processes relevant to all schools; the latter are extensions of the district document permitting each principal to infuse initiatives beneficial to a specific school.

School-based PR programs require support and nurturing from district-level officials. For example, the school board should provide appropriate policy and encouragement; the superintendent should provide overall direction and fiscal resources; and the PR director should provide counsel and direct assistance. In addition, central office personnel contribute to effective PR by promoting values and beliefs foundational to open, two-way communication. Even the best-conceived plan is likely to fail if it must be used in an organizational culture that restricts the principles of modern PR.

Garnering Support

A principal cannot hope to create staff support for a PR program instantly because an effective program can only develop over time. Although system policy may specify certain parameters in which any school PR program can operate, practices at individual schools are what really determine program effectiveness. At the school level, an effective PR program is not an "add-on" but a reflection of a shared vision predicated on egalitarianism, and extensive opportunities for participation, trust, and open channels of communication. Because informed and involved staff members are more supportive of administrative decisions (Brown, Burkhalter, & Schaer, 1996–1997), the first task for a principal is to ensure that there is a climate that supports the development of such a staff.

As with creating other desirable behaviors, modeling appropriate PR behavior is an effective step toward getting others to reciprocate. It is also important to recognize and reward such behavior when others demonstrate it. Only when the organizational climate is conducive to good human relations, in general, is it appropriate to launch a concerted PR effort that will involve planning and identifying people to carry out the required actions.

DEVELOPING A PR PROGRAM AT THE SCHOOL LEVEL

Both board policy and a district-level plan are important to successful practice at the school level. They are especially crucial for those principals who have a limited understanding of the PR process. In the absence of direction and encouragement, these administrators are apt to either ignore this administrative responsibility or to approach it haphazardly. Although some better informed principals are able to develop reasonably good PR programs without direction from central administration, they too will eventually have problems. In a crisis situation, for example, a principal may follow the school plan in dealing with the media only to discover that the school board and superintendent disagree with the content of the school's plan. Thus, principals working in districts without a centralized plan or without policy ought to have their individual school plans approved by the superintendent after they are developed.

Creating a Building-Level Committee

A number of popular initiatives, such as total quality management and strategic planning, have begun to modify traditional top-down management approaches in education. Authoritative school administrators are being replaced by school officials who believe in governance councils, school-based management teams, strategic planning committees, and similar groups of stakeholders; in some states, these efforts are mandated by the legislature. This focus on collaborative decision making is based on the principle that all individuals affected by decisions (stakeholders) should share in the decision-making process. Although not all school decisions need to be made by a committee, PR is, by its very nature, an area that can be served well by the committee process.

The school-level PR committee should be large enough to provide representation for all groups, but not so large that communication and decision making suffer. Although not designed to be comprehensive, the following list identifies different groups that should be considered for PR committee participation:

- ◆ *Teachers.* Teachers should be chosen to represent a cross section of the faculty. For example, are grade levels and academic areas represented? Do you have a special education representative? An athletics representative?
- ◆ *Administration and professional support services.* These may include media specialists, guidance counselors, assistant principals, and other professional employees.
- ◆ *Parents.* With a vested interest in their school-age children, parents represent a crucial connection to the public.
- ◆ *District-level PR representative.* To ensure that school-level and district-level plans are aligned, the district director of PR (or designee) should be on the committee.
- ◆ *General support staff.* Representatives of transportation, food service, and custodial services should be included.
- ◆ *Business partner or business community representative.* Business partners have a vested interest in their future employees and customers, and they may be able to make valuable contributions.

Regardless of who is chosen, the underlying selection principle should be stakeholder representation. Balance within racial, philosophical, gender, and other areas should be established to ensure adequate representation and political acceptance. A diverse committee brings different attitudes, opinions, and solutions to the table, and this condition often strengthens the quality of decisions. In our increasingly pluralistic society, schools are facing significant demographic shifts that require ongoing attention. Many areas are seeing their Latino/Latina population expanding rapidly, but there are often influxes of other ethnic groups as well; for example, a city of 100,000 in Massachusetts recently saw its Cambodian population grow by 10,000 in a single year.

A PR program functioning at its optimal level has a systemwide PR committee ideally comprising about 15 members: administrators, staff, students, parents and nonparents, senior citizens, and business and industry leaders (West, 1985). There should also be parallel committees for each school. Although the systemwide committee is commonly chaired by the school district's PR director, the school committee may be led by the principal, assistant principal, or a designee (e.g., a teacher with abbreviated duties).

Both the district and school committees should meet separately about once a month throughout the school year. Then in fall and spring, it is a good idea to bring together members from all of the district's PR committees to share concerns and ideas. Such interaction strengthens the focus on PR and provides a bridge between the centralized and decentralized elements of the program.

Joint meetings for the PR committees are instrumental in assessing the extent to which individual schools are contributing to systemwide PR goals, and they provide an opportunity to evaluate. These meetings also serve to keep the lines of communication open among the committees, a factor that is essential to systemic program development.

To ensure continuity, the terms of committee members should be staggered, ensuring that no more than one-third of the membership changes from year to year. This staggered approach gives new members the benefit of always having experienced members on hand to assist them in learning committee fundamentals.

Developing a PR Plan

A crucial step in developing an effective PR program at the school level is the creation of a PR plan. Often, building-level PR plans are not developed properly for two reasons: a lack of commitment from the school's administration, and the failure to provide ample time for preparation. Principals should recognize that, in addition to allowing members opportunities to analyze data and to complete other vital tasks, providing time also symbolically communicates commitment. An effective PR plan usually requires staff development and research, both of which must be supported by the principal to be perceived as important.

In developing either school-level or district-level PR plans, Grossman (1998) recommends following a basic four-step process:

1. *Research*—providing an in-depth analysis of relationships with all internal and external publics
2. *Action plan*—developing PR goals, objectives, and strategies that are aligned with the overall mission and goals
3. *Communication*—performing the necessary tasks to successfully complete the outlined objectives and goals
4. *Evaluation*—investigating past decisions to determine their impact on the future

With these four concepts in mind, Grossman offers a 10-step process to develop public relations plans for school districts. With a few alterations, this can be an effective process for a building-level PR committee. The steps of the process are:

1. *Assess board or management*—Begin by meeting with the district's public relations department to determine priorities for school-level PR. Consider district- and school-level mission statements, goals, and objectives. PR goals should assist in achieving these goals and objectives. Answer the question: How do we want to be perceived by our publics?
2. *Conduct internal and external research*—Before developing the plan, the committee must research to determine how they are viewed by both internal and external publics. Using surveys, census data, feedback from parents and community, and other forms of research, determine the school's current reputation by analyzing information developed through the following questions: What are the current issues in the community? Who are our publics, and what are their images of our school? What new issues may arise in the future?

3. *Develop public relations goals and objectives*—Using the assessment and research from the initial steps of the process, develop short-term and long-term goals for public relations. These goals should be developed by a committee representing the school administration, faculty, parents, community members, and others who have a vested interest in the school.

4. *Identify target publics*—The target publics are those groups in the school community that need to be approached in order to achieve the goals and objectives of the PR committee. At the school level, target publics primarily consist of staff, students, and parents. Secondary target publics include those members of the community who are not directly reached by school-level PR.

5. *Identify desired behavior of publics*—Grossman (1998) identifies this as a critical step in the process. In this step the PR committee must determine what they want the program to do. Is the objective to disseminate information? To establish support for restructuring initiatives?

6. *Identify what is needed to achieve desired behavior*—Using information from the committee's previous research, decide what actions need to take place to create the desired behaviors. For example, your high school faculty has decided to implement block scheduling. During your research, it was determined that only 40% of the parents supported the transition. To implement block scheduling, the PR committee selected an approval rate of 85%, so what will the PR committee do to reach the desired approval percentage? Perhaps a survey will determine the reasons why parents are not supportive of the change. An information campaign directed at those parents may help to ease their concerns and increase support for the new schedule.

7. *Create strategies and tactics for reaching publics*—As defined by Grossman, strategies are overall procedures (such as creating a packet of information on the merits of the block schedule). Tactics are the actions that must occur to carry out the procedures (such as distributing the information through the media or mail).

8. *Put your plan on paper*—In this step, the school-level committee should develop a budget, create a timeline, and assign responsibility for strategies and tactics.

9. *Implement the plan*—After completion of the plan and receiving any necessary approval, activate the plan. Make sure to include the committee in the implementation process and to update members on progress.

10. *Evaluate your efforts*—To determine the effectiveness of your efforts, evaluate the plan. The planning process should be evaluated to determine areas of improvement for the future; the actual plan should be analyzed during implementation to determine any necessary revisions; and goals and objectives should be reviewed to determine whether they have been met.

Armistead (2002) has outlined a similar approach, emphasizing the use of "message points" that should be carefully developed. A focused PR campaign should lead to a few key phrases that are simple to remember and easy to comprehend. The most effective message points will apply to a diverse audience and should be repeated often enough that they are ingrained.

Identifying the Elements of an Effective PR Program

According to Gronstedt (1997), effective public relations is practiced in four steps: planning and goal setting, implementation and monitoring, evaluation, and acting on the evaluation to make improvements. In step 1, planning and goal setting, five strategic questions should be answered:

1. *What are our most significant strengths, weaknesses, opportunities, and threats?* The strengths, weaknesses, opportunities, and threats (SWOT) strategy analyzes the organization's strengths and weaknesses in meeting the opportunities and threats in the external environment.
2. *Who are our most important stakeholders?* Each organization must identify its stakeholders and prioritize their importance to the organization.
3. *What are the most important needs of each of the stakeholder groups that our organization can address?* The answer to this question requires research to be conducted to determine the needs of each stakeholder group. Questions to be asked during this research include the following: Why should I send my children to your school? What does this stakeholder group need from our school?
4. *What are the behavioral and communication objectives?* Based upon the research of stakeholder needs, behavioral objectives should be created to identify each stakeholder group. For example, when discussing the ever-controversial topic of ability grouping, it may be necessary to persuade key groups of parents to support heterogeneous grouping. After specific objectives have been developed, communication objectives can be created to support them.
5. *What is the "personal media network" of a typical target audience member?* The final step of the planning process is to determine the personal media network (PMN) for each stakeholder group. The PMN can be determined by mapping a typical day in the life of an individual stakeholder. By completing the mapping, information is generated identifying the best opportunities for the individual to be receptive to the idea being promoted.

In step 2, implementation and monitoring, the results of the research and the final product are implemented. The key to this step is monitoring the plan's effectiveness to determine if adjustments are necessary. Possible techniques include surveys, telephone polls, stakeholder feedback, and media perception.

In step 3, evaluation, the effects of the implemented plan should be evaluated periodically to measure behavior changes. Both qualitative methods (interviews, focus groups, observations) and quantitative methods (mail surveys, telephone surveys, exit polls) may be used to measure previously established benchmarks for success. In step 4, acting on the evaluation, the information received from the evaluation process in step 3 is used to determine needed changes in strategies and must be shared with the rest of the organization. Often in education, research and its finding are placed on bookshelves or in file cabinets. In this stage, however, the research should be used to indicate directions for the future and any needed present changes within the current public relations strategy.

Another measure of effectiveness can be employed by evaluating the school-level PR plan using the following interpretation from the National School Public Relations Association (NSPRA) *Standards for Educational Public Relations Programs* (1998a):

> Educational public relations is a planned and systematic management function designed to help improve the programs and services of an educational organization. It relies on a comprehensive two-way communications process involving both internal and external publics, with a goal of stimulating a better understanding of the role, objectives, accomplishments, and needs of the organization. Educational public relations programs assist in interpreting public attitudes, identifying and helping shape policies and procedures in the public interest, and carrying on involvement and information activities which earn public understanding and support.

Addressing the Unique Needs, Interests, and Aspirations of School Clients

The needs of school clients may vary from school to school. Whereas latchkey programs may be vital in one school, a program to prevent student dropout may be crucial in another. Whereas the former may entail enlisting volunteers or hiring paraprofessionals to operate these programs, the latter may suggest a whole array of activities to involve parents in the education of their children. Another challenge for many schools is finding ways to meet the needs of linguistically different students and families who are moving into their areas.

The interests of clients in various schools may also differ. Some clients are enamored with a school's athletic opportunities for their youngsters, whereas others favor a school's academic offerings. However, if a community education program is in place for community members, some of the school's clients may deem computer training as a desirable course for the school to make available; others may reveal a strong interest in aerobics, ceramics, or stained glass courses.

The aspirations of a school's clients may be largely contingent on their success or their children's success in the school. If an adult successfully completes a high school equivalency program, he or she may give much consideration to entering college or some specialized technical school. If a youngster repeatedly experiences success in a writing program, he or she may aspire to become a professional writer or to go on to college to major in English.

With this wide variance among a school's clients, schools would be well served to periodically conduct comprehensive assessments of their community to determine their particular publics. This can be accomplished through telephone surveys, mailouts, informal feedback, and interviews with appropriately selected focus groups that accurately represent the many demographics found in a school community's population.

Multicultural Public Relations

A discussion of the unique needs of school clients would not be complete without a discussion of multicultural public relations and the need to address the changing demographics among today's school populations. Without addressing all school clients, schools may face racial and cultural differences that contribute to negative interaction. The necessity of a multicultural public relations approach is well documented in the literature (e.g., Banks, 1995; Grunig & White, 1992; Kern-Foxworth & Miller, 1992).

Banks (1995) analyzes effective multicultural public relations and offers his Social-Interpretive Communication Theory as a model of implementation. He writes that effectiveness in multicultural public relations is evaluated by the degree to which communication

- reinforces participants' self-concepts
- affirms participants' cultural identities
- enhances the parties' relationship
- accomplishes the parties' strategic goals
- embraces the constitutive nature of communication
- recognizes the contextual nature of meanings
- accepts the diversity of interpretations
- remains open to reinterpretation

Banks concludes his study of multicultural public relations by offering advice on how to foster effective multicultural public relations. He states that "practitioners and educators must become more sensitive to this immense environmental change by enacting diversity as a concern relevant to their professional lives and responding to it interactively" (p. 11).

Principals can begin a multicultural public relations approach by first determining the social makeup of their school population. The more that is known about a school's external publics, the better the chance for success. A sociological inventory is one method of determining a school population's social composition. Gallagher, Bagin, and Kindred (1997) recommend determining the following pieces of information through the inventory: population characteristics, customs and traditions, political structure, social tensions, economic conditions, community groups, communication channels, and previous community efforts. Once again, the starting point of multicultural public relations lies in determining the social composition of the school's population. With knowledge of these external publics, specific considerations and objectives can be directed at these populations to foster better school–community communication.

The fact that an effective PR program is an outgrowth of an open school climate, that is, truly a climate that welcomes students, parents, and others, needs to be reiterated. Unfortunately, many schools sustain relatively closed climates. For example, during interviews with the Latino Commission, high school students reported feeling left out when their curriculum contained nothing related to their own culture (Rodriguez, 1992). School officials also need to be sensitive to the range of ideas about education that exist in almost every district and that often diverge from what is expected by most educators. Punjabi immigrant parents in California were found to believe that they should not be directly involved in what goes on in school—it is the teachers' job to provide education. However, these parents insisted that their children concentrate on school, to the extent that parents would work more than one job to allow children to focus on homework (Gibson, 1983, 1987). Consequently, Punjabi students have higher rates of graduation and postsecondary acceptance than other immigrant groups.

Gathering such data in a proactive fashion would be indicative of a school that is making the kind of outreach efforts that underlie an open climate and an effective PR program. Williams and Chavkin (1989) note that successful programs for community involvement tend to share a number of characteristics, including:

- guidance by written policies
- support from school administration
- training of both staff and parents
- use of a partnership approach
- maintenance of two-way communication
- encouragement of networking
- constant modification by ongoing evaluation

Schools Within a Choice District

The majority of school principals in a typical school district would admit they do not spend enough time on PR. However, many principals across the country are being forced to take a more active role in this administrative function because of reform initiatives encouraging competition among schools. School choice, for example, creates new conditions in which students and parents make choices based on what they perceive to be the best schools.

Awarded with the National School Public Relations Association's 1997 Gold Medallion Award, the Red Clay Consolidated School District in Wilmington, Delaware, developed an aggressive marketing plan to establish itself as the premier "choice" district in the state. In response to statewide choice for the 1996–1997 school year and the resulting competition for students, the district proposed the following objectives:

- To maintain and increase current student enrollment
- To establish Red Clay as the district of choice in Delaware
- To capture students currently attending parochial and other private schools
- To educate the community about school choice

The marketing strategy included the slogan, "Red Clay Consolidated School District . . . The First Choice." Several different strategies, such as identifying immediate target audiences, participating in a communitywide educational expo, districtwide open houses, radio spots, and several mailouts, were used. The results were impressive. After implementing the plan, evaluation showed that the district had received more than 60% of the school choice applications for the 1996–1997 and 1997–1998 school years. In addition, nearly 600 students from private and parochial schools and from other districts applied for admission into Red Clay. As a reward, the district received an additional $600,000 in tax revenues for 1997 and expected a similar amount for 1998.

In some districts, even without the pressure from choice plans, schools are finding that they are under increasing competition from charter schools. Although many of the nation's 1,700 charter schools market themselves as "niche" institutions that can better serve a specialized clientele, they still represent at least an implicit criticism of existing public schools and a challenge for regular schools to find a way to better tell their story in the competition for student enrollment. Other recent developments that bring market forces to bear on the issue of school choice are the provision in H.R.1 (the no Child Left Behind Act of 2001) for parents to transfer their students from "failing schools," and the U.S. Supreme Court decision supporting the Cleveland voucher plan. Given this more competitive environment, a strong PR program is even more of a necessity for every school.

SHARED GOVERNANCE AND PUBLIC RELATIONS MANAGEMENT

Total quality management, site-based management, shared decision making, strategic planning, empowerment, consensus decision making, charter schools, school choice, participatory management, and decentralization are a few of the concepts and ideas advanced for local school governance. These proposed arrangements can change the relationships among school-community members, and in this vein, they can influence PR programming. Concepts such as professionalism and democratic governance are congruous with collaborative organizational culture. Sashkin (1993) posits that effective school leaders must be able to create a vision, a cultural ideal for the school or district. The leader generates support for the vision by "involving others in articulating a philosophy that summarizes the vision and by creating policies and programs that turn the philosophy into action" (p. 84).

Site-Based PR Management

Site- or school-based management (SBM) plans are now required in several states. For example, school systems in Kentucky and Texas must develop and implement SBM plans annually as a way of decentralizing control. Proponents of decentralized governance believe that people affected by educational decisions ought to be involved in making decisions because involvement leads to greater commitment to the eventual success of the decision (McNergney & Herbert, 1998); thus, SBM committees often are given the power to make final decisions in certain areas.

Flattening the hierarchy, encouraging and fostering consensus decisions, and communicating frequently with diverse community groups are, therefore, among the leadership challenges for educational administrators in the new millennium. The shift in power from the central office to the school is framed by strategies to improve schools and student learning. In their book, Schwahn and Spady (1998) analyze and recommend the best future-focused change strategies for education. They echo the recommendation of Peters and Waterman (1982) who urged that visionary leaders "get close to their customers." The philosophy of a client focus encourages leaders to ask their colleagues and themselves repeatedly if they meet or exceed their customers' needs, present, emerging, and future (Schwahn & Spady, 1998). Exceptional principals work hard to find opportunities to form and discuss school goals and purposes, as well as mission with staff, parents, students, community members, and others in the school system (Ashby & Krug, 1998). In those districts where SBM, total quality management, and strategic planning are reinforced by broadening dramatically the circle of participation, public relations skills become even more important.

Traditionally, superintendents and principals have depended on legal and organizational authority. Under SBM, they are expected to support decisions made by others. However, citing a common misunderstanding that decentralization reduces the role of administrators, Thompson and Wood (1998) assert that all site powers ultimately derive from central office decisions that support site leadership. After certain labor management, control, continuity, and workload issues are resolved, they agree with Baldwin (1997), who, in a recent study of support staff views on SBM, concluded that students benefited from SBM. Other studies have shown different results (Hannaway & Carnoy, 1993) and the complexity of the factors involved in such a change suggest that this is an area in which much more research is needed (Björk, 2001).

Regardless, as both internal district initiatives and public policy directives lead to more attempts at implementing SBM, school leaders will find it necessary to focus additional resources on PR about these projects. Ideally, at the district level, superintendents should assign a full-time communications person to the executive staff, create a communications team, and ask the school board to approve a communications policy (Gallagher et al., 1997; Ledell, 1996; Norton, Webb, Dlugosh, & Sybouts, 1996). The emerging role of the PR director (and school-community relations specialist or other such roles) is to coach and advise school personnel in matters that deal with public relations (NSPRA, 1992). The PR director can help SBM councils and teams develop both communication strategies and mission statements to guide them in relationships with each other and other groups (NSPRA, 1993). Other system support and uses of a PR director include dealing with the media (NSPRA, 1992), recognizing the diversity of publics (Norton et al., 1996), change strategies (Swaim, 1996), conducting a communications audit (Ledell, 1996), and developing collaborative public relations programs (Leichty, 1997).

THE MARKETING OF EDUCATION

A discussion of educational marketing should begin by distinguishing this term from public relations. Although many see the terms as interchangeable, in fact, they are different. Hanson and Henry (1993) distinguish the two by defining public relations as a broad-based, multifaceted approach to building understanding for the full range of activities going on within an institution such as a school system; marketing is viewed as "developing or refining specific school programs in response to the needs and desires of specific target markets . . . , and using effective means of communication to understand those needs and inform and motivate those markets" (p. 81). Educational marketing can further be defined as working toward fostering support from the community for a "focused" project such as expanding PTA participation, fostering support for a bond referendum, or creating support for a curricular change. The use of strategic marketing, typically associated with the private sector, can be of significant value in school public relations when attempting to develop public confidence and support. Hanson and Henry pointed out that many schools are already conducting educational marketing activities. The missing ingredient in these efforts has been the ability to plan and work within a strategic marketing framework.

As a method for the planning process of a marketing plan, Hanson and Henry developed a 12-step process (designated as research and operational steps) for strategic educational marketing. Beginning with a focused project, the strategic marketing plan should be tied to a strategic plan (specific measure).

Step 1—Market analysis (research step). This step involves the marketing team researching the demographics of the community to determine the needs and expectations of the community. It also includes researching to determine the current community perceptions of the school or school system. This step can be carried out by interviewing a focus group of 7 to 10 community members, representing a cross section of the population. If the process is conducted appropriately, this step will provide information on community attitudes and perceptions of the school system.

Step 2—Establish organizational objectives (operational step). Using the information gathered from the market analysis in step 1, the marketing team must determine whether the gathered information is valid and, if valid, what changes or new programs need to be offered.

Step 3—Define new offerings (research step). After the objectives have been established in step 2, the marketing team must develop new programs or initiatives to respond to the community needs established in step 1. This stage is difficult because of the lack of funding in most districts. In essence, community desires and needs must be prioritized according to financial and other constraints.

Step 4—Develop programs and policies (operational step). After defining new programs and initiatives in step 3, the marketing team must establish new policies and guidelines for the implementation.

Step 5—Define the marketing mission (research step). The marketing team now creates clear objectives for the marketing campaign. The team will focus only on broad objectives at this point. The specific objectives of the marketing campaign will be created in the next stage.

Step 6—Organize the campaign leadership structure (operational step). Prior to continuing with the process, the marketing team must now create a leadership structure to define the strategies and plans for the marketing campaign. The leadership structure should include a combination of school system employees and representatives from segments of the community. Their objectives are to plan for how the marketing mission will be carried out.

Step 7—Campaign planning market mix (research step). Using the four P's created by McCarthy (1960), the marketing team must develop information on product, price, place, and promotion. *Product* relates to the basic worth of whatever is being described to the public (e.g., lower teacher-student ratio); *price* refers to the financial impact felt by community members (e.g., $10 additional property tax); *place* refers to analyzing the costs associated with different means of communication and publicity (e.g., radio stations, newspapers); and *promotion* refers to how target marketing will be conducted (e.g., bond referendum).

Step 8—Campaign trials (operational step). Using a random, representative sample of the community, pretest the strategic market plan and its components to determine areas of improvement. As Hanson and Henry (1993) note, "if it doesn't work on representative small samples, it won't work on the parent population" (p. 86).

Step 9—Define specific tactics (research step). The marketing process evolves from its broad-based approach to specifics. Who will accomplish what? How will this be accomplished? Specific details to accomplish the marketing mission will be discussed and recorded.

Step 10—Carry out the campaign (operational step). The specific components of the strategic marketing plan are executed.

Step 11—Determine performance benchmarks (research step). Benchmarks need to be created to assess the campaign as it develops. Considerations for review throughout the campaign include brochures distributed, mailouts conducted, public meetings held, and other benchmarks for assessment.

Step 12—Evaluate the plan and the campaign (operational step). In an effort to gather information for future marketing initiatives, committee members should analyze the campaign for future improvement. Regardless of positive or negative results, a review of the marketing process will produce much-needed information for the next initiative.

Faced with problems of declining enrollment and inaccurate reporting by the media, the Rowland Unified School District in Rowland Heights, California, implemented a comprehensive marketing plan to dispute inaccurate reporting by media concerning crime and violence in surrounding neighborhoods, the implementation of choice, aggressive marketing by local private schools, and a 3-year declining enrollment. After completing an assessment, district personnel determined a campaign was needed to redirect the word-of-mouth communications concerning the district.

Target audiences were determined to be current and prospective clients living in the surrounding areas, parents of private school children, realtors and real estate developers, Chinese and Korean parents, and parents from the feeder elementary and intermediate schools. In addition to a concentrated media relations effort, parents were trained to be ambassadors so they could communicate with target audiences. Other communication strategies included hosting a breakfast and school tours for realtors and developers, mailing a marketing brochure to parents who recently withdrew their children from the district, developing key communicator groups, and releasing newspaper stories on the academic programs and unique aspects of the school district. To evaluate the campaign, feedback from target audiences and anecdotal data were used to evaluate success. The evaluation revealed two positive outcomes: an increase in enrollment for the first time in 3 years and more balanced media coverage.

A leader does not have to wait until there are negative indicators in the community before developing a PR campaign. In fact, in this area as in many others, excellent programs are often built before the need is apparent to everyone, and a proactive rather than a reactive approach allows the school to be more thoughtful and ultimately more effective.

PUBLIC RELATIONS ROLES OF SCHOOL-LEVEL PERSONNEL

When a school district has a good PR program, it usually is because there is close coordination between systemwide and individual school efforts. The day-to-day accomplishments that build successful practice usually occur within schools, and it is within schools that the most compelling stories are to be found.

Role of School Principals

The role of a school principal is much like that of a superintendent. Both should be instrumental in getting a board to adopt a PR policy: the superintendent directly, principals indirectly through the superintendent. The principal focuses on improving relations with and among building-level personnel and between the school and its neighborhood. The superintendent concentrates on improving relations with employees and the broader district community. Both deal with the media: a principal periodically, the superintendent fairly often. As a consequence, both are obliged to develop good relations with the media. Both must also have the necessary personal attributes to relate to people effectively (West, 1985).

A survey taken in Texas (Schueckler & West, 1991) to assess the perceptions of both principals and PR directors concerning the actual and ideal PR role of senior high school principals found that the principals saw themselves as doing a better job than did the PR directors. Five areas in which principals thought they needed to improve their PR role were:

◆ Strive to operate an effective school office
◆ Possess common sense, judgment, discretion, and a sense of proportion
◆ Listen carefully when others speak with him or her
◆ Be tactful and diplomatic in all relationships
◆ Promote an open-door policy with students, teachers, parents, and others (p. 25)

Interestingly, two of these areas were also among the top five areas in which PR directors perceived a need for improvement among principals. Three other areas where PR officers saw a need for improvement in principals were:

◆ Continually strive for the best public relations program possible
◆ Recognize the accomplishments of individuals and groups
◆ Strive to keep the superintendent informed of any potential problem in the area of public relations (p. 25)

Assistant principals in high schools also have an important PR role to play, as indicated in a recent Delphi study that had a panel of experts identify critical tasks for Texas assistant principals in two time periods: in the next 5 years and for the following 10 to 20 years (Eaton & West, 1988). In the first time period, or the immediate future, there were six critical PR tasks for assistant high school principals:

◆ Maintain rapport with teachers (agreement among experts on the importance of this task was 83%)
◆ Motivate students and faculty (78%)
◆ Communicate with parents and students (78%)
◆ Present professional demeanor to faculty (72%)
◆ Maintain rapport with students (72%)
◆ Improve teacher morale (66%) (p. 31)

In the second time period, or more-distant future, there were eight critical tasks to be performed by assistant high school principals, six of which also appear in the first time period, with about the same degree of group consensus. The remaining two were "improve school climate" (78%) and "elicit parental cooperation" (66%) (p. 31).

Elementary school principals also have a significant PR role. According to West (1993),

> they communicate with a variety of groups daily, most typically students, teachers, support staff and parents, but also central office personnel, their peers, and sometimes their superintendents, depending on the size of the system. They also communicate with business/industry representatives engaged in adopt-a-school programs. In these relationships they may at one moment assume an instructional leadership posture and at another an entrepreneurial stance. As entrepreneurs they strive to communicate their school's excellence to the neighborhoods that support them. (p. 10)

Role of Teachers

As the largest category of employees in a school system, the impact of teachers on public relations is immense. As the individuals on the frontline, interaction with parents, students, and the community occurs on a daily basis. For example, each secondary teacher can interact on a daily basis with up to 150 students, thus having indirect contact with as many as 300 parents. Teacher impact is further magnified because large percentages of them live in communities in which they teach.

   One of the most effective PR postures teachers should assume is treating students as clients. This means that teachers must know their subject matter and be able to deliver it in a manner that is educational and interesting. It also means that teachers must have high expectations for students, and that they must recognize and reward appropriate behaviors. In carrying out this PR role, teachers should model behavior that they would like their students to emulate. It is also very important that lines of communication between teacher and parent be kept open. Perhaps the most important factor that creates satisfying relationships between home and school is a properly qualified and proficient teacher of high moral standing who works hard and cares about children (Swink, 1989). A teacher also has to be a good listener, maintain a professional and caring demeanor, and never minimize the parent or the child (Ediger, 2001). By welcoming parents into classrooms they have made appealing for learning and by getting involved in a school's PR program, teachers further enhance their role.

Role of Other School Personnel

All school personnel have a PR role. Guidance counselors, for example, often develop close relationships with students and parents through their aid and advice in academic matters. They help both student and parent realize educational aspirations. School nurses may also develop close relationships with students through frequent school contacts and with parents through notes carried home by students, occasional phone calls, and home visitations. Librarians open up a world of books to children and sometimes prepare annotated reading lists for faculty members to make them aware of new library holdings. They are also involved in the sensitive issue of making library acquisitions that might incur community disapproval. Working just outside the principal's office, secretaries and clerks generally are the first school contact for a large number of visitors, and their attitudes toward and treatment of these people—be they staff, students, or visitors—tend to characterize the kind of morale existing within a school (Ediger, 2001). Because an attractive and well-kept building reflects a school family's pride of ownership, and because this pride typically encourages better care of the school facility by the rest of the community, a custodian surely has an important PR role to play.

Even what is served daily in the school's cafeteria, and how it is served, affects public perceptions. In this regard, cafeteria workers can enhance the morale of virtually the entire school. Bus drivers are also potential PR emissaries, who gain the respect and confidence of parents by showing concern for their children while transporting them safely along busy streets or highways in all kinds of weather. School employees, regardless of their position, are representatives of the organization and contribute to institutional image.

IDENTIFYING THE SCHOOL-LEVEL PR PERSON

Principals face a number of difficult questions relating to PR at the school building level. Three are especially cogent: Should the school PR coordinator be full time or part time? What relationship should the school coordinator have with the district PR director? What qualifications are needed for this position?

Part Time or Full Time

A national study (Genzer, 1993) that sought to determine actual and ideal workloads of PR directors found that 90% of responding PR directors were employed full time, and 64% had a staff of more than one. In contrast, a much earlier study by West in 1980 revealed that only 67% of the PR directors sampled were employed full time.

Over the years, it has been quite commonplace for part-time PR directors to work themselves into full-time jobs as a district expands and PR responsibilities multiply. Today, as districts continue to grow and a variety of site-based management approaches are implemented, the importance of having someone function in that position at the school level, at least part time, is almost as great as having someone do the same at the system level full time. This is especially true if districts adopt a school PR advisory committee to network with a system's PR advisory committee or, for that matter, with the system PR director.

According to Kendall (1986), site coordinators are the key to an effectively networked communication program. For example, once trained in the fundamentals of communications, 50 site coordinators—60% of them secretaries, 35% of them teachers, and the rest school managers—in California's Vallejo City Unified School District helped the district move from a centralized form of reporting information to one that coordinated and networked all its communication efforts and charged each school with the responsibility of planning and disseminating through a variety of information channels.

A number of building administrators have manipulated teacher allocation points to appoint part-time teachers to the task of public relations. Many of these site PR coordinators are assigned a smaller teaching load in exchange for their PR efforts. In determining their need for PR and, subsequently, their allocation of time for the task, principals should consider the following three concepts promoted by the NSPRA (1998b):

1. This is the media age. School communication needs have increased dramatically and become more complex. A school needs a PR person to develop and execute its communication plans through both print and electronic media.

2. Education is under attack from taxpayers, business groups, and others. A school needs a PR person to publicize the positive news about student and staff achievement programs, and to develop a coordinated proactive, rather than reactive, approach that anticipates problems before they develop. If there is no positive communication from the school, the critics' voices are the only ones that will be heard.

3. The scope of successful school public relations has expanded greatly from what in the past was mostly written communication to a greatly increased need for face-to-face communication with the many publics in your community. A school needs a PR person to schedule community relations programs and to build informed support and solid community relationships.

These concepts, originally written for the district level, have been paraphrased to emphasize the school level, but certainly they are applicable to all levels of PR in these changing times.

Relationship With the System-Level PR Director

An individual given released time to perform school PR responsibilities may report to both the school system director and the site-based management team (if one exists). This person provides leadership and serves as a resource person for the school PR advisory committee. Typically, the relationship between school coordinator and system director is collegial rather than supervisory with regard to school PR matters. This type of relationship allows schools to communicate directly with their publics. However, in those PR matters that affect the total system, the district PR director usually has authority.

Qualifications for the School-Level PR Position

In performing their jobs, PR directors usually stress the need for both training and experience in journalism (West, 1980). Most school personnel, however, often find that they must acquire this knowledge and skill through inservice or staff development. For example, NSPRA has an annual seminar that brings together experienced and novice PR directors to exchange ideas and obtain needed skills. NSPRA's state chapters provide similar training opportunities. NSPRA also has an array of publications designed to help all educational PR directors do their jobs better. Useful ideas may also be gleaned from the *School Journal of Public Relations*, a quarterly publication directed toward meeting the needs of educational PR specialists.

Individuals chosen to assume the public relations responsibilities should possess excellent writing and speaking skills. Other desirable competencies include photography, a working knowledge of how the various media operate, leadership skills, and the ability to work well with others, especially in the increasingly multicultural environments in which schools function. A study of PR directors in the early 1990s found that these individuals had majored in a variety of disciplines at both the undergraduate and graduate levels (Genzer, 1993), an indication that focus has been more on skills than on formal training.

CULTIVATING INFORMATION NETWORKS

Two-way communication, horizontal and vertical, is vital in any organization. If information channels are not kept open, rumors flourish (perhaps especially on employee e-mail) and morale suffers. The flow of information within schools and between schools and the system is crucial to goal assessment and continuous improvement. Without information, schools function in a vacuum. When communication breaks down between school and community, the school becomes isolated. Hence, information networks are at the very core of PR practice.

School to School (Formal and Informal)

Although there are many formal ways to communicate, perhaps the best way for schools to exchange information is through the individuals who preside over each school's PR advisory committee. Through periodic meetings, these coordinators have an opportunity to share information and to collaborate. Summaries of their meetings can be shared with individual school advisory committees and with SBM councils.

A monthly school newsletter is another way schools can share information. Ideally, these newsletters are prepared by the school PR coordinator in consultation with the school's PR committee and principal and endorsed by the school council. Other sources of communication between and among schools include activity schedules, publications, cable television programs, and Web pages on the Internet. As we begin the new millennium, the expectation is that each school will have an attractive and efficient home page for students and parents to access for information on programs, special events, and even help with homework.

Informal opportunities for information exchanges occur many times during a school year. Staff members working in the district may be neighbors, with informal exchanges taking place over backyard fences, in neighborhood socials, or through the ubiquitous e-mail exchanges. Students also serve as information carriers. Because virtually everyone is an information carrier, the school PR coordinator should keep staff constantly in touch with accurate and up-to-date information.

School to District (Formal and Informal)

The same kind of periodic meetings that bring school PR coordinators together can be used between school coordinators and the system PR director. These encounters can also serve as learning experiences as school coordinators draw upon the expertise of the system PR director to design information plans and networks that establish and cultivate media contacts. Perhaps most important, these meetings provide an opportunity for school coordinators to receive advanced notices of press releases or information that affect school employees and students. Informal information exchanges can occur on the system level in many different ways: before and after periodic PR meetings with the system PR director; during staff development PR sessions over which the system PR director presides; and on picnics instigated by the local teachers' association where all school personnel have an opportunity to visit with one another. Administrators and teachers almost always have informed networks that permit them to exchange information.

Determining Other Information Channels

In every neighborhood, there are formal leaders to whom residents turn for information and advice. They may have a seat on the city council or on the school board, or be a minister in a church or a leader of a local scout group. Easy to target and eager to accept civic responsibilities, these people can serve as information agents for the school PR coordinator. Each community also has its own unique network of informal leaders (for example, the local barber or beauty shop owner/employee, service workers, small business owners/employees, and the like) who serve as information sources for neighborhood members (Norton et al., 1996). One needs only to query a random selection of residents and members of local service clubs to determine each community's set of key communicators. Once identified, this ever-expanding list of key communicators can serve as a formal community network between the school and the community. The key communicators personalize the message and help community members understand and accept change (Gallagher et al., 1997). The downside for the school is that these key communicators, like all of us, filter messages based on their perceptions and support for school programs; nevertheless, given their importance, it is a mistake to ignore these individuals.

Utilizing Technology

Technology leaders are those who see technology as a central tool for transforming teaching and learning (Bailey, 1996). Although teaching and learning are primary considerations in public education, administrative uses of technology enhance the development of school and system PR. Most organizations believe that the more value that is added by a tool, the less the tool is perceived as costly (Rhodes, 1997); more important, technology should be used in ways that allow us to be more human centered (Reiman & Thies-Sprinthall, 1998).

By networking, school PR persons can transmit information via computer to each other and the system PR director almost instantly. They can have online conferences without ever leaving their work sites. They can leave electronic messages (e-mail and fax) and keep a record of all electronic exchanges. The need for hard copies of messages has been reduced and eliminated in a few institutions. Electronic scanners and dictating software for computers reduce our dependence on secretarial assistance, and notebook computers increase mobility and flexibility, and virtually eliminate distance as a limitation between respondents.

Some school systems have used cable television to link their schools with each other and the community. In these systems, the camcorder takes its place alongside the camera for recording information about the schools for media dissemination. Fax transmissions of pictures and words make communication between parties instantaneous. With the everyday use of projection television and 100-inch screens, every member of an SBM team, not just its PR designee, can be networked for video-conferencing.

In recent years, however, perhaps the valuable PR tool for a district or individual school is its Web site. Even remote rural schools have effectively incorporated technology into their instructional and communication plans. For example, in the Humboldt County School District in Nevada, six rural schools have combined to serve not only their own students but the surrounding region as well by providing Internet services. The McDermitt Consolidated School in Nevada was listed by *PC Magazine* as one on its top 100 "Wired Schools" with a computer-to-student ratio of 1:2.25 and 100% Internet access (WestEd, 2000).

Many schools now have their own Web sites that provide information on programs and policies, and as the number of families with home computers increases, there will be expanded opportunities for schools to utilize these for much of their PR needs. That said, schools need to move into this area with a good deal of caution. As noted by Levine (2001), a school needs to develop a comprehensive Web policy to guide decisions related to its Web site. These decisions will relate to the following:

1. *Roles and responsibilities*—Three roles are crucial: a webmaster to oversee the technical aspects of the site, an editor to monitor the content that is published, and an instructional development specialist to provide training of district staff.

2. *Education value*—The Web site is intended to support the PR function that, in turn, supports the school's teaching and learning objectives. Content must be regularly reviewed for value as well as to be sure it is accurate, fair, and not damaging to anyone's reputation. Libel suits are painful and expensive.

3. *Student privacy*—While most school personnel are familiar with the Federal Education Rights and Privacy Act, the FBI and the recent Children's Online Privacy and Protection Act provide even more safeguards that must be followed. In the fall of 2000, for example, the FBI urged schools not to use student photos on their Web sites. A district policy should be adopted regarding student confidentiality before a Web site is allowed to post information, and, as a minimum, photo release forms should be revised to include use in electronic formats.

4. *Copyright laws*—Most schools already have policies regarding adherence to fair use provisions of copyright laws, but this will need to be revisited to ensure awareness that Internet publishing is considered a "public performance" and that stricter guidelines pertain.

5. *Technical standards*—Among the issues to consider here are the size of files that will be permitted and if your school site must be hosted on an official district server. Although many districts use the "schoolname.K12.state.us" designation, others purchase a .com or .org domain name. Levine (2001) recommends that districts also purchase similar names to protect against those who might wish to parody your site or to use it for anti-educational messages. The 2000 presidential campaign by George W. Bush experienced this problem, as did a district in Connecticut when an angry parent used a similar site to post negative information about the district.

6. *Commercial sites and services*—A school's Web policy should forbid the use of third-party sites that have not been approved by school personnel. Sometimes business enterprises manage to create sites or fundraising programs with no official ties to the school. These can create problems with posting of inaccurate information or by siphoning off funds that donors believed to have been donated to the school.

Given these cautions, however, each school should consider the valuable uses that a Web site can offer, especially in an era in which calls for accountability are paramount. Many schools publish their "report card" online, and a Web site can be an effective method for communicating about awards your staff or students have received. It can help personalize the school experience for parents and communicate the issues that are not covered in other media, such as the local newspaper. With effective translations, a Web site can help a school reach out to minority parents, and it can reach those who no longer have children in school but whose support might be crucial in bond elections and tax levy issues that are needed to improve local education.

ASSESSING THE SCHOOL-LEVEL PROGRAM

A school's PR program cannot be deemed effective or in a continuous state of improvement unless there is ongoing assessment. McGhan (1998) urges the development of a robust system that measures school quality in fair, honest, and meaningful ways and distributes that information widely. Although there are many ways to access a PR program, the most productive way is to direct all efforts toward achieving predetermined and concrete goals (West, 1985). Because school and district are linked in PR goal accomplishment, there is considerable overlapping in most assessment procedures. Inventories, for example, that target system PR programs typically include sections that have relevance for school PR assessment. Bortner (1979) offered 168 items that can be used to evaluate a system PR program, including an array of items that are applicable to school PR programs. The Texas School Public Relations Association (1991) provides an evaluation of the school's PR program by the principal, staff, parents, and students. Using a six-item Likert scale (5 = always or superior, 1 = never or inferior, 0 = unknown or undecided) for each item, average rating for specific category sections or all sections collectively can be calculated. The NSPRA (1984) has developed a PR checklist, and several of its items are applicable for evaluating a school PR program. Holliday (1987), in his PR climate-assessment inventory, offered a specific section for building-level evaluation. An assessment inventory called PROWESS, developed by Oberg and West (West, 1985), also provides items that can be adapted for school PR use.

Feedback is crucial to the assessment process. It can be formal or informal, planned or unplanned. Schools often are convenient targets of criticism by special-interest groups who generally promote a single-issue agenda to the exclusion of other patrons' interests. In the past two decades, schools have done a better job of obtaining broad-based client input. The use of advisory committees, public forums, crisis communication teams, and key communicators has contributed to a client-focused PR program. Educational policy is increasingly framed by the use of demographically balanced focus groups. The topic of program evaluation is addressed in greater depth in Chapter 15.

Using Opinionnaires

Easy to construct and just as easy to administer—by telephone, mail, or face to face—the opinionnaire can serve as a relatively easy method of assessing a school PR program. Opinionnaires can target any or all aspects of a school's program, at one time assessing the perceptions of staff as to PR program effectiveness; at another time, students; and at still another, community members.

The items for an opinionnaire may be generated from the school PR advisory committee, key communicator groups, and SBM focus groups and teams. PR consultants may be asked to assist, but the best approach is to rely on those individuals who are most committed to making the school PR program a success. Chapter 13 addresses the topic of collecting and analyzing survey data.

Quantifying Levels of Involvement

Levels of involvement, usually an indicator of PR effectiveness, are determined by a quantitative assessment. For example, how many parents attend school functions or are involved in the school's PTA or PTO? How many accolades or criticisms does a school receive from its constituents? How many parents, nonparents, and senior citizens are involved in its volunteer program? How many local businesses have pledged support to the school's adopt-a-school program?

The number of articles about a school published in the local press and the number of public service announcements about a school aired on radio and television also are quantitative assessment points. In effect, virtually anything associated with PR that can be counted serves as a way of quantitatively assessing a school PR program. Although not everything that can be measured is necessarily important (and, indeed, the most important things are difficult to quantify), school leaders should be aware that we participate in a culture with a high regard for the "bottom line" and statistics can be very useful in building support for a program.

Cost–Benefit Analysis

Planning, teamwork, and period assessment are integral to a successful PR program. A critical public evaluates the ability of school officials to cope with day-to-day concerns and to resolve crises and problems. Cost and value, although often used interchangeably, are not the same thing. PR value is based on a belief or perception fueled by a school's response to a problem and the subsequent communication of the event and action taken. Cost usually represents the money spent on the PR program.

The monetary cost of an educational PR program is often debated by board members and administrators. However, the debate usually confuses the abstract concept of PR value with actual funds budgeted and spent for PR programs. This problem is exacerbated by the tendency to spend too much time responding to critics and not enough time improving program deficiencies. National PR consultant Ledell (1996) recommends that schools spend 70% of their PR time with "silent majority" concerns.

After supplies and equipment are recorded and the percentage of personnel time devoted to PR programs is calculated, most schools and districts can make an accurate estimate of PR expenditures. Additionally, it is possible to place "fair cost" on the amount of volunteer time and donations received to support school PR efforts. As a percentage of the total school budget, PR amounts typically are small. Unfortunately, the cost of a PR program is easier to determine than is the benefit, but this should not excuse a school leader from the responsibility for making a determined effort to win support for this important aspect of the educational endeavor.

SUMMARY

The need for PR programs at the school level has never been greater. Long-term efforts to foster broad and meaningful participation within school districts have given rise to site-based management and the resurgence of a grass-roots philosophy that invites community involvement at the local level. To ensure that the outcomes of shared decision making are carefully planned and implemented and are of the highest quality, school administrators have employed strategic planning and total quality management as management tools. Finally, to convey the message to the school district's various publics that system and unit goals are being accomplished and that district needs are being met, administrators have begun to market their schools.

Because the success of site-based management and the management tools it uses are largely contingent on how well school personnel and community people work together and how well they communicate and market their achievement and innovations, effective PR becomes critical at the unit level. In every school, someone should coordinate the PR responsibility, and this individual should work closely with school committees, the district PR director, and the principal.

| CASE STUDY | Marijuana Madness |

Carson High School (CHS) is located in an affluent suburb of a southern metropolitan city. With an enrollment of 2,400 students, CHS is perceived as an effective school whose clientele are primarily college bound. Often referred to as the school for preppies, CHS has been successful in academics and athletics. Because of the school's successes, families have begun to relocate to this area in an effort to enroll their students in the already overcrowded school.

Unfortunately, in the past 6 months, the media have reported several on-campus drug-related arrests of students, ranging from simple possession of marijuana to possession of marijuana with intent to distribute. One of the students arrested was Stanley Washington, a highly regarded athlete and student leader. Washington was arrested for possessing more than 2 ounces of marijuana packaged for distribution in varying amounts. After his arraignment, his mother was interviewed by a local television station. She claimed that drugs, specifically marijuana, are pervasive at CHS. The arrest of Washington and the negative media coverage raised community awareness about the drug problems at the school. In the brief span of 6 months, the reputation of CHS changed from a highly regarded high school to that of a drug-infested school. Largely because of its negative image, parents started to withdraw their children from the school.

Dr. Robert Wickert, principal of the school for the last 12 years, was understandably concerned. In the weeks following the arrest of Washington, principal Wickert and the school governance council developed a three-step strategy to correct the drug problem. First, Wickert employed two additional guidance counselors to advise students on drug-related issues and to improve communication between faculty and students. Second, a school resource officer was hired to assist James Padgett, vice principal for discipline, in developing strategies to resolve the drug problem. Finally, Martha Reynolds, a veteran English teacher and member of the community, was selected as the school's first PR coordinator. Despite these measures, Dr. Wickert continued to receive reports that drugs were being sold and used on campus.

In an annual school board survey, parents were asked to rate CHS's effectiveness in academics, teacher–student relationships, school climate, security and maintenance, instructional management, student discipline, and parent and community–school relations. Despite small increases in standardized test scores from the previous year, parents rated academics, instructional management, and teacher–student relationships significantly lower than the previous year. In the categories of school climate, security and maintenance, student discipline, and parent and community–school relations, the school received the lowest marks since the survey's implementation 9 years ago. The principal and staff were disappointed that many achievements had been overshadowed by the continuing drug problem.

QUESTIONS AND SUGGESTED ACTIVITIES

CASE STUDY

1. To what extent was this school prepared to deal with negative news?
2. Assume you are the principal of CHS. You are going to develop a committee and implement a PR plan to improve public opinion. Who should be on the committee? What should be the committee's primary objectives?
3. If you were the principal, what resources might you seek from central administration to deal with the drug issue?
4. Can public relations be used to hide school problems from the community? Should it be used for this purpose?

CHAPTER

5. Why is it important to have a building-level PR program? What should such a program look like? What is the principal's role in preparing the plan?

6. Develop a list of qualifications for the building-level PR person and a job description for the position.
7. Consider the financial costs of a school-level PR program. Create a sample 3-year budget designed to fund the PR program.
8. To what extent is a building-level PR program compatible with the concepts of decentralization and democratic governance?
9. What is the ideal relationship between a district PR plan and a school PR plan?

SUGGESTED READINGS

Armistead, L. (2000). Public relations: Harness your school's power. *High School Magazine, 7*(6), 24–27.

Bruckner, M. (1998). Make friends before we need them: Operating a key communicator program. *Journal of Educational Relations, 19*(1), 6–12.

David, J. L. (1995–1996). The who, what, and why of site-based management. *Educational Leadership, 53*(4), 4–9.

Gronstedt, A. (1997). The role of research in public relations strategy and planning. In C. L. Claywood (Ed.), *The handbook of strategic public relations and integrated communications* (pp. 47–59). New York: McGraw-Hill.

Grossman, J. W. (1998). *Public relations plans.* Rockville, MD: National School Public Relations Association.

Holliday, A. E. (1996). 99 ways to increase/improve school-community relations. *Journal of Educational Relations, 17*(3), 2–6.

McLaren, P. (1998). *Life in schools.* New York: Longman.

McNergney, R. F., & Herbert, J. M. (1998). *Foundations of education.* Boston: Allyn & Bacon.

Ordovensky, P., & Marx, G. (1993). *Working with the news media.* Arlington, VA: American Association of School Administrators.

Plucker, J. A., & Slavkin, M. L. (2000). No school is an island. *Principal Leadership, 1*(1), 48–53.

Schmoker, M. J., & Wilson, R. B. (1993). *Total quality in education.* Bloomington, IN: Phi Delta Kappa.

Schwahn, C. J., & Spady, W. G. (1998). *Total leaders.* Arlington, VA: American Association of School Administrators.

Sharp, W., Sharp, H. M., & Walter, J. K. (1995). An excellent public relations program can begin with low-cost methods. *Journal of Educational Relations, 16*(2), 8–12.

Watson, A. (1998). The newspaper's responsibility. *Phi Delta Kappan, 79*(10), 728–734.

REFERENCES

Armistead, L. (2002). Ten steps for planning public relations. *Education Digest, 67*(6), 57–61.

Ashby, D. E., & Krug, S. E. (1998). *Thinking through the principalship.* Larchmont, NY: Eye on Education.

Bailey, G. D. (1996). Technology leadership: Ten essential buttons for understanding technology integration in the 21st century. *Educational Considerations, 23*(2), 2–6.

Baldwin, G. H. (1997). Support staff's views on site-based management. *School Business Affairs, 63*(1), 27–32.

Banks, S. P. (1995). *Multicultural public relations: A social-interpretive approach.* Thousand Oaks, CA: Sage.

Björk, L. (2001). The role of the central office in decentralization. In T. J. Kowalski & G. Perreault (Eds.), *21st century challenges for school administrators* (pp. 286–309). Lanham, MD: Scarecrow Press.

Bortner, D. M. (1979). Benchmarks for school public relations. *Journal of Educational Communications, 3*(2), 8–19.

Brown, J. A., Burkhalter, B. B., & Schaer, B. B. (1996–1997). Job stress and coping strategies for public school superintendents. *Record in Educational Leadership, 16 & 17*(1&2), 146–153.

Eaton, E. R., & West, P. T. (1988). Assistant high school principals will have an important PR role. *Journal of Educational Public Relations, 11*(1), 31.

Ediger, M. (2001). Effective public school relations. *Education, 121*(4), 743–750.

Gallagher, D. R., Bagin, D., & Kindred, L. W. (1997). *The school and community relations* (6th ed.). Boston: Allyn & Bacon.

Genzer, S. M. (1993). *Actual and ideal workloads of educational public relations directors in the United States.* Unpublished doctoral dissertation, Texas A&M University.

Gibson, M. A. (1983). *Home-school-community linkages: A study of educational opportunity for Punjabi youth. Final report.* Stockton, CA: South Asian American Education Association.

Gibson, M. A. (1987). The school performance of immigrant minorities: A comparative view. *Anthropology and Education Quarterly, 18*(4), 262–275.

Gronstedt, A. (1997). The role of research in public relations strategy and planning. In C. L. Caywood (Ed.), *The handbook of strategic public relations and integrated communications* (pp. 47–59). New York: McGraw-Hill.

Grossman, J. W. (1998). *Public relations plans.* Rockville, MD: National School Public Relations Association.

Grunig, J. E., & White, J. (1992). The effect of world views on public relations theory and practice. In J. E. Grunig (Ed.), *Excellence in public relations and communication management* (pp. 31–65). Hillsdale, NJ: Erlbaum.

Hannaway, J., & Carnoy, M. (Eds.). (1993). *Decentralization and school improvement: Can we fulfill the promise?* San Francisco: Jossey-Bass.

Hanson, E. M., & Henry, W. (1993). Strategic marketing for educational systems: A guide for implementation. *NASSP Bulletin, 77*(556), 79–88.

Holliday, A. E. (1987). What's your public relations/communications/relationships climate? *Journal of Educational Public Relations, 10*(1), 10–15.

Kendall, B. E. (1986). Breaking with tradition. *Journal of Educational Public Relations, 9*(3), 4–9.

Kern-Foxworth, M., & Miller, D. A. (1992, May). *Embracing multicultural diversity: A preliminary examination of public relations education.* Paper presented at the annual conference of the International Communication Association, Miami.

Ledell, M. A. (1996). Common ground: A way of life. *School Administrator, 53*(10), 8–11.

Leichty, G. (1997). The limits of collaboration. *Public Relations Review, 23*(1), 47–55.

Levine, E. (2001). A web policy primer. *American School Board Journal, 188*(7).

Martinson, D. (1995). School public relations: Do it right or don't do it at all! *Contemporary Education, 66*(2), 82–85.

McCarthy, B. J. (1960). *Basic marketing: A managerial approach.* Homewood, IL: Irwin.

McGhan, B. (1998). Choice and compulsion. *Phi Delta Kappan, 79*(8), 610–612.

McNergney, R. F., & Herbert, J. M. (1998). *Foundations of education.* Boston: Allyn & Bacon.

National School Public Relations Association (NSPRA). (1984). *Evaluating your school PR investment.* Arlington, VA: Author.

National School Public Relations Association. (1992, October). Site-based management changing school PR role. *Network,* 1–3.

National School Public Relations Association. (1993, October). The care and feeding of school-site councils. *It Starts on the Frontline,* 1.

National School Public Relations Association. (1998a). *Standards for educational public relations programs*. Rockville, MD: Author.

National School Public Relations Association. (1998b). *Why do you need a school PR practitioner now more than ever?* Rockville, MD: Author.

Norton, M. S., Webb, L. D., Dlugosh, L. L., & Sybouts, W. (1996). *The school superintendency*. Boston: Allyn & Bacon.

Peters, T., & Waterman, R. (1982). *In search of excellence*. New York: Harper & Row.

Reiman, A. J., & Thies-Sprinthall, L. (1998). *Mentoring and supervision for teacher development*. New York: Longman.

Rhodes, L. A. (1997). Building leadership technology. *School Administrator, 54*(4), 12–16.

Rodriguez, C. E. (1992). *Student voices: High school students' perspectives on the Latino dropout problem*. Report of the Fordham University, College at Lincoln Center Student Research Project. New York: Latino Commission on Educational Reform.

Sashkin, M. (1993). The visionary principal: School leadership for the next century. In M. Sashkin & H. J. Walberg (Eds.), *Educational leadership and school culture* (pp. 75–85). Berkeley, CA: McCutchan.

Schueckler, L. P., & West, P. T. (1991). Principals and PR directors mostly agree on the ideal PR role for senior high school principals, but substantially disagree on their PR performance. *Journal of Educational Public Relations, 13*(4), 24–26.

Schwahn, C. J., & Spady, W. G. (1998). *Total leaders*. Arlington, VA: American Association of School Administrators.

Swaim, S. (1996). The central office role in middle-level school reform. *School Administrator, 53*(6), 6–9.

Swink, E. (1989). What factors in a school create satisfying home–school–community relations? *Journal of Educational Public Relations, 12*(1), 19–20.

Texas School Public Relations Association. (1991). *Campus level public relations assessment process*. Austin, TX: Author.

Thompson, D. C., & Wood, R. C. (1998). *Money and schools*. Larchmont, NY: Eye on Education.

West, P. T. (1980). The making of a school PR director. *Journal of Educational Communication, 4*(1), 28–29.

West, P. T. (1985). *Educational public relations*. South Beverly Hills, CA: Sage.

West, P. T. (1993). The elementary school principal's role in school–community relations. *Georgia's Elementary Principal, 1*(2), 9–10.

WestEd. (2000). *CSRD footprints*. Retrieved August 2002 from http://www.wested.org/csrd/ newsletter/ spring00/page2state.html

Williams, D. I., Jr., & Chavkin, N. F. (1989). Essential elements of strong parent involvement programs. *Educational Leadership, 47*(2), 19–20.

9

Practice in Private and Nontraditional Public Schools

Theodore J. Kowalski

Over the past two decades, interest in private schools and alternative forms of public education has grown considerably. The reasons are varied and often inextricably intertwined. Consider just three supporting arguments for providing parents with more education options:

1. Students from low-income families, trapped in areas served by the most ineffective and troubled public schools, could benefit from having options that are otherwise unavailable to them (Hill, 1996; Viteritti, 1996).
2. Reformers embracing market mechanisms[1] (Friedman & Friedman, 1981) believe that ineffective public schools will either improve or close if they must compete for students. Moreover, competition spawned by choice programs is seen as a relatively inexpensive reform strategy.
3. Reformers guided primarily by the value of liberty believe that parents across all income levels should have the freedom to select schools for their children. In the eyes of these change agents, school choice produces greater parental support, and therefore, benefits students (Vasallo, 2000).

Ideas promoting more alternatives to traditional public schooling have not gone unchallenged. Consider some of the more prevalent criticisms:

♦ Teacher unions and political leaders sympathetic to them have been especially vocal in denouncing programs such as vouchers, tuition tax credits, and charter schools. They see these ideas as merely diversions that further reduce public education's scarce resources and that potentially diminish the political influence of unions (Brouillette & Williams, 1999).
♦ Less educated parents with more modest means are less likely to exercise choice. Therefore, choice systems could lead to less equity and greater racial, ethnic, and socioeconomic stratification (Goldhaber, 1999; Good & Braden, 2000).
♦ Market-driven reform strategies have spawned ideological concerns related to the concept of school as community (Bryk, Lee, & Holland, 1993) and to the potential for greater racial (Smith & Meier, 1995) and social segregation (Walford, 1996).
♦ Rather than serving the needs of inner-city students from low-income families, choice caters to families in the middle and upper classes (Witte, 1995).
♦ Private schools can and do reject students. The propensity to attend them increases with both income and ability, and in private schools tuition declines with student ability—a factor making private schools attractive to higher achieving students. Hence, choice programs, and especially those funded through vouchers, can entice these students to leave traditional public schools (Epple & Romano, 1998).
♦ Choice programs raise fundamental legal questions; if legislation promoting this concept is enacted without corresponding revisions to school finance laws and policies, local control over public education will be eroded (Hilton, 1994).

Despite myriad economic and philosophical concerns, the movement toward establishing more alternatives to traditional public schools is still gaining momentum.

---

[1]Defined as the concepts central to the marketplace economy where competition among providers is believed to produce organizational change and development.

This chapter examines the application of public relations in institutions that directly compete with traditional public schools for students. Private schools and then nontraditional public schools are discussed. The number of administrators working in both types of institutions has been increasing and this trend is expected to continue. In addition, the nature of these schools is now being addressed in most adminstrator preparation programs because they compete with traditional public schools.

PRIVATE SCHOOLS

The popularity of private schools is attested to by the fact that the rate of enrollment increases in these institutions is getting larger; between 1970 and 1986, private school enrollment in the United States increased by 2% but rose 6% between 1986 and 1996 (Smith, 1997). During the period of 1997 to 2007, total private school enrollment is expected to increase 3%, rising from 5.9 to 6.1 million (Smith). Overall, about 12% of all elementary and secondary school students attend private institutions. Consequently, the percentage of graduates from school administration programs who obtain employment in private schools is expected to increase for the foreseeable future.

Nature of Private Schools

Although state governments have virtually ensured the continued existence of public schools, private schools have had to rely on attractive programs, values, and aspects of climate and culture to recruit and retain students. Success has usually depended on the delivery of a challenging, personalized, academic curriculum in a socially defined atmosphere. Therefore, compared to public schools, private schools have had to exist in a more competitive environment—a condition that elevated the importance of public relations for their administrators.

Generalizations about private schools are precarious because these institutions have different missions and serve different clientele. They can be distinguished from each other by using the following criteria.

- *Religious affiliation.* This criterion identifies whether a school is affiliated with or subsidized by an organized religion, a religious order, a parish, church, synagogue, or other religious institution. Schools having such an affiliation are generally referred to as *parochial schools;*[2] those that do not are classified as *independent* or *nonsectarian schools.*
- *Cost.* The cost of sending a student to a private elementary and secondary school varies markedly in this country. Generally, secondary schools cost more than elementary schools, and geographic location, mission, and economic realities play some part in determining tuition and fee rates. High-cost schools, usually found in urban and suburban locations, have distinctive student populations generally characterized by students from high-income families. They rely heavily on tuition

[2]Parochial schools also are defined more narrowly to include parish-sponsored schools.

revenues and private gifts. By comparison, moderate-cost and low-cost schools typically are parochial schools that rely on a mix of tuition revenues, private gifts, and subsidies provided by the sponsoring parish or religious group.

◆ *Religious admission criteria*. Not all parochial schools use religious-based admission criteria. Most Catholic and Lutheran schools, for example, accept students of different faiths. Fundamentalist schools, however, purposefully restrict enrollment based on adherence to religious tenets, values, and beliefs. These schools typically require parents or students to sign contracts stipulating acceptance of religious principles and a commitment to abide by those principles; the intent is to socialize students to think and behave according to the dictates of the sponsoring religion's doctrine (Peshkin, 1986). Conservative Christian schools sponsored by various Protestant denominations constitute the vast majority of fundamentalist schools in this country. Muslim academies and some Hebrew day schools also are in this category.

◆ *Academic admission criteria*. Private schools often have different admission standards based on student ability and past achievement. Some are highly selective, whereas others have open admission policies with respect to this criterion.

◆ *Student residence*. A small percentage of private schools are boarding schools; these are institutions requiring students to live on campus in dormitories or other facilities.

The National Center for Education Statistics utilizes a nine-category typology to report private elementary and secondary school statistics:

1. *Catholic Parochial Schools:* schools affiliated with a parish. (This is a narrower definition of "parochial school" than commonly used in the literature.)
2. *Catholic–Diocesan Schools:* schools associated with a larger diocesan unit (e.g., a diocesan high school).
3. *Catholic Private Order Schools:* schools owned and operated by religious orders (e.g., Jesuit, Marianist, or Christian Brothers schools).
4. *Other Religious–Conservative Christian Schools:* includes only conservative Christian schools, whereas a general reference to "fundamentalist schools" is usually broader.
5. *Other Religious–Affiliated Schools:* includes Lutheran, Episcopal, Seventh-day Adventist, Hebrew, and Muslim schools.
6. *Other Religious–Unaffiliated Schools:* schools that have a religious mission and philosophy but are not affiliated with any particular religion, church, or denomination.
7. *Nonsectarian Regular Schools:* private schools without a religious affiliation and without a special focus.
8. *Nonsectarian Special Emphasis Schools:* private schools without religious affiliation but having a special mission or philosophical focus (e.g., Montessori schools).
9. *Nonsectarian Special Education Schools:* private schools without religious affiliation and serving only special needs students (http://nces.ed.gov/pubs/ps/).

Historically, religiously affiliated schools have accounted for the vast majority of private elementary and secondary schools in the United States, with a high percentage being Catholic schools. In 1965, Catholic schools educated 88% of the students attending this country's private schools; from that year to 1983, however, the number of Catholic schools declined by 30%. In 1983, only 46% of the students enrolled in private schools were attending Catholic schools (Cooper, 1984). Responding to declining enrollments and rising costs, Catholic schools across America launched a marketing campaign in the early 1990s called "Discover Catholic Schools 1992" (Rist, 1991). This effort helped to reverse the declining enrollment trend. In 1993–1994, just under 5 million elementary and secondary school students were enrolled in 26,093 private institutions. The Catholic Church operated about one-third of the private schools (32%) and enrolled slightly more than half (51%) of the nation's students attending private schools (McLaughlin & Broughman, 1997). In the fall of 1999, there were 27,223 private elementary and secondary schools in the United States. Among the three primary types of private schools—Catholic, other religious, and nonsectarian—other religious schools were the most numerous, followed by Catholic schools and then nonsectarian schools, representing 49, 30, and 22% of all private schools, respectively (Broughman & Colaciello, 1999).

Although Catholic schools were declining in number, other types of private schools were growing. The most dramatic increase in the number of schools in the last quarter of the 20th century was experienced among those identified as "conservative Christian." However, Jewish schools, Montessori schools, and special education schools also have multiplied since 1960 (Broughman & Colaciello, 1998; McLaughlin & Broughman, 1997). Interest in parochial schools has been most apparent in urban areas, largely because many minority families have lost confidence in their local districts. Even when religion is not a factor, some families have selected parochial schools because they thought that the public schools lacked discipline and academic focus. Some studies (e.g., Convey, 1991) have even found academics to be the prime motivator for parents enrolling their children in religiously affiliated schools.

Since the early 1980s, interest in entrepreneurial schools also has grown. These institutions operate as a business; that is, their primary goal is to produce profits. For-profit private schools are different from public schools operated under contract by private businesses and charter schools in that they are not required to abide by policies and regulations governing public schools, nor do they receive public funding. Private for-profit schools are most likely to be found in urban areas where they attract affluent parents dissatisfied with their other school choices. Lieberman (1986), a leading spokesperson for entrepreneurial schools, argues that these institutions create levels of competition with public schools that have not been achieved by other types of private schools. He noted, for example, that competition between Catholic and public schools is often "genteel" (p. 216) because Catholic leaders do not want to risk alienating church members who send their children to public schools by labeling public schools ineffective. Lieberman observes that officials in entrepreneurial schools have fewer inhibitions in this regard; their marketing and recruitment strategies often aggressively point out public education's perceived deficiencies.

Financial Realities of Private Schools

Generally speaking, private schools receive no direct tax dollars to support operations. They rely primarily on the following funding sources:

◆ Tuition and fees
◆ Capital campaigns and other forms of annual fundraising

♦ Major private gifts and endowments
♦ In the case of religiously affiliated schools, fiscal support from parishes, congregations, or religious orders

Compared with public schools, private school funding is less assured and more sporadic. Private school administrators, however, typically have more flexibility to make resource allocation decisions, to initiate fundraising activities, and to invest funds.[3] Seeking greater flexibility in using fiscal resources, many public districts and schools have established their own educational foundations in recent years. These separate legal entities allow foundation boards to expend money collected from private donors (Merz & Frankel, 1997).

Virtually all private schools are experiencing cost increases, the most significant of which involve personnel costs. Catholic schools, for example, used to be staffed primarily by men and women in religious orders, employees who received little compensation. As the number of religious vocations declined, personnel budgets had to be increased significantly so that lay teachers and administrators could be hired. Even so, public school teachers still earn more and receive more benefits than private school teachers (Choy, 1997). A study in the mid-1990s, for example, found that public elementary schools generally spent twice as much per pupil as did religiously affiliated elementary schools—and much of the difference was attributable to personnel costs (Larson, 1995). Many parish-sponsored schools, funded heavily by weekly collections, suffered considerably as personnel costs escalated. Unable to divert more parish revenues, pastors faced the difficult choice of raising tuition or closing the school. For many schools, higher tuition produced a seemingly hopeless cycle of budget-enrollment decline problems.

In addition to personnel, operating costs in private schools have been affected by the following conditions:

♦ *Capital improvements:* Many private schools have had to enlarge, renovate, or replace their facilities.
♦ *Risk management:* Many private schools have had to expand liability coverage and pay higher insurance premiums.
♦ *Technology:* In order to remain competitive, private schools have had to divert resources to the deployment of technology in classrooms and in administrative offices.
♦ *Rising energy prices:* In many parts of the country, the cost of heating and cooling school buildings has gotten progressively higher.

Public schools facing similar fiscal challenges often secured added funding either through state or local tax revenues. Private school officials had to rely on a mix of tuition increases, budget cuts, and fundraising activities to survive.

Independent schools and some parochial schools, especially those in the high-cost category, almost always have endowments. Revenues for them are raised through periodic capital campaigns, annual alumni contributions, and grants and gifts from philanthropic organizations and foundations. This is one area where public relations plays a vital role in private school administration.

---

[3]States laws govern the types of investments that may be made by public agencies, including school districts.

Interest in Private Schools

A number of writers (e.g., Greeley & McManus, 1987; Rothstein, Carnoy, & Benveniste, 1999) have pointed out that private schools, and especially those with a religious affiliation, view organizational climate as an asset. "Climate" refers to the general characteristics of a school, including its physical attributes, social structure, organizational design, and culture (the values and beliefs held in common by those who constitute the school community). Parochial schools, in particular, are often able to provide a "family atmosphere" congruent with the philosophical convictions of the families represented by their students. Even lay administrators and teachers are expected to be role models in these cultures, symbolically expressing through their dress and their behavior the school's moral values and beliefs (Kelly & Bredeson, 1991). In addition, researchers (e.g., Choy, 1997; Kowalski & Swaringin, 1982; McLaughlin, O'Donnell, & Ries, 1995) have found that the sense of community, levels of job satisfaction, and morale were higher in private schools.

Public perceptions of private schools often depend on the nature of comparisons being made. When private schools are compared to urban public schools, for instance, most people believe that private schools are more academically effective, safer, and more orderly. Even when comparisons are made with all public schools, many people view private schools as setting higher student expectations, tolerating less misbehavior, and requiring more academic tasks. Some researchers (e.g., Convey, 1991; Crawford & Freeman, 1996) have found that instruction and discipline often outweigh religious considerations when parents opt for parochial schools. Yet, attitudes about instruction and discipline are not easily separated from religious convictions. Parochial schools are formed to promote a central (frequently spiritually oriented) mission or set of values that get translated into learning and behavior expectations (Kowalski, 2003).

In the final analysis, parents choose private schools for many reasons (Newman, 1995). Dissatisfaction with public schools, commonly expressed in terms of inadequate discipline and low academic standards, is certainly one of them. Closer scrutiny, however, reveals that dissatisfaction is rooted in a broader and more abstract issue. Put simply, many parents have decided that public schools lack a sense of purpose. This conviction is certainly reinforced when parents believe that their values are ignored, or even worse, openly ridiculed. Philosophical and political differences over the purposes of public education have presented a challenge to educational leaders from the very beginning of this nation's public schools.

Table 9–1 provides a list of general comparisons between public and private schools. These factors help to frame the context of practice in private schools.

NONTRADITIONAL PUBLIC SCHOOLS

Charter schools became a major reform initiative in the 1990s. Although it is difficult to precisely define these institutions because of varying state statutes (Good & Braden, 2000), they basically are hybrids. They are funded much like public schools but operate much like private schools. A primary intent of charter schools is to balance freedom (by virtue of being excused from traditional state policies and rules governing public schools)

TABLE 9–1

Public and Private Schools: Key Considerations

Factor	Comparison
Structure	Laws and regulations largely shape public schools: distinctive missions and philosophies largely shape private schools.
Funding sources	Public schools rely on tax revenues; private schools rely on a combination of tuition gifts, subsidies, and grants.
Expenditure decisions	Public school administrators are restricted by laws and state policies governing the expenditure of tax revenues and by local school board approval; private school administrators are typically restricted by board or pastor approval.
Students	Mandatory attendance laws and little competition ensure clientele for public schools; private schools must compete for students. Public schools must serve all eligible students: private schools can be and often are selective in admitting students.
Market status	Public schools are considered quasi-monopolies: private schools function in a competitive market in which the future is not assured.
Mission	Public schools typically have broad missions reflecting a range of purposes and expectations; private schools typically have a narrow mission based either on religious or academic criteria.
Programming	Public schools offer a wide range of programs intended to serve student needs and interests; private schools programs are often more basic and focused serving the needs of a more homogeneous population.
Parents/volunteers	In many public schools, parent and volunteer involvement is viewed as a luxury; in many private schools, this involvement is viewed as a necessity.
PR structure	In public schools, PR responsibilities exist at both the district and school levels: in private schools, school administrators rarely have support from a larger organizational structure.
PR program foci	Public schools tend to concentrate on information exchanges between the schools and the community; private schools focus largely on marketing, recruitment, and fundraising.

and accountability (by virtue of producing evidence of sufficient student performance). Proponents argue that charters offer parental choice and a way to restructure public schools by creating competition while avoiding conflict related to funding private schools (Vergari, 1999). With respect to public relations, these institutions are included in this chapter because they resemble private schools in two important ways.

> First, they are self-governing institutions with wide-ranging control over their own curriculum, instruction, staffing, budget, internal organization, and much more. The second similarity is that nearly all of them are schools of choice. Nobody is assigned against his or her will to attend (or teach in) a charter school. (Manno, Finn, & Vanourek, 2000, p. 737)

By 2002, 38 states had enacted charter school laws. Basic variations in the statutes exist in the following areas:

♦ *Authority to grant a charter:* Typically, charters must be granted by a state agency (e.g., department of education or state board of education); however, some states allow local school boards to grant charters.

- ◆ *Eligible recipients:* Whereas some states grant charters only to licensed teachers, other states have much broader eligibility criteria that allow businesses, parents, and community groups to receive a charter.
- ◆ *Time limits:* Because accountability is a focal point of charter schools, charters are typically granted for only a few years. Some states, for example, Michigan, essentially do not place a time limit on a charter.

In 2002, it was estimated that over 1.5 million parents, students, educators, and other employees were involved with charter schools. There were nearly 2,400 schools operating in 34 states[4] and they enrolled approximately 576,000 students—a figure that increased nearly 12% from 2001 (Center for Educational Reform, 2002). These figures are expected to increase, perhaps significantly, in the near future as a result of a recent U.S. Supreme Court ruling in *Zelman v. Simmons-Harris et al.*—a case challenging the constitutionality of a voucher program in the Cleveland, Ohio, public schools. On June 27, 2002, the Court ruled that vouchers as they were being used in that school district did not violate the U.S. Constitution. In so ruling, the Court lifted a cloud regarding federal constitutional questions on this matter and opened the door for state legislatures to pursue voucher legislation. Passage of state voucher laws is expected to accelerate the growth rate of charter schools and increase private school enrollments.

Some of the most vocal critics and opponents of charter school laws have been teacher unions. The Ohio Federation of Teachers, for instance, sued the state challenging the constitutionality of its charter school law. The following are some of the condemnations leveled at these schools:

- ◆ Charter schools reduce state fiscal allocations to regular public schools.
- ◆ The fundamental promise of charter schools—that they will improve public education through competition—is an unproven hypothesis.
- ◆ Race and economics and not curricula or policies influence many families enrolling children in charter schools. Therefore, these institutions could contribute to the greater levels of segregation.
- ◆ In some states, virtually anyone can get a charter.
- ◆ Many charter schools began operating without sound management and without a financial plan.
- ◆ Charter schools often operate in unsafe environments that are not conducive to effective teaching.
- ◆ Many charter schools practice selective admissions; for example, students with special needs are often not admitted.
- ◆ Despite accountability rhetoric, states do not always have a well-conceived evaluation plan. Consequently, more emphasis is placed on process than on progress.

Although charter school advocates disagree with most or all of these criticisms, they acknowledge that outcomes have not always been glowing. Statewide test scores in Ohio, for instance, suggest rather poor academic performance in these schools. Whereas 43% of

---

[4]As of June 2002, Indiana, New Hampshire, and Wyoming had charter school laws but no charter schools.

TABLE 9–2
Nontraditional Public Schools

Institution Type	Unique Public Relations Challenges
Charter schools	Imaging and marketing are especially important because the schools must recruit a sufficient number of students to survive. In addition, the concept has many critics, including certain education groups.
Magnet schools	Imaging and marketing are especially important because the schools must recruit a sufficient number of students to meet their goals. In addition, these schools are not always understood or supported by the public.
Area vocational schools	Imaging and marketing are especially important because funding depends on enrollment. As America moved from a manufacturing to an information-based society, the value of these schools has been increasingly questioned. In addition, many vocational schools have been perceived as having poor academic standards. Hence, revamping curricula and rebuilding image are often essential to survival.
Alternative schools	Alternative schools also have had to deal with image problems (Raywid, 1995). In many districts, they enroll students who have had difficulty functioning in regular programs—mostly because of discipline-related problems. Although recruiting students is not an issue, administrators in these schools usually have to cope with less than enthusiastic support from the public and from educators.

all fourth graders passed all five tests required by the state in March 2002, only 6% of charter school fourth graders achieved these results.[5] In addition, some charter schools have ceased operation after a relatively short time. Common reasons for charter school closure have included mismanagement, financial difficulties, unsuitable facilities, and failure to meet the academic goals stipulated in the charter (Paglin, 2001).

Three other types of public schools—*magnet schools, area vocational schools,* and *alternative schools*[6]—also face the reality that their future is not guaranteed. Table 9–2 shows a summary of four nontraditional public schools discussed in this chapter.

SELLING PRIVATE AND NONTRADITIONAL PUBLIC SCHOOLS

Positioning is a technique used in the commercial sales world to associate a product with consumer needs. Being able to maintain adequate enrollment levels in private and nontraditional public schools depends largely on the ability of school officials to position their institutions appropriately so that they are attractive to consumers. In the case of private schools, administrators are expected to ascertain and evaluate market conditions (marketing) and convince parents that tuition is a beneficial investment (selling). In the

---

[5]The vast majority of Ohio's charter schools are located in urban areas and a substantial portion of the students come from low-income families.
[6]Magnet schools use academic themes to recruit students on a districtwide basis. Area vocational schools are usually confederations of several districts, and administrators recruit students across the member districts. Alternative schools are often established to serve the needs of students who are having difficulty in a regular program.

case of nontraditional public schools, administrators must also engage in the same activities; however, their efforts typically extend beyond parents to include entire communities. They are expected to demonstrate that their schools are beneficial to students and, more generally, to the community and public education.

Having to compete for students requires most private school administrators to sell their programs to multiple publics spanning age groups and interest levels. Brochures, newsletters, buttons, wearing apparel, bumper stickers, and even athletic teams have been used to build and advertise an all-inclusive image. Public school administrators, by comparison, have not commonly developed effective sales strategies, and this fact became painfully apparent as they tried to counter a confidence crisis that intensified during the 1980s as a result of stinging criticisms contained in reform reports (Hanson, 1992).

For contemporary private schools, advertising foci typically have included educational (and religious) philosophy, tuition, discipline, financial aid, athletic programs, social standing of the student population, and average ability and achievement scores. Nontraditional public schools have been more likely to emphasize curriculum, human and material resources, educational philosophy, and student achievement. Administrators have a responsibility to maintain high ethical standards when promoting their institutions. As examples, issuing false promises, denigrating other schools, and using high-pressure tactics to recruit students are considered unethical acts. More pragmatically, unscrupulous advertising and recruiting tactics have proven to be ineffective most of the time, and they have the potential to destroy a school's reputation (Barbieri, 1991).

Defining the School

To be successful, both private and nontraditional public schools need to establish a market niche. To do this, administrators must develop defining statements—testimonials that realistically and accurately give a school a special identity. The purpose is to highlight differences between a particular school and other schools in the vicinity. Defining statements should be based on actual experiences as characterized by current and former students or by other verifiable evidence. Some private high schools, for example, use alumni testimony appearing in paid media ads as a defining device. Typically these ads feature a graduate who attributes her or his career success to study skills, moral values, and self-discipline acquired in high school. Schools also define themselves symbolically—through logos or mottos—or through well-developed brochures (Abella, 1989).

Effective schools that have defined themselves positively overshadow schools that have not. Identity communicates a deep commitment to an educational (and possibly religious) philosophy. In defining a school, administrators should be guided by three objectives (Cheney, 1991):

1. *Coherence*—the image is presented clearly and comprehensively.
2. *Symbolism*—the image represents values and attitudes.
3. *Positioning*—the image differentiates the school from other institutions.

The importance of being able to connect to potential consumers has prompted private and nontraditional public school officials to rely less on their own judgment and more on techniques such as focus groups. A focus group infuses the opinions and sentiments of actual and potential stakeholders into the defining process. Parents, for instance, may be asked to talk about what they like best about the school; they may be urged to identify problems and other elements of the school that may alienate other parents and students. Ideally, all groups connected to a school should have an opportunity to participate in image building for two very important reasons. First, broad participation enhances the likelihood of an accurate image. Second, participation fosters ownership; participants are more likely to play an active role promoting the image. Proven educational benefits, properly articulated by the school's staff, alumni, and parents, often override concerns and doubts.

Continuously revising image statements is also important because conditions in society are dynamic. At one time, religiously affiliated schools relied entirely on values to sell their institutions to parents; more recently, academic excellence (Leahy, 1989) and discipline (Meade, 1991) have become equally or more attractive issues. Some inner-city parochial school administrators, for example, have argued that moral values and discipline philosophy are preconditions for productive teaching and learning as well as providing distinguishing characteristics for their institutions (Meade).

Interrelating Marketing, Public Relations, and Student Recruitment

Largely because a steady flow of students is not guaranteed for either private or nontraditional public schools, marketing and public relations are treated as interrelated functions. The two functions require administrators to address the following activities simultaneously:

- ◆ Interpreting known needs and wants
- ◆ Monitoring the environment to detect changing needs and wants
- ◆ Defining the school
- ◆ Communicating information about relevant programs and building goodwill

Student recruitment (i.e., selling the product) is an extension of marketing and public relations. Except in large-enrollment private schools and nontraditional public schools that function within the framework of a large local district, one administrator or staff member usually has responsibility for all three functions.

Selling or student recruitment typically receives the most attention from administrators because they know that continued operations depend on having a sufficient number of students. Recruitment has both quantitative and qualitative dimensions. Whereas the former (securing a sufficient number of students) is readily recognized, the latter is less understood. Both private schools and nontraditional public schools usually want to attract the "right types" of students. Consider these examples:

- ◆ A high-tuition private school targets its recruitment activities at upper-income families.
- ◆ A charter school emphasizing family involvement seeks to connect with parents willing to do volunteer work.
- ◆ The recruitment efforts of a Lutheran high school are focused on families who are members of local parishes.

In other words, administrators in these schools really have two recruitment goals: enroll a sufficient number of students and enroll a sufficient number of the preferred types of students. The quantitative dimension addresses an economic goal; the qualitative dimension addresses philosophical and programmatic goals.

The qualitative dimension of student recruitment can be an especially sticky wicket for charter school administrators because legal parameters and political community expectations often constrict them. For instance, they often are expected to enroll a sufficient number of preferred students while maintaining racial and economic balance equal to or greater than other public schools in the same district. Or they may be expected to provide a broad curriculum to serve the needs of all types of students, including special education programs. Nontraditional public school administrators also face important questions about admission decisions that are less likely to create conflict for private school administrators. For instance, under what circumstances may a charter school deny admission to an applicant? A recent study of the 36 state charter school laws revealed that all but two contained some provision with regard to ensuring that underrepresented groups have equal access to these institutions (Ausbrooks, 2001). So although charter schools can and do deny some students admission, administrators in these institutions typically have less latitude in this regard than do their private school peers.

Parental commitment is arguably important in every school, but it is particularly critical in schools of choice. When parents select a school, they usually feel a special sense of responsibility. In the case of private schools, tuition payments almost always deepen this feeling. Consequently, parents who become disillusioned, disappointed, or mistreated often act swiftly to transfer their children to another school. Recognizing this proclivity, administrators in schools of choice often attempt to continuously reinforce the convictions that initially influenced parents—action that requires them to know the reasons and to validate them after the students are enrolled.

ORGANIZING THE PUBLIC RELATIONS FUNCTION

In traditional public schools, marketing and PR activities are often divided between district and school initiatives. In schools of choice, these responsibilities often belong entirely or primarily to the principal or assistant principal. The greatest challenges related to providing a coherent PR program are commonly faced by principals in small parochial schools. These administrators rarely have administrative support staff, yet they are expected to build and maintain community relations and recruit students in addition to their other managerial and leadership duties. Unfortunately, preparing newsletters, issuing press releases, scheduling promotional activities, and seeking community input are not necessarily easier or less time consuming in these schools.

Some private school principals have relegated marketing and PR responsibilities to teachers or parent volunteers, but this option has usually been ineffective for three reasons:

1. The individuals selected are not prepared adequately for the assignments.
2. The individuals selected end up devoting insufficient time to these essential tasks.
3. Marketing, PR, and recruiting get fragmented because each task is being executed by a different employee or volunteer.

TABLE 9–3
Organizational Options for Administering Public Relations and Marketing

Option	Advantages or Disadvantages
Not assigning responsibilities to an employee	Ignoring these responsibilities or addressing them on an ad hoc basis by assigning them to employees or volunteers almost always leads to serious problems. Neither coordination nor continuity is likely. Minimal resources are allocated.
Assigning responsibilities to the principal	Principals already have myriad leadership and management duties; overloading them with additional assignments may detract from their primary responsibilities in areas such as curriculum development and instructional leadership. Minimal resources are allocated.
Distributing the duties among two or more existing employees or volunteers	Public relations and marketing are likely to get fragmented; these two duties may be low priorities for the individuals who are assigned. Minimal resources are allocated.
Employing a PR or marketing specialist	This option requires considerable resources, but it is likely to provide the most comprehensive and effective leadership. Combining public relations and marketing with fundraising and student recruitment responsibilities may reduce costs.
Employing a PR or marketing consultant	Resources required vary depending on quantity and quality of service provided. Administrators lose some control over these functions.

Recognizing these possible problems, some administrators have tried to amalgamate marketing and PR with recruiting and fundraising. Combining these duties makes it more likely that either a half-time or full-time specialist can be employed. In some instances, this goal has been accomplished by having the specialist raise funds for his or her salary. Table 9–3 contains information about different organizational options for addressing these responsibilities.

BUILDING AND USING A PUBLIC RELATIONS CALENDAR

A public relations–marketing–recruitment calendar is one tool that helps principals to deal with conditions caused by less than adequate resources. The calendar is a guide for daily, weekly, and monthly activities. A sample calendar is illustrated in Table 9–4. All events and responsibilities pertaining to public relations, marketing, and recruitment should be placed on the calendar and updated daily or at least weekly.

Internal and external audiences should be considered when preparing the calendar. Within the school, all officials, including members of the governing board, should receive periodic updates of the calendar to ensure that they are aware of scheduled activities, programs, and communication efforts. Pertinent parts of the calendar should also be shared with teachers, support staff, and relevant external audiences. Thus, parts of the calendar should be shared with parents, local government officials, fundraising groups, the media, and even other school administrators.

The calendar also is used to ensure that communication exchanges are occurring between appropriate parties and that potential scheduling conflicts are avoided. For instance, the calendar can be used to monitor schedules for college recruiters and the

TABLE 9–4
Sample Public Relations–Marketing–Recruitment Calendar

Program/Event	Date	Start/End Time	Target Audience	Objective
Alumni reception	9/22	6:00–9:00 p.m.	Alumni in local area	Communicate goals for annual fund drive
TV program	9/23	4:00–4:30 p.m.	Potential students	Promote the school
Parent advisory meeting	9/23	7:00–9:00 p.m.	Parents	Get information about problems, positive experiences, etc.
Deadline for newsletter copy	9/24	5:00 p.m.	Potential contributors	Get materials on time

number of alumni relations activities in a given school year. The PR calendar also provides a composite of activities, and therefore, it indirectly aids the principal or others working with PR to allocate resources effectively.

COMMUNICATING WITH EXTERNAL PUBLICS

The political environment of public education prompts administrators in these schools to maintain contact with external audiences. Less obvious is the need for private school principals to do the same. Contact with external groups requires knowledge, skill, and effort because both motive and product are likely to be evaluated. Communicating with the public only when the school needs or wants something (e.g., fundraising) typically is judged negatively by community members. Likewise, a poorly prepared newsletter filled with grammatical errors or misspelled words may spawn negative perceptions.

Communicating with external publics serves several purposes. For example, the process may sustain interest in the school, provide information about accomplishments or activities, or call attention to planned actions, such as fund drives, athletic events, or school social events. Generally, each communication should focus on two overarching goals: reinforcing the school's effectiveness and reminding the public of the school's special role in the local community.

Two-way communication with the public also produces information that can be used by principals to make a variety of decisions (Tarter & Hoy, 1996). Often referred to as *environmental scanning*, monitoring the community helps administrators to engage in organizational development. Changing economic, social, and political conditions, for example, can affect the welfare of schools of choice in a relatively brief time. A downturn in a local economy may negatively influence parental decisions about keeping their children in private schools; the addition of new programs or the realignment of attendance boundaries in the local public schools may negatively affect charter or vocational school enrollments.

Identifying targeted audiences (i.e., individuals and groups with whom school officials should exchange information) is a key element of external communications. Knowledge of the community is vital to both inside-out and outside-in communication. In the former, school officials disseminate messages through outlets such as newsletters, recruitment brochures, press releases, public service announcements, outdoor advertising, open houses, community service projects, and lectures. In the latter, community input is gathered and analyzed by using opinion surveys, telephone interviews, and focus groups (Carroll & Carroll, 2001).

STUDENT AND PARENTAL INVOLVEMENT

In business, selling a product is easier when a potential buyer knows a satisfied consumer. The same principle is true for schools of choice. Students and parents who praise the school, who talk about the successes, are often the best recruiters. Satisfied students and parents are, therefore, ambassadors for the school because they independently relate positive attitudes to friends, neighbors, and relatives. These individuals also can contribute to the planned PR program by providing testimonials that appear in ads and publications (Warner, 1994).

A school advisory committee is another way to broaden participation in a PR program. Students and parents serving on the committee usually have valuable insights about the following topics:

- ◆ How the school's PR efforts are received in the community
- ◆ The school's strengths and weaknesses
- ◆ Ways that parents can become more involved in the school's operations
- ◆ How marketing, recruiting, and fundraising could be improved
- ◆ Family-oriented social events that build goodwill

Involving parents and students on the PR committee conveys the message that the school engages families—a factor that is often interpreted positively by parents who place a great deal of importance on education. This is the very reason why parent–teacher associations in public schools have been a potent force for developing school image over the years. Most parents react positively to messages that tell them that they are welcome in the school and that their direct involvement is welcomed and appreciated.

Many parochial schools depend on parent volunteers (including grandparents) to offset resource deficiencies. Some schools have even developed volunteer "gift option" booklets— a communication device that details volunteer opportunities. Further, the booklets provide specifications for time and talent so that parents can select an activity that fits their schedule and interests or abilities.

Parental involvement is truly a win-win situation because the benefits extend beyond PR to the students themselves. Research indicates that parental involvement and home-learning activities positively influence student grades, attendance, and behavior (Simon, 2001). Hence, the high rate of parental involvement in schools of choice may partially explain the relatively high rates of student success reported by many of these schools.

FUTURE ISSUES AND PROBLEMS

Because their future is not ensured, private schools remain highly dependent on effective strategic planning and PR. Having to compete for students affects virtually every aspect of their operations, and this reality has been magnified by the uncertain future of school reform. Initiatives such as school choice, charter schools, vouchers, and tuition tax credits remain popular topics. The widespread adoption of charter school laws, for example, already has created new issues for both private and public school administrators.

The success and possibly future existence of both private and nontraditional public schools depends largely on how these schools are defined. If present political trends continue, all elementary and secondary schools are likely to face more competition than they have in the past. Consider some of the ongoing developments that support this conclusion:

- ◆ Interest in parochial schools has been revitalized in recent years. In Indiana, for example, three new Catholic high schools were scheduled to open between 2003 and 2004—the first new Catholic high schools created in that state in several decades.
- ◆ Parental dissatisfaction with traditional urban public schools has led to enrollment increases in many urban private schools and efforts to create urban charter schools.
- ◆ Entrepreneurial schools are being created in many parts of the country. Although their primary targets are children in public schools, they also may siphon students from existing private schools.
- ◆ Efforts to pass voucher and tuition tax credit legislation could dramatically affect the demand for private education, especially among low-income families.

These and other realities discussed in this chapter indicate that private school and nontraditional public school administrators will be required to spend considerable time and effort on PR activities. Doing this will require several improvements. Principals will need to be properly prepared to assume these assignments; stakeholders must understand the true meaning of PR and provide support for its various functions; marketing, recruiting, and fundraising need to be integrated with PR to ensure that these functions are not fragmented.

SUMMARY

From a process perspective, PR principles are applicable to private schools and public schools because all of these institutions are more effective when they maintain a symbiotic relationship with their external publics. In private and nontraditional schools, however, the immediate need to recruit students elevates certain aspects of PR. For example, marketing and imaging are absolutely essential to schools of choice.

Current economic and political policy trends suggest that market-driven reform ideas will be increasingly adopted by state legislatures. Approximately 75% of the states, for example, have already promulgated charter school laws. Adoption of voucher or tuition tax credit legislation is expected to have an even more dramatic effect on private school enrollments—and consequently, on the level of competition between public and private schools.

In the past, many parochial schools have attracted students largely on the basis of religious values. Today, academics and discipline are more likely to attract parents to these schools. This change reflects the dynamic nature of market conditions and points out why it is essential for schools of choice to engage in marketing, imaging, and two-way communication. In this vein, strategic planning and other PR-related activities will become increasingly essential.

CASE STUDY	Selling a School

Selling a School

Located in an established area of a northeastern city, Metropolitan Hebrew High School has a tradition that dates back to 1951. Many of the alumni are prominent citizens in the community and regular contributors to the school. Until recently, the school's principal has not had to worry about enrollments because a new generation of alumni children always filled the available spaces and the enrollment remained stable at about 300 students. In the past 3 years, however, the incoming first-year students have declined about 5% each year.

Urged by the school's board of directors, the headmaster has conducted a study to determine why the school is losing enrollment. He cited three factors as being most responsible.

1. There has been a gradual exodus of Jewish families from the immediate community. Although most of the families have remained in the metropolitan area, they have moved to affluent suburbs where the public schools have a more positive reputation.
2. The public school district in which Metropolitan Hebrew High School is located has just opened a new mathematics and science magnet school. Housed in a new building just blocks away, the magnet school is equipped with modern computers and science laboratories.
3. A group of teachers has opened a charter school in the community. Although housed in an old elementary school being rented from the local school district, the charter school has developed a positive reputation for maintaining small classes and high academic standards.

In addition, the headmaster's report included the following related information:

◆ Metropolitan Hebrew High School defines itself both as a religious and an academic school. In the past, parents have paid more attention to religious values, but presently, they appear to be placing more emphasis on academics.
◆ Restricted resources have limited both improvements to the facility (now more than 50 years old) and the acquisition of technology.
◆ In the past 5 years, 20% of the faculty have resigned to accept positions in other schools.
◆ A school newsletter is mailed to both parents and other donors twice each year. The primary purpose is to solicit donations. Annual contributions stemming from the newsletter for the last 3 years have averaged about $54,000, or about $200 per pupil. Last year, about 85% of the total amount came from just 11 donors.
◆ The school's last capital campaign occurred 26 years ago and raised $1.5 million. About half of the funds were used to start a foundation account; the other half were used to pay for facility improvements.

♦ Tuition is currently $7,200 per year, and annual increases over the past decade have averaged 3%.

♦ In addition to tuition revenues and annual donations, the school receives support from two local synagogues; each contributes $25,000 per year. These funds are used for operating expenses and several tuition scholarships.

♦ The school's foundation account has a balance of just under $4 million. Nearly half of this amount was donated by one individual 12 years ago. The balance in the account has decreased from its peak level of $4.3 million 7 years ago because funds had to be used to offset unanticipated building repairs.

♦ The school does not have either a PR or a recruitment plan due to a lack of operating funds. Parent volunteers assist the headmaster with sending recruitment letters to potential students.

♦ The school does not employ teacher aides and there is only one secretary in the school. Twenty-one volunteers work one day per month in the school—primarily assisting teachers. The number of volunteers has declined about 10% over the last 4 years.

After reading the principal's report, the board of directors has decided to embark on a 5-year program to reverse enrollment trends. They have instructed the principal to outline a plan of action, advising him that a failure to reverse enrollment trends will likely mean the demise of the school. They also have expressed fears that additional tuition increases will do more harm than good.

QUESTIONS AND SUGGESTED ACTIVITIES

CASE STUDY

1. Assume you are the headmaster of the Metropolitan Hebrew High School. What steps would you take to meet the board's directive?
2. Is it possible that the absence of a PR plan has contributed to enrollment declines? Why or why not?
3. Evaluate the school's newsletter. How could you change it to make it more effective?
4. In light of increased competition and a dwindling population of Jewish families, what information should the headmaster obtain to define the school?
5. In what respects are the problems facing the Metropolitan Hebrew High School typical for urban parochial schools?
6. Develop a list of actions that might increase parental involvement in this school's activities.

CHAPTER

7. Why are charter schools and area vocational schools similar to private schools with respect to developing a PR plan?
8. Why is it important for schools of choice to define themselves?
9. Why have market-driven reform ideas such as school choice been so popular in the past 10 to 15 years?

10. What factors have contributed to the increasing popularity of private schools in recent years?
11. Why does the assignment of marketing, recruiting, and PR to staff and volunteers tend to lead to fragmentation?
12. A connection to fundraising could enhance PR planning and programs in private schools. Why?
13. Why should public school administrators understand how private schools are organized and operate?

SUGGESTED READINGS

Bushweller, K. (1997). Working miracles: Catholic school's success formula. *American School Board Journal, 184*(1), 14–19.

Coleman, J. S., & Hoffer, T. (1987). *Public and private high schools: The impact of communities.* New York: Basic Books.

Convey, J. J. (1992). *Catholic schools make a difference: Twenty-five years of research.* Washington, DC: National Catholic Educational Association.

Cooper, B. S., & Gargan, A. (1996). Private, religious schooling in the United States. Emerging trends and issues. *Journal of Research on Christian Education, 5*(2), 157–178.

DeBlois, R. (1997). Public vs. private: Time for an honest discussion that could benefit all schools. *NASSP Bulletin, 81*(589), 90–98.

Gestwicki, C. (1992). *Home, school, and community relations: A guide to working with parents* (2nd ed.). Albany, NY: Delmar.

Henry, M. E. (1993). *School cultures: Universes of meaning in private schools.* Norwood, NJ: Ablex.

Hess, F. M. (2001). Whaddya mean you want to close my school? The politics of regulatory accountability in charter schooling. *Education and Urban Society, 33*(2), 141–156.

Hogan, S. D., & Knight, H. (1988). *Successful planning for private schools: The administrator's guide.* Arlington, VA: Thornsbury Bailey & Brown.

Holcomb, J. H. (1993). *Educational marketing: A business approach to school–community relations.* Lanham, MD: University Press of America.

Holland, P. B. (1997a). Catholic school lessons for the public schools. *School Administrator, 54*(7), 24–26.

Holland, P. B. (1997b). The folly of public/parochial comparisons. *School Administrator, 54*(7), 28–31.

James, C., & Phillips, P. (1995). The practice of educational marketing in schools. *Educational Management and Administration, 23*(2), 75–88.

Reid, K. S., & Johnson, R. C. (2001, December 5). Public debates, private choices. *Education Week, 21*(14).

REFERENCES

Abella, M. (1989). The exciting world of public relations. *Momentum, 20*(1), 38–39.

Ausbrooks, C. Y. (2001, April). *How equal is access to charter schools?* Paper presented at the Annual Meeting of the American Educational Research Association, Seattle, WA.

Barbieri, R. (1991). Morality in marketing. In R. Cowan (Ed.), *The next marketing handbook for independent schools* (pp. 14–17). Boston: National Association of Independent Schools.

Broughman, S. P., & Colaciello, L. A. (1998). *Private school universe study, 1995–96.* U.S. Department of Education, National Center for Education Statistics. Washington, DC: U.S. Government Printing Office.

Broughman, S. P., & Colaciello, L. A. (1999). *Private school universe survey: 1997–98.* U.S. Department of Education, National Center for Education Statistics. Washington, DC: U.S. Government Printing Office.

Brouillette, M. J., & Williams, J. R. (1999). *The impact of school choice on school employee labor unions: Unionization rates among private, charter, and traditional government schools suggest reason for union opposition to school choice.* Midland, MI: Mackinac Center for Public Policy.

Bryk, A. S., Lee, V. E., & Holland, P. B. (1993). *Catholic schools and the common good.* Cambridge, MA: Harvard University Press.

Carroll, S. R., & Carroll, D. (2001). Outside-inside marketing. *School Administrator, 58*(7), 32–34.

Center for Education Reform. (2002). *Education reform update.* Retrieved June 10, 2002, from http://edreform.com/press/2001/010917.html.

Cheney, C. (1991). In other words. In R. Cowan (Ed.), *The next marketing handbook for independent schools* (pp. 36–44). Boston: National Association of Independent Schools.

Choy, S. P. (1997). *Public and private schools: How do they differ?* Findings from *"The Condition of Education, 1997."* Washington, DC: U.S. Government Printing Office.

Convey, J. J. (1991). Catholic schools in a changing society: Past accomplishments and future challenges. In *The catholic school and society.* Washington, DC: National Catholic Educational Association.

Cooper, B. (1984). The changing demography of private schools. *Education and Urban Society, 16*(4), 429–442.

Crawford, J., & Freeman, S. (1996). Why parents choose private schooling: Implications for public school programs and information campaigns. *ERS Spectrum, 14*(3), 9–16.

Epple, D., & Romano, R. E. (1998). Competition between private and public schools, vouchers, and peer-group effects. *American Economic Review, 88*(1), 33–62.

Friedman, M., & Friedman, R. (1981). *Free to choose.* New York: Avon Books.

Goldhaber, D. D. (1999). School choice: An examination of the empirical evidence on achievement, parental decision making, and equity. *Educational Researcher, 28*(9), 16–25.

Good, T. L., & Braden, J. S. (2000). Charter schools: Another reform failure or a worthwhile investment? *Phi Delta Kappan, 81*(10), 745–750.

Greeley, A. M., & McManus, W. (1987). *Catholic contributions: Sociology and policy.* Chicago: Thomas More Press.

Hanson, E. M. (1992). Educational marketing and the public schools: Policies, practices, and problems. *Educational Policy, 6*(1), 19–34.

Hill, P. T. (1996). The educational consequences of choice. *Phi Delta Kappan, 77*(10), 671–675.

Hilton, J. J. (1994). Local autonomy, educational equity, and school choice: Constitutional criticism of school reform. *New England Journal of Public Policy, 10*(1), 293–305.

Kelly, B. E., & Bredeson, P. V. (1991). Measures of meaning in a public and in a parochial school: Principals as symbol managers. *Journal of Educational Administration, 29*(3), 6–22.

Kowalski, T. J. (2003). *Contemporary school administration: An introduction* (2nd ed.). Boston: Allyn & Bacon.

Kowalski, T. J., & Swaringin, C. (1982, Spring). Measured differences in public and non-public elementary school teacher morale. *Private School Quarterly,* 25–32.

Larson, M. (1995). *Public and religious elementary school costs and programs.* Unpublished Ed.D. dissertation, Arizona State University.

Leahy, M. A. (1989). A new determination. *Momentum, 20*(3), 48–51.

Lieberman, M. (1986). *Beyond public education.* New York: Praeger.

Manno, B. V., Finn, C. E., & Vanourek, G. (2000). Beyond the schoolhouse door: How charter schools are transforming U.S. public education. *Phi Delta Kappan, 81*(10), 736–744.

McLaughlin, D. H., & Broughman, S. (1997). *Private schools in the United States: A statistical profile, 1993–94.* U.S. Department of Education, National Center for Education Statistics. Washington, DC: U.S. Government Printing Office.

McLaughlin, D. H., O'Donnell, C., & Ries, L. (1995). *Schools and staffing in the United States: A statistical profile, 1993–94.* U.S. Department of Education, National Center for Education Statistics. Washington, DC: U.S. Government Printing Office.

Meade, J. (1991). Keeping the faith. *Teacher Magazine, 3*(1), 34–36, 41–45.

Merz, C., & Frankel, S. S. (1997). School foundations: Local control or equity circumvented? *School Administrator, 54*(1), 28–31.

Newman, J. W. (1995). Comparing private schools and public schools in the 20th century: History, demography, and the debate over choice. *Educational Foundations, 9*(3), 5–18.

Paglin, C. (2001). Why charter schools stumble—and sometimes fall. *Northwest Education, 6*(3), 20–25.

Peshkin, A. (1986). God's choice: The total world of a Fundamentalist Christian School. *Educational Leadership, 43*(4), 36–41.

Raywid, M. A. (1995). Alternative schools: The state of the art. *Educational Leadership, 52*(1), 26–31.

Rist, M. C. (1991). Parochial schools set out to win their share of the market. *Executive Educator, 13*(9), 24.

Rothstein, R., Carnoy, M., & Benveniste, L. (1999). *Can public schools learn from private schools? Case studies in the public & private nonprofit sectors.* Washington, DC: Economic Policy Institute.

Simon, B. S. (2001). Family involvement in high school: Predictors and effects. *NASSP Bulletin, 85*(2), 8–19.

Smith, K. B., & Meier, K. J. (1995). School choice: Panacea or Pandora's Box? *Phi Delta Kappan, 77*(4), 312–316.

Smith, T. M. (1997). *The pocket condition of education, 1997.* Washington, DC: U.S. Government Printing Office.

Tarter, C. J., & Hoy, W. K. (1996). Toward a contingency theory of decision making. *Journal of Educational Administration, 36*(3 & 4), 212–228.

Vasallo, P. (2000). *More than grades: How choice boosts parental involvement and benefits children.* Policy Analysis No. 383. Washington, DC: Cato Institute.

Vergari, S. (1999). Charter schools: A primer on the issues. *Education and Urban Society, 31*(4), 389–405.

Viteritti, J. P. (1996). Stacking the deck for the poor. The new politics of school choice. *Brookings Review, 14*(3), 10–13.

Walford, G. (1996). Diversity and choice in school education: An alternative view. *Oxford Review of Education, 22*(2), 143–154.

Warner, C. (1994). *Promoting your school: Going beyond PR.* Thousand Oaks, CA: Corwin Press.

Witte, J. F. (1995). Three critical factors in the school choice debate. *Social Science Quarterly, 76*(3), 502–505.

Part III
Administrator Responsibilities

10

Planning in Public Relations
Setting Goals and Developing Strategies

Robert H. Beach

The forces impacting education have, over the past three decades, increased both in number and in scale. Differing cultural expectations for schools, a concern over violence, and the demand for school safety are examples of problems that now necessitate responses by school leaders—responses that were hardly national in scope 30 years ago. A superintendent in the 1960s often attended to the public relations needs of a small district by going to the Lions Club lunch, talking with people at the barber shop, and networking with community leaders. Although these classic methods are still valid, such an ad hoc approach would now be considered inadequate, especially if it constituted the total public relations program.

Issues of national diversity and safety, and of controversy surrounding other social problems, have reached even the small district. Consequently, effective school public relations should go beyond intuitive actions and focus on a coherently guided system for managing inter- and intradistrict information flows.

As education's problems have expanded and become more complex, the public relations efforts made by school administrators have had to expand. These broader efforts have required a more sophisticated and comprehensive perspective of school public relations, such as the one presented in this book. Within this perspective, planning assumes a central role in determining goals and prescribing strategies to achieve them.

Historically, emphasis on education planning was rudimentary, highly authoritative, and inflexible. But with social change, this rigid approach has proven to be less than successful. Over time, multiple planning theories have evolved and some have been quite successful. The dominant planning tool in use today is known generically as *strategic planning*, but it has multiple forms. From the early, overly structured attempts to control the planning process, modern versions of strategic planning now emphasize adherence to process, flexibility, and stakeholder involvement.

A sound approach to planning will assist in positioning the school to meet new issues prior to their becoming problematic. An effective public relations program can assist with that positioning. An effective planning-based public relations program will better prepare schools for a future that the district's public relations effort has helped shape.

PLANNING IN EDUCATION

Planning has long been considered a management function and, therefore, an area of interest for educational administrators. As a discipline, educational planning can trace its roots to the work of Simon (1955), who created a theory of planning known as *rationalism*. This theory views the organization as a highly rational entity that seeks a series of logically derived linear steps to a "best" solution. Today, rationalism is referred to as "traditional planning" and is the underlying structure for both long-range and strategic planning. Simon's theory, however, had several problems related to (a) a natural confusion between ends and means, (b) the organization's inability to produce truly rational outputs, (c) the inability to define a "best" solution, and (d) normal human limitations. As a result, a competing perspective, known as *incrementalism*, was proposed by Lindbloom (1959). Incrementalism accepts the organization as it is and, within this context, proposes accepting opportune increments to a loosely defined objective. But, it too was flawed; over time, the fuzziness related to processes and objectives subjects the organization to political activism and a loss of focus.

Yet another approach to planning grew out of the organizational development movement and related disciplines. It became known as the *goal-free* or *developmental* perspective and received attention in education as a result of the work of Clark (1981). Here the organization recognizes that an early focus on goals can lead to conflict; goals are therefore given attention only later in the planning process. The involvement of stakeholders has become an axiom of this planning approach. However, this theory also tends to suffer from ambiguity in process and goals.

Concerns for plan implementation and the readiness of the organization to undergo a proposed change process may be more important to success than a purist application of specific theories. In most change settings, one can simultaneously find applications for rationalism, incrementalism, and developmental approaches to planning (Beach, 1993).

Growth in district size (enrollment) elevated demands for accountability, and business methodology was adapted by many administrators to guide education planning. Although rational models were initially used, educators sought ways to operationalize more systematic approaches to shaping a positive future. Eventually, more rigid forms of strategic planning were employed. The primary difference between these two approaches is that long-range rational models are more internally focused and based on an extrapolation of trends from past organizational data. Strategic planning has an internal focus (trend analysis), but it also explores external issues (environmental scanning) with an analysis of their potential organizational impact (Howell, 2000). With time, strategic planning came under extensive criticism because of a perceived lack of adequate attention to the human aspect of planning. Such criticism has contributed to the infusion of developmental theory resulting in "softer" models of strategic planning. Now it is generally accepted that all planning theory can be relevant, regardless of which perspective one uses as a basic model: "mix and match" to suit each unique problem has become standard. Bryson (1999) noted that there must be a "willingness to be flexible regarding what constitutes a strategic plan" (p. xv).

The development of a public relations program involves several elements that are in the domains of educational planning and organizational change. Planning, as noted, is future oriented—seeking to achieve a better future than any anticipated. Change involves the institutionalization of planning products—the public relations management system or program. A traditional planning process begins with the goals of the system having been articulated in relation to the overall organization's vision and mission. At some point a problem set presents itself; this is simply the recognition, by individuals in the organization, that one or more issues needing resolution exist. Such awareness can occur in many ways, including tirades by irate citizens or a recognition derived from internal data analysis. Additional information is then developed relating to the problem set, the organization, outside forces, and similar factors. A search for potential solutions is initiated in conjunction with an examination of available resources and possible constraints or barriers. A solution is eventually selected and implementation initiated. Finally, an evaluation is conducted to determine the effectiveness of the process and preferred solution.

Two major problems have plagued educational planning at all levels. First, each division of a district or school tends to view public relations as the responsibility of someone else; many opportunities for productive planning and programming are lost as a result of this thinking (Cochran, Phelps, & Cochran, 1980). Although every group—teachers, administrators, and boards of education—agrees that effective planning is vital, each group thinks that the responsibility for planning rests elsewhere. Obviously, this viewpoint is counterproductive. Everyone in the school community has to work together to develop a common vision and plan. Networks of concerned citizens, internal and external to schools, should combine their efforts and resources to set future goals.

The second planning problem involves a reliance on top-down planning approaches. It has become clear that the "We'll tell you what you need to know" approach is no longer acceptable. Modern public relations programs, especially in public schools, encourage total school and community involvement.

The potential value of public relations is addressed by Kaufman and Herman (1991). They distinguished between "inside-out" and "outside-in" planning. Inside-out planning makes the organization the primary client, "as if one were looking from within the organization outside into the operational world where learners graduate, and where citizens live, play and work" (p. 7). Outside-in planning views society as the primary agent and beneficiary, "as if one were looking into the organization from outside, from the vantage point of society, back into the realm of organizational results and efforts" (p. 8). Kaufman and Herman indicated that the difference between the two perspectives is how one views the world. In the inside-out mode, the client (and beneficiary) is the organization; its survival and well-being will likely be paramount. The outside-in mode sees the basic client (and beneficiary) as society, and anything the school can or should contribute is identified and considered in that light. A comparison of "what is" may be made against "what should be" in order to determine what to keep and what to change (p. 9).

Educational leaders seeking to develop and legitimize a school system's public relations program should strongly consider a planning system that incorporates the following characteristics:

Simplicity: Most school systems simply do not have the resources to establish a full-time planning position. This being the case, an effective system will involve planners who hold other full-time professional positions. Time constraints will require a planning system that is simple, straightforward, and easily managed.

Visibility: An effective plan should establish both the purpose and underlying principles that ground a public relations program. Visibility should be a prime consideration in communicating key elements of the program and in shaping public expectations related to the public relations function.

Accountability: Outcomes of the plan should be tangible and measurable. Planning raises expectations that outcomes will be achieved. Planners must be sensitive to the need to visibly demonstrate planning outcomes.

Brevity: An effective plan should communicate with a wide variety of constituents. It should be succinct and to the point, with language and structure appropriate to a wide audience.

Gallagher, Bagin, and Kindred (1997) provided a planning checklist that suggests a way to determine where to go and how to get there in school public relations planning:

1. A legally adopted policy in school-community relations is indicated.
2. The larger goals and specific objectives of the program must be consistent with the philosophy of the school system and the laws of the state.
3. To the extent possible, the larger goals and specific objectives must be stated in measurable terms.
4. The strategies for attaining the objectives must involve members of various special publics when such involvement is feasible.
5. A distinction must be made in the plan between short- and long-term objectives.
6. The objectives of the school-community relations program must reflect an assessment of need or the gap discovered between what is and what should be.
7. The program must be planned and tailored to the nature of the school and the community with which it is identified.
8. The communication channels selected for disseminating various kinds of information must be appropriate for the audiences involved.
9. The program must involve a continuing audit of the results it produces.
10. Each individual having responsibility in the program must know exactly what he or she is trying to accomplish.
11. The plan must include guides for resolving issues of emotional and intellectual concern to members of the community.
12. To the extent possible, provision must be made in the plan for long-range inservice education of the staff.
13. Program strategies and activities must be adapted to available human resources, funds, and facilities. (pp. 47–48)

A workable planning format requires a projection of future trends and the development of a long-term vision for the program. Plans must be realistic and make sense to a wide variety of school constituents. These considerations suggest involving both members of the school family and members of the community in the planning process. Typically, a planning team should range between 15 and 25 people, at least half of whom represent the community. Teams should be broad enough to be representative, but not so large as to make consensus difficult. Membership of the typical planning team often includes central-office administrators, building administrators, teachers, and noncertified staff. Community representatives may include both parents and nonparents. Representatives may also reflect constituencies that have a strong vested interest in education: business, government, human services, ministerial, and industrial constituencies. The planning team is led by the school system administrator responsible for planning and typically includes the superintendent of schools. The superintendent's presence lends credibility and reinforces high priority for the public relations planning function.

Although it is unlikely that all planning team members will be experienced planners, it is desirable to select participants who have strong people skills and a commitment to working together. Staff development efforts can create an awareness of the major processes and issues in planning. In their research, Brown, Perry, and McIntire (1995) found that while "teachers and principals . . . desire significantly more participation by students, parents and community members . . . " educators must realize that "team building is a prerequisite. . . ." (p. 3). Individuals should be selected who can work toward consensus, which requires an ability to put aside individual biases and agendas and to base decisions on objective data.

STRATEGIC PLANNING

Strategic planning emerged in the 1980s but has roots in the rationalism movement that developed much earlier. Cook (1995) was a major figure in adapting this tool to educational use. He saw strategic planning as "the means by which an organization continually recreates itself toward extraordinary purpose" (p. 41). This planning methodology is presented here as a context for developing a public relations program in that a considerable body of literature and professional materials exist that can be used in supporting public relations planning efforts. However, it must be noted that this is only one tool among many and it is an elaborate tool for which consultant assistance might be needed. Also, many published materials present the topic as a very formal, rigid, and document-burdened model. As Black and Gregersen (2002) pointed out, "the eight mistakes, twelve steps, and so on offered by others about change are often correct in direction but overly complicated in reality" (pp. 8–9).

How does strategic planning differ from traditional planning and how can the process be utilized in the development of an effective public relations program? Strategic planning attempts to predict the external environment that the organization will have to deal with in order to accomplish its goals. Too often organizations focus inwardly and, thus, they fail to see outside their boundaries—a process that is essential to predicting the future. Strategic planning recognizes that significant change is likely to come from outside the organization. Few parallels can be drawn between traditional public relations programs and the current practice of having more involvement from people outside the organization (Ricks, 1992). Educators have too often assumed what the public wants or needs to know about schools rather than asking that public what it needs or desires.

Byars (1987) defined strategic planning as the process of clarifying the nature of the organization, making decisions about its future direction, and implementing such decisions. Organizations do not exist in a vacuum; rather, they exist in both internal and external environments that continually change. As Byars observed, strategic planning attempts to anticipate change over time, project the future, and develop organizational direction based on agreed-upon visions of what the future environment will look like. Public relations planners should use the same strategic process for clarifying the present, assessing future possibilities, deciding what should happen next, and implementing the plan.

Interest in planning has grown in virtually all segments of American society. Advocacy for its use in public education has been tied to school reform ideas, such as decentralized control. As strategic planning, where an awareness of the environment and of the importance of value differences and broadened participation are focal points, replaces traditional long-range planning, school public relations becomes the operational means to engage school employees, parents, and others in the community in the decision-making process.

Effective planning is associated with effective leadership. The leader who is committed to strategic thinking and planning understands the difference in the two processes. Fenwick English made the point that most practitioners get bogged down in activity and see planning as the doing as opposed to the thinking (Kaufman, 1992). Thinking "strategically" requires a mind-set different from that typical of many traditional planners: it requires flexibility as a key ingredient. The same shift in mind-set is needed in the development and implementation of a public relations program. Public relations involves much more than "informing the public." Effective public relations programs now reach out to parents, the community, businesses, and other constituencies for total involvement in planning, decision-making, and evaluation. Crowson (1998) has pointed out that considerable community support for schools can be an indirect product of participation strategies.

In order to plan strategically for public relations, one should recognize the unique properties of strategic planning: it links the purpose and beliefs of the organization to its goals over time; it requires a clear, collective understanding of internal and external environments as they presently exist and enables planners to objectively position the organization as future trends are projected; it projects a future based on the assumption that the internal and external environments continually change; it requires reaching out beyond the boundaries of the organization to identify the perceptions of external constituents; and finally, it involves an ongoing, continuous process of reshaping the direction of the organization so that it can effectively respond to change.

Kaufman (1992) cited six critical success factors for thinking and planning strategically: (a) being willing to move out of today's comfort zone to use new and broader limits for thinking, planning, doing, and evaluating; (b) distinguishing between ends and means by focusing on what, not how; (c) utilizing all three levels of results (mega, macro, and micro); (d) using an ideal vision as the underlying reason for planning without being limited by current restraints or naysayers; (e) developing objectives that will include measures that tell you what you have accomplished; and (f) defining "need" as a gap in results, not as insufficient resources, means, or methods.

THE STRATEGIC PLANNING PROCESS

In adopting a strategic planning process, an administrator should recognize that most school systems have limited planning resources, including time. Figure 10–1 illustrates a process that is straightforward, yet features the essential strategic planning steps. These seven steps include database development, strategic analysis, development of the strategic plan, capacity analysis, the finalized plan, action planning, and establishing an annual review.

When undertaking the following steps, take the opportunity to involve various stakeholders in the actual work processes. The developmental theorists believe that this has a powerful social benefit. Not only can this involvement help with simple labor concerns, it also becomes an opportunity for faculty and other groups to become familiar with the details of the organization. Most faculty do not have an understanding of the school at these levels. As individuals learn about the organization, there tends to develop a simultaneous growth in their personal understanding relative to how they fit within the school—an understanding that transcends a focus on just the teaching function and creates a perception of the individual's place in the whole.

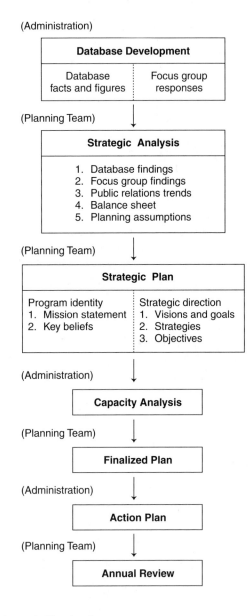

FIGURE 10–1
The Public Relations Strategic Planning Process

Step 1: Database Development

Bernhardt (1998) stated that "Data provide power . . . to make good decisions . . ." (p. xiii).
As you will note, the process recommended here is data based. As a first and ongoing step, the
school system's administration assembles hard data relative to the organization and its external environment. Database sources cited by Gallagher et al. (1997) and Kaufman and Her-

man (1991) suggest that strong emphasis be placed on assessing both the internal characteristics of the school system and external demographics. In addition, the authors recommended organizing community and school focus groups to better understand values, attitudes, and expectations regarding public relations. Focus groups may be organized by identifying constituent groups that interact with the schools and scan their respective memberships to identify each group's perception of the public relations function.

Three problems will present themselves at this point. The first relates to what data will be useful; the second is how best to collect this data in an ongoing fashion; and the third is how to engender unbiased responses to questions from participants. These concerns will be answered over time. If expertise is not available locally, then perhaps a local university or business partner can assist in this effort as part of service activity. Some expertise is required for minimizing concerns in these three areas and should, therefore, be worked through in advance.

Step 2: Strategic Analysis

Strategic analysis, the second step in the strategic planning process, represents the first activity of the planning team. Beginning with the assessment of the database and an analysis of focus group responses, planning team members develop findings for each category of data and each focus group's responses.

An analysis of data from both internal and external sources is undertaken to identify trends that will impact planning. Emphasis must be placed on reaching consensus through answering questions similar to the following:

1. Finding: What do the data show has occurred over time? Specific pieces of data are examined over a five-year period to identify trends.
2. Projected future: What do these data imply in a 3- to 5-year future? What future trends may be predicted?
3. Comments/qualifications: What scenarios/events may intervene to impact the data? What does the projected future assume and depend upon? (Ricks, with Carr & Buroker, 1991, p. 66)

Figure 10–2 illustrates a possible format for the results of a typical data analysis related to public relations.

Focus group activity within the community is a second data type that can be utilized. Data are gathered by asking open-ended questions of constituent groups and then extracting information on values, attitudes, and expectations reflective of the group response. Figure 10–3 presents output from an organized focus group response.

Obtaining unbiased responses can be a problem: in this case, one solution may be anonymous responses. This option is more plausible with technology. A local school computer laboratory can be used, when networked, to provide an anonymous response system for a small group. Proprietary software materials such as BlackBoard, Web CT, FrontPage, and others can be used to serve the same purpose with larger groups.

Database analysis serves two important purposes in the strategic planning process: it provides planners with a common understanding of the organization and suggests trends that must be planned for or planned around. In the typical district, most analysis can be done using desktop technology. Spreadsheet software such as Excel, Access, and PowerPoint, which can be found in almost all districts, can provide powerful analysis, data

Database: Demographics

Finding (summary)
A review of demographic data over a 5-year period reveals a dramatic decline in the percentage of families in the community with children in school. From a high of 31% in 1993, the 1998 data imply that only 22% of the district's families now have children in school: a 9% decline.

Projected future
This trend is projected to continue in the future as the population ages. It does not appear likely that younger families will immigrate into the district as a result of new business and industry expansion.

Comments and qualifications
Fewer families will have a direct stake in the educational process. This will lessen support for schools.

FIGURE 10–2
Output Format from an Analysis of Hard Data

Constituent group: Chamber of commerce
Question: What is the primary purpose of a school public relations program?

Response priority
1. Sell the public on the value of school
2. Keep the public informed about school events
3. Promote school levies or bond issues
4. Communicate about school life
5. Promote extracurricular athletics
6. Involve parents in school activities
7. Communicate school policy

Values and attitudes (summary)
Local businesspeople value public relations for a wide variety of reasons. Selling the public on the value of school—the number-one priority—reflects business's desire to support excellence. Attitudes are positive, with substantial support present for a public relations program.

Organizational expectations (summary)
The business community will expect a diverse, multifaceted approach to public relations to effectively market the schools to the community.

FIGURE 10–3
Output Format for an Analysis of Focus Group Responses

management and presentation tools that someone in the district will be able to use. More powerful software, such as SPSS (Statistical Package for the Social Sciences), will handle most districts' needs. Although a standard analysis tool, SPSS requires a greater level of knowledge to use and it is somewhat expensive.

After completion of the database analysis, planners examine public relations trends and the mandates imposed by federal regulations, the state department of education, or the local board. More specifically, planners identify trends related to the database, project action to be taken, estimate impacts on the organization, consider the probability of occurrence, and project trend duration. The potential impact upon planning decisions is also cited. Figure 10–4 illustrates a format for organizing the results of a typical trend analysis.

Once trends and mandates are analyzed, it is essential to monitor future directions and to reassess trend data over time. An analysis of important trends and mandates is followed by the development of an organizational balance sheet designed to assess organizational strengths and weaknesses. The balance sheet provides planners with the opportunity to classify certain key factors:

Trend   [X]   [X] National
Mandate [ ]   [ ] State

Description
Telecommunication holds promise for new methods of communicating with households. Public-access channels offer school systems an opportunity to better communicate with constituents.

Required action
Innovative programming suitable for a wide audience needs to be developed to effectively compete with commercial channels.

Impact
Low   X   High

Probability
Low   X   High

Duration (in years)
Short term   X   Long term
2   4   6   8   10

Potential planning impact

FIGURE 10–4
Format for an Analysis of Trends and Mandates

1. *Assets:* Advantages enjoyed over time and likely to continue in the future.
2. *Liabilities:* Temporary negative conditions that may be overcome in the short term.
3. *Barriers:* Disadvantages experienced over time and likely to continue in the future.
4. *Threats:* Predictable future conditions that may jeopardize the organization's capacity to meet its purposes.
5. *Favorable probabilities:* Future advantages the organization may exploit to strengthen its position. (Ricks, with Carr & Buroker, 1991, pp. 88–90)

Figure 10–5 illustrates an organization of these factors into a typical balance sheet.

A final step in strategic analysis involves the development of planning assumptions. A *planning assumption* is a simple statement predicting a future condition that will need to be planned for or planned around. It is not a goal or action statement that addresses how a problem will be met. A planning assumption is a predicted condition, usually identified by examining data over time and projecting how related external and internal variables may impact future data. Examples of planning assumptions are given below:

Data: Five-year data trends show that the number of families in the community without children is increasing.

Assumption: There may be some erosion in future support for schools.

Data: Demographic data and projections indicate a stable population base with insignificant population in-migration.

Assumption: There may be little change or a slight decline in the number of children entering school in the future.

Data: Economic data project the slow growth of new industry in the community.

<table>
<tr><td colspan="2" align="center">*Present*</td></tr>
<tr><td>*1. Assets*

Financial support has been and will be present to support a public relations program.</td><td>*2. Liabilities*

A lack of public relations expertise exists in the school system.

3. Barriers

Historically, some segments of the public have been resistant to supporting a public relations plan.</td></tr>
<tr><td colspan="2" align="center">*Future*</td></tr>
<tr><td>*5. Favorable probabilities*

Technological advances in communications will open new awareness to better communication with the public.</td><td>*4. Threats*

Educational restructuring may demand resources that might otherwise support public relations efforts.</td></tr>
</table>

FIGURE 10–5
A Typical Balance Sheet

Assumption: There may be some improvement in the tax base supporting the schools.

Data: National and state data indicate a dropping birth rate.

Assumption: Competition for state educational dollars may be reduced.

Step 3: Development of the Strategic Plan

Completion of the strategic analysis phase leads planners to the development of the actual plan. The plan consists of two components: identifying the program and determining a strategic direction.

Developing the Program Identity.   Development of a program identity serves to establish both the purpose of and the key beliefs about the public relations function. This process is essential in establishing the program in that it serves to shape the expectations of the school's public and to set parameters that will guide in developing the strategic direction. Establishing an effective program requires a sustained effort on the part of the organization to communicate both the program's purpose and its key guiding principles to all involved. The development of a program mission statement and a belief system provide the primary communication channels in this process.

The development of a clear, concise *mission statement* is essential for organizational planning. A mission statement should be structured in a fashion that will maximize its impact on both the members of the organization and its external constituents. The following guidelines should be observed in developing an organizational mission statement:

1. Keep the statement as brief as possible. An effective mission statement should not exceed one or two paragraphs, and should provide guidance for a sense of organizational purpose and direction, a definition of operational scope, resource allocation parameters, and a foundation for strategic goals and objectives.
2. Use language that is understandable to the constituencies being addressed. The mission statement should be readily understood by members of the organization and to the people external to it.
3. Make sure the mission statement contains all required elements. Check the statement to see that it captures all dimensions of the organization.
4. Design and construct the statement for widespread dissemination. The statement should appear throughout the organization and should be predominantly displayed through organizational publications and posted in public areas.

A sample mission statement is found in Figure 10–6.

The development of a *belief system* represents a second step in clarifying the identity of the program. The primary purpose of a belief system is to establish the relationship between the program and its employees, clients, and external constituents. A belief system meets this purpose by establishing values and philosophies that provide the parameters for the way the program operates in practice. It serves to define the culture of the program while setting expectations for conduct. It also provides basic premises around which policies, rules, and regulations are developed.

The public relations program of the Ashtown Community School is intended to involve, educate, and inform parents and community of the school system's purposes, program, and activities. Through the program, the public will develop greater understanding and insight into the schools, which will lead to greater appreciation of the school's contribution to the community. The program is structured to offer greater opportunity for expanded school communication to ensure community input in school activity.

FIGURE 10–6
Sample Mission Statement

Effective public relations requires two-way communication between the school and community.

FIGURE 10–7
One Tenet of a Belief System

Beliefs serve as constants as the program responds to internal and external challenges. The strength of the program is established through actualization of the school's belief system. In developing a belief system, the program should be described as it is, as well as the way it aspires to be. The belief system cannot be imposed on the organization externally but rather should be articulated from the traditions that are held within the organization itself.

The belief system should set clear expectations *for the behavior of all who interact with the program.* The behavior of employers toward all individuals should maintain an underlying consistency.

Typically, programs are encouraged to build their belief systems on a maximum of 10 major tenets. Keep it simple and clear. Shared belief systems are a basic element in school culture and will take time to emerge. A typical tenet is illustrated in Figure 10–7.

Determining the Strategic Direction. A second activity in the development of a strategic plan is a goal-setting process; this involves drafting strategic visions, establishing strategic goals, devising strategies, and setting measurable objectives. The process relies on information found in the database and conclusions drawn through strategic analysis. Information from both of these sources must be continually referenced throughout the goal-setting process.

The identity established for the program is equally important to the process. All outcomes of the strategic goal-setting process must be congruent with previously developed elements that define the organization's identity. In the strategic planning process, each step builds on previous steps and moves sequentially in establishing and defining a direction for the organization.

The first task in determining strategic direction is the development of strategic vision statements that predict the future environmental conditions to which the program must respond in meeting its purposes. A vision statement should be framed to address both

Population trends in the nation and in our service area will continue to show an increase in the percentage of families without school-age children. Families of this type have less vested interest in participating.

FIGURE 10–8
A Strategic Vision Statement

The school system shall place increased emphasis on keeping those without school-age children well informed about the schools, their programs, and their importance to the community.

FIGURE 10–9
Sample Strategic Goal

desired educational outcomes and the conditions that must be met if the program is to retain its capacity to meet its purposes. An example of a vision statement is provided in Figure 10-8.

Most strategic plans feature four to seven vision statements. Because vision statements drive the plan's development, it is necessary to limit them to what is deemed most significant to the program.

Once strategic visions are formed and adopted, they are directly linked to the purposes of the program through the development of goals. Strategic goals constitute a broad general future for the program based as they are on projections of variables that will impact the program's future. Each goal should clearly indicate a priority direction for the organization that is based on the vision statements. A sample strategic goal is given in Figure 10–9.

Historically, a superintendent could establish the goals for a district's public relations program simply by decree. Largely due to changes in the way we perceive organizations, this is now a sure way to doom any planning effort in just about any large, especially public, organization. Examples of this are easy to find. Assume an administrator does, in fact, set a goal for a public relations program such as *increase public receptivity to higher fiscal support for the school district*. This, of course, is read as *higher taxes*. Teachers are members of the community—that is, the public. If the teachers do not agree with raising taxes, improved salary and working conditions aside, then the goal comes into conflict with the beliefs of some of the very people who will be involved with its successful attainment. When asked by other members of the community if new funding really is needed, some teachers will present an individual perspective, perhaps masked by other issues—"not if they would stop spending on those computers"—which is at variance with district efforts. An important and needed goal can become a source of contention within the school itself and within the community.

Goals are better established by a process of articulation where the teachers and other members of the organization and community (stakeholders) have input into their formulation. It is difficult to move an educational institution to a place where it does not wish to go. If a goal is important for an organization, yet does not arise naturally from within the stakeholder group, then it may be that time must be given by the administration to preplan. This is simply a term for improving stakeholders' understanding of the organization. Why are new moneys required, how will this improve instruction, how will the children benefit, and so on? This process can be undertaken by creating task forces that focus on a problem; problem investigation and solution build a stronger understanding of the institution among task force participants.

An additional problem can be associated with goal formation: a beautiful solution is stated, but no goal. Take, for example, the goal *establish better relationships with the press*. This looks like a natural, even required goal, but it is not. It is one means (solution) to some other goal, perhaps the fiscal support goal above. Better press relationships are necessary for some larger end. This is end-means confusion and a pit that even experienced planners fall into. The goal is the end; the solution strategy is the means of achieving the end. When solutions are substituted for goals, the process of finding better alternatives is truncated and unexplored, with many potentially better solutions overlooked. Consider a teacher who has the goal of obtaining a new text for a reading class. The text is, of course, a means to better student reading performance. Other methods of reading improvement, such as a pull-out program, are not examined when the textbook "goal" is accepted.

In any serious program there usually will be more than one goal. In addition, because goals tend to be of a general nature, a greater degree of specificity must be supplied. This is done by establishing objectives in support of each goal, as noted, thus creating a cascade or hierarchy from goals to objectives. Objectives are usually stated in performance terms. Figure 10–10 shows an illustration of two objectives related to a goal.

The goal and objectives illustrated in Figure 10–10 should have been developed through a process of problem articulation, data generation and analysis, and a search for

---

Problem: The print media publishes articles related only to district problems.

Goal A: Increase the number of publicized columns that present district achievements and successes.

Objective 1:
Within 3 months have established a file on each major local print media provider and subfiles within each to include the name, address, phone numbers, topical areas of interest, etc., for each educational correspondent and reporter.

Objective 2:
Within 6 months ensure that 90% of the local print media's educational correspondents and reporters have met personally the district's public relations officer.

FIGURE 10–10
A Goal-Objective Hierarchy

What is our organization doing now?
The school district currently sends a newsletter to citizens of the school system featuring school programs.

What are the deficits of our current activity?
Many residents do not read the newsletter because they do not perceive school news to be important to them.

What needs to occur to overcome deficits?
The readership base of the newsletter needs to be significantly expanded.

Strategy
The district newsletter shall be expanded to include other information of vital community interest as a means of expanding the readership base.

FIGURE 10–11
The Strategy Development Process

By 1997, the school system shall effectively communicate information about district programs to 60% of all families without children in school.

FIGURE 10–12
Sample Objective

alternative solutions. This latter element, developing alternative solution strategies, requires specific attention.

Each goal should be linked by one or more strategies that, in turn, shape the objectives that define component activities related to the goal. In forming strategies, the organization concentrates on identifying alternative actions that hold promise for maximizing the organization's likelihood of reaching its goals. Strategy formulation may be accomplished by addressing the sequence of questions shown in Figure 10–11.

Problems can arise in many ways. They may come "out of the woodwork," be the result of a review of instructional test scores or other data analyses, or in a public relations program, may arise from reflections on what must be accomplished in meeting the institution's public relations goals. In the last case, there will be a series of linked problems, each requiring a solution. The linking of individual problems and their solutions ultimately becomes the program itself. Solving these problems requires the development of a set of possible solutions and choosing the "best" solution for each problem.

Strategies are alternatives the organization selects to best enable it to meet its objectives. These objectives are most often programmatic aspects of the total organizational effort, constituting the substance of what it will take to make the projected future a reality (Ricks, with Carr & Buroker, 1991).

Objectives should be measurable and feature a clearly defined time frame (See Figure 10–12). Typical time frames for objectives are from 1 to 5 years.

Projecting time lines and establishing ways to measure the achievement of objectives involve a "best guess" consideration of how effective the previously developed strategy will be in driving the desirable programmatic outcome. In setting objectives, you have to project the impact of the strategy you will apply in shaping both standards for measuring success and projected time lines.

Step 4: Capacity Analysis

Prior to a final adoption of the strategic plan, consideration must be given as to whether or not the organization has adequate resources to carry it out. To this end the organization is charged with the responsibility of conducting a capacity analysis to determine the plan's viability.

The capacity analysis is a preliminary examination of the ability of the organization to support plan objectives. "Capacity" comprises two elements. *Fiscal requirements* are defined as the amount of money needed over time to accomplish each objective. *Human requirements* are an estimate of the personnel required to conduct plan activities. Each variable should be projected for each objective (Ricks, with Carr & Buroker, 1991). Figure 10–13 represents a typical capacity analysis.

Close attention to capacity analysis is critical if credibility is to be preserved. Planning raises expectations in the community and in the schools. Credibility is damaged if the organization does not have the capacity to move its public relations plan forward. Consequently, failing to conduct capacity analysis properly can result in serious problems after planning.

Step 5: Action Planning

Each adopted objective in the strategic plan should be finalized and forwarded for action planning to the administrator responsible for public relations. Action planning consists of identification, in chronological order, of activities that must be initiated to satisfy the objective. Prior to initiating an action plan, the administrator in charge should carefully examine the vision statement, goal, and strategy related to each objective. The action plan should be consistent with both the vision statement and the goal and should directly reflect the strategies around which the objective is based.

The development of action plans can be accomplished through the steps outlined in Figure 10–14. Each step included represents a specific activity taken over the course of approximately 1 year of the planning cycle. Evaluation of the cycle will drive an annual review of objectives requiring more than 1 year of activity.

Step 6: Establishing a Planning Cycle

To maximize the effectiveness of a public relations strategic plan, the planning process should be ongoing. Unlike more traditional long-range plans, the components of a strategic plan are considered dynamic. As the future unfolds, they must be revisited, readjusted, and updated. Changes in both the internal and external environments over

Goal
The school system shall place increased emphasis on keeping those without school-age children informed about schools, their programs, and their importance to the community.

Objective
By 1999, the school system shall effectively communicate information about district programs to 60% of all families without children in school.

Anticipated activity

1. Evaluate newsletter content
2. Assess public views and needs
3. Reformat newsletters
4. Bid graphics/printing
5. Assemble mailing list

Anticipated outcome

Fiscal requirements

Supplies	$ 5,000.00	Reallocated	50%
Equipment/printing	$120,000.00	Reallocated	65%
Personnel	$ 53,000.00	Reallocated	100%
Construction	$_____	Reallocated	____%
Maintenance	$_____	Reallocated	____%
Total cost	$178,000.00	Total new monies $47,550.00	

Human resources

Director John Doe   % time 100%

Other participants (describe)   Secretary 100%

                                          Newsletter editor 25%

% workday   2–100% Estimated additional cost $15,000

                 1–25%

FIGURE 10–13
Capacity Analysis

time require flexibility. An annual planning cycle is necessary to ensure that the plan becomes a part of the culture of the public relations program.

In establishing an annual planning cycle, it is considered most desirable to annually reconvene the original planning team to review progress on the plan and to reconsider its viability in the face of changing conditions. Figure 10–15 presents a simple flowchart illustrating the annual planning cycle. The figure illustrates a cycle that features flexibility in promoting termination, modification, or regeneration of objectives on an annual basis. Through this configuration, the plan becomes dynamic over time as changes in the environment will result in restructuring activity each year.

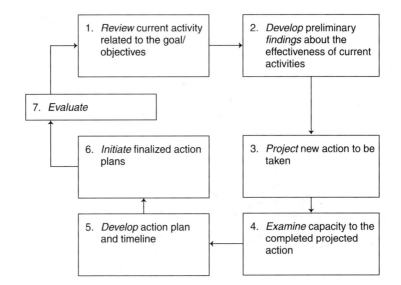

FIGURE 10–14
Steps in Developing an Action Plan

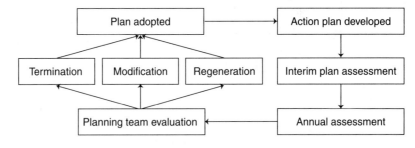

FIGURE 10–15
Annual Planning Cycle

PITFALLS WHEN PLANNING

Even though the strategic planning system presented in this chapter is intended to provide planners with a simple, straightforward tool, users should be aware of pitfalls that may be encountered in its implementation. Even the best-planned efforts may become bogged down unless careful attention is given to avoid the following problems:

1. *Overreliance on data*—Databases utilized in strategic planning should be designed to lead to the identification of general conditions that must be planned for or planned around. Adding extensive, detailed information to databases may not contribute to drawing accurate generalizations and may, in effect, bog down planners in trivia.

2. *Compromised analysis*—Planners often differ in their perceptions of what major priorities ought to be. All too often competing views may be adopted in the same plan because of the planner's inability to reach consensus. When this happens, plans soon proliferate and often exceed the capacity of the organization to complete.

3. *Strained resources*—Planners are urged to consider the importance of tailoring the scope of plans to available resources. Resources include faculty and staff time. Exceeding available resources will lead to unmet objectives and goals and, as a consequence, unmet public expectations.

4. *Failure to consider mandates*—Educational reform often leads to mandates for change outside the control of local planners. Failure to project such mandates and incorporate them appropriately in plans may lead to overextension and competition for resources.

5. *Overly complex language*—Overly complex language may take several forms. Extensive use of "educationese" (complicated language understood only by educators) will confuse readers. Complex sentence structure and long, wordy sentences will discourage careful reading (Ricks, 1992).

6. *Assumptions about the future*—The future is not fixed. It can change in an instant and assumptions made from trend analysis and environmental scanning can become invalid within months or even within a shorter time period. The pace of change may outpace projections and may be sufficiently complex so that it is not predictable with any precision. Be flexible and alert (Napier, Sanaghan, Sidle, & Saraghan, 1997, p. 14).

7. *Assumptions about citizens*—Just because citizens desire involvement in school affairs does not mean that they will be willing to participate and independently seek relations with the school (Snowden & Gorton, 2002, p. 239).

Careful consideration of the pitfalls outlined above will help ensure a timely planning process that will generate a high-utility product.

SUMMARY

Public relations is an often overlooked but very important component of any successful organization. School systems have not given it enough attention because of the lack of resources, knowledge, or skill levels—or because of failure to realize the impact that a good public relations program can have on the employees, clients, and external constituents. Boards of education and superintendents, because of the attention being given to education by the media, much of which is negative, have begun to focus on better ways of communicating with the public.

The development of a public relations program requires careful planning that not only takes into account current activities in the organization, but also focuses on the future. It is important to understand the community both internally and externally, as it now exists, but it is just as important to project the future environment that will have to be dealt with in order for the organization to meet its purpose. The image of the organization can be significantly enhanced through an effective and efficient public relations program.

Even at a time when educators are expected to do more with less, a public relations strategy will be invaluable to a school district. It is not a matter of whether one is needed, but rather a matter of getting started, moving forward in explaining to the constituents, employees, and clients where the system is, where it wants to go, and how it expects to get there. A positive image takes time, resources, and effort to establish, but the dividends are endless.

CASE STUDY

A Cold Night . . . Getting Colder

Ira Hoskins, standing by his window in a cold sweat, had just returned from a very hot board meeting. It was cold outside. A light rain was falling and the mist was beginning to rise. For the first time in his superintendency he had been threatened with a revocation of his contract. Marshal had expressed his belief that the failure of the county to raise the half-cent sales tax for the school district was Ira's fault. Marshal had said it was "a direct result of the superintendent's lackadaisical approach to getting people behind the district's efforts." But Ira felt that he had kept on top of this.

The intercom buzzed and Alice said that Bill Watson was on the phone. Ira picked up the phone, "Hi, Bill, quite a board meeting."

Bill responded, "Ya, well Ira, I just wanted to let you know that I'm 110% with you on this."

"Thanks, Bill," Ira responded, "any suggestions?"

"Well, things can't go on the way they are now. It's just a matter of time before the board will act and, well, when that begins to happen, even I will have to side with the majority—but I know you'll get things cleaned up. And remember, we can go back to the commission in 6 months, so you have a good shot at this. Got to go, Ira."

"Thanks, Bill," and Ira punched off.

Ira felt he had made many contacts within the community, even to the point of being out of the house four nights a week. Things were okay at the *Dispatch*. Mabel Blane, at the paper, called Ira whenever questions on school issues were being covered. True, they had printed Pete Johnston's comment that the real problem in the district was the "pigheaded nature of the county commission and a lack of gray matter on the part of the older elements in the community," which, when coming from the principal of the district's newest school, was not as helpful as it might have been. With the families having kids in school down to 20% and about 35% of the community's citizens being older than 65, this comment had created quite a flurry. Still, the *Tribune* and the two TV stations rarely covered stories about the district. Ira had formed a PR task force just after this incident, and they had been charged with providing his office with suggestions for improving community relations. They had come up with two or three good ideas.

Well, with Henry and Mary supporting Marshal and with Bill moving to the middle of the road, things looked as bleak as the outside weather. Thinking of his new principal who had become well known in PR circles, Ira checks his rotary file and dials your number.

QUESTIONS AND SUGGESTED ACTIVITIES

CASE STUDY

1. What seems to be the central problem for this district?
2. How would you proceed to change the PR planning process in the district?
3. What PR goals and objectives would you develop for the district?
4. In response to Ira's call, what will you tell him about the problem?

CHAPTER

5. Why is it important to scan the environment when planning strategically?
6. What are the four characteristics of a good planning model?
7. Assume that you are a superintendent of a district with 3,500 students. Who would you involve in the public relations planning process?
8. Discuss potential barriers that may prevent school administrators from properly planning a public relations program. What actions can be taken to overcome these barriers?
9. What problems might occur if capacity analysis is not completed?
10. What is a mission statement?

SUGGESTED READINGS

Bradford, R. W., & Duncan, J. P. (2000). *Simplified strategic planning: A no-nonsense guide for busy people who want results fast.* Worcester, MA: Chandler House Press.

Corrado, F. (1993). *Getting the word out: How managers can create value with communications.* Homewood, IL: Business One Irwin.

Fearn-Banks, K. (1995). *Crises communications: A casebook approach.* Mahwah, NJ: Erlbaum.

Grunig, L., & Grunig, J. (Eds.). (1991). *Public relations research annual* (Vol. 3). Hillsdale, NJ: Erlbaum.

Long-range planning manual for board members. (1993). Frederick, MD: Aspen Publishers.

Peccolo, D., Dlugosh, L., & Sybouts, W. (1997). What makes strategic planning work. *Planning and Changing, 28,* 246–253.

Simsek, H. (1997). Paradigm shift and strategic planning: Planning and management in a turbulent decade. *Educational Planning, 10*(3), 21–35.

Stone, N. (1995). *The management and practice of public relations.* London: Macmillan.

Tucker, K., Derelian, D., & Rouner, D. (1997). *Public relations writing: An issue-driven behavioral approach.* Englewood Cliffs, NJ: Prentice Hall.

REFERENCES

Beach, R. (1993). Emerging perspectives on planning and change processes. *Journal of School Leadership, 3,* 646–665.

Bernhardt, V. (1998). *Data analysis for comprehensive schoolwide improvement.* Larchmont, NY: Eye on Education.

Black, J. S., & Gregersen, H. B. (2002). *Leading strategic change: Breaking the brain barrier*. New York: Prentice Hall.

Brown, D., Perry, C., & McIntire, W. (1995). Parents, students, community members: Teachers and administrators desire their increased participation in making educational decisions. *Journal of Educational Relations, 16*(4), 2–8.

Bryson, J. M. (1999). *Strategic management in public voluntary service: A reader*. New York: Pergamon.

Byars, L. (1987). *Strategic management: Planning and implementation*. New York: Harper & Row.

Clark, D. (1981). In consideration of goal-free planning: The failure of traditional planning systems in education. *Educational Administrative Quarterly, 17*(3), 42–60.

Cochran, L., Phelps, L., & Cochran, L. (1980). *Advisory committees in action*. Boston: Allyn & Bacon.

Cook, W. (1995). *Strategic planning for America's schools*. Arlington, VA: American Association for School Administrators.

Crowson, R. (1998). *School-community relations, under reform*. Berkeley, CA: McCutchan.

Gallagher, D., Bagin, D., & Kindred, L. (1997). *The school and community relations*. Boston: Allyn & Bacon.

Howell, E. (2000). *Strategic planning for a new century: Process over product* (Report No. EDO-JC-00-08). Los Angeles, CA: ERIC Clearinghouse for Community Colleges. (ERIC Document Reproduction Service No. ED447842.)

Kaufman, R. L. (1992). *Mapping educational success: Strategic thinking and planning for school administrators*. Newbury Park, CA: Corwin Press.

Kaufman, R. L., & Herman, J. (1991). *Strategic planning in education: Rethinking, restructuring, revitalizing*. Lancaster, PA: Technomic.

Lindbloom, C. E. (1959). The science of muddling through. *Public Administration Review, 19*, 79–88.

Napier, R., Sanaghan, P., Sidle, C., & Saraghan, P. (1997). *High impact tools and activities for strategic planning: Creative techniques for facilitating your organization's planning process*. New York: McGraw-Hill Trade.

Ricks, J. (1992). Strategic planning. In J. Kaiser (Ed.), *Educational administration* (pp. 151–182). Mequon, WI: Stylex.

Ricks, J. (with Carr, P., & Buroker, C.). (1991). Strategic planning for schools: A manual designed for school district organizational planning. In *Record in Educational Administration and Supervision*. Dayton, OH: Wright State University.

Simon, H. A. (1955). A behavioral model of rational choice. *Quarterly Journal of Economics, 69*, 99–118.

Snowden, P., & Gorton, R. (2002). *School leadership and administration*. (6th ed.) New York: McGraw-Hill.

11

Working With the Media

Theodore J. Kowalski

A 1997 report by Public Agenda, a nonpartisan public-opinion research firm, confirmed that administrators were very displeased with the quality of press coverage being given to public education (Batory, 1999). This general perception helps explain why district and school officials usually view working with the media to be an unpleasant assignment. The following are other factors that contribute to apprehensiveness.

1. Administrators often do not have a positive relationship with reporters assigned to cover schools—a condition that leads them to see journalists as adversaries.
2. Reporters typically seek information under negative circumstances; that is, they come knocking on a superintendent's or principal's door after a serious problem or conflict has surfaced. Interaction with reporters under these conditions almost always places the administrator in a defensive posture.
3. Reporters covering schools often have little understanding of the professional and political dimensions of school administration. Those who lack this knowledge tend to view superintendents and principals as bureaucrats—managers intent on blocking the flow of information.
4. Efforts by administrators to produce positive stories have often been rebuffed by reporters antagonistic toward public officials attempting to engage in public relations. These reporters have tended to define public relations narrowly as attempts to create or overstate positive information and to restrict or conceal negative information (Spicer, 1997).
5. Most administrators know little or nothing about journalism and journalists. Colleagues who have had disagreeable experiences with reporters in the past are often the primary source of information for new administrators about media relations.

Over the past few decades, books and journal articles have encouraged practitioners to reconsider their attitudes about working with reporters and about the value of having schools in the media spotlight. From a professional perspective, administrators are taught that public schools should be open organizations accessible to all segments of the community being served. Blocking media access to district employees is clearly incongruous with this belief.

Pragmatically, maintaining a positive relationship with reporters is likely to reduce tensions that surround unpleasant situations when administrators must respond to intense criticism or a crisis situation (Polansky & Montague, 2001). The advice that administrators should place and keep schools in the news is predicated on the following conditions pervasive in an information-based society:

1. The public demands accurate, complete, and timely information about governmental agencies.
2. In the current school reform environment, administrators need to introduce and explain improvement initiatives to the public.
3. Nearly two decades of intense criticism make it imperative that administrators are able to build public confidence and support.

Wallace (1990) noted that everyone benefits when education business is dealt with forthrightly and candidly. Proper information exchanges with the community, he concluded, are far more likely to occur when school officials have developed both a positive disposition toward the media and a relations program for working with reporters. More specifically he urges three objectives:

1. Administrators should establish realistic expectations of the media.
2. Media relations should be personalized so that school officials know the reporters who are assigned to cover them.
3. Administrators should maintain some control over access to the media and messages that are transmitted. This means that administrators generate stories as well as responding to media inquiries.

This chapter addresses organizational and personal decisions related to media relations. Two goals frame the discussion. First, the intent is to identify ways that administrators can take advantage of the media to enhance the image and effectiveness of districts and schools. Second, the intent is to identify ways that administrators can be better prepared to react to potentially threatening situations when the media is demanding data and comments.

ORGANIZATIONAL DECISIONS

The term *media relations* refers to the patterns of communication that occur between organization members and media personnel (Ridgway, 1996). Working without a media relations plan is like tightrope walking; administrators have to make spontaneous decisions about what to communicate and how to communicate. The result is usually inconsistent, unpredictable, and largely negative interactions (Gonring, 1997).

A Media Relations Plan

An organization's media relations plan should be shaped by four basic considerations (Gonring, 1997):

1. *Organizational purpose*—Why does the organization exist? Purpose raises questions about the organization's value to society. In the case of schools, the overarching purpose is to provide an essential service.
2. *Ownership*—Who owns the organization? In the case of schools, ownership is either public or private. This consideration is especially pertinent to determining the extent to which the organization is expected to interact with the publics being served.
3. *Media interest in the organization*—To what extent does the media seek to report on the organization? In the case of schools, interest is typically high. This variable prompts administrators to think about circumstances that cause media interest to fluctuate.
4. *Organizational expectations*—What does the organization hope to accomplish by interacting with the media? In the case of schools, building a positive image, producing political support, and securing economic resources are almost always cogent objectives.

In order to develop a plan, administrators must know the district or school public relations goals, the relevant publics that should receive information, and the resources available to support media relations.

The formation of a media relations plan is enhanced when the following attributes are present:

◆ *Direction:* The district or school has a policy that provides parameters for the plan's goals and strategies. As an example, policy should detail expectations regarding the exchange of information between the organization and its multiple publics.
◆ *Clarity:* The plan is written in language readily understood by those affected.
◆ *Unity:* The plan is an extension of a more comprehensive public relations plan to ensure that interactions with media personnel are connected to more global communication and information management objectives.
◆ *Sponsorship:* The plan is supported and approved by the superintendent and school board.

The relationship between the basic considerations and these attributes is shown in Figure 11–1.

Basic considerations

Organization type   **Ownership**

Key attributes

Direction—Plan is guided by policy.

Clarity—Plan is written in unambiguous language.

Unity—Plan is an extension of the district PR plan.

Sponsorship—Plan is supported by the school board.

Media interest   **Organizational expectations**

FIGURE 11–1
Media Relations Plans: Considerations and Attributes

Since contextual variables differ from school to school, simply adopting a successful media relations plan developed by another institution is not advisable. This is because an innovation's success is attributable to the circumstances under which it was developed and implemented as well as the innovation itself (Fullan, 1999). Therefore, you should not assume that a plan proven to be highly effective in one setting would be equally successful in another. In the case of districts and schools, internal (philosophy, goals) and external (local media, community needs and wants) conditions are rarely the same; the presence of even small differences can determine if a media relations plan will produce its intended results.

Although there is no universally effective recipe for media relations, effective plans usually include several basic procedures (see Figure 11–2).

◆ A *needs assessment* is a process used to identify gaps between ideal and real practices related to dealing with the media. For example, school officials want more positive than negative media coverage. As part of a needs assessment, articles are collected, sorted, and quantified so that the gap between the ideal and real conditions can be quantified.

◆ *Problem identification and analysis* is a process used to make judgments about identified needs. Assume that 65% of the media stories about a school were negative over the past year. Obviously, the school district has not achieved its goal of generating more positive than negative articles. At this stage, administrators seek to determine whether problems (e.g., lack of voter support for a tax referendum) resulted from not having achieved the ideal and to estimate the effects of those problems.

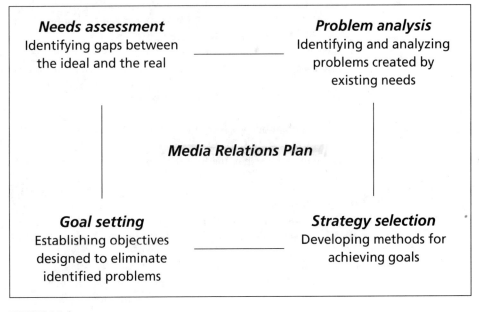

Needs assessment
Identifying gaps between
the ideal and the real

Problem analysis
Identifying and analyzing
problems created by
existing needs

Media Relations Plan

Goal setting
Establishing objectives
designed to eliminate
identified problems

Strategy selection
Developing methods for
achieving goals

FIGURE 11–2
Basic Elements of a Media Relations Plan

TABLE 11–1

Key Questions for Developing a Media Relations Plan

Question	Relevance
What has been the history of media relations?	Discovering the past so that ideal and real performance can be compared
What media have a primary interest in the schools?	Identifying the media that have the most contact with the greatest impact on schools
Which journalists are assigned to cover schools?	Identifying reporters who have the most contact with and greatest impact on schools
What messages need to be delivered?	Setting goals based on identified needs
What are the interests and goals of the targeted media?	Selecting strategies that maximize opportunities for desired coverage
What do targeted media deem as newsworthy?	Informing staff of the areas that are likely to receive coverage
Who will assume management of the plan?	Identifying one individual who assumes overall responsibility for implementation and who serves as a resource person to other administrators
Who will receive or use the media relations plan?	Ensuring that the plan is written appropriately for those who use and are affected by it
How often will the plan be revised?	Ensuring that the plan is evaluated and that goals and strategies are revised periodically

♦ *Goal setting* entails replacing, reaffirming, or modifying existing objectives to increase the probability that identified needs could be met in the next year. In the district where two-thirds of the media stories over the past year were negative; for instance, administrators may decide to add the goal of producing at least one positive story monthly over the course of the next year.

♦ *Strategy development* focuses on prescribing actions and behaviors intended to enhance goal attainment. For instance, what actions are recommended to ensure that one positive story will be produced each month? Key questions surrounding the plan's development are listed in Table 11–1.

The philosophy and biases of the planners affect both media relationship goals and role expectations for those responsible for executing the plan. Thus, it is imperative for planners to recognize that media relations plans ought to serve the needs of three clients:

1. The district or school
2. The print and electronic media
3. The publics served by the media and schools (Kosmicki & Bona, 1996)

Without a plan, administrators may not treat the media as well as they treat the school board or the general public. Yet, the media often influence public opinion because reporters and editors can shape and control information (Gonring, 1997).

A well-conceived media relations plan should benefit every district administrator because it contains needs, problem statements, goals, and strategies. Updated local, regional, and state media lists should be developed as an appendix to the plan. This information can be used both to initiate and to respond to media contacts. Properly designed and implemented, the plan serves organizational as well as individual purposes. The value of having established positive media relations becomes most apparent when school officials face crisis situations such as shootings or disasters (Cook, 2001).

Determining Responsibility

Larger school districts usually employ specialized personnel to operate a public relations or community relations office. In these situations, a person assigned to that office is likely to be responsible for both developing and implementing a media relations plan. Often this person is called a *public information officer*. Most school districts, however, are small; only about 10% of the nation's approximately 14,000 local school districts enroll more than 5,000 students (Kowalski, 1999). Because most districts are relatively small, superintendents do not have a full-time communication specialist on staff. Consequently, the responsibility is either ignored or added to the duties of an existing administrative position. When the employment of a media relations specialist is not possible, the school board and superintendent should provide resources necessary for the designated person to perform the duties adequately (e.g., staff development or university courses). Primary responsibilities associated with the position of media relations director typically include:

- ◆ Developing a media relations plan
- ◆ Administering and evaluating the plan
- ◆ Providing consultation for employees regarding their interactions with the media
- ◆ Planning staff development activities to prepare them to interact effectively with the media
- ◆ Adjudicating conflict between the district and the media
- ◆ Developing and supervising press releases and press conferences
- ◆ Preparing and disseminating positive stories that detail district accomplishments
- ◆ Advising the superintendent (or designee) on relevant policy and regulations

The media relations director is the most likely person to serve as the district's contact person for media inquiries. Districts that do not enjoy the luxury of specialized PR personnel must find another employee who is capable of assuming this assignment. Selecting someone is a critical decision because the performance of the media contact person can affect the district's reputation or the reputation of employees. The following criteria are useful in guiding this decision.

- ◆ *Knowledge of the issue or crisis:* The spokesperson should possess the knowledge necessary to respond to media inquiries or the knowledge necessary to direct the inquiries to others. In the case of a tax referendum, for example, the superintendent may appoint the business manager or treasurer as the spokesperson.
- ◆ *Knowledge of the district's policies and plans concerning communication:* The spokesperson should be familiar with all policies and plans that affect communication so that interactions with the media are carried out properly.

♦ *Information management skills:* The spokesperson must be well informed with respect to information sources and the methods required for retrieving information.
♦ *Communication skills:* The spokesperson's knowledge and information-gathering skills are of limited value if he or she is unable to communicate effectively.
♦ *Trust of district officials:* The spokesperson should have the confidence of the superintendent, administrative staff, and school board.
♦ *Personal relationship with the media:* The spokesperson should have credibility and a good relationship with reporters.

In several instances, school board members have been designated as spokespersons. Although unusual circumstances might explain such an assignment, having a board member serve in this capacity is generally not a good idea. Board members do not possess individual authority, nor do they report to the superintendent. If a board member spokesperson errs or fails to fulfill assigned responsibilities, the superintendent is left with difficult choices for adjudicating the resulting problems.

Given the importance of the media spokesperson, designating one individual to serve in this capacity for all crisis situations is recommended. This assignment should be listed in the district's crisis plan so that all personnel have access to the information (Armistead, 1996). Having a single crisis spokesperson also reduces costs associated with preparing the person to fulfill job expectations (e.g., staff development costs).

SUGGESTIONS FOR WORKING WITH REPORTERS

As in all professions, school administrators share accumulated wisdom commonly referred to as "craft knowledge." One pearl commonly passed from generation to generation is the caveat—a paraphrase of Mark Twain—that educational leaders ought not to fight with persons who buy their ink by the barrel (Akers, 1983). While serving as executive director of the American Association of School Administrators, Paul Salmon developed a list of old-fashioned, commonsense guidelines for successful practice. Among them were the following two pieces of advice: recognize the importance of empowerment and effective communication and develop a positive relationship with the media (Shannon, 1994). But seasoned administrators are quick to point out that these goals are much easier to set than they are to accomplish. Good media relationships, even in the presence of a well-developed media relations plan, require nurturing. In addition to time, the parties involved must be sufficiently open-minded and trusting so they can overcome misperceptions and prejudices about each other.

Developing Positive Relationships

Administrators cannot prevent media contacts, but they can affect the conditions under which they occur. Many superintendents and principals make the mistake of not initiating the first contact with reporters. When reporters make the first move, they usually are not seeking to socialize; rather, they probably want to interview the administrator about a problem, a crisis, or a scandal. Meeting a reporter for the first time under these conditions can be highly stressful because the interviewee does not know if the interviewer is trustworthy. If the meeting does not go well, the relationship between the administrator and reporter may already be headed in a negative direction. When inviting a reporter to a get-acquainted meeting, the administrator should be clear about purpose; media personnel are generally wary if they think an administrator is trying to manipulate them (Bridges & Nelson, 2000). Once the administrator and reporter are acquainted, they can move forward to build credibility and trust. An open-door policy that gives the reporter access to the administrator is an important step toward achieving this goal (Sielke, 2000).

A positive relationship with reporters also depends on the parties understanding and respecting each other and each other's roles (Raisman, 2000). Treating journalists as professionals and being courteous toward them is indicative of this condition. Unfortunately, many administrators typecast reporters as troublemakers—individuals who are interested only in covering negative stories (McQuaid, 1989). This skewed perspective is less likely among administrators who understand journalism and the common role expectations of media personnel. Discussing expectations during the initial meeting is an opportune time to exchange information on these topics.

Accommodating Deadlines

Administrators should know that reporters routinely have deadlines—times established for a reporter to complete his or her research, writing, and editing. Stories typically must be submitted hours before publication or airing because the copy may require the approval of several editors as well as technical development (e.g., determining where and how the article will be placed in the newspaper). Time parameters necessitate expeditious information exchanges, thus reporters are often aggravated when school officials fail to return telephone calls or when they return them only after deadlines have passed. Some administrators wrongly assume that ignoring a reporter's inquiries ensures a story's demise. When inquiries are not answered within the requested time frame, reporters are likely to write the story sans the school district's perspective. Responding within requested time parameters is a safeguard against one-sided reporting and a courtesy that strengthens personal relationships between administrators and reporters (Frohlichstein, 1993).

Obviously, being able to respond within certain time frames may not be possible. For example, asking an administrator to compile a summary of student test scores in one or two days may be an unrealistic request. Under such circumstances, the administrator should give the reporter an honest explanation and an estimate of time needed to fulfill the request. An ethical reporter should then explain why certain information is not included in his or her article, and arrangements should be made for a follow-up story so that data can be reported accurately.

Working With New Reporters

As noted, the press can be an administrator's ally in communicating the school's message to the public (Shaw, 1987). Collaboration between administrators and media personnel is most likely when the parties trust each other. Unfortunately, two conditions often impede such relationships.

1. At low-circulation newspapers,[1] reporters assigned to education rarely have a single assignment. Responsible for covering multiple beats, they have only a limited amount of time for interacting with school administrators (Posner, 1994).
2. Education assignments are low-level appointments at many newspapers, often given to the least experienced reporters. Those who do well covering schools generally get promoted out of the assignment (McQuaid, 1989).

Most media personnel know little about the inner workings of schools and even less about the history, culture, or current problems of a specific district or school when they are initially assigned to this beat. Consequently, helping them to learn about education in general and about the local schools specifically is one way to build trust. In terms of building relationships with administrators, media personnel are much like new teachers: both are more apt to trust administrators who are sincere in helping them become more proficient.

Assisting media personnel to cover school board meetings—a difficult assignment for those who know little about the structure and politics of public education—is one way to build trust. Typically, a reporter's article must be prepared right after the meeting ends. Faced with a tight deadline, there is little or no opportunity to conduct postmeeting interviews, to check name spellings and titles, or to confirm statements. Anticipating these conditions, administrators could aid the media personnel in the following ways:

- Send the reporter an agenda several days in advance of the meeting.
- Highlight and explain action items.
- List the names and titles of individuals scheduled to participate in agenda items.
- Offer to meet with reporters prior to the board meeting to answer questions they may have about the agenda.

In addition to assistance for covering board meetings, administrators can build trust by helping media personnel in the following ways:

- Identify and explain pressing education issues of the day. Often reporters are unaware of emerging issues, and even when they are aware, their understanding of them is often shallow.
- Provide research and related information. Reporters appreciate receiving background material that potentially strengthens their articles or reports.
- Direct reporters to outside sources. Reporters usually appreciate receiving tips about individuals outside the school district who could provide additional or different perspectives.
- Share documents when permissible and appropriate. Often administrators have access to documents that can clarify or validate an issue; reporters appreciate having material that adds accuracy to their coverage (Rhoades & Rhoades, 1991).

---

[1] These are newspapers with a circulation of less than 75,000. Newspapers of this type cover the vast majority of the nation's school districts.

Dealing With Negative News

What is negative news? It is any report or article that focuses on a problem, conflict, or scandal that places a district or school in a less-than-favorable light. Negative news frustrates administrators because long-term efforts to build a positive image may get attenuated by just one incident. Negative media stories may focus on the organization (e.g., the unsafe conditions in a school building) or people in the organization (e.g., violent acts by students or employee misconduct). When faced with these stories, administrators may become defensive. As an example, they may claim unscrupulous reporters trying to advance their own careers are victimizing them or the schools. Even if true, expressing such feelings does not make the negative story disappear, nor does it neutralize the story's effects. Reporters, including those having a positive relationship with administrators, are trained not to look the other way when problems surface. Media personnel see themselves as public watchdogs—individuals with the responsibility to reveal and report on problems in public institutions.

Choosing to ignore negative news is a big mistake (Shaw, 1987). Most observers will view silence as either an admission of guilt or as evidence of incompetence. The following guidelines facilitate the formulation and issuance of a managed response.

- ◆ Never try to suppress a story by lying or refusing to comment.
- ◆ If a problem really exists, share your perspective on the issue as quickly as possible and make yourself accessible to the media.
- ◆ Have the top-ranking administrator speak to the media. Hearing from the superintendent conveys the message that the school district is not taking the matter lightly.
- ◆ Have an action plan to deal with the problem. Negative reactions are often attenuated when school officials exhibit that they are prepared to deal with the situation.
- ◆ Communicate the action plan in language that can be understood by the reporter and readers. Unless the public understands the district's response, they are not apt to focus on it.

Like all organizational conflict, negative news can lead to positive change if it is managed properly. As an example, consider an elementary school principal faced with the problem of crowded classrooms. After several parents wrote letters to the newspaper editor complaining about the situation, the education reporter was directed to do a series of articles on the topic. Instead of being defensive, the principal admitted the problem existed and acknowledged that the parental concerns had merit. He also accommodated the reporter's information requests by including the district's long-range facility plan calling for an addition at the school within 2 or 3 years. Last, the principal carefully explained that state law required taxpayers to approve the planned addition via a tax referendum.

Skillfully, the principal capitalized on the conflict initiated by the parental complaints. He acknowledged that the problem was real; he focused on the fact that the district officials already had a plan to resolve the problem; and he pointed out that taxpayers, including the complaining parents, would play a pivotal role in determining if the district's solution would be implemented.

Speaking Off the Record

Speaking off the record means different things to different people; more important, the rules regarding such communication vary among reporters. Thus, the general rule is to "never say anything to a reporter you are not willing to see in print or hear on the evening news" (Howard & Mathews, 1994, p. 113). Despite this caveat, experienced reporters have been able to get administrators to speak off the record, usually by promising them anonymity or confidentiality. That is, the administrators are assured that they will not be identified as the source of the information or they are assured that the story will be pursued through other sources. Even when such promises are honored (and at times they are not), the story frequently gets traced back to the administrator who agreed to speak off the record.

Some administrators have gone off the record believing that such conversations strengthened their relationships with media personnel. The outcomes, however, were frequently quite different. Some reporters lost respect for the administrators and started treating them as informants. Others concluded that the administrators were being manipulative; that is, they were attempting to selectively disclose information. This judgment evoked suspicions about the truthfulness of the administrators (Howard & Mathews).

Avoiding "No Comment"

When confronted with difficult questions or accusations, administrators have often responded by saying "no comment" or "I can neither confirm nor deny your accusation." Although these responses appear to be safe and uncomplicated, they usually convey negative messages. Reporters, for example, may conclude that an administrator is trying to cover up something; instead of retreating, they usually dig deeper. The public may interpret these responses to mean that administrators refuse to disclose information they possess; they draw their own conclusions about the administrators' motives.

Rather than refusing to comment, the following responses are usually more effective:

- ◆ "I don't have the details to answer your question at this time. Can I get back to you later?" This response is effective when the administrator needs to collect and analyze data. An example would be answering questions about an accident in a science lab before school district officials have concluded an investigation of the matter.
- ◆ "Can I have _____ contact you regarding this issue?" This response is effective when the question pertains to a matter that could be better addressed by another school official (e.g., the school's attorney or the business manager).
- ◆ "I am not at liberty to provide this information because _____." This response is effective when the administrator knows that the requested information is protected by law (e.g., the contents are from an employee's personnel file).
- ◆ "I am not sure the information you want can be revealed. I'll check and get back to you promptly." This response is effective when the administrator is uncertain whether the requested information can be made available (e.g., details of an out-of-court legal settlement).

♦ "I need to confirm the information before I respond. I'll contact you as soon as I am able to do that." This response is effective when the administrator is unaware of the situation raised by the reporter (e.g., being asked to comment about an employee being arrested).

In some cases, administrators cannot respond to reporter questions because the information being sought is legally protected. Consider a case where parents accuse administrators of unfair discipline practices. The administrators feel helpless to respond to the media inquiries because federal laws prohibit them from releasing discipline information contained in a student's record (Surratt, Majestic, & Shelton, 1998). But rather than saying "no comment" to reporter questions, the administrators could either explain why they cannot discuss information in the student's file or they can request that the parents sign a release allowing them to do so. A refusal to sign such a release often conveys a message that the parents are the ones who do not want all the facts presented to the media (Surratt et al.).

Avoiding Lies

One of the cardinal principles of public relations for administrators is to never lie to the media. School officials often find it tempting to mislead reporters, especially when the circumstances are personal or when the officials believe that reporters are their adversaries. An administrator who lies or obscures facts rarely prevents a good reporter from finding the real story (Posner, 1994). Although answering certain questions is painful, giving untruthful answers can be deadly. Experience has proved that lies come back to haunt those who tell them. If caught lying, administrators can lose credibility, public trust, and positive relationships with the media that took years to build—a tremendous price to pay for having gained the convenience of keeping reporters temporarily at bay (Howard & Mathews, 1994).

Staying on Track

When reporters contact administrators, they usually have a specific topic in mind and a deadline to meet. Consequently, they get frustrated with school officials who meander to other subjects, avoid questions, or answer questions with questions during the interview. If there is another story that merits media attention, the administrator can make this suggestion at the end of the interview (Ordovensky & Marx, 1993). Administrators should answer questions directly and avoid being evasive; their purpose should be to facilitate, not hinder, communication (Parker, 1991).

Getting the School's Story to the Media

As noted earlier, administrators often lament the lack of positive stories about schools. What educators see as news, however, may be of little interest to reporters—not because the story is positive but simply because it is not news. If administrators want to get their stories in the media, they have to know what reporters will find worthy of their attention. Asking and answering the following questions can be helpful in this regard:

- ◆ Would I want to hear this story?
- ◆ Who is the audience for this story?
- ◆ Why should taxpayers care about the story?
- ◆ Can the story be connected to larger issues currently in the news?
- ◆ Are there interesting photo opportunities that accompany the story? (This is a factor that can be crucial with television.)

Frequently, stories that administrators want to see in print simply do not lend themselves to newspaper articles. A folk dancing group at a high school and a Thanksgiving skit at an elementary school exemplify activities that reporters may not see as newsworthy, but they could make their way into publication because they are suitable for stand-alone photos—that is, photos that are used without accompanying stories. Media coverage for schools is enhanced when administrators understand how news stories and features are used, but it is also enhanced when administrators understand the importance of timing. Features that are not suitable for news stories can attract media attention if they are brought forward at an opportune moment. If stories can be linked to current events, they often have a better chance of being published. For example, a story about an outdoor science laboratory might be used in conjunction with the state legislature's deliberation of an environmental protection bill.

Besides understanding the nature of news and the value of timing, administrators need to know their local media markets. Consider, for example, the tremendous differences that usually exist between urban and rural areas. A small-town newspaper is usually more willing to cover "puff" pieces—stories that have no news value and little human interest but are published to keep good relations between the newspaper and the school district. Hence, reporters for these papers might do a photo and short story about a principal having lunch with the straight-A students, whereas a big-city paper is likely to reject the idea. In addition, reporters are often the friends and neighbors of school officials in smaller communities. These contacts can serve to draw the reporter's attention to a desired story (Parker, 1991).

Fallon (1993), a former public information officer with the California School Boards Association, noted there are many activities, such as presenting certificates to outstanding students, that are important to the school's mission but are rarely newsworthy. He suggested that school officials concentrate on other areas where they have an opportunity to get news in print:

> At the local school district level, some examples come immediately to mind . . . scores (good or bad) on standardized state and national tests, violence or drug abuse on a campus, the impact of budget cuts, school closures, attendance boundary changes, collective bargaining that goes awry. At the state level, trends in admission of students to state universities, the influence of the legislature in setting educational policy, and research reports on a range of topics . . . from students with a limited knowledge of English to student performance comparisons in other states. Surveys and research reports at the local level also can have a strong news value, particularly reports of educational innovations and new school programs that produce successful results.

In discussing ways to gain positive media coverage, he offered the following suggestions:

- ◆ Understand that there are slow and busy news days. This can make a difference in covering education stories.
- ◆ Do not hesitate to make suggestions for future stories. Reporters like to receive ideas from administrators, and though they may not act on them immediately, they may place the ideas in their file for future reference.
- ◆ Realistically, schools should expect a combination of positive and negative stories. Unfortunately, positive stories are more quickly forgotten. But some negative stories can lead to positive stories, for example, a plan of action for a particular problem or how a problem was eradicated. Always look for public relations opportunities—even in negative stories.

School officials who are uncooperative when the media are probing into problems ought not to expect reporters to be accommodating when the issue is positive publicity.

Press Releases and Conferences

Writing a press release is a relatively simple process and a good way to eliminate misunderstandings. Timing is an important consideration for news releases. At the top of the release, the reader should be informed if it is an "immediate" or "embargoed" release. An immediate release is intended to have the information disseminated to the public as soon as possible; an embargoed news release[2] is provided to the media for use at a later time or date specified by the school officials. The release should be typed and include the full name and telephone number of the contact person the reporter can call for additional information. Experts (e.g., Albrecht, 1997) recommend using a headline that grabs attention and gets to the point. According to Ordovensky and Marx (1993), the release should be written in journalistic style and address the following five W's:

- ◆ *Who* is issuing the release?
- ◆ *What* is the release about?
- ◆ *When* will the event in question take place?
- ◆ *Where* will the event in question take place?
- ◆ *Why* will the event in question take place?

The effectiveness of a press release is enhanced when the most important information is placed at the beginning. Larger circulation newspapers and broadcast media outlets often receive multiple press releases from public agencies, so placing basic information first helps reporters to sort through them in a timely manner.

Press releases may contain facts and opinions. Facts should be stated concisely, and if opinions are included, quotes from individuals expressing the opinions should be provided. Since press releases should not be very long (typically two or three pages), only the most important or effective quotes should be used. The release should be written just as you

---

[2]Embargoed news releases are typically used to give reporters advance notice so that they have ample time to prepare an article for publication on a predetermined date.

TABLE 11–2
Guidelines for Preparing Press Releases

Guideline	Benefit
Identify the issuing organization immediately.	Reporters or editors know the source before reading the document: identification can provide credibility.
Identify the contact person.	Question, comments, and decisions are directed to the appropriate person.
Provide a headline.	The reader is able to discern the nature of the release immediately; in large media markets, this can be critical.
Keep it brief and concise.	Reporters or editors are more likely to read the entire release.
Double-space the document.	The reader has room to do editing.
Provide time information.	Clearly stating the date the release was issued and the date of intended publication or broadcast increases the effectiveness of the document.
Write "more" at the end of a page if the release continues to the next page, and the pound symbol (###) at the end.	The reader knows whether additional information follows at the end of each page.
Attribute opinions to individuals by using quotes.	Opinions are properly identified with the individuals offering them.
Before developing the release, predetermine distribution.	The release will reach its intended audience.

would like to see it appear in the newspaper the next day. Table 11–2 contains more basic guidelines that can be used to structure press releases.

Press conferences present a greater challenge for administrators. This may explain why school personnel do not use them as often as press releases. There are three primary reasons for having a news conference:

1. School officials need to communicate with multiple media outlets simultaneously.
2. Reporters indicate that they need to ask questions about breaking news.
3. A knowledgeable source needs to be available to the media, but he or she has only a limited amount of time to devote to such interactions. (Ordovensky & Marx, 1993)

Since one of the goals of a press conference is to communicate with representatives of multiple media outlets simultaneously, giving them as much notice as possible is advisable. A media advisory containing basic information about the purpose of the conference and logistics (date, time, location, and parking) should be sent to reporters at least several days in advance.

A press conference is more likely to be successful when it is planned properly. Here are some suggestions:

◆ Select a time of day and a location that is convenient for reporters.
◆ Select a site that (a) can accommodate media equipment, (b) is convenient for reporters, and (c) is appropriate for the topic.
◆ The morning of the conference, contact reporters and politely ask them if they will be attending. The call serves as a reminder and also symbolically conveys the fact that you consider the conference to be important.
◆ Have materials ready for distribution at the start of the conference. This includes one or more relevant press releases and information packets containing data.

- Anticipate reporter questions and be prepared to answer them.
- Inform attendees how they can get additional information.
- Avoid confrontational encounters with the media and have a contingency plan if one or more of the district representatives become emotional.
- Determine a procedure for conducting the conference so that the process is orderly.
- Have a planned ending for the conference. The preferred method is to announce that only one more question can be asked.
- Make sure that school personnel do not leave the conference abruptly.

Press conferences should be used sparingly because reporters are likely to ignore frivolous events. Therefore, the administrator's very first task is to determine whether the issue underlying the conference is indeed newsworthy.

Making Corrections

As in all human endeavors, mistakes are made in media stories about schools, and these errors are made on both sides of the fence—by reporters and by school officials. When they occur, administrators ought not ignore them. Even slight errors, such as misstating a person's official title, could have repercussions. Regardless of who is at fault, the administrator should point out the problem directly to the reporter. Lodging a complaint with an editor may create the perception that primary intent is to discredit the reporter and not to correct the error. If sloppiness or unfairness persists, the editor should be informed.

Several years ago, a newspaper story mistakenly reported that a school district had paid $250,000 to a junior high school girl who had sued her teacher for sexual harassment. After the story broke, school officials filed their own complaints against the teacher and disciplinary action took place. Countless stories followed in the city's two newspapers. Reporters came and went, relying on previous stories for historical background to cover the story. Not until 5 years later did the superintendent tell an education reporter that the insurance pool, and not the school district, had paid the $250,000 in damages to the girl. Despite taxpayer complaints spanning 4 years, school officials had never set the record straight. As it turns out, the superintendent had not made the correction because he feared that it would damage the reporter and he wanted their positive relationship to remain intact.

Printing corrections ought to be determined jointly by the reporter and the administrator. In some instances, corrections will only repeat damaging or negative information that the educational organization prefers to avoid. But even in these situations, the error should be pointed out to the reporter. If not, it is likely to recur in subsequent stories.

WORKING WITH BROADCAST MEDIA REPORTERS

Working with mainstream broadcast media—television and radio stations—presents several additional challenges for administrators. When interviews are conducted by broadcast media reporters, school officials not only have to be concerned about what they say but also how they speak, and in the case of television, how they look when they speak. In addition, administrators often find that these reporters are more likely to be confrontational than their print media peers (Walker, 1990).

Television

The tenor of a live or taped interview is crucial because both the administrator and reporter communicate with audiences nonverbally as well as with words. Consequently, dress, gestures, and facial expressions can be more powerful than words. Given the special challenges presented by television, administrators should heed the following recommendations.

- ◆ Before you agree to do an interview, find out if it will be live or taped. Taped interviews allow you to pause before answering or to stop and start over if you decide to rephrase your answer.
- ◆ Anticipate the interview questions that will be asked and have prepared responses.
- ◆ Focus on the nonverbal behavior of the reporter as well as your own nonverbal behavior. Smiling before you answer, for example, helps to build rapport with the interviewer and audience.
- ◆ Avoid one-word and excessively long answers.
- ◆ Focus on a message that you want to present; deciding on two or three key points prior to the interview is helpful.
- ◆ Dress appropriately. Overdressing for television may place more attention on the interviewee than on the message and underdressing may reduce credibility.
- ◆ Suggest questions that the interviewer might ask. This allows you greater opportunity to present your message (Ordovensky & Marx, 1993).
- ◆ Maintain eye contact with the interviewer and try to ignore the cameras. The only exception would be a satellite interview without a reporter present.
- ◆ Be careful what you say during a commercial break; the interviewer could repeat your comments after the cameras are rolling.
- ◆ Avoid being manipulated or intimidated by the interviewer (Howard & Mathews, 1994).
- ◆ Use related questions to make points. If you are trying to stress the importance of passing a bond referendum for a new school, you may ask: "What programs will have to be curtailed if the referendum fails?"
- ◆ Build a cutoff into an answer as a mechanism for dropping a topic.
- ◆ Avoid repeating hostile questions and attempt to remain focused on the message you want to transmit.
- ◆ Avoid appearing defensive. If you are asked an inappropriate question or a question for which you have no answer, try to redirect your comments to the key points you want to discuss.
- ◆ Avoid nervous habits such as tapping your fingers on the table or shuffling papers.
- ◆ If the reporter keeps interrupting you, politely request that you be given adequate time to answer questions.
- ◆ Use visuals to enhance critical points (Parker, 1991).

Television reporters who cover school board meetings usually look for short pieces that can be integrated into the nightly news broadcast. These spots provide opportunities for administrators to deliver a message, but the time is limited—maybe only 45 seconds or less. Thus, words must be chosen very carefully (Parker).

Radio

Reporters working for radio stations often contact administrators without advance notice seeking a few sound bites that can be used to enhance a story. Most often these interviews are conducted via telephone and the reporter should ask if it is permissible to tape the conversation. Radio offers an excellent opportunity for direct audience involvement via call-in shows (Austin & Pinkleton, 2001). Consequently, station personnel may invite administrators to participate in scheduled programs where the purpose is an in-depth interview coupled with audience participation. If you are contacted to do such a program, you should have extensive knowledge on the topic(s) to be discussed. If you do not, arrange for one or more other administrators to do the program.

Although many of the suggestions for appearing on television are relevant to radio, there are some basic differences between these two mediums.

- ◆ Administrators typically are able to use notes and prepared statements to respond to radio interview questions.
- ◆ Nonverbal behavior and dress are important in a radio interview only if a live studio audience is present.
- ◆ Administrators usually have greater opportunity to discuss essential points in detail on radio because the time frames generally are longer than they are on television.
- ◆ Presenting statistical data on the radio is more difficult because charts or other visual aids are not possible.

SUMMARY

In an information age, school officials are expected to provide information frequently, accurately, and honestly. Their ability to do so usually depends on their associations with journalists. Effective relationships occur when both parties are willing to learn about each other's work and there is a mutual appreciation of responsibility. Table 11–3 includes a summary of media relations suggestions discussed in this chapter.

Being criticized by the media, directly or indirectly, is painful for administrators. Although it may appear that reporters are interested in covering only negative school stories, the media actually reports both positive and negative stories; over time, the two types of articles usually balance out (Shaw, 1987). When facing negative press, administrators are often tempted to hide, express indifference, or make excuses. These actions are nonmanagement responses because they do nothing to improve the situation. Effective practitioners recognize that problems can be friends; they offer an opportunity to improve schools and community relations. Superintendents and principals with this disposition focus on solutions and detail not only how a problem will be resolved, but also on how the organization is likely to become stronger because of the problem.

TABLE 11–3
Summary of Media Relations Suggestions

Issue	Suggestions
Making organizational decisions	Develop a media relations plan that is connected to the district's public relations plan; determine who will be responsible for administering public information functions; determine who will serve as spokespersons.
Understanding the work of reporters	Learn about journalism and journalists; gain insight into the job descriptions for reporters.
Building and maintaining positive relationships	Take charge: don't wait for reporters to make the first move.
Being accessible to answer questions	Be sensitive of deadlines and respond to telephone calls in a timely manner.
Answering reporters' questions	Never lie or use evasive statements like "No comment."
Speaking off the record	Don't do it.
Dealing with negative news	If the problem is real, admit it: focus attention on a solution.
Issuing press releases	Use journalistic style: include pertinent and accurate information; be concise and brief; make the objective of the release clear.
Holding press conferences	Conduct them only when necessary; schedule to accommodate key school officials and media representatives; make sure the session is well planned and under control.
Conveying the school district's message	Structure stories to take advantage of media interests and prevailing news interests.
Dealing with errors	Always bring errors to the attention of the reporter; determine if a printed or broadcasted correction is in the best interests of the school district.
Working with broadcast media	Be cognizant of nonverbal communication; anticipate questions; stay focused on a predetermined message.

CASE STUDY

Mismanaging a Sensitive Situation

School administrators face many unforeseen situations, but the most anxiety producing are those involving an inappropriate relationship between teacher and student. Not long ago, a high school football coach was placed on paid leave after one of his players reported that the coach had asked him to have sex with the coach's wife. The story made its way to school officials who then acted to remove the coach from the school environment pending a legal investigation.

Knowing that rumors would fly as soon as reporters started asking questions about the coach being placed on leave, the school's principal called a faculty meeting. Without releasing details of the problem, he emphasized to the staff that they should keep personnel matters confidential—in essence, he urged them to refrain from talking about the matter. Following the general faculty meeting, the principal met with the school's counselors and told them to be alert for relevant student problems.

Despite efforts to keep the matter private, the story was leaked to a local newspaper prior to the conclusion of a police investigation and the eventual arrest of the coach. On the very day law enforcement officials took the coach and his wife into custody, a story confirming the investigation and the alleged sexual misconduct became front-page copy.

Faced with a media crisis, the school board designated one of its members as the official spokesperson. This board member was to field all media inquiries, including those made to school district employees. But this action did not deter television crews and newspaper reporters from descending on the high school. Interviews were sought with students and teachers. Unable to control conversations with the media, school officials were stunned to watch students who had no real knowledge of the incident embellish tales on the nightly news; they were dismayed by anonymous quotes appearing regularly in the local newspaper.

Information in one of the articles was clearly wrong, but school officials decided not to call the matter to the reporter's attention. The newspaper that printed the story was a small local publication and they figured that making a correction was not worth the effort. But shortly after the story appeared, the Associated Press picked it up and ran it across the country. The error was now compounded.

Another major decision made by the school board was to hire a private investigator for $10,000 to determine whether any employees had prior knowledge of the sexual misconduct involving the coach and his wife. This decision sparked a good bit of criticism because the district was in poor financial condition. Taxpayers' anger only increased when they learned that the private investigator had found nothing to show that any employee had advance knowledge of the coach's misconduct.

Eventually, the coach and his wife pleaded guilty to the crimes. Two teenagers who were found to be victims in the crimes then sued the school district, alleging that school officials had failed to adequately protect them from the coach. When asked about the lawsuits, school administrators and the board member spokesperson uniformly responded, "No comment."

Many disgruntled patrons cited school officials for three failures. First, many concluded that proper supervision of employees could have averted the incident in the first place. Second, the problem should not have been compounded by spending money for a private detective. Third, the school district now faced more financial losses because of the suits filed by the students.

QUESTIONS AND SUGGESTED ACTIVITIES

CASE STUDY

1. Was it a good idea for the school board to name one of its members as the official media spokesperson to deal with this scandal? Why or why not?
2. Evaluate the principal's decision to urge the faculty to remain silent.
3. What actions should the principal have taken to control media access to students?
4. Should the superintendent have been more visible in making media statements with regard to this case? Why or why not?
5. Evaluate the impact of not having corrected an inaccurate story published by a small local newspaper.

6. By refusing to comment about the scandal, did school officials contribute to taxpayers' anger?
7. If you were a consultant to this district, what advice would you give regarding being better prepared for such situations in the future?

CHAPTER

8. What is the purpose of a media relations plan?
9. What information should be contained in a media relations plan?
10. What factors should be weighed in naming an official spokesperson for a crisis or problem situation?
11. When and how should administrators point out errors in stories that appear in the media?
12. Why is it important for principals to have a basic understanding of journalism?
13. What can an administrator do to prepare for a television interview?
14. When is it appropriate for an administrator to speak to a reporter off the record?
15. What are some effective ways of responding to negative news?

SUGGESTED READINGS

Burgess, D. (2000). Managing public scrutiny. *American School and University, 72*(5), 38–40.
Cook, G. (2001). The media and the message. *American School Board Journal, 188*(6), 16–22.
Engeln, J. (2000). A complete turnabout. *High School Magazine, 7*(6), 28–31.
Fox, J. A., & Levin, J. (1993). *How to work with the media.* Newbury Park, CA: Sage.
Frohlichstein, T. (1993). Dealing successfully with media inquiries. *NASSP Bulletin, 77*(555), 82–88.
Hennessey, A. (1992). Getting the word out: Working with your local school reporter. *Phi Delta Kappan, 74*(1), 82–84.
Lyons, C. (1990). Getting the ink. *American School Board Journal, 177*(11), 37.
Ordovensky, P., & Marx, G. (1993). *Working with the news media.* Arlington, VA: American Association of School Administrators.
Owen, A. R., & Karrh, J. A. (1996). Video news releases: Effects on viewer recall and attitudes. *Public Relations Review, 22*(4), 369–378.
Paciancia, D. (1995). Getting out the good news. *American School Board Journal, 182*(6), 39–40.
Pohl, R. J. (1994). Beyond confrontation. *American School Board Journal, 181*(2), 54.
Polansky, H. B., & Montague, R. (2001). Handling an emergency: A defining moment. *School Business Affairs, 67*(7), 13–15.
Raisman, N. A. (2000). Building relationships with the media: A brief working guide for community college leaders. *New Directions for Community Colleges, 28*(2), 21–27.
Sielke, J. (2000). So, you want positive press? An in-depth look at what the media really want when they come knocking. *School Business Affairs, 66*(10), 26–29.
Smith, A. (1991). How to be a great communicator. *American School Board Journal, 178*(8), 31–33.
Sperbeck, J. M. (1997). Some media relations success stories. *Journal of Applied Communications, 81*(3), 24–39.
Townsend, R. (1993). Coping with controversy. *School Administrator, 50*(9), 24–27.

REFERENCES

Akers, J. T. (1983). *Don't fight the man who buys his ink by the barrel.* (ERIC Document Reproduction Service No. ED246553.)

Albrecht, D. G. (1997). *Promoting your business with free (or almost free) publicity.* Englewood Cliffs, NJ: Prentice Hall.

Armistead, L. (1996). What to do before the violence happens: Designing the crisis communication plan. *NASSP Bulletin, 80*(579), 31–37.

Austin, E. W., & Pinkleton, B. E. (2001). *Strategic public relations management: Planning and managing effective communication programs.* Mahwah, NJ: Erlbaum.

Batory, J. P. (1999). The sad state of education coverage. *School Administrator, 56*(8), 34–38.

Bridges, J. A., & Nelson, R. A. (2000). Issues management: A relational approach. In J. A. Ledingham & S. D. Bruning (Eds.), *Public relations as relationship management: A relational approach to the study and practice of public relations* (pp. 95-116). Mahwah, NJ: Erlbaum.

Cook, G. (2001). The media and the message. *American School Board Journal, 188*(6), 16–22.

Fallon, M. (1993, November). Written interview.

Frohlichstein, T. (1993). Dealing successfully with media inquiries. *NASSP Bulletin, 77*(555), 82–88.

Fullan, M. (1999). *Change forces: The sequel.* Falmer Press.

Gonring, M. P. (1997). Global and local media relations. In C. L. Caywood (Ed.), *The handbook of strategic public relations and integrated communication* (pp. 63–76). New York: McGraw-Hill.

Howard, C. M., & Mathews, W. K. (1994). *On deadline: Managing media relations.* Prospect Heights, IL: Waveland Press.

Kosmicki, R. J., & Bona, F. E. (1996). Media relations: How to relate to the press. In R. L. Dilenschneider (Ed.), *Dartnell's public relations handbook* (4th ed., pp. 59–75). Chicago: The Dartnell Corporation.

Kowalski, T. J. (1999). The school superintendent: Theory, practice, and cases. Upper Saddle River, NJ: Merrill/Prentice Hall.

McQuaid, E. P. (1989). The rising tide of mediocre education coverage. *Education Digest, 54*(8), 7–10.

Ordovensky, P., & Marx, G. (1993). *Working with the news media.* Arlington, VA: American Association of School Administrators.

Parker, J. (1991). *Accessing the media.* (ERIC Document Reproduction Service No. ED339337)

Polansky, H. B., & Montague, R. (2001). Handling an emergency: A defining moment. *School Business Affairs, 67*(7), 13–15.

Posner, M. A. (1994). Read all about it. *Case Currents, 20*(1), 8–13.

Raisman, N. A. (2000). Building relationships with the media: A brief working guide for community college leaders. *New Directions for Community Colleges, 28*(2), 21–27.

Rhoades, L., & Rhoades, G. (1991). Helping the media add depth to education news. *Clearing House, 64*(5), 350–351.

Ridgway, J. (1996). *Practical media relations* (2nd ed.). Brookfield, VT: Gower.

Shannon, T. A. (1994). Salmon's laws. *Executive Educator, 16*(4), 52–54.

Shaw, R. C. (1987). Do's and don'ts for dealing with the press. *NASSP Bulletin, 71*(503), 99–102.

Sielke, J. (2000). So, you want positive press? An in-depth look at what the media really want when they come knocking. *School Business Affairs, 66*(10), 26–29.

Spicer, C. (1997). *Organizational public relations: A political perspective.* Mahwah, NJ: Erlbaum.

Surratt, J., Majestic, A., & Shelton, S. (1998). Both sides of the story. Media relations. *American School Board Journal, 185*(2), 47, 52.

Walker, K. B. (1990). Confrontational media training for administrators: Performance and practice. *Public Personnel Management, 19*(4), 419–427.

Wallace, R. C. (1990). Greet the press! *School Administrator, 47*(7), 1–17, 19.

12

Responding to Crisis

Edward H. Seifert

As principal of Cameron Elementary School, you cannot feel it! You cannot touch or taste it. But you do smell it. The smell, however, is alien to your senses. You ask yourself if you might be inhaling something that is harmful, even life threatening. Your eyes start watering, but you are not sure if this symptom is connected to the smell or just your nervous state. You start to wonder if the building is safe. You think to yourself, "Please let there be no problem!" Should you order the evacuation of the 500 students and their teachers? Should you call the superintendent? How do you contact parents? Should you call the media first? Call the Cameron fire department—what's the number? "Oh yes, 911 is the number." Where do we take the children? It seems a hundred questions are racing through your mind.

When facing a crisis, an administrator is bombarded by dozens of stimuli. They often send conflicting messages and serve to further cloud one's thinking. But despite these adverse conditions, the administrator knows that decisions must be made quickly. More important, there is the realization that these decisions may affect the welfare of hundreds of other people.

Situations such as the one at Cameron Elementary School are not uncommon. Principals and superintendents across the country can attest to the fact that crisis occurs with regularity; for some administrators, they occur so frequently they are actually anticipated. For seasoned school officials, panic and fear have been replaced by psychological coping mechanisms that treat crisis as an inevitability, as something that happens in schools across this nation on a daily basis.

As principals ponder the safety of students, it is important to keep in mind that practice and preparation for crisis events are the only way to make sure teachers, students, and staff react in a positive manner to crisis events. The 24-hour television news channels trying to fill airtime have brought school incidents to millions of viewers across the nation and around the world. These media outlets tend to focus on the perpetrators and not the victims. For example, there was the incident in February 1996 in Moses Lake, Washington, where a 14-year-old boy wearing a trench coat and carrying a hunting rifle walked into an algebra class and killed his teacher and two classmates. The media attraction generated by the Columbine massacre, the incident at Heritage High School in Conyers, Georgia, followed by a 6-year-old first grader murdering another 6-year-old has created the impression that schools are nothing but centers of violent crime. In December 2000, however, the United States Justice Department reported a decline of 68% in juvenile homicides between 1993 and 1999, whereas the Federal Bureau of Investigation (FBI) reported a 36% decline in violent juvenile crime (Knutson, 2001).

The Safe Schools Survey (1998) revealed that 60% of the respondents had observed violence between one and five times during the school year. This violence included such things as verbal abuse, stolen property, and physical assault. More than 59% of these same respondents acknowledged having been victims of violent acts, and they failed to report these incidents to teachers or administrators.

Is school violence increasing or decreasing? The evidence seems to indicate a decrease in school violence, but Volokh and Snell (1998) reported that 1,000 crimes per 100,000 students occurred in public schools. The highest crime rate occurred in high schools where 103 crimes per 100,000 students occurred, whereas only 13 crimes per 100,000 students were reported in elementary schools.

In a 1999 survey of high school principals, 88.1% of the respondents indicated they had been threatened physically or verbally by parents and 53.3% indicated that abusive language was directed at them by parents. Fifty-eight percent of these same respondents indicated that students had verbally or physically threatened them (Seifert, 2000).

More likely than not, a principal will never face students shooting students and teachers. He or she probably will face teacher and student injuries and deaths from automobile accidents, deaths due to catastrophic illnesses, weather-related disasters, and teacher and student suicides. The magnitude of a school crisis is measured by the level of preparation each school attains. Crisis by its very nature is unpredictable, making preparation the single most important element in eliminating student, teacher, and staff injury.

How prepared was the principal at Cameron Elementary to cope with the uncertainty of the moment? It is possible the principal will make the appropriate decisions for the welfare of students, teachers, and staff, but the probability of a successful outcome decreases as the level of preparation decreases. Banking on good fortune is a risk that no principal should be willing to take in light of his or her responsibility to students, teachers, and the community (Seifert, 2000).

DEFINING CRISIS

When attempting to conceptualize crisis management, it seems appropriate to define the word *crisis. Merriam-Webster's Collegiate Dictionary* (1993) defines *crisis* as a "turning point for better or worse," as a "decisive moment" or "crucial time," and goes on to reveal that crisis is a "situation that has reached a critical phase." Poland and McCormick (1999) stated that crisis is a "temporary breakdown of coping" (p. 6) surrounded by anger, anxiety, and grief. The individual or group's outlook and response to the event most often determine crisis. Guetzloe (1997) noted that crisis occurs anytime a student's behavior requires instant attention to protect the safety of others. Most of the time, these events are unanticipated and require an immediate administrative response.

Crisis is, by its very nature, unpredictable; it may not always be bad. Fink (1986) observed that outcomes are almost equally divided between those that are desirable and those that are not. He suggested that the key to shifting the percentages in favor of desirable outcomes is preparation. Such preparation entails three elements: (a) designing a crisis management plan, (b) teaching the plan to employees, and (c) reinforcing the system's effectiveness through rehearsal. The intent is to make the plan an integral part of the organization so management control over crisis is maximized.

A school safety plan comprises self-correcting, interrelated parts that direct employees toward desired actions. It is predicated on the anticipation that there will be future events that are potential turning points for the school and that when such situations occur, the maintenance of the organizational homeostasis requires purposeful, planned action. Administrators who develop such plans and monitor the environment in an effort to predict crisis are more likely to influence outcomes positively (Fink, 1986).

In the example presented at the beginning of this chapter, the principal, has no crisis plan in place to give direction. It is possible that the administrator will make appropriate decisions and protect the welfare of those under his or her supervision even without a plan of action. However, it is foolhardy and dangerous to rely on good fortune; even if outcomes are not damaging to the school, students, and employees, the process of facing crisis unprepared may take its toll on the administrator's well-being.

All too often, administrators think about plans of action after they have already reached a crisis situation. Typically, this is too late. The school safety plan should be molded in periods of tranquility when administrators have the opportunity to identify contingencies and reflect on their potential effectiveness. This chapter provides strategies for developing and implementing such plans.

SCHOOL SAFETY PLANNING TASK FORCE

The school safety planning task force is responsible for creating policy statements concerning student, teacher, and staff safety. Keeping these groups free from fear ensures that more teaching and learning will take place in school. It is important for community stakeholders, first responder agencies, and school personnel to participate in the development of a school safety plan. The leadership of the planning task force is critical and the individual chosen to fill this responsibility must have the time and expertise to guide a large and diverse task force.

Stephens (1998) provided direction in developing a safe schools planning task force. These steps include:

- ◆ Select team members that represent and are influential in the community.
- ◆ Invite all community stakeholders to an open forum on school safety, making sure all of the members of the task force are present.
- ◆ Schedule the forum far enough in advance so that all interested individuals may attend.
- ◆ Notify all stakeholders of the anticipated date for completing the safe schools plan.
- ◆ Make sure all forum attendees are notified of the times, dates, and places for the task force meetings.
- ◆ Ensure that all first responder agencies participate in the forum.
- ◆ Videotape the forum rather than assigning someone to take copious notes.

In creating a safe schools plan one size does not fit all. The school's context dictates the policies and procedures that need to be implemented. The biggest problems in putting together the planning team will be the egos and strained relationships that are by-products of activities that occur outside of the school setting (Seifert, 2001).

Selecting task force members can be accomplished in several ways, but it is important to remember that those selected must be willing and able to serve. Task force members can be nominated by school organizations, such as the PTA or PTO, district school board members, community service organizations, and first responder agencies such as police, fire, and the emergency medical service (EMS). Establishing times, dates, and places to meet will be key factors in determining who will be able to participate. The task force should represent a broad spectrum of individuals; in addition, they must have status in the community. Selecting the right people to accomplish this task will go a long way toward making sure the finished product will be acceptable to community stakeholders.

Hosting an open forum on the topic of school safety allows all segments represented by the school to participate in the development of the safety plan. Make sure the forum design allows all who want to speak an opportunity to be heard. Cautioning speakers to make sure their comments are on the topic helps structure the listening process for members of the task force. The chairperson of the task force must be willing to stop speakers who attempt to stray from the topic. One way to make sure that individual speakers stay on topic is to force them to address specific questions structured by the task force. For example, one of the questions that needs to be addressed by the stakeholders might be, "What type and level of safety training do teachers and students need to help ensure their safety?" Listing a maximum of three questions to be addressed keeps the forum focused.

It is critical that the planning task force receive wide-ranging publicity for the open forum utilizing all available news outlets. This publicity should include such items as the time, date, and place of the open forum. If the school has the capacity, the entire open forum should be videotaped for the purpose of recording what was discussed. Task force members that were unable to attend the forum in person could view this tape. Another strategy that should be used is making sure that the school mission statement references school safety. For example, the mission statement might read:

> Cameron Elementary School will provide students with an opportunity to obtain a quality education in a safe environment.

In addition, the task force should release the times, dates, and places for their regular meetings. All meetings of the task force should be open to the public, and making sure community stakeholders have the information necessary to attend all meetings is a must.

First responder agencies have a plethora of information that all members of the planning task force can utilize. Police, fire, and emergency medical service (EMS) agencies work with safety and crisis situations on a regular basis, and they have information that will make the planning task force's job much easier. Although these agencies should be *part* of the planning process, the task force must maintain control of the process. The lynchpin for success in controlling the participation of first responder agencies is the chairperson of the task force. This person must make sure these individuals function within the structure of the task force.

THE SAFE SCHOOL PLAN

Planning for the safety of children is a task that most principals understand as part of their role, but they generally don't believe that the school where they work will have a crisis. The most efficient way to ensure a principal considers the well-being of students is to have a comprehensive school safety plan. Preparation is the most important aspect of any plan. The first 60 minutes of any crisis will be chaotic and fluid (Poland & McCormick, 1999), and this is why preparation is essential for student safety. Principals must recognize that personal emotions play an important part in the principal's ability to cope with the situation. In any crisis situation a principal will experience the arrival of the first responders such as police, fire, and EMS personnel, followed by a surge of media, and then the crush of parents (Peterson & Straub, 1992). In order to minimize the emotional stress of the crisis event, Rettig (1999) developed the following safety plan.

1. Create a school safety team.
2. Conduct a school safety audit.
3. Develop procedures for as many crises as you can imagine, adding contingencies for each situation.
4. Provide all school personnel with safety training.
5. Make sure students understand that they should share safety information and help each other.
6. Provide students with coping skills for violent events.

The school safety team should be created with the utmost care and concern for students, teachers, and staff. This team must have the ability to carry out all of the tasks required during any type of crisis. The principal has the responsibility of choosing the members of the safety team. Not every faculty or staff member is equally prepared to deal with the stress and chaos of a crisis situation. This is particularly true when dealing with crises such as student or teacher suicide, catastrophic illness, violence against children, and automobile accidents. For these situations, it is imperative that team members are calm and emotionally stable. Safety team members should be chosen because they are good communicators, listeners, and negotiators in addition to being emotionally stable. The team members should receive the majority of the professional development that is devoted to school safety, but the entire faculty must be instructed in all aspects of the safety plan. The key to implementing an effective plan, is practice, practice, practice.

The school safety team should be composed of the following members:

◆ The principal as the safety team leader
◆ First responder coordinator
◆ First-aid responders
◆ Sweep team coordinators
◆ Media spokesperson
◆ Parent liaison

The building administrator should be the safety team leader. An assistant team leader should be appointed in the event that the team leader is away from the building during the crisis. The team leader is responsible for directing and coordinating all emergency response activities, and remains in the emergency command center in order to direct the activities prior to the arrival of the first responder personnel. The team leader will remain in control of the dissemination of information to all media outlets, including the release of student, teacher, and staff member names.

The first responder coordinator is responsible for meeting all first responder personnel and directs them to the crisis area. In addition, this team member directs the media, parents, and central administration to their appropriate locations. Although this person is not involved with the on-site operations of the police, fire, or EMS personnel, he or she provides maps and gives directions. No special training is needed to perform this task other than the training all safety team members should receive.

First-aid responders must be trained in first-aid techniques and must continually upgrade skills and knowledge. Many times athletic trainers, physical educators, or athletic coaches have first-aid knowledge. These individuals can fill this safety team position. First-aid responders render emergency medical assistance to individuals in need until the highly trained first responder groups arrive on the scene. If there are no certified first-aid providers in the school, it is the principal's responsibility to find teachers and staff members to become certified first-aid providers. The school should reimburse the individual for the cost of the training and the time spent on training.

The sweep team coordinators are the last individuals out of the building when an evacuation is instituted. They check the hallways, restrooms, and other nonclassroom areas for students, always being vigilant for any unusual-looking packages, misplaced items, and other strange phenomena. Make sure the sweep team members make their rounds immediately after the building evacuation is executed.

The media spokesperson must work directly with the safety team leader and is responsible for all media briefings, both electronic and print. The spokesperson needs some experience in working with all forms of media. This is generally not a problem in medium-sized to larger school districts, but in small districts a teacher spokesperson needs to be selected and trained. The media spokesperson provides support to the school by preparing press releases, arranging interviews, and providing background information when appropriate. A major focus of the media spokesperson must include knowledge of ethical and legal issues surrounding information and dissemination about students, teacher, and staff. It is important that the media spokesperson be located away from the crisis site. This helps prevent the media from participating in the crisis and disrupting the emergency workers' activities.

The parent liaison responds to parents who arrive at the crisis site, directing them to the area where they may be united with their children. Depending on the structure of the safety team, the parent liaison may be the person who informs parents of children directly involved in the crisis. The parent liaison should be located away from the crisis site, to ensure the liaison's and the parents' safety. It is critical that the parent liaison be emotionally stable, with the ability to work with parents who are emotionally distressed.

The safety team is most effective when all roles are assumed by properly prepared individuals and when it functions consistently without regard to the type of crisis being faced. The only way to ensure the members are capable of working as a team is to practice the safety plan simulating various crisis situations. These simulations must include participation by all first responder agencies. To make sure all safety team members are able to fulfill their assigned duties, each member will carry a credit card-sized information card with his or her responsibilities printed on it. Below is an example of what these safety information cards might look like:

Safety Team Leader

Emergency Tel. 817-258-0001, Emergency fax No. 817-258-0002
Pager Nos. 817-258-0003, 817-258-0004, 817-258-0005, 817-258-0006
Safety Team Leader: Judy Boswell, Pager No. 817-258-0007

1. Declare a crisis and activate the safety team.
2. Notify first responder agencies, as appropriate.
3. Notify the central administration.

4. Collect facts for accurate information dissemination.
5. Arrange for the spokesperson to meet the media.
6. Arrange for faculty and staff information.
7. Remain calm and keep your emotions under control.

These cards should be carried at all times by the safety team members. The information provides secure telephone and pager numbers to be used by team members in a crisis; individuals tend to forget such critical information when placed under extreme stress and chaos.

Examples of quality school safety plans can be found at the following Internet sites:

◆ School Safety Plan, Pearl School District, Pearl Mississippi http://www.wa.gov/ago/ourschools/5_plan/pearl.htm
◆ School Safety Response Plan, Wayne Township, Indianapolis, Indiana http://www.wa.gov/ago/ourschools/5_plan/responplan.htm
◆ School Safety Plan, Oconomawac, Wisconsin http://www.wa.gov/ago/ourschools/5_plan/Excepts.htm
◆ Crisis Response Plan, Nettleton Public Schools, Jonesboro, Arkansas http://nettleton.crsc.k12.ar.us/crisis.htm

SCHOOL SAFETY AUDIT

The school safety audit is a tool that can pay dividends for student, faculty, and staff well-being. The safety audit is intended to examine the structure and design of the school building. The procedures contained in the safety plan are directly related to the results of the safety audit. A team of experts, including local law enforcement, engineers, and security professionals, as well as school district personnel perform this audit. This safety audit addresses topics such as:

◆ Design and location of restrooms, including ease of supervision, entrance and exit doors, or lack of doors.
◆ Access to windows—limited window access to the building is essential.
◆ Control of the building entrance with video cameras—electronically controlled doors must be locked at all times with panic bars and not secured with other devices.
◆ Lighting on the exterior of the building—trees and shrubs around the building look nice but should be limited to keep vandals from hiding in the vegetation.
◆ The use of 24-hour surveillance cameras—these can be utilized inside and outside the building to provide information about what is happening in and around the building.
◆ Structurally unstable areas in the building—especially during severe weather, these areas should be identified and avoided in the severe weather plan. Structural engineers should be consulted to identify areas of the building that appear to have structural problems.

◆ The building evacuation plan—observe building evacuation in order to discover flaws in the plan. Plans for building evacuation call for students to move to an athletic field, stadium, playground, or parking lot. All of these areas are logical sites for students to gather but they also carry a significant level of danger for students, teachers, and staff. If building evacuations are designated for one specific spot each time the plan is practiced, it is not unrealistic to think that perpetrators could place explosive devices in that area. The evacuation plan should include several sites.

◆ An internal and external video of the building—this video should be supplied to all first responder groups and a special emphasis of the video should include all hidden areas inside and outside the building.

The safety audit should include community and school data, such as community crime data. The school district and each individual school should compile information on the types and magnitude of crimes committed in the community. In addition, vandalism data should be collected by reviewing district repair requests.

The audit should address the number and types of communication devices that are available during a crisis. Every classroom, office, and occupied area should have an in-house talkback intercom system that is accessible to students, teachers, and staff. Even better than the intercom is an in-house telephone system that places a telephone in all areas of the building and on play fields. Many principals utilize FM two-way radios to communicate because of the ease of operation and maneuverability.

Perhaps the most important piece of the safety audit is the manner in which building key control is exercised. One of the discoveries of the Columbine High School crisis was the suggestion that one of the teachers gave his or her keys to one of the perpetrators to go to a storage area to bring an item back to the classroom. It is highly possible that when teachers give students their keys, the student may have the ability to copy the key. Most faculty members would like the principal to believe that they spend many hours on weekends working in their classroom preparing for the next week, thus justifying the need for an exterior door key. The reality is that few teachers need exterior door keys because few teachers use or need to use the building on weekends and holidays. The best way to manage building keys is with "smart card" controlled electronic locks. The main advantage to this locking system is the ability to identify each person entering the building and the time he or she entered and exited, thus providing a record of who was in the building. In addition, this system allows the principal to control the active entrance to the building by changing the code on the locks via a computer.

POLICY AND PROCEDURE DEVELOPMENT FOR THE SAFETY PLAN

Each safety plan requires the creation of policies and procedures that address every conceivable crisis (Schwartz, 1997). These policies and procedures need to focus on violent events, zero tolerance for drugs, drug paraphernalia, weapons, a dress code, and an unknown persons policy (Rettig, 1999). Crises may involve medical emergencies, student runaways, student and teacher deaths, and bomb threats. Others may be caused by natural disasters such as gas leaks, explosions, and power outages.

Dealing With Violent Events

It is just a matter of time before a violent event occurs in a school; only a toss of the dice distinguishes those who have experienced violent school events from those who have not (Frisby & Beckham, 1993). In the most recent past, schools have had to work through bomb explosions, children shot by people walking onto the campus, children being taken hostage by parents and others, teachers being murdered in front of children by their students, administrators gunned down in school hallways or offices, and students as young as 11 years of age carrying out plots with automatic weapons to slaughter their classmates and teachers. FBI Special Agent O'Toole (2000) revealed that teenage violence and homicides have decreased since 1963 but the incidence of public shootings has created the perception that teenage violence was increasing. She noted that the media's perception of increased violence was often accompanied by erroneous conclusions such as these:

- ◆ School violence is constantly increasing
- ◆ All student shooters have the same psychological profile
- ◆ Student shooters are loners
- ◆ Students shoot other students to get even
- ◆ Unusual behaviors are the key to violent students

Nevertheless, a police liaison should have input into the school safety plan and he or she may even be a member of the safety team. Many administrators and teachers have resisted the presence of law enforcement personnel in schools and their involvement in developing a safety plan, and in so doing, they have ignored the realities of modern society. In violent situations, the primary focus is on the delineation of responsibilities among the police department, fire department, EMS, and the school. Without a well-coordinated plan detailing the responsibilities of each first responder agency, chaos may occur. For example, each agency may attempt to take charge of the crisis, causing turf battles that direct energy away from the crisis itself.

Student fights constitute the vast majority of violent school events. In the 1996–1997 school year, 190,000 student fights were reported by public schools (National Center for Education Statistics, 1998). School officials need to be prepared for these situations by being aware of the following tactics:

1. Analyze the situation to determine the level of physical danger the combatants are perpetrating on each other and to the intervener. Are the students in a physical or verbal confrontation or is there a weapon involved?
2. Have a student go for help from the closest adult.
3. Intervene verbally by calling the student by name, announce to the students who you are by name (for example, Principal Smith, Assistant Principal Johnson, Teacher Woodbury, or Custodian James).
4. Try to get the crowd to disperse by calling students you know by name.
5. Make sure you remain as calm as possible, continually telling the combatants to stop.

6. When the physical confrontation stops, separate the combatants as quickly as possible.

7. All combatants should be escorted to the principal's office in the company of a teacher, staff, or administrator. Never send students unattended.

8. The principal should contact the police for assistance. In some school districts the police issue citations for fighting in school. Make sure you follow the procedures established by your district (Poland & McCormick, 1999).

A major problem facing schools after a violent event is responding to the public's immediate need for more precautions, much more stringent law enforcement, and more surveillance equipment (O'Toole, 2000). This is especially true when there is a shooting.

The National Threat Assessment Center of the U.S. Secret Service determined the following characteristics about violent students and specifically the student shooter:

◆ Shooters are rarely impulsive; they generally plan their actions.
◆ Shooters most always tell someone else.
◆ There is no accurate way to profile student shooters.
◆ Most shootings are over in less than 20 minutes.
◆ Shooters almost always contemplate suicide. (Vossekuil, Reddy, Fein, Borum, & Modzeleski, 2000)

Students must be educated to report acts of violence. Teachers must be more diligent in observing changing student behavior in order to minimize student violence. Warning signs of aggressive behavior include poor grades and lack of interest over time, drug or alcohol abuse, uncontrolled anger, school discipline problems, affiliation with gangs that support violence, and extreme feelings of rejection (Dwyer, Osher, & Warger, 1998).

Dealing With Crisis Events Involving People

One of the more destructive activities perpetrated against schools is bomb threats. The destruction comes in the form of facility destruction should a bomb detonate or psychological damage to students created by fear. Most bomb threats are called in by students enrolled in the school receiving the threat. Estimates are that 500–1,000 threats are reported for every real bomb. Each and every threat must be taken seriously, however; following are suggestions to help the school deal with the call announcing a bomb threat:

1. Train the person answering the call to remain composed asking these questions:
   ◆ What is the location of the device?
   ◆ When will it detonate?
   ◆ What is your name?
2. Keep the caller on the line and call the police.
3. Decide whether the building should be evacuated.
4. Determine which evacuation areas should be selected for students. (Poland & McCormick, 1999)

Decisions about evacuation depend on the weather, the information gathered, the amount of community violence, and perhaps input from the police and fire departments. Some districts have chosen to ignore bomb threats, believing that most bombs are planted in restrooms or hall lockers; thus, moving students out of the building through the halls exposes them to greater danger than keeping them in the classrooms. Administrators should consult with experts to determine which procedures are most effective for a specific school.

The newest and the least known of these crisis events is the threat of bioterrorism. Most schools have had to add strategies for working through situations such as students bringing unknown substances to school in order to simulate anthrax hoping for a day off from school. The prudent principal facing unknown substances will have a decision-making plan that includes the following steps:

1. Get reliable information before making any decision.
2. Have two or three physicians with whom you can consult about biological or chemical events.
3. Secure the building by closing all doors and shutting off the HVAC system and window units.
4. Do not evacuate, especially if the threat of further biological or chemical attacks is possible. (Kentucky Center for School Safety, 2002; The Safety Zone, 2002)

The Safety Zone (2002) provides the following Internet addresses for chemical and biological terrorism:

◆ US Postal Service Guidelines for Dealing with Potential Mail Attacks http://www.usps.com/news/2001/press/pr01_1010tips.htm
◆ FBI Advisory for Suspicious Packages http://www.kysafeschools.org/pdfs&docs/safemail.pdf
◆ CDC Chemical/Biological Terrorism Strategies http://www.bt.cdc.gov/Documents/BTStratPlan.pdf
◆ Suggested Emergency Guidelines for Anthrax Threats http://ideanet.doe.stat.in.us/isssa/lawrencegdlsanthrax.html
◆ School Safety Issues Related to the Terrorist Attacks on the United States http://www.schoolsecurity.org/terrorist_response.html

Weather-Related Events

Tornados and snowstorms can happen with little or no advanced warning. It is very important for each school to have access to weather-related information; this can be accomplished by purchasing a National Oceanographic and Atmospheric Administration (NOAA) weather radio that sounds an alarm in the event of severe weather in the area. In some jurisdictions the county sheriff's department broadcasts weather-related information on special radios supplied to each school. It is the school's responsibility to make sure it can receive as much advanced warning for these events as possible. It is also important to have the telephone numbers of the police, sheriff, fire departments, local radio and television stations, and the nearest office of the National Weather Service as a backup system to the weather radios. The "GO Bag" is a suitcase type container capable of holding information and equipment useful during a crisis. It is a portable operations center containing cell phones, first-aid equipment, a bullhorn, student and teacher rosters, safety team assignments, safety team telephone numbers, and other equipment that may be useful during a weather-related crisis (Seifert, 2000). In addition, a prudent principal would purchase or lease the following items for his or her campus:

♦ A private telephone line that can be accessed only by members of the school safety team.
♦ A cellular telephone or two-way radio for each member of the safety team (Cell phones provide greater security.)
♦ A fax machine in the area where the safety team will establish a command center.
♦ Bullhorns for each member of the safety team.

The equipment listed above is the minimum that principals should have at their disposal for any type of crisis. The use of palm pilot technology that transmits written messages wirelessly is available and might be used in lieu of cell phones or two-way radios. New technology surfaces periodically and the proactive principal should be aware of them and know how they could be used to communicate during a crisis.

Tornados are unpredictable weather phenomenon and it is mandatory that schools have a plan to protect students. The plan should include a strategy for moving students from the classroom to structurally safe areas in the building. In most schools the closest safe area is the interior corridor. Students should move quickly and quietly to the corridor, kneel facing the corridor wall, then cover their heads with their arms and hands. This strategy should be practiced to the point where students feel comfortable assuming this position. If at all possible, have students take large textbooks with them to help cover their heads. Some students and even some teachers may become emotionally upset during this exercise; it is the teachers' responsibility to ensure that the exercise is completed safely. Tornados generate flying debris which could be a major concern, thus students should stay away from rooms with windows.

In some states the most important weather-related event is caused by severe snow and ice. Snow and ice can accumulate at such a rapid rate that schools become unable to transport students back home before roads or visibility deteriorate and safety is jeopardized. In these situations the school safety plan must include the storing of blankets, food, and heating devices should students be trapped at school. Provisions for 3 to 5 days should be accumulated in order to meet the needs of students, teachers, and staff. It is much more responsible to be safe in a building than stranded on a school bus with limited resources.

Perhaps the least known of weather-related crisis events are earthquakes and landslides. These events do happen in many parts of the United States, but little attention is paid to these acts of nature. Strategies for monitoring these events are accomplished in the same manner as for snow and tornados—via police, weather, television, and radio reports. Preparation and practice for these events is the key to student, teacher, and staff safety (*Focus on Critical Issues*, 1998).

NOTIFICATION OF FACULTY OF A CRISIS EVENT

When responding to all types of crises, the safety plan must include a system for notifying faculty and staff of the crisis event in a way that triggers action to protect students and school personnel. If you have an intercom system in the school, voice commands are the best and most efficient way to inform teachers what to do. If there is no intercom, a system of bells could be used to let the faculty know of the crisis. A bell system can create chaos, however, especially if the crisis occurs at about the same time as a passing period bell is designated to ring. The following voice command examples activate the safety plan:

- *Code yellow:* classroom lock-down; an unauthorized person is in the building.
- *Code blue:* a catastrophic medical event is occurring in the building.
- *Code red:* a weather-related event is imminent; move to your assigned safe area.
- *Code purple:* evacuate the building and proceed to student holding area 3 (play field)
- *Code green:* general all clear; return to your classroom.

When the voice command "code yellow" is sounded, each teacher must take quick action. The teacher instructs the students to move quickly, to get on the floor and crawl toward the outside wall of the building, and the teacher goes and locks the door. If the door has a window, a covering for the window should be used. The teacher positions the students next to the exterior wall so that anyone looking through the windows will be unable to see the children. If the room is equipped with window blinds, these blinds should be pulled down or twisted shut. In most cases, concrete block or brick walls serve as the best protection against bullets and bullet fragments. Placing students against the interior wall puts them in danger of being hit by bullets coming through structurally less substantial walls.

"Code blue" tells the teacher that someone in the building is experiencing a catastrophic medical event. When hearing this command the teacher knows to ignore any passing bells or student dismissal tones and to hold the students in the classroom. Keeping corridors clear for emergency medical personnel and keeping small children isolated from this trauma is important. During any "code blue" situation, a designated person should be placed in each major corridor to remind teachers and students to remain in the classrooms until the "code green" command is given.

A "code red" command may require teachers to move quickly in evacuating their rooms to a safe area of the building. Tornados are the most likely weather event that requires the quickest action. The aftermath of a tornado that hits a school building will create chaos, but it is the principal's job to move the students out of the building rubble when possible. Move quickly around the building, assessing student and teacher injury. If possible, activate the school safety team and begin utilizing the plan.

"Code purple" tells the teachers and staff to evacuate the building and to proceed to a specific gathering area. Numbering each gathering area helps reduce the probability that students will be directed to a gathering area that has been planted with explosive devices. For example, area 1 is the football stadium or field, area 2 is the parking lot, area 3 a park across the street from the school, and area 4 might be the softball field. Each school should designate a minimum of three gathering areas to ensure student safety.

"Code green" is the all-clear command that instructs teachers and students to return to their classrooms. Teachers need to take student attendance to make sure all students are back in a safe environment if they have had to evacuate the building. This command officially ends the crisis.

SCHOOL SAFETY TRAINING FOR FACULTY AND STAFF

Precrisis planning and faculty and staff training are key elements to successful implementation of any school safety plan. Training and more training will help all participants if, or when, a crisis occurs. Training will not prevent crisis situations, but it will reduce the likelihood of panic mentality becoming the overriding emotion during the initial stages of any crisis. This point was reinforced in a document prepared by the North Carolina State Department of Public Instruction (1988): "When crisis occurs," the agency warned, "it can be magnified or minimized depending on how well the school staff follows the appropriate policies and procedures. For that reason, the school system should have annual in-service concerning the procedures that relate to various crisis situations" (p. 4).

Training in small groups, with a presenter who is sensitive to faculty and staff responses to crisis situations, helps ensure a positive result from the initiation of a school safety plan. School safety training according to Serafin (1990) should include:

◆ The duties of each member of the school safety plan
◆ The referral process to be used by all members of the system
◆ An understanding of the grief process
◆ The process of networking in the community
◆ Legal issues surrounding liability and student confidentiality
◆ Evaluation and assessment review
◆ Specialized training in working with the media
◆ Specialized training for secretaries in handling telephone-related threats, media referrals, and issues of confidentiality
◆ Specialized training for students who will be involved in peer counseling or student-staffed hotlines.

As stated earlier, members of the school safety team should receive the most intense training, but all faculty and staff should be instructed in some aspects of the safety plan. The safety team should meet 6–8 times per year to practice various aspects of the plan in order to create continuity, review situations, make recommendations, and plan training. At the beginning of each year, all employees should be reminded of their roles and responsibilities in the event of crisis. This is a time when new and changed procedures in the safety plan should be discussed and described to all employees. Using simulations is one way of helping faculty and staff understand and practice their roles for crisis situations. These simulations should be as accurate and realistic as possible in order to test the safety plan.

Staff training is imperative if the safety plan is to be implemented successfully. Most faculty and staff do not enter the teaching profession with the necessary skills or training to carry out any type of school safety plan. Even if they do, they will benefit from interfacing their skills with a specific school safety plan. Most faculty members do not understand how tragedy affects people and what it takes to serve traumatized individuals.

POSTCRISIS PLANNING

One of the most overlooked aspects of crisis policy is the postcrisis planning. The development of an aftercare safety team is designed to work with students, teachers, and parents in a mental health environment. Once the crisis is under control, it is time to bring in mental health workers, counselors, and clergy. It is important to ensure that clergy and mental health workers are licensed professionals. The principal should contact all the mental health professionals at the beginning of each school year to make sure adequate staffing will be available should a crisis event occur. If you wait until the crisis occurs it may be too late.

The aftercare safety team is directly related to the context of the school. In most small- to medium-sized school districts, the aftercare team should be comprised of counselors and mental health workers that are external to the school district. In larger districts all of the mental health workers could come from within the district. The team should be composed of:

◆ A *team leader:* this individual is usually a principal from another campus. This allows the building principal to work with the crisis while the team leader principal operates the school.
◆ *Counselors:* these counselors are trained in grief counseling techniques.
◆ *Social workers:* the social workers serve as liaisons between the school and the families of the injured or deceased students or teachers.

The aftercare of teachers and students is dependent upon the crisis and can be accomplished in several different ways. After the loss of a student or teacher, the aftercare team provides mental health support for all members of the school family. For example, after the death of a student, the aftercare team moves onto the campus to provide support for teachers and students by creating a dedicated space called a "safe room." The purpose of this room is to provide a space for students who are distracted by a crisis event. The room is equipped with beanbag chairs, small stuffed animals, snacks, and blankets for students to use while sitting on the floor. Students could come and go from this room after talking with a fellow student or one of the counselors. The safe room allows students to grieve the loss of a friend in a mentally safe environment.

INFORMING FACULTY, STAFF, STUDENTS, AND PARENTS

Various groups need to be notified when the safety plan is activated. In most cases, the principal is the key communicator, but someone else at the school should be designated to serve as a backup if the principal is away from the campus.

The first group that should be informed during a crisis is the faculty. Telling the teachers first allows them to adjust to the situation and to prepare themselves emotionally to meet with students, parents, and colleagues. According to Peterson and Straub (1992), the principal should never use the intercom system to relay critical information because teachers and students would receive the information at the same time. Faculty notification should be made in person, if possible. This could be accomplished through a general faculty meeting, a meeting of all grade-level or department chairs, a telephone tree, or a one-on-one meeting between a teacher and the principal (or designee).

As noted, rumor control is a primary concern. A general meeting of all employees is a way to communicate accurately. In this setting, the principal needs to remind faculty and staff of their responsibilities and lets them know how students will be informed. This general meeting also allows administrators and counselors to identify faculty and staff who may not be capable of working with students during this stressful period. The school safety team leader may use the meeting to announce schedule changes (e.g., altering the class schedule) as well.

Warner (1994) believed that school officials should be open and honest about a tragedy because this approach helps ensure a higher level of trust among students and parents as they begin the healing and coping process. The preferred method of announcing tragic news to the general student population is through a carefully prepared, factually based, written statement that is read in individual classrooms. All students should receive the same, accurate information simultaneously. Providing information to smaller (such as classes) groups gives students the opportunity to grieve and share feelings in a more intimate environment. It also gives them greater opportunity to ask questions.

Students should be made aware of available counseling services, and they should be told how the services can be accessed. The more individuals in an organization are informed, the more likely they will support the organization. When employees are informed and respond in caring ways, the organization is more likely to exhibit characteristics of a family (Overman, 1991).

Informing students, teachers, and staff of traumatic events affecting other students and teachers is a task that requires a great deal of empathy and understanding. Some guidelines that might be used to provide information are:

◆ Teachers or principals should provide information concerning catastrophic events that happen to students and teachers. A way to accomplish this task is by creating written statements that can be read to students by their teacher. This technique ensures that all students and teachers get the information at the same time and helps control rumors. It also helps students begin the grieving process while among their peers.
◆ When a student is told that a member of his or her family has been involved in a serious accident, a school counselor should be on-site when the student receives the news.
◆ Information should be given to students and other school personnel in a straightforward, nonemotional manner while eliminating specific details.
◆ The person delivering the tragic news must be prepared for a variety of student emotions.

In-Classroom Statement
Death of a Parent

As you know, Janey is absent from school today because her mother and father were involved in a vehicle accident that killed them both. Janey will not be returning to class for several more days, but when she does return to our class, she will feel very sad. As members of this class and Janey's friend, what can we do to help her when she returns?

In-Classroom Statement
Catastrophic Illness of a Student

Many of you know that Mary Elizabeth has been very sick, and I have been told by her parents that she will not be back at school for several more weeks. Mary Elizabeth is being treated for her illness at Seven Seas Hospital in Cameron and will be at the hospital for the next several days. Please think of some things that we can do to help Mary Elizabeth feel better, so that she can return to our class as soon as possible. Please share your ideas with me.

In-Classroom Statement
Schoolwide Loss of a Teacher

Our principal Dr. Milton Reese has been very sick the past 6 months. His wife had told us that his illness took his life last night. As a tribute to Dr. Reese for all of the students he inspired and the community he served for 25 years, we will celebrate his life next Wednesday morning with a gathering at the school flagpole. Students, please think about how your class might participate in this celebration. Share your ideas with your teacher and your classmates.

FIGURE 12–1

In-Classroom Statements to Be Read to Students and Teachers

- Silence is the norm when students receive bad news.
- If a student is involved in a serious accident, make sure any brothers and sisters are notified, whether at the same school or at different schools. (Fiore, 2002)

Figure 12–1 contains examples of statements that could be read to students if necessary.

If a school district has a media spokesperson the principal will be responsible for writing and communicating the statements to teachers and students. Utilizing these statements will help develop trust between the school and the parents. It is very important for parents to be able to participate with their child in the grieving and healing processes. Principals can use a variety of tools to provide information to parents and all other community stakeholders. Some of the communication tools that might be appropriate for schools to use include letters sent home via students, print media, electronic media, a school Web page, and in many situations, the school will have student e-mail addresses that can provide instant information to many parents. Regardless of the communication tool used, parents must understand that the school is providing counseling for students and how that service can be accessed.

MEDIA RELATIONS

A major component of every school safety plan is the development of a strategy for working with the print and electronic media. The media plan should be an integral part of the school safety plan as it is being developed. The plan should clearly spell out who will be the media spokesperson and where the press briefings will be located, preferably away from the crisis scene. Depending on the type of crisis event that occurs, it may be necessary to make arrangements for the spokesperson to be on duty around the clock to work with the media. Regardless of the extent of the crisis, the media center should be open extended hours in order to answer questions and provide accurate information.

The media center provides a place where all media personnel and visitors can gather to receive briefings. The size and extent of the crisis determines the need for a media center, but one should be established for even the smallest crisis. The person in charge of the media center should

- ◆ create a working relationship with reporters from the print and electronic media outlets.
- ◆ concentrate on reporters' questions.
- ◆ make available facts about the ongoing situation.
- ◆ make sure all information that is disseminated is kept in a release log.
- ◆ always be honest with reporters.
- ◆ not let reporters attack or bully him or her.
- ◆ always answer questions from written statements and never deviate from the statement.
- ◆ repeat the message over and over.
- ◆ be aware of his or her nonverbal communication.
- ◆ never release names of students or teachers. (Fiore, 2002)

As discussed in depth in Chapter 11, the creation of a working relationship between the school's media spokesperson and reporters is done prior to any crisis event. It is important to develop this relationship on the basis of mutual trust. Providing reporters with interesting storylines prior to a crisis will help the working relationship during the crisis. Make sure reporters know they can trust the media spokesperson to provide information in a timely manner. As the media spokesperson, never tell reporters that you will get them specific information and then fail to do so.

Create a fact sheet about the school that includes demographic information, current accomplishments of the school and students, and the grade configuration of the school. Provide facts about the crisis, only after having those facts cleared through the safety team leader and law enforcement if on site. Do not release names or provide background information for teachers and students involved in the crisis. Never speculate about the situation with reporters.

All information to be released to the public must be read and approved for release by the safety team leader in conjunction with the media spokesperson. Prior to releasing the information it should be logged out in order to avoid redundancy and the changing of facts. Prior to logging the news release, all facts must be checked and double-checked.

The perception among many reporters is that half-truths, made in multiples of two, equal truth. It is up to the school's media spokesperson to make sure the facts surrounding the situation become known. Always be honest with reporters, never allowing yourself the luxury of stretching the truth. Avoid saying "No comment" to the media because it gives the impression you have something to hide. Instead, explain the reason you cannot address the question. Questions that address personnel or legal issues are examples of questions that cannot be answered and would require an explanation of why they would not be answered.

Reporters who attempt to intimidate or bully the media spokesperson should be ignored. In some instances it may be necessary to tell the reporter that you are not going to answer his or her questions. Should this continue to occur during media briefings, the safety team leader may be required to contact the director of the media outlet where the aggressive reporter works and ask to withdraw the reporter from the story.

Always answer reporters' questions from written statements that have been prepared for release to the media. *Never* answer questions off the top of your head. It is the responsibility of the media spokesperson to anticipate questions that will be raised by reporters and to prepare answers. Safety team members may be helpful in identifying such questions and, in addition, they may help structure responses. Reporters at an initial media briefing might ask the following questions:

- ◆ Who was injured or involved in causing the crisis event?
- ◆ Will you provide us with the details of the event as you have them?
- ◆ When will the media be able to view the area where the crisis occurred?
- ◆ What specifically caused this event?
- ◆ Has the crisis been resolved or stabilized?
- ◆ When will more information be available?
- ◆ When will a school spokesperson be available for an on-camera interview?

A television or radio interview can be intimidating even to the most seasoned school personnel. Amid microphones, lights, and cameras, having reporters peppering you with questions is an unnerving experience. Most school personnel have had little experience with these situations, so it is imperative for those to be interviewed to practice their comments before moving in front of the microphone. Effective performance entails emotional control, knowledge of the situation, and an understanding of how the electronic medium works. Most television news segments last no longer than 30–40 seconds and, in some cases, only 15–20 seconds. Radio segments are even shorter. Since electronic news reports typically are edited for time, the spokesperson needs to focus solely on one or two points. Key messages should be repeated as often as possible, with no deviations. The media spokesperson must learn to talk in sound bites in order to get the intended message out—not an easy take for the untrained media person.

CRISIS PREVENTION PLAN

When a crisis occurs at school, students and teachers frequently say to the media, "I was fearful this might happen." The ongoing solution to crisis management is preparation and prevention. To this point, the chapter has focused on activities that must occur when a crisis actually happens. The development of a prevention plan is essential in a safe schools plan. Incidents such as student suicide, teacher suicide, alcohol abuse, drug abuse, gun violence, and student-on-student attacks might be reduced if a prevention plan were implemented. This plan should include (a) suggested activities; (b) pertinent information; and (c) identities of individuals with helping skills who can assist students, faculty, and staff.

The major goal of the prevention team is to collect and provide information about students and, in some cases, teachers who need emotional or psychological help (Psychological Services Crisis Intervention: Grant JUHSD, 1998). The gathering of information can be accomplished by asking students, faculty, and staff to make referrals to the crisis prevention group concerning behavior abnormalities. Because of the potential for a crisis, administrators and teachers should realize the importance of threatening words. A student who says "I am going to shoot Old Man Jones for giving me an F in science this quarter" should not be ignored and should be referred to the campus administrator immediately. The student should be interviewed, his or her parents contacted, and the teacher who is the target of the threat notified.

Stephens (1998) suggested that principals and teachers talk to troubled students and find out what is worrying them. This type of intervention could stop a tragedy. Each referral to the prevention team should be reviewed and an action plan created that puts into place an emergency action. The process for prevention referrals includes:

- Intervention strategies that have worked in other communities
- A plan that provides for immediate intervention
- An action plan is completed that outlines strategies to help the individual
- The referral is given to the prevention team leader
- The team leader monitors processes and resources for the person being referred
- All referrals are reviewed at the crisis prevention team meetings (Dwyer et al., 1998)

The prevention process includes strategies that bring together the person in question and another who can help the individual. The prevention team should comprise teachers, parents, peers, or members of the community with the skills to work with students and teachers (Psychological Services Crisis Intervention: Grant JUHSD, 1998). The team may elect to meet weekly or only when referrals have been made.

All teachers need to be reminded yearly about the activities and availability of the prevention team. Teachers new to the campus must be provided staff development in the referral process. Faculty and staff should realize that overacting is better than saying nothing when a potential problem occurs. Extending information to parents also helps. Information concerning these staff development opportunities needs to be made known to all campus stakeholders through school newsletters, print media, electronic media, and Web pages.

Peer groups working with students demonstrating depression and other behavioral changes can provide support and assistance during a crisis (Psychological Services Crisis Intervention: Grant JUHSD, 1998). Implementing a "buddy system" to support students in crisis is an example of a peer group intervention strategy. However, students who assume such roles require extensive training. Perhaps the most crucial aspect of a peer counseling program is the selection of the peer counselors: they should come from all segments of the student population. If all of the peer counselors are seen as the "good kids" at school, the program will surely fail.

A club for students new to the school can provide a feeling of security for new students. It can also be an opportunity for students already assimilated into the student body to support the new students. A strategy that may prove helpful is the creation of wallet-sized cards with telephone numbers of agencies that provide help for problems such as drug and alcohol abuse, as well as agencies focusing on suicide prevention, pregnancy prevention, legal counseling, runaway services, and psychological counseling.

EVALUATING THE SAFETY PLAN

Evaluating the safety plan is of utmost importance to determine how well the plan functions. In the absence of a real crisis, this evaluation can be accomplished through simulation. An evaluation team, consisting of community members, agency members, and safety team members, should be activated to study the safety plan and evaluate the various crisis simulations that might be utilized. This group has the responsibility for recommending changes in the safety plan. The plan needs to be evaluated on a yearly basis and after every crisis event. The time spent reviewing the process pays dividends the next time the plan is operationalized. The following questions may serve as a beginning for creating an evaluation instrument:

- ◆ What was the nature of the crisis?
- ◆ What steps did the safety team undertake?
- ◆ What additional steps could the safety team have taken?
- ◆ Did the plan function as it was designed? If not, describe the malfunction(s) in detail. (Seifert, 2000)

SUMMARY

Developing a school safety plan may seem like an exercise in fear, but the fact is that it is better to be in a state of readiness than in a state of panic. This is especially true when facing a panel of five reporters from various media outlets and parents whose child was injured or killed. Creating the safety plan is the first and most crucial step in preparing for the unexpected. Planning, staff training, and practice become the guides for successful implementation of the plan. Selecting faculty and staff members for the safety and after-care teams is critical to the plan's functioning successfully.

It is imperative that the building principal take responsibility for directing the operation of the safety plan, and it is his or her task to provide a spokesperson for the school, should the crisis event warrant such action. The spokesperson must be prepared to coordinate all media contacts, press releases, and press conferences. This person should attempt to control rumors by providing accurate information for community consumption. The plan must include a procedure for mobilizing and activating community resources, such as mental health workers, clergy, counselors, and social workers; bringing closure to the crisis; and evaluating how well the plan functioned. These steps form the structure for a school safety plan. Expanding each step with roles, responsibilities, training, practice, and evaluation will provide each school with a desired level of confidence and security. Every principal will use the school's plan sometime during his or her career, but it is not clear when or where. Prepare for the worst and hope for the best.

CASE STUDY	**Crisis at Cameron Elementary School**

Principal Beth Rodriguez arrived at Cameron Elementary School at about 7:15 a.m. She was startled to find three police cruisers and an EMS unit sitting in front of the building. She wondered what the problem could be this early in the morning. Perhaps someone had come to work early and activated the security alarm by accident or maybe a break-in had occurred. Perhaps the fire alarm had malfunctioned for the third day in a row. As she moved quickly to the main entrance, Rodriguez heard the sound of sirens in the distance. In her office, she found Pasha and Mary, the building custodians, talking with Detective Mario Mangioni, whom she knew from activities in the community. As the principal approached the three individuals, she knew from the looks on their faces something must be very wrong.

Taking Rodriguez into her inner office, Detective Mangioni told her that the custodians had called 911 about 6:00 a.m. after finding the body of Bill Block, a science teacher, hanging from one of the rafters in the gymnasium. Rodriguez could hardly believe the news. Block was one of the best teachers on the faculty; he was very popular with the teachers and students. Mangioni told Rodriguez that his investigation indicated suicide because there was no evidence of murder.

Rodriguez was unsure of how to deal with this crisis event. Students and teachers would be arriving at school soon. Suicides were not supposed to happen in Cameron. She had no crisis intervention or safety plan at hand, and she could not recall the plan that had been used in the school district where she had been an assistant principal.

In the midst of anxiety and stress, Rodriguez tried to recall Block's attitude last Friday when she met with him about the life science curriculum. She remembered nothing strange or different about his behavior. She wondered if she had contributed to this awful tragedy, and thought about what could be so wrong in his life that he would leave his wife and children this way.

As Rodriguez began to get her emotions under control, she realized it was now 7:45 a.m. and students would be arriving on the first buses in 10 minutes. They'd normally go to the gymnasium to wait for the bell to go to the classrooms at 8:12 a.m. Panicked, the principal rushed to the bus unloading zone. By this time, arriving teachers were abuzz about the emergency EMS and police units in front of the building. With the buses pulling up, the teachers arriving for work, and her staff in a state of shock, Rodriguez faced a situation she had never faced before. What should she do?

QUESTIONS AND SUGGESTED ACTIVITIES

CASE STUDY

1. What information does Beth Rodriguez need to deal with the immediate problems at Cameron Middle School?
2. Which faculty and staff members should she meet with immediately?
3. Where should she send the arriving children? How can she keep this tragedy from becoming traumatic for all children, especially Block's students?

4. What must she do to solve the long-range problem of no school safety plan at Cameron Middle School?

5. Once this crisis event is over, what research should she do in beginning to create a school safety plan?

CHAPTER

6. What process should a principal use to create a school safety plan?

7. As a principal, how should you develop faculty and staff ownership of a school safety plan?

8. What steps can be taken to involve the community in dealing with potentially violent situations at school?

9. Identify individuals that could become a member of your school's safety team and outline the criteria you would use in selecting these members.

10. Develop the duties for each member of the school safety team and discuss those responsibilities with a colleague.

SUGGESTED READINGS

Fiore, D. J. (2002). *School community relations*. Larchmont, NY: Eye on Education.

National Center for Education Statistics. (1998). *Violence and discipline problems in U.S. public schools: 1996–97*. Washington, DC: Author.

O'Toole, M. E. (2000). *The school shooter: A threat assessment perspective*. Federal Bureau of Investigation. Washington, DC: National Center for the Analysis of Violent Crime.

Poland, S., & McCormick, J. S. (1999). *Coping with crisis*. Longmont, CO: Sopris West.

Rettig, M. A. (1999). Seven steps to schoolwide safety. *Principal, 71*(9), 10–13.

Stephens, R. D. (1998). Ten steps to safer schools. *American School Board Journal, 185*(3), 30–33.

REFERENCES

Dwyer, K., Osher, D., & Warger, C. (1998). *Early warning, time response: A guide to safe schools*. Washington, DC: US Department of Education.

Fink, S. (1986). *Crisis management*. New York: American Management Association.

Fiore, D. J. (2002). *School community relations*. Larchmont, NY: Eye on Education.

Focus on critical issues. (1998). When crisis hits in our schools. Retrieved from http://www.osbu.org/Pubs/critiss/crisiscr.pdf.

Frisby, D., & Beckham, J. (1993). Dealing with violence and threats of violence in the school. *National Association of Secondary School Principals Bulletin, 77*(552), 10–15.

Guetzloe, E. (1997). *Developing a plan for crisis intervention*. Retrieved from http://www.wm.eda/TTAC/articles/challenging/developing.htm.

Kentucky Center for School Safety (2002). Responding to biological and chemical emergencies. Retrieved from http://www.safetyzone.org/bio_chem_emergencies.html

Knutson, L. L. (2001, January 14). Clinton says hot line, site to help teens resolve disputes. *Fort Worth Star-Telegram*, p. 23A.

Merriam-Webster's collegiate dictionary. (1993). Springfield, MA: Merriam-Webster.

National Center for Education Statistics. (1998). *Violence and discipline problems in U.S. public schools: 1996–97.* Washington, DC: Author.

Nettleton Public Schools. (2000). *Crisis response plan.* Retrieved from http://nettleton.crsc.k12.ar.us/crisis.htm.

North Carolina State Department of Public Instruction. (1988). *Guidelines for handling crisis situations in the schools.* Raleigh, NC: North Carolina Department of Public Instruction. (ERIC Document Reproduction Service No. ED297233.)

Oconomawac, Wisconsin. (2000). *School safety plan.* Retrieved from http://www.wa.gov/ago/ourschools/5_plan/Excepts.htm.

O'Toole, M. E. (2000). *The school shooter: A threat assessment perspective.* Federal Bureau of Investigation. Washington, DC: National Center for the Analysis of Violent Crime.

Overman, S. (1991). After the smoke clears. *HR Magazine, 36*(11), 44–47.

Pearl School District. (2000). *School safety plan.* Retrieved from http://www.wa.gov/ago/ourschools/5_plan/pearl.htm.

Peterson, S., & Straub, R. (1992). *School crisis survival guide.* West Nyack, NY: Center for Applied Research in Education.

Poland, S., & McCormick, J. S. (1999). *Coping with crisis.* Longmont, CO: Sopris West.

Psychological Services Crisis Intervention: Grant JUHSD. (1998). *Guidelines for establishing crisis intervention teams in local schools.* Retrieved from http://www.grant.K12.Ca.us/grant_html/risk%20management/Crisis%20Intervention.html.

Rettig, M. A. (1999). Seven steps to schoolwide safety. *Principal, 71*(9), 10–13.

Safe Schools Survey 1998. (1998). *Safe schools.* Retrieved from http://www.ag.state.mn.us.

The safety zone. (2002). *Responding to biological and chemical emergencies.* Retrieved from http://www.safetyzone.org/Pdf/winter.

Schwartz, W. (1997). *An overview of strategies to reduce school violence. ERIC clearinghouse on urban education.* Retrieved from http://ericweb.tc.columbia.edu/digests/dig115.html.

Seifert, E. H. (2000). Responding to crisis. In Theodore J. Kowalski (Ed.), *Public relations in schools* (2nd ed., pp. 294–314). Englewood Cliffs, NJ: Merrill Prentice Hall.

Seifert, E. H. (2001). *Crisis management strategies.* Unpublished manuscript.

Serafin, J. (Ed.). (1990). *Be aware be prepared: Guidelines for crisis response planning for school communities.* Denver, CO: Office of Federal/State Programs and Services.

Stephens, R. D. (1998). Ten steps to safer schools. *American School Board Journal, 185*(3), 30–33.

Volokh, A., & Snell, L. (1998). *School violence prevention: Strategies to keep schools safe.* Reason Public Policy Institute. Retrieved from http://www.rppi.org/ps234.html.

Vossekuil, B., Reddy, M., Fein, R., Borum, R., & Modzeleski, W. (2000). *U.S.S.S. safe school initiative: An interim report on the prevention of targeted violence in schools.* Washington, DC: U.S. Secret Service, National Threat Assessment Center.

Warner, C. (1994). *Promoting your school: Going beyond PR.* Thousand Oaks, CA: Corwin Press.

Wayne Township, Indianapolis, Indiana. (2000). *School safety response plan.* Retrieved from http://www.wa.gov/ago/ourschools/5_plan/responplan.htm.

13

Collecting and Analyzing Decision-Oriented Data

A. William Place

Maryanne McNamara

James F. McNamara

The definition of public relations given in Chapter 1 includes providing vital and useful information to the public and employees and serving as an integral part of the planning and decision-making functions. This chapter is most concerned with the concepts of two-way communication and using data for the purposes of planning and decision making. *Decision making* is defined as a process of generating an outcome based on a variety of cognitive, social, and contextual influences (Jones & Beck, 1996). Administrators can make better decisions when they collect and analyze data directly related to these three areas (McNamara, 1993b, 1994a).

Many leadership concepts promote data-driven decision making. For example, Total Quality Management (TQM) includes data-based decisions as a key element. In fact, data-based decision making has been called the "statistical process control movement, which was the precursor of the Total Quality Management movement in industry and education" (Bonstingl, 1992, p. 62). Gathering and analyzing information, however, is not merely a trend; it is an essential component of modern leadership. This process, like other elements of public relations, entails effective two-way communication.

Gathering and analyzing data about the thoughts, feelings, and characteristics of a community is even more important today because of increased diversity in society. In the past the dominant culture has sometimes emphasized one-way communication. Today in our multicultural society, one-way communication, even if it is well intentioned with a good message, is not sufficient for good leadership. Successful practice must include collecting and analyzing data from the various community groups and perspectives. One of the issues addressed in the case study at the end of this chapter is an understanding of why different cultures affect schools in both dramatic ways.

As administrators collect data, they should start with the basics. For example, to measure anything, even a child's height, the assessor should have a clear understanding of purpose (why the measurement is being done) and process (how the measurement will be done). In the case of children's height, the researcher may simply be interested in the distance from the bottom of the children's feet to the top of their head. One accurate way to collect these data is to have each child take off his or her shoes and stand up straight with their back to a tall enough measuring stick. Even with the rather simple task, the researcher must make important decisions that may influence how data will be used, for example, deciding whether to report data in inches or meters.

For educational leaders, decision-making data are often complex and difficult to access. For instance, determining community perceptions of a particular program can be a very intricate assignment. First, the administrator must understand interactions between the program being studied and other programs. That is, how does the program affect other programs, and how do other programs affect this program? Second, the administrator must answer basic questions: What population or sample of a population will be studied? What measure of perception will facilitate making a decision? Third, the administrator must determine whether qualitative data, quantitative data, or both are needed. Whereas quantitative data deal with numbers, qualitative data typically entail thick and rich descriptions, often of situations that are difficult or impossible to study quantitatively.

Qualitative approaches may be preferable when the population or sample is quite small and when the variable being measured is complex (i.e., involving interrelated variables that cannot be neatly separated). If, however, population or sample is large and data can be isolated and clearly defined, then quantitative methods are likely to be more useful. Qualitative approaches are preferable when depth understanding is important; quantitative approaches are preferable when ascertaining general perceptions is the goal. Selection of methodology ought not to be based on the evaluator's preference, but rather should be determined by the type of information needed.

In modern organizations, there is a large inventory of tools that can be used to formalize the collection and analysis of relevant information. It is helpful to think of these tools as systematic procedures used to complete tasks associated with one or more of the major phases in a decision model (McNamara & Chisolm, 1988). When used as intended, these tools improve the capacity to make more effective managerial and policy decisions.[1]

Public relations is viewed here as an organizational activity whose purpose is to provide relevant information assisting policy makers and practitioners in all phases of decision making. From this perspective, public relations plays an instrumental role in *creating* a shared vision among all organizational stakeholders, *designing* a plan of action, and *evaluating* the organization's progress toward reaching its agreed-upon goals.

SOCIAL SCIENTIFIC SURVEYS

In examining the ways in which one can use tools to collect, analyze, and share relevant decision-oriented information, the public relations specialist should look at social scientific surveys as a valuable tool. Conducting a survey prior to making certain administrative decisions may improve the process and outcomes of those decisions. For example, restructuring efforts, adjusting to new state mandates, and determining whether to keep a long-standing program are difficult decisions that should be based on accurate information. In conducting surveys, the identification of key stakeholders helps to determine the population for a study. For example, the planning group considering year-round schooling might want to know the preferences of students, parents, teachers, and voters in the district, stakeholders who are affected if a year-round school calendar is adopted.

When researchers and policy analysts introduce the topic of social scientific surveys, two questions naturally arise. The first is: What is the difference between a *survey* and a *poll*? Some authors (e.g., Bradburn & Sudman, 1988) treat these two terms as being interchangeable; differences usually relate to application. For example, polling involves surveying the public. Education researchers and practicing administrators typically use the term *survey*, or they use yet another synonym, *questionnaire*.

The second question that arises is: What is the difference between a *social scientific survey* and a *probability sampling survey*? Put briefly, these two terms are also interchangeable. Social scientific surveys use probability sampling to ensure that the sample is an accurate representation of the population to which the survey researcher wishes to

---

[1]Surveys, like other scientific and technical tools, can be well or poorly made and can be used in appropriate or inappropriate ways. In their widely referenced book, Bradburn and Sudman (1988) discuss wide-range survey uses and provide excellent examples of appropriate, inappropriate, and questionable usage.

generalize (Babbie, 1990). A *margin of error* (an essential feature of social scientific surveys) can be constructed *only* when a true probability sampling plan is implemented (O'Shea, 1992; Williams, 1978).[2]

Sampling Issues

Most often it is not necessary to survey an entire population to get an accurate measure of opinions, because a scientific random sample may produce results very close to those obtained from an entire population. This is because a scientific random sample, by definition, provides an equal chance that every individual in a population will be chosen (Krathwohl, 1998). A true random sample is free of bias or predetermined purpose that would skew the results. It is far different from the case where only people who happen to be at a particular place are asked to complete a survey (e.g., the mall, or even an open forum held at one of the schools). Random samples are systematically selected through a computer or a table of random numbers that matches an individual in the population with a selected number. Often a simple random sample is sufficient to produce the desired information. However, if the administrator seeks to produce information about subgroups, a stratified random sample may be more appropriate. This technique produces separate samples of proportional size so that the subgroups are representative of the whole population. As an example, a stratified random sample is the appropriate choice if a planning committee wants to compare the preferences of stakeholder groups (e.g., parents versus nonparent taxpayers). To ensure adequate statistical power (i.e., the ability of the survey to detect true preference differences), at least 100 randomly chosen survey respondents are recommended for each stakeholder group.[3]

If the planning committee wished to compare the preferences of two or more stakeholder groups using formal statistical tests (e.g., a t-test of proportions from two independent groups or an F-test of proportions of two or more independent groups entered in an analysis of variance model), then the sample sizes should be based on sample size formulae used in hypothesis-testing designs to ensure adequate statistical power. Differences in the rules between formulae used elsewhere to determine sample size and those used in hypothesis testing can be found in research method books (e.g., McNamara, 1994b).

If a population is small (e.g., 100 or 200), random sampling may not always be a good choice. For example, a principal surveying the parents of fifth-grade students should include all of them. When all individuals in a group are included you have a population (see Table 13–1 for examples of the differences among samples and populations). With small populations, scientific random sampling excludes a relatively small number of people. Any cost savings associated with using random sampling (e.g., as a result of having to send out fewer surveys) may be outweighed by the ill feeling of those individuals who

---

[2]To learn more about basic survey operations, see McNamara (1994b).
[3]The specific reason for recommending at least 100 respondents in each stakeholder group is to ensure that the survey sampling design and the corresponding test statistics are able to detect real and meaningful group differences. For a brief overview of statistical power and its sampling requirements, see McNamara (1991, 1994b, Chap. 3).

TABLE 13–1

Examples of Populations and Samples

Category	Examples
Population	All parents of students in a school; all parents of students in a grade within a school; all adult residents in a school district
Random sample	Every third parent from an alphabetized list of all parents in a school district; 20% of the parents from a middle school selected through a random drawing
Stratified random sample	Every third male parent and every third female parent from an alphabetized list of all parents in a school district; 10% of parents in each of three income categories (high, average, low) selected through a random drawing
Nonrandom sample	Every individual who physically visits a school and completes a survey there; parents who actually file a complaint with a school official

were not included. Stratified random sampling can be viewed as a series of simple random sampling designs with each person in the population appearing on only one list.[4]

In a policy preference survey of members in each of several stakeholder groups, some of the names will appear on more than one list. For example, a teacher may also be a parent. This poses no real problem, however; if a teacher's name were selected from the population list of teachers, the response requested would be from a teacher's perspective. If the teacher's name were also selected from a population list of parents, the parent's viewpoint would be requested.

In situations where sampling is a preferred approach, the researcher must determine a reasonable margin of error as well as a reasonable level of confidence. The margin of error is a measure of how closely the information obtained from a sample represents the entire population. The level of confidence deals with acknowledging that in a few cases it is possible that the results are not as close to the population as the margin of error adopted. If the results of a survey indicated that 80% of the parents were in favor of the new plan, the margin of error indicates how close to exactly 80% of the population is actually in favor. Specifically, a margin of error of plus or minus five percentage points would mean that the 80% result would be an estimate that ranges from 75 to 85% for the actual results that would be obtained if the whole population were surveyed. In many cases this would be close enough, but if for another question there was a need to be more exact, then a smaller margin of error would need to be set (e.g., a margin of error of plus or minus two percentage points would mean that with an 80% result, the estimate would range from 78 to 82%).

This level of confidence is typically stated in terms of *error probability*. For example, if the researcher sets the probability of sample data being in error at .05, he or she is accepting the fact that there are 5 chances in 100 that the results obtained from the sample are not accurate (defined by the margin of error) for the entire population. This is also referred to as a 95% confidence level. Although not a universal standard and not something that should be accepted lightly or without thoughtful consideration, that is a commonly used confidence level. Many researchers would say that 95% allows enough confidence that the

---

[4]On the use of stratified sampling in policy preference surveys, see McNamara (1994b). For an easy-to-read treatment of all essential features of stratified random sampling see Sheaffer, Mendenhall, and Ott (1990, Chap. 5).

results obtained are very close to the results that would have been obtained if everyone in the population had been asked and therefore is acceptable for purposes of administrative decision making. To put it another way, a 95% confidence level indicates that in less than 5 out of 100 samples you would obtain the 80% results if the population were more than 85% in favor or less than 75% in favor.

Return Rates

Another important aspect of using surveys to collect data is the return rate. The size of a sample is important, but the return rate of your survey is even more crucial in the interpretation of the results. Although the size of the population can make some differences for any large population, a sample of 384 will be sufficient to obtain a .05 level of confidence with a 5% margin of error. However, it is the return rate that is used to estimate how much the results can be generalized (i.e., for interpreting what the population response would have been had the entire population been surveyed). Private businesses often are willing to make decisions based on surveys with relatively low return rates (e.g., 20% or less) because the risk does not involve a public interest. However, the type of decisions (e.g., marketing) made in the private sector are quite different from those that educational administrators make that involve the expenditure of public funds and, more important, influence the future of students.

When an educational decision is made based on survey data, the administrator should remember that the information collected provides no insights about those who did not respond. Therefore, with a 40% response rate, no conclusion can be made about the other 60%. If information about nonrespondents is needed, follow-up studies may be necessary. However, it is less expensive to properly design surveys to enhance return rates. Educators often seek return rates of 60–80% or more so that the known outweighs the unknown. Schools have an advantage over other groups doing surveys if they include information identifying that it is important to get input from *all* citizens. However, it does need to be emphasized that even those without children need to give input on certain issues. Most people will respond to a short survey (something that takes 5 minutes or less) if it is from the schools because many people do care about kids or at least the tax dollars needed to support the kids. The survey's clarity, length, design, and interest that it holds for the respondents as well as the method of implementation can greatly impact the return rate.

In addition to the practical considerations of aggravating people, there are ethical considerations involved in survey research. Since ethical concerns are sometimes not considered to be part of scientific methods, researchers and practitioners look to another set of guidelines. These guidelines are given in the *Code of Professional Ethics and Practices* published by The American Association of Public Opinion Research (AAPOR), an interdisciplinary association of both academic and commercial survey researchers.[5]

---

[5]A reprint of the AAPOR code can be found in Babbie (1990). On the use of ethical guidelines for survey research in educational organizations, see also McNamara (1994b).

Method of Implementation

There are four methods of using surveys to collect data: (a) the personal face-to-face interview, (b) the written form dropped off to be picked up later or the mailed questionnaire, (c) the telephone interview, and (d) the Internet or e-mail survey. Each has strengths and weaknesses, which should be considered. The wording of questions is important in all four methods.

There are strengths associated with face-to-face interviews that other approaches lack. As an example, clarifying questions can be asked when the information being considered is complex or detailed. In addition, this method typically produces a high return rate, which as noted is very important. However, the personal face-to-face interview often has serious limitations and problems associated with it. Consider some of the more prevalent concerns:

♦ Unless the interviewer is properly trained, face-to-face interviews may produce unreliable data. An inadequately prepared interviewer may behave inconsistently. For example, the interviewer's nonverbal behaviors or verbal inflections may be uneven across the interviewers—a condition that could result in varying levels of influence on the respondents. Put another way, inconsistencies in the questions or interviewer behavior are very likely to produce reliability problems for quantitative data.

♦ Validity (i.e., accuracy) is also a potential concern with face-to-face interviews. Specifically, interviewees often feel compelled to give socially acceptable responses (or politically correct responses). When the interviewer and interviewee know each other, the interviewee may be reluctant to provide any answer that he or she believes will offend or anger the interviewee. For example, some citizens may tell an administrator that they support a tax referendum for a new school building when they do not.

♦ The environment in which data are collected may influence answers. For example, an interviewer may conduct the sessions in the interviewee's home. A noisy or messy environment may influence the tone of the communication (e.g., influence eye contact or candidness). In a true random sample, some respondents may reside in geographic areas where the crime rate is high or security restricts access; consequently, interviewers may be reluctant to or unable to interview everyone in the sample.

A written form dropped off and picked up by the researcher also requires communication skills. For example, the respondent may ask questions about the survey or the meaning of some of the items on the survey. Therefore, it has some of the disadvantages of face-to-face interviews, but to a lesser degree.

The mailed questionnaire is very popular largely because it is time efficient. A big advantage of this method is candidness, especially if anonymity is ensured. In addition, all individuals in the population or sample probably can be reached via mail, and this option is relatively inexpensive. The technique, however, has three noteworthy potential problems:

1. The technique tends to have the lowest return rate among primary survey methods.
2. A person other than the intended respondent could fill out the questionnaire and return it.
3. Pressure groups may try to influence respondents.

There are some things that can be done to increase the return rate. Specific strategies can be found in most basic survey research texts.

The e-mail survey is a variation of the mailed questionnaire. It has become increasingly popular because of its low cost and relative speed. Because anonymity cannot be ensured, some members of the population or sample refuse to respond or give less than honest answers. In certain school districts, a significant portion of the population, those without e-mail addresses, may be automatically excluded if this technique is used. As the volume of e-mail increases, many individuals quickly sort incoming communications or have list servers sort them. Thus, a survey could be discarded before the interviewee even sees it.

The telephone interview is another inexpensive way to collect data in a relatively short time, especially if all the calls are toll-free or made with a special long-distance line. This option, however, also has several limitations.

♦ Some residents may have unlisted phone numbers, making them ineligible to participate.
♦ Some residents may not have a telephone.
♦ Some residents may hang up immediately after receiving an interview call because of their attitude toward telemarketing.

Training is a key variable for success with telephone interviews. Such preparation helps ensure interviewer consistency.

Survey Question Development

Incorrectly wording survey questions can waste time and effort. For example, answers to poorly worded questions are generally unusable. Designing a survey question may seem like a simple task, but it is not. Often questions do not ask what is intended or the question is ambiguous. Consider, for example, the *double-barreled question*—a question that asks two things at the same time. For example, "Do you favor year-round schools and longer school days?" The respondent may be confused if he or she agrees with one part of the question, but not the other.

There are several other pitfalls to be avoided. One of the most common is the *ambiguous* or *unclear question*. Here a problem results because the researcher and respondent are using different frames of reference. For example, a respondent may not understand a question that reads: "Is the principal doing a good job?" This question could be interpreted in many different ways because performance criteria are not identified.

Another concern is the *esoteric question*. This problem involves using words or concepts not understood by some or all of the respondents. For example, one superintendent surveyed parents about their support for year-round school calendars, but never described or defined the concept. Most parents simply failed to respond to the survey. Because education surveys are intended to obtain accurate data for the entire community, great care should be given to drafting questions in language that can be understood across social, economic, and cultural groups.

Response options also are another important consideration. A principal, for example, distributed a survey to parents asking, "How long have you lived in this district?" A blank space was provided for the answer, but neither instructions nor response choices were listed. Consequently, the respondents answered in many different ways ranging from exact quantitative data to very general statements (e.g., "a very long time"). As a result, the principal was unable to tabulate the answers. This principal should have provided a finite number of response choices (e.g., less than 1 year, 1 to 3 years, and so forth). When establishing response choices it is essential to consider the type of information needed. Also, the options need to be clear. An example of unclear choices would be: from 0 to 10 years; 10 or more years. A person having lived in the district for 10 years could select either option.

Researchers obviously cannot respond to clarification questions raised by respondents using a written survey. For this reason, these instruments usually contain instructions and clarifying information, such as definitions of key terms. But, such additions to a survey can cause problems. For example, clarifying information suggesting that a proposed program will result in cost savings may strongly influence the level of support for the program. For this reason, definitions and clarifications should be as neutral and accurate as possible.

Asking leading questions is another potential problem. These are questions designed to encourage the respondent to give the researcher answers he or she prefers. Most people resent being manipulated; therefore, even the mere suggestion of manipulation may result in a loss of trust and unreliable responses.

Conducting pilot studies—collecting data from a group of individuals who are similar to the targeted population—can be very helpful in survey research. Such studies, for instance, may reveal if certain survey questions are leading, ambiguous, or double-barreled. A pilot study also may uncover questions or wording that are or may be potentially offensive. Conversely, results from these studies may reveal the need to add additional questions to the survey before it is used with the targeted population. The effectiveness of a pilot study depends largely on whether the researcher selects a group of respondents who are reasonably similar to the targeted population. If a researcher's ultimate goal is to poll taxpayers in a school district, he or she must use a group of respondents in the pilot study who possess characteristics representative of those taxpayers (e.g., income level, political persuasion, education level).

Other considerations administrators should make about using surveys include the following:

◆ Respondents often believe that the researcher has an implied obligation to share the outcomes of the survey with them. For this reason, the researcher should inform participants regarding this matter at the time that their participation is requested. The AAPOR has set both ethical guidelines and scientific standards for reporting survey research findings. In addition to reporting the margin of error, seven other items should appear in a publication reporting survey results: *sample size, sponsor, response rate, dates when the data were collected, an accurate definition of the population, how respondents were contacted,* and the *precise wording of questions used in the survey.* See Babbie (1990) and McNamara (1994b) for more complete information about these topics.

◆ Because information gathered by public schools is almost always in the public domain, consideration should be given to how data will be analyzed and reported before they are collected.

◆ Survey instruments should be "user friendly." That is, they should be concise, clearly worded in language that the respondents can comprehend, and printed at a level of quality allowing respondents to read them without difficulty. Many respondents will elect not to complete a survey if it requires more than 10 minutes of their time or if completing it requires special effort.

- The purpose and importance of a survey need to be explained. In the case of education, such information often is a deciding factor determining if a person will respond. If the project is quite large, purpose and importance can be conveyed to the entire population through press releases or public service announcements.
- Providing a prepaid postage envelope (or a one-page fold-over form with prepaid postage) can be a determining factor in getting a respondent to complete and return a survey. Consequently, such return envelopes should be used in direct-mail surveys.
- Researchers should include an introductory letter to the survey that states (a) the purpose and importance of the study, (b) conditions of anonymity (it is almost always preferable to provide anonymity unless there are ethical reasons not to do so), (c) an explanation of how the results will be used, and (d) a statement of appreciation for the respondent's cooperation.

QUALITATIVE RESEARCH STRATEGIES: THE CASE STUDY

In keeping with the rich historical overview provided by Lancy (1993), most social science researchers and program evaluators acknowledge the case study to be an integral part of the qualitative research tradition. Along with Stenhouse (1985) and Patton (2002), Lancy argues that case studies conducted in educational research share a common purpose: they all address directly the improvement of practice. Accordingly, case studies in education are designed to influence important educational policy decisions.

Yin (1984) suggests that the case study has at least four applications:

1. *Explaining* the casual relationships in real-life interventions that are too complex for the survey or experimental strategies
2. *Describing* the real-life context in which an intervention has occurred
3. *Creating* a rich illustration or journalistic account of a specific intervention
4. *Exploring* situations where a promising intervention has no clear, single inventory of outcomes

Case studies (usually conducted using open-ended interviews with individuals or groups) are also often used as an initial step in the design of a standardized instrument or a custom-made questionnaire to be used later in a social scientific survey. The use of focus groups is one of the prevalent methods for this activity; the use of focus groups is explained in a number of research methodology books (e.g., Morgan, 1997; Stewart & Shamdasani, 1990).

Using the first two phases of Simon's (1977) decision model, a case study focusing on collaboration between schools and universities is developed here to demonstrate how data can be collected, analyzed, and reported. The two phases are an *intelligence activity*, which focuses on problem-defining tasks, and a *design activity*, which focuses on problem-solving tasks.

Setting Up the Case Study

Over the past decade, school and university collaborative arrangements have been under-taken as a means to bridge the gap between theory and practice, as well as the gap between public schools and teacher training. Although it has become commonplace for public schools and universities to agree to become partners, getting a productive venture started requires answers to several key questions: How do people come together? Who provides the leadership for a collaborative? Who initiates and who responds? What problems can best be solved using collaborative strategies? How are prospective collaborative research projects identified? How are proposed new collaborative search projects approved?

Assume that these policy questions pertain to a newly formed venture in which educa-tion school professors and public school practitioners in a single district intend to conduct joint research and development projects. Also assume that the university collaborators were asked explicitly by their school district colleagues to take the lead in two areas: *designing* the organizational governance structure for the partnership and *identifying* prom-ising cooperative search and development projects.

One way the university collaborators could be responsive, but not prescriptive, would be to use the case study as a decision tool to uncover *how* school partners would prefer to interact with key players in the collaborative and *what* real-world problems these school district practitioners would like to research together.

In the case study offered below, the superintendent was chosen to be the school partner whose views were to be collected, analyzed, and ultimately shared with those having the responsibility to shape a productive partnership. Obviously, other school partner case study efforts could be (and more than likely would be) conducted following the four-phase strat-egy elaborated below. Put briefly, these phases are collecting the data, analyzing the data, verifying the findings, and sharing the report.

Using the Case Study in Decision Making

Phase 1: Collecting the Data.   The collaborating school district superintendent was interviewed on a Friday morning, June 18, 1993. The interview started at 9:15 and was concluded at 10:15. A semistructured instrument was used, containing a few general questions designed to elicit the superintendent's perspectives on school and university col-laboration in her school district. The overall issue in the protocol dealt with collaboration. What follows is a transcript of the one-hour interview.

> *Question: What role do you (as superintendent) play in school-university collaboration in your district?*
>
> First, I want to make it clear that any collaboration between the school and univer-sity must be a good fit with our district's mission. I want to assure you that *all* of our students receive the best education—not just a select few.
>
> *Question: How do you interact with key players in the collaboration? What communication strategies do you use?*
>
> My role involves setting up communication channels that are formal. For example, it is my understanding that there is a subgroup—namely, the Administration Council

(10 key players in our collaborative)—that is cochaired by my assistant superintendent for instruction. He informs me about the goings-on of the collaborative, and I, in turn, keep the board of trustees updated.

Question: How do you do this—communicate with the board, that is?

I brought this idea with me from my last superintendency in [another city]. I personally write a formal update of issues to be shared with the board in a weekly written report called *Board Notes*. Board notes are separated into two categories. One includes ongoing activities that the board needs to know about—such as details about what is happening at our partnership middle school. The other focuses on separate issues that require board action. I have a senior administrative staff member who helps me on this. This is my way of informing *all* board members. In other words, *no* single board member receives information that is not provided to other board members. This is a kind of one-on-one, almost face-to-face communication strategy. It avoids the common problem that many superintendents have when some board members receive more information than others do. I also have a CONFIDENTIAL stamp that I use for information that should not go beyond their purview. This way we have a common level of understanding about confidentiality.

Question: Do you have a screening procedure for collaboration with the university?

Yes, we are now involved with another collaborative at a second partnership school (an elementary school that is operating as a professional development school). This partnership will involve a host of projects that must be screened. My assistant superintendent for instruction will be responsible for this. Again, let me say that collaboration ventures are messy and I understand and welcome that.

Question: What do you mean by "messy"?

Any effort to change the way things have always been done is messy. If we expect innovation, then we have to be able to tolerate ambiguity, and I have a high tolerance for ambiguity. However, I know when to draw the line. If I believe that any of these programs are counter to our mission, then I put a halt to it.

Question: What are your thoughts on the university's ultimate goal—to involve other professionals from health care and human services in the collaboration?

I feel that this will take time, and I'll tell you why. There is some confusion among parents and board members about issues like condom distribution. That's the bottom line. Sadly enough, whenever parents hear about health services coming into the school, they believe that their morals will be compromised. This is unfortunate because our goal is to have students coming to school ready to learn, and they can't do this when they aren't healthy—physically or mentally healthy. In my last superintendency, we had a health center located on our high school campus. It worked beautifully. The students who used it were for the most part—and I mean about 95%—students that had stomachaches, sore throats, toothaches, and so on. Normally they would stay home for at least a day, and in the case of sore throats, they'd be out for a week if an infection occurred. This way, with a health center, they came to school knowing they'd get help. They'd miss only an hour or so of school. Schools need to take the position that a health center facilitates bringing service to where the customer is. We can serve kids best by keeping them in school. This is why stores like Randall's have film developing and flower delivery services located right in the store. It's good business!

Question: Do you see moving toward full-service schools anytime soon?
This will take time. We need to work on our constituency. Educate them. Get them to understand the need. They must understand that schools are not insular. [The city where I previously had a superintendency] already has networks with a variety of other groups. I realize, though, that this community is conservative and will reject this move. We need to build trust. Explain that only a small number of cases deal with the issues they fear most.

Question: Do you have any other concerns that you want to discuss about the superintendent's role in collaboration?
Yes. The district and the university need to get together and sit down and say we won't have things done the way they're being done in the language arts area. Our students deserve a better program—not one where reading and writing and grammar are separated into different classes. I see this as urgent and critical. It's a travesty that these subjects are taught separately. We must put a stop to it. This idea of separate subjects is one of the keenest instructional issues I've had to face.

Question: Why is it so difficult to change? Can't you just demand a change?
Again, here is something that will take time and training. I was shocked at the initial response I received when I proposed an instructional change with teachers. One teacher actually said, "We see ourselves as grammarians, not as remedial teachers." They confuse reading classes with remediation—a carryover from the past. We are giving one more year to allow teachers to adjust to the idea of teaching in another way. We'll provide training. We'll seek a waiver for certification problems, and we'll provide a safety net for teachers. But change they must!

Question: Do you see collaboration with the university as help with this?
Yes. Together maybe we can change teacher attitudes. We need to sit down together—all of us—[this city], the university, *and* [another major city in the region that also has its own independent school district]. We need to show teachers and principals evidence that these areas—reading, writing, literature, grammar—are interdependent. They must be taught together, not in unrelated packages. We want our schools to produce clear thinkers, and one way to do this is to provide students with more than we presently offer. This is our challenge. [End of the formal interview.]

Phase 2: Analyzing the Data. In analyzing the data from the superintendent's interview, the case study researcher uncovered six emergent themes that help clarify how the superintendent views her role in school and university collaboration arrangements.

1. *Promoting the district's mission*—The superintendent was clear about the necessity for a good fit between university goals and the mission of the district. As superintendent she believes her role is to ensure that the district's mission is the driving force behind collaborative activities.
2. *Respecting community values*—The superintendent respects the values and beliefs of all stakeholders in her community. She understands that the community values

cannot be compromised. Implementing collaborative programs involving health care and human services in the schools will work *only if* the community believes that the effort is meaningful.

3. *Communicating with the school board*—The superintendent's role includes following an organized strategy for informing board members about collaborative activities. In addition to meeting with them monthly, she sends each board member a weekly copy of the *Board Notes*.

4. *Defining problems*—The superintendent's role as problem definer is reflected in her description of instructional changes that she hopes to implement. Although she welcomes input from university personnel, it is clear that she will *not* allow them to dictate what changes are necessary in district classrooms.

5. *Empowering key players*—The superintendent's role in collaboration includes sharing power with her assistant superintendent for instruction, her special council members, principals, and teachers. In accordance with this role, the superintendent promotes staff development and other workshops for training teachers. Her goal is to encourage teachers to assume ownership and leadership in efforts toward change. She is sensitive and responsive to their concerns.

6. *Reaping benefits*—The superintendent sees school and university collaboration as a way to effect positive change in teaching and learning in her district. For example, she suggested that a collaborative effort would be an excellent way to solve the school district's instructional problem regarding the need to integrate reading, literature, writing, and language arts. It is also of interest to note that she believes collaboration efforts can involve several school districts working together with the university to solve problems of mutual interests. For example, in the interview she suggested that both her school district and the other major school district in the regional area might both join with the university to work on a curriculum project devoted to integrating instruction in reading, literature, writing, and language arts.

Reanalysis of these six themes indicated that they were consistent with the literature on successful collaboration. Most important among these themes is the superintendent's insistence that school-university collaboration be based on a shared vision of the outcomes to be produced by their joint efforts.

Phase 3: Verifying the Findings. Once the initial draft of the case study report is prepared, the next step is to share this written record with the superintendent, who should verify the accuracy of both the interview text and themes that were uncovered in the phase 2 analysis of the data.[6] Also to be accomplished in phase 3 are two additional important

[6]In naturalistic inquiries, the phase 3 verification activities described here are seen as "carrying out a member check." The purpose of a member check is not only to test for factual and interpretative accuracy, but also to provide evidence of credibility (a criterion of quality research analogous to internal validity in conventional quantitative studies such as scientific surveys). On member checks, see especially Lincoln and Guba (1985, Chap. 11) and Erlandson, Harris, Skipper, and Allen, (1993, Chap. 7).

concerns. First, the superintendent and the case study researcher should discuss any special circumstances (ethical and legal issues) that might require revision before the report is shared in a public meeting.[7]

Once the case study report is revised and meets with the approval of both the university researcher and the school district superintendent, the researcher should exercise professional courtesy and formally request the superintendent's permission to go public with the final draft of the report. Going public at this point means sharing the case study report with school district and university collaborators.

Phase 4: Sharing the Report.   When the case study is used as a decision tool, it is essential that the report be written and shared with the intended audience. In many circumstances, the format used to report case study results can vary. For example, Merriam (1988) suggests that one might consider executive summaries or specialized condensations. Yin (1984) offers another suggestion: replace the narrative with a set of open-ended questions and answers drawn from the data.

For this case study on the superintendent's position regarding school-university collaboration, the report probably should remain in the format presented here. Accordingly, the first part of the report is in question-and-answer form (using the actual semistructured questions raised in the interview) and the second part provides brief analytic summaries of themes uncovered in data analysis. To maximize the value of this information in a planning work session, the case study report would be distributed to work session participants about a week prior to the actual session. Moreover, having the superintendent present as a participant in the session is advantageous.

Essential Characteristics of a Case Study

The unique value of the case study as a decision tool can be recognized by reflecting on its essential characteristics. Merriam (1988) has pointed out four properties of case studies that are especially important:

1. *They are particularistic.* This implies that case studies focus on a particular situation, event, program, individual, or group. They can suggest to the reader what to do or what not to do. They can concentrate on a specific instance but illuminate a general problem or outcome.
2. *They are descriptive.* This implies that case studies yield a rich description of the event or entity being investigated. They can illustrate the complexities of a situation, identify differences in opinion on an issue, and suggest how these differences might influence the actual decision reached. Most important, they can describe the views of a wide array of organizational stakeholders.
3. *They are heuristic.* This implies that case studies extend the reader's understanding of the issue or entity selected for inquiry. Accordingly, they can explain the reason

---

[7]On dealing with the issues of validity, reliability, and ethics in qualitative case study research, see especially the treatment of these issues in Merriam (1988, Chap. 10).

for a problem, lead to the discovery of new relationships, verify (or negate) an informed speculation, and most important, explain why an innovative program worked or failed to work.

4. *They are inductive.* This implies that case studies rely on inductive reasoning. As such, they begin with collection of data (empirical observations of interest) and then identify theoretical categories and patterns (trends or propositions) from relationships uncovered in data analysis.

Two additional points deserve mention. First, the case study does not claim any particular method for either data collection or data analysis. However, qualitative methods are most often chosen in conducting case studies because researchers or policy analysts are primarily interested in insight, discovery, and interpretation rather than in testing hypotheses or estimating parameters. Second, it should be kept in mind that the case study is just one of many qualitative decision tools that can be used to inform administrative decision making.

SUMMARY

Three essential ideas were advanced in this chapter. First, both the selection and application of either the social scientific survey (a quantitative method) or the case study (a qualitative method) as a decision tool can be linked directly to administrative decision making. Second, collecting and analyzing data are necessary activities but not sufficient in themselves to inform decision making. These two essential functions must be followed by a formal effort to prepare and share a written report that effectively communicates the findings of the inquiry with the intended audience. Third, the decision-making tools discussed in this chapter can be used by administrators to create a shared vision, design a plan of action, and evaluate progress toward reaching agreed-upon goals.

Administrators interested in taking the lead in the use of modern decision tools in districts and schools should heed the words of Machiavelli in *The Prince*:

> There is nothing more difficult to take in hand, more perilous to conduct, or more uncertain in its success, than to take the lead in the introduction of a new order of things, because the innovator has for enemies all those who have done well under the old conditions and lukewarm defenders in those who may do well under the new law.

CASE STUDY

Good Intentions Aren't Always Enough

Having to spend extra time hunting for a parking space at the John F. Kennedy Elementary School was not in Jane West's plan for this April evening. As director of communications for the Lancaster School District, Dr. West was ending a 2-week marathon of scheduled meetings in each of the district's seven elementary schools. The purpose of these meetings was to share information with parents about a proposed new year-round calendar to be piloted in the district beginning in September.

Persons attending each elementary school campus meeting had been asked to fill out and return a questionnaire related to their interest in having their children participate in the new year-round school pilot program. Questionnaire responses from previous elementary school meetings indicated that, in general, parents were supportive of the program. However, West was cautious about this finding because she realized that (a) attendance at the previous meetings had been low, (b) those in attendance had come from what is considered to be more affluent sections of the district, and (c) many of those attending had not returned their questionnaires.

After searching several minutes for a parking spot, West was convinced that the low attendance would not be an issue at tonight's meeting. As she entered the cafeteria, she saw that all seats were taken and that a few parents were standing. She was surprised to see the large numbers of preschool children accompanying their parents.

The audience was largely Hispanic, and West was pleased that she'd had the good sense to arrange to have a translator at the meeting, since many of the residents in this area of the school district were new immigrants.

When West turned on the overhead projector and began her presentation, she heard shouts coming from several areas of the room. "No! We don't want to hear about something that you've already decided for us." "We can't afford to have our children out of school at odd times of the year. How will we find babysitters?" "We've heard rumors that you're going to force all of the children in *this* neighborhood to go to school this summer." "Why is it that no one has asked *us* what we think about a year-round school program?"

West, though startled, recovered quickly: "Your children brought information home last month, and the local newspaper published two articles on this pilot program just last week. We're now asking you to fill out this questionnaire so that we'll *know* how you feel." But her enthusiasm to share more information about the program was quickly eroded as she realized that the angry questions and comments were not going to stop.

At the close of the meeting, a frustrated West had her assistants pass out the questionnaires. "Before you go home could you please fill these out?" she asked. "We'll pay close attention to your responses."

Several parents had already left the building before the questionnaires were distributed. A few people crumpled the sheets when they saw that the forms were written in English. Most people, however, simply left the questionnaires on their empty seats. As the last of her audience filed out, West leaned over and dejectedly picked up a few of the questionnaires that had floated to the floor.

Early the next morning, Jane West sat in her office thinking about the series of meetings she had conducted on the year-round school pilot program. Last night's meeting at the John F. Kennedy Elementary School had made it clear that something more needed to be done to get clarity on whether or not families with children in district schools were interested in exploring year-round schools. What should she do to get accurate information on how the pilot program could best work for them? Would "working best for them" be different for different types of families?

QUESTIONS AND SUGGESTED ACTIVITIES

Four specific activities are offered below to link the quantitative and the qualitative strategies detailed in this chapter with problems encountered in practice. Each of these suggested activities can be conducted by individual students or carried out by one or more groups.

CASE STUDY

1. You are the new incoming principal of the John F. Kennedy Elementary School and you were just hired last month. A local state university that has an excellent record of collaborating with school districts is located just 20 minutes from your school. Given the problems described in the case study, Jane West, the director of communication, has expressed an interest in having you and the field studies research group from the local university conduct a needs assessment for the district.

   You meet with Dr. West and learn that the needs assessment must answer two policy questions: What percentage of the families residing in the Kennedy School boundaries with school-age children are interested in participating in a year-round school program? Do the families express a preference for a type of year-round calendar (e.g., single track or multiple track)? In addition, Dr. West lets you know that she is agreeable to using both a social scientific survey and a set of case studies to explore these two policy questions in detail.

   With this information in hand, you agree to prepare a two-page needs assessment proposal elaborating a specific research plan for the Lancaster School District and forward it to Dr. West. Prepare the proposal. You may include some draft questions (as an appendix) and rationale for each question that you think could provide useful data for your decisions.

2. Was Dr. West properly prepared for the meeting with parents? Why or why not?

3. Why did so many parents elect not to fill out the survey?

CHAPTER

4. Invite an educational research methods professor to join one of your public relations classes. Prior to the professor's visit, each student should develop at least one question to ask the professor about collecting, analyzing, and reporting data for a district or school.

5. What are some common errors that can be made in constructing questions for a survey?

6. What is a pilot study? What are the purposes of a pilot study?

7. What are some of the advantages and disadvantages of conducting face-to-face interviews?

8. Should a researcher always convey the purposes and importance of a study to potential respondents? Why or why not?

9. What is the basic difference between quantitative and qualitative data?

10. How can collecting data from the public enhance public relations programming in a school or district?

SUGGESTED READINGS

Bradburn, N. M., & Sudman, S. (1988). *Polls and surveys: Understanding what they tell us.* San Francisco: Jossey-Bass.

Carbonaro, M., & Bainbridge, J. (2000). Design and development of a process for Web-based survey research. *Alberta Journal of Educational Research, 46*(4) 392–394.

Jacobs, L. R., & Shapiro, R. Y. (1996). Toward the integrated study of political communications, public opinion, and the policy-making process. *PS: Political Science and Politics, 29*(1), 10–13.

Jaeger, R. M. (1984). *Sampling in education and social sciences.* New York: Longman.

Krejcie, R. V., & Morgan, D. A. (1970). Determining sample size for research activity. *Educational and Psychological Measurement, 30* (6), 607–610.

McNamara, J. F. (1994). *Surveys and experiments in educational research.* Lancaster, PA: Technomic.

McNamara, J. F. (1997). Parental views on the biggest problems facing public schools: National versus local findings. *International Journal of Educational Reform, 6*(3), 377–389.

Merriam, S. B. (1988). *Case study research in education: A qualitative approach.* San Francisco: Jossey-Bass.

Newman, I., & Benz, C. R. (1998). *Qualitative-quantitative research methodology.* Carbondale, IL: Southern University Press.

Tacheny, S. A. (1997). Polls are useful: Yes, no, or maybe? *Educational Leadership, 54*(5), 49–51.

REFERENCES

Babbie, E. (1990). *Survey research methods* (2nd ed.). Belmont, CA: Wadsworth.

Bonstingl, J. J. (1992). *Schools of quality: An introduction to Total Quality Management in education.* Alexandria, VA: Association for Supervision and Curriculum Development.

Bradburn, N. M., & Sudman, S. (1988). *Polls and surveys: Understanding what they tell us.* San Francisco: Jossey-Bass.

Erlandson, D. A., Harris, E. L., Skipper, B. L., & Allen, S. D. (1993). *Doing naturalistic inquiry: A guide to methods.* Newbury Park, CA: Sage.

Jones, R. A., & Beck, S. E. (1996). *Decision making in nursing.* Albany, NY: Delmar.

Krathwohl, D. R. (1998). *Methods of educational & social science research: An integrated approach* (2nd ed.). New York: Longman.

Lancy, D. F. (1993). *Qualitative research in education: An introduction to the major traditions.* New York: Longman.

Lincoln, Y. S., & Guba, E. G. (1985). *Naturalistic inquiry.* Newbury Park, CA: Sage.

McNamara, J. F. (1991). Statistical power in educational research. *National Forum of Applied Educational Research Journal, 3*(2), 23–26.

McNamara, J. F. (1993a). Ethical guidelines in survey research. *International Journal of Educational Reform, 2*(2), 213–223. (Reprinted in McNamara, 1994b.)

McNamara, J. F. (1993b). Administrative decision making: Part one. *International Journal of Educational Reform, 2*(4), 465–474.

McNamara, J. F. (1994a). Administrative decision making. Part two. *International Journal of Educational Reform, 3*(1), 113–121.

McNamara, J. F. (1994b). *Surveys and experiments in educational research.* Lancaster, PA: Technomic.

McNamara, J. F., & Chisolm, G. B. (1988). The technical tools of decision making. In N. J. Boyan (Ed.), *Handbook of research on educational administration (pp. 525–567).* New York: Longman.

Merriam, S. B. (1988). *Case study research in education: A qualitative approach.* San Francisco: Jossey-Bass.

Morgan, D. L. (1997). *Focus groups as qualitative research* (2nd ed.). Thousand Oaks, CA: Sage.

O'Shea, D. W. (1992). Survey design. In M. C. Alkin (Ed.), *Encyclopedia of educational research* (6th ed.,) (pp. 1323–1331). New York: Macmillan.

Patton, M. Q. (2002). *Qualitative research and evaluation methods* (3rd ed.). Thousand Oaks, CA: Sage.

Sheaffer, R. L., Mendenhall, W., & Ott, L. (1990). *Elementary survey sampling* (4th ed.). Boston: Duxbury.

Simon, H. A. (1977). *The new science of management decision* (Rev. ed.). Englewood Cliffs, NJ: Prentice Hall.

Stenhouse, L. (1985). A note on case study and educational practice. In R. G. Burgess (Ed.), *Field methods in the study of education* (pp. 263–271). London: Falmer Press.

Stewart, D. W., & Shamdasani, P. N. (1990). *Focus groups: Theory and practice*. Newbury Park, CA: Sage.

Williams, B. (1978). *A sampler on sampling*. New York: Wiley.

Yin, R. K. (1984). *Case study research: Design and methods*. Newbury Park, CA: Sage.

14

Public Relations in a Funding Campaign

Glenn Graham
Gordon Wise

One of the most critical tests of public relations activities conducted by and for public schools comes at those inevitable times when the schools must turn to the community of voters for financial support. In most of the United States, the level of state financial support has failed to keep pace with increases in the cost of public education. In recent years, many states have made substantial cuts in financial support. Increasingly costly and rigorous mandates for programs and facilities are commonly thrust upon schools, typically without accompanying budgets to fund them.

All this leads to more frequent trips by the schools to the public funding well. In most states, such a trip is successful *only* if the voters in the district approve some form of tax levy or bond issue. It is in this all-too-common and frequently dreary scenario that the public relations activities (both long term and short term) are vital.

Let it be said up front that a school district that reaches for its public relations tools only at times when a funding election approaches is not worthy of the support of its community. A basic theme of this entire book, and certainly of this chapter, is that an effective public relations effort must be *ongoing*. The promotion and public relations efforts undertaken during funding campaigns will ideally reinforce, support, and supplement the regular links already in place between the community and the schools.

MARKETING VERSUS SELLING

The ongoing public relations effort, including those activities used during funding campaigns, should be an integrated part of a broader marketing commitment of the schools. In the past (and, sadly, too often at present), schools have tended toward a more traditional selling approach in their promotional efforts, which may include some nod toward the public relations area.

Schools that are the most successful at funding campaigns are also the most successful at discerning the differences between a marketing and a selling approach. When "selling," the attempt is to "get rid of what one has"—for example, the grocer who has a surplus of produce needs to "sell" it to the buyer to get it off his or her hands. "Marketing" is having what one "knows one can get rid of."

This distinction may sound overly simple, but the difference is profound. In the former (selling) posture, the focus is on the *product* (the program, the curriculum, the levy campaign) in an effort to convince the *market* (students, parents, voters) that they must accept or vote for that product. In the latter (marketing) posture, the focus is on the market. Here the primary efforts are devoted to determining what constitutes "value" to that market: what are its needs, wants, desires? What perceptions and expectations does that market have? Then—and only then—does the school that practices a marketing approach attempt to put together its product. This revised focus allows the astute marketer to combine the resources he or she controls into a bundle of satisfactions that has the best chance of gaining acceptance from the market.

THE FOUR P'S OF MARKETING

The tools of a marketing approach used by a school are very similar to the marketing tools used by a business firm. They include the following:

1. The *product*, or the "bundle of satisfactions" developed from the resources the organization controls.
2. The *price*, or the sacrifice of resources required to access that bundle of satisfactions. This may be found in fees and taxes but also in time, effort, and energy provided to the school by the person who chaperones the band bus or the prom or who serves at a PTA function.
3. The *promotion*, or the application of both personal and nonpersonal efforts to expand awareness, interest, and support for the product. This area of marketing encompasses the public relations effort.
4. The *place* (physical distribution), or the actual delivery of the bundle of satisfactions. Schools find "place" activities in such areas as boundaries, districts, bus routes, and the grouping of students or classes. (Should the sixth grade be in the elementary school or in the middle school/junior high?)

The successful ongoing marketing program of a school uses these tools in appropriate and often-changing proportions to develop and direct its *controllable* marketing efforts in response to those *uncontrollable* variables it must confront. Included in those uncontrollables are such things as changing populations and demographics; the emergence of "competitors" (private schooling, home schooling, open enrollment, as well as anything that competes for the time and resources the school would normally attract from its students, parents, and taxpayers); and the wide range of environmental variables (economic, social-cultural, legal-public policy) that can thwart the objectives of the schools. (The authors have treated this subject in greater depth in a specialized article addressing the need for school administrators to adopt an ongoing total marketing approach. See Graham and Wise, 1990.)

THE SCOUTING REPORT AND GAME PLAN

Consider approaching a campaign for a school tax levy or bond issue as a coach approaches an upcoming game. You scout the opposition, ascertain their strengths and weaknesses, and from this scouting report, develop a game plan to achieve victory.

The Market Report

The "scouting report" here is a survey of the market—the voting-age population of the school district.

The market survey that works best is the door-to-door, structured, personal interview method. This format is preferred over mail or phone surveys for several reasons:

1. With mail surveys, one risks hearing primarily extreme positions and not those in the middle, yet those in the middle are often critical to the campaign's success.
2. The response rate of mail surveys is notoriously low—usually about 20%.
3. With both mail and phone surveys, it is much more difficult to tell if respondents are being honest.
4. Many people react negatively to phone surveys, and this disposition might translate into a negative vote.

In a structured interview, all questions are predetermined; the interviewer merely reads them and records interviewee responses. Because the campaign strategies and tactics—that is, the game plan—depend on the information obtained from these interviews, they must be carefully planned.

Initially, meetings should be held with a school committee consisting of school administrators and board members to determine components of the interview. This committee might ask itself: Are specific school programs to be evaluated? Are attitudes to be evaluated? What are the issues that influence people to vote yes or no? What demographics should be obtained?

Following this process, three or four focus groups should be established from a cross section of the voting-age population of the school district. In order to gather input from all segments of the community, composition of the focus groups should be as diverse as possible. The authors typically provide the following checklist to clients to assist them in creating the greatest possible diversity in the focus groups: Each focus group should have from 8 to 12 people. Included in the total composition of all groups should be representatives from

- both genders
- all age groups (high school students through senior adults)
- clergy
- blue collar/white collar (barbers and hairdressers are good sources)
- school personnel (staff, teachers, administration)
- professionals (attorneys, doctors, dentists)
- school critics (we need to hear from this side of the issue)
- the various geographic regions of the school district
- racial/ethnic groups
- politicians
- realtors
- people who do/do not have children in school

Focus group members should be invited by a phone call and a follow-up reminder call the day before the focus group. They should be invited to come and share, not only their perceptions, concerns, issues, and so forth, but also those of the people with whom they have contact.

In recruiting focus group members, it is critical that direct contact is made with each person. DO NOT simply send a letter to prospective participants. Contact in person or by phone should be made with the invitation to participate, and the dates and times of focus group sessions. Persons who commit to participate should then be allowed to choose a session convenient to them. A follow-up letter of confirmation should be sent, followed by a reminder phone call the day before the focus session. (Always remember a thank-you note following their participation.)

There should be two focus-group leaders to take notes and keep the discussion going (Wise & Graham, 1993; Wise, Graham, & McCammon, 1994). Encourage honest, open dialogue; no tape recorders or video recorders should be used. With two people taking notes, not much will be missed. Some focus-group questions might include: What are the strengths and weaknesses of the schools in this district? Why was the operating levy defeated in the last election? What reasons do people give for being for or against the upcoming levy? An hour to an hour and a half of open-ended discussion should generate many positive and negative concerns from focus-group members. This input provides the basic ingredients for the structured interview.

The question format for the structured interview should utilize forced-choice items: the interviewer reads a statement to which the interviewee responds according to a scale such as strongly agree, agree, neutral, disagree, strongly disagree. This type of response mode is good for obtaining attitudes toward the schools and school programs. In the next section of this chapter, there is a discussion of how two other types of forced-choice items are used to deal with positive and negative perceptions.

Once the first draft of the interview guide has been prepared, it should be shared with the school committee for possible revisions. The next step is to select about 10 people to field-test the interview. These persons should be given the instrument so that they have an opportunity to discuss the questions and to ensure that the content is clear and unbiased. The final version of the interview guide evolves from this process. An interview should take about 15 to 20 minutes, and it is always advisable to field-test the instrument before actually doing the survey. Before administering the survey, interviewers need to be trained so they are thoroughly familiar with it.

It is critical that interviewers understand their role is reaching into the community for information. The following "ten commandments" for interviewers should be considered as guidelines:

1. Go to neighborhoods where you are not known. Do not interview friends, relatives, or acquaintances.
2. Read through the survey questions several times until you are thoroughly familiar with them. Do a few practice interviews before starting with the real ones.
3. Do not discuss the results of your interviews with anyone except those analyzing the results. If word gets out about what was said or who said it, the credibility of the survey is compromised.
4. Be courteous. The respondents will view you as an extension of the schools. Your actions could possibly affect how someone will vote.
5. Do not express agreement or disagreement with the respondent's answers. Assure them there are no right or wrong answers; your only function is to record their answers.
6. Do not campaign. If a respondent is negative, so be it. Do not try to change his or her mind during the interview. The campaign comes later.
7. Avoid nonverbal and body language cues. Do not smile when they say something you like and frown when they say something you don't. Be pleasant and noncommittal.
8. If someone refuses to be interviewed, be gracious and do not plead. Thank them and leave. If someone is hesitant, explain the importance of the survey and ensure their anonymity. If suspicious, suggest they call the police and verify your legitimacy.
9. Keep a count of the number of refusals. These may be indicative of a negative attitude toward the bond or levy.
10. Be sure to record the demographic data on your sample. Those who analyze the survey data not only want to tabulate the percentage of responses to each question, but also need to be able to cross-tabulate answers by demographics: Do men and women respond differently? Are there differences depending on age? Do registered voters differ from those unregistered? Are there differences between high- and low-income neighborhoods?

The names of the interviewers should be given to the local police department, and interviewers should wear an identification badge when collecting data. Should anyone be concerned about the survey, interviewers can suggest that the police be called for verification. This will help them access people who might otherwise refuse to be interviewed.

Interviewees should be determined as randomly as possible. One approach is the stratified random sample. This can be done by dividing the school district into voting blocks (precincts or townships). Using results from the last two or three school votes, for example, board elections or referenda, determine what proportion of the total vote came from each voting block. If, for example, 4% of the vote came from precinct 1A, then 4% of the sample should come from 1A. Next, number all the streets and roads in *each* precinct, starting at 1 each time. Using a table of random numbers (which can be found in most statistics texts or can be computer generated), select the streets and roads for your sample. Each time the street number comes up in the table, select one residence from it. A residence can be a house, apartment, or mobile home. For example, if Plum Street is number 15 on the list, and 15 occurs in the random number table, then pick a residence on Plum Street; should 15 occur again, pick a second residence. Which *specific* residence is picked is up to the interviewer, for if no one is at home at one location or if a person refuses to be interviewed, the interviewer can go to another residence on the same street. If no interview can be obtained on the street selected, the interviewer should go to the next closest street.

The size of the sample to be interviewed depends on the population of the school district and the amount of error with which the district is comfortable. Typically, in school districts of 5,000 to 100,000, sample sizes will range from about 300 to 400 people, for an error rate of plus or minus 5%.

Identifying and Dealing With Positive and Negative Perceptions

Identifying the Issues That Influence a Vote.   Using the focus groups as the source, an administrator can identify the issues that potentially have a positive influence (encourage a vote for the levy or bond) or a negative influence (encourage a vote against the levy or bond). These issues are incorporated into the market survey by means of a statement such as:

> In any levy (bond) election, there are certain issues that may influence you to vote for it, some issues that may influence you to vote against it, and there are some issues that would have no influence on how you vote. For each of the following, please tell me if it would:
>
> 1. Influence you to *vote for* the levy (bond).
> 2. Have *no influence* on how you would vote.
> 3. Influence you to *vote against* the levy (bond).

The interviewee is then handed a sheet with the preceding response options, and each of the issues is read. Once the list of issues has been covered, each issue can be classified as positive and negative or as a nonissue. But if the administrator stopped at this point, he or she would miss a crucial piece of the information; that is, what is the *relative strength* of each issue? Which issues will have the *most influence* on positive or negative votes? After the list of issues has had its initial reading, the interviewer proceeds to give these directions:

> I am going to show you the issues from this list that you picked as influencing you to vote for the levy (bond). Of these issues, which is the *single most important* in influencing you to vote for the

levy (bond). [Pause] Which is the *second most important?* [Pause] Which is the *third most important?* [Pause] Now I'm going to show you those issues you picked as influencing you to vote against the levy (bond). Of these issues, which is the *single most important* in influencing you to vote against the levy (bond). [Pause] Which is the *second most important?* [Pause] Which is the *third most important?*

Weight each of the ranks, giving issues ranked as "most important" 3 points; "second most important," 2 points; "third most important," 1 point. Total the points for the positive issues and for the negative issues. From these, the top five or six of both positive and negative issues become those issues that will drive the campaign.

Dealing With the Positive and Negative Issues. In the words of an old song, you must now "accentuate the positive and eliminate the negative." To eliminate the negative does not mean to ignore the negative issues and hope they will go away. Those issues influencing a "no" vote need to be explained carefully and honestly in order to weaken their impact. For example, although people do not want to pay more taxes, they typically like increased property values. By emphasizing a nexus between the quality of schools and increased property values, the impact of the tax increase may appear less severe.

The lists of top issues should serve as a screen for any campaign materials, whether they are ads, brochures, or letters to the editor. After all, these are the issues that the community has said will influence their vote; therefore, all campaign materials should focus on these. If at least one of the top positive or top negative issues is not addressed, then that campaign material should not be used.

Projecting the Election Outcome

Many school systems have run campaigns based on a false optimism that is trampled by harsh reality on election day. Afterward, district leaders will hear comments from the campaign committee such as, "But they told us they'd vote for it!" The problem may have been that the questions were asked in the wrong way. Take the question, "Will you vote for or against the levy (bond)?" This question requires a socially acceptable answer; most people will not admit that they voted against the schools. Therefore, a question designed to help project the voting outcome must allow for the respondent to say "no" in a socially acceptable way. The question could have been phrased as follows:

If an election were held today, and you were asked to vote on a five-million dollar levy to increase property taxes to support operating expenses of our school district, how would you most likely vote:

1. I would *certainly vote for* the levy.
2. I would *almost certainly vote for* the levy.
3. I would *probably vote for* the levy.
4. I am *uncertain* as to how I would vote.
5. I would *probably vote against* the levy.
6. I would *almost certainly vote against* the levy.
7. I would *certainly vote against* the levy.

People who respond that they will "certainly vote for" have put themselves on the line, and in most cases, they will be supportive. In projecting the vote, 90% of those who give this response can be believed. If they choose the "almost certainly vote for" option, they are hedging a bit; 60 or 70% of these responses can be believed. (If more than 30% of those asked to take the interview refuse to do so, use the 60% value.)

Those who respond "probably vote for" will probably vote against. This is one of the socially acceptable "no" options. Such persons have passed over two more positive options to give this response. When projecting the vote, 30 or 40% of these responses can be regarded as voting for the tax. (Use the lower percentage if more than 30% have refused to be interviewed.) Those who are "uncertain" really aren't uncertain; they will almost certainly vote "no." When projecting this vote, count only 10 or 20% of these responses as voting for the tax. Obviously, those who say they will vote against are to be believed. The projection of those voting for is found by adding the following: (1) 0.90 times the number of people responding "certainly for"; (2) 0.60 or 0.70 by the number responding "almost certainly for"; (3) 0.30 or 0.40 by the number responding "probably for"; (4) 0.10 or 0.20 by the number responding "uncertain." This sum is then divided by the total number of all responses to give the proportion projected as voting for (Graham, Wise, & Bachman, 1990; Wise, Graham, & McCammon, 1994).

Although there is no highly scientific or mathematical defense for the percentages used, experience provides support for their validity. The procedure rarely projects less than 30% voting for, which is consistent with election results. Also, in those elections where little or no campaign was conducted, the voting outcome on each of these has been plus or minus five percentage points of the prediction.

Since a good campaign can easily turn on 10% of the voters in the middle, any projection of 40% or more means the bond (levy) has a good chance of passing; a projection of 35 to 39% means there is a moderate chance; 30 to 40% connotes a high risk; and anything less means the bond (levy) has almost no chance of passing (Graham, Wise, & Bachman, 1990; Graham, Wise, & McCammon, 1994). If the last projection occurs, this does not mean that the bond or levy should be taken off the ballot. It is quite common for a bond or levy to fail in several elections before passing. The issues simply need to be thoroughly debated before some voters are convinced of the need.

Funding the Market Survey

Although a school board can fund the market survey, there are times when it might not be politically expedient to do so. Some opponents may charge, "If they can afford to spend the money for the survey, they don't need more money for the schools!" This argument is commonly presented in focus groups. Where such sentiment exists, administrators may want to look to outside sources to fund the market survey. The following sources may be especially helpful in this regard:

1. Individuals or groups of individuals—private citizens who see the importance of the initiative and are willing to contribute to or fund the survey entirely.
2. Chambers of commerce—many local chambers have education subcommittees and support education. This agency may be willing to underwrite the project.
3. Local business and industry—schools throughout the country are establishing business advisory councils. These groups often are willing to fund special projects.
4. Grants from education-supporting organizations.

The bottom line—do not be afraid to ask.

Developing a Plan and Strategies for the Campaign

A funding campaign is brought closer to success through thorough, timely planning. A marketing plan that identifies appropriate strategies, tactics, and timetables should be employed.

The plan ought to include the following components:

1. Identifying the objective (e.g., figuring out the proportion of votes needed for passage of a school levy).
2. Identifying strategy options (determining the range of possible strategies, such as running a positive versus negative campaign or relying on personal contact instead of the media).
3. Evaluating all strategy options (determining costs, feasibility, strengths, and weaknesses of each option).
4. Developing tactics to support strategy (e.g., identifying who will do what and how things are to get done).
5. Developing a timetable for the campaign (deciding the sequence and time parameters for each task to ensure that they get done on schedule).
6. Developing a campaign budget (identifying activities, revenues, and expenditures associated with the campaign).

Organizing Public Relations for the Campaign

Campaign Leadership: The Organizational Chart.   Many school tax issues fail because administrators did not plan properly. The campaign organization should be in place and functioning 4 to 6 months before the election. Figure 14–1 shows a suggested organizational chart for this task.

The steering committee provides direction for all aspects of the campaign. It comprises the campaign cochairs; treasurer; consultant(s), if any; the four division chairs; and representatives from the school board, school administration, teachers and staff, students and parents, and the local media. Having representation from the local media might not be readily considered; however, a campaign should have nothing to hide. Keeping a media representative informed can actually be beneficial. In some instances, reporters may decline to serve in this capacity.

Representatives of the clergy also can be helpful. Having access to church bulletins, newsletters, and sermons provides additional avenues for the campaign message.

The steering committee should meet biweekly at the outset and weekly during the final 2 months of the campaign. A noon or evening dinner meeting (the pay-your-own-expenses type) works well.

The concept of a steering committee at the top of the organizational structure for a levy campaign is recommended regardless of the size of the community or school district. However, for smaller or more rural districts, there may be substantial differences in the organizational structure. The manufacturing division simply may not exist—or it may be replaced by an agricultural division. The business/professional division may be structured differently to reflect the community's business and professional segment. For example, representatives from service clubs may replace business representatives. Regardless of the size of the community, efforts

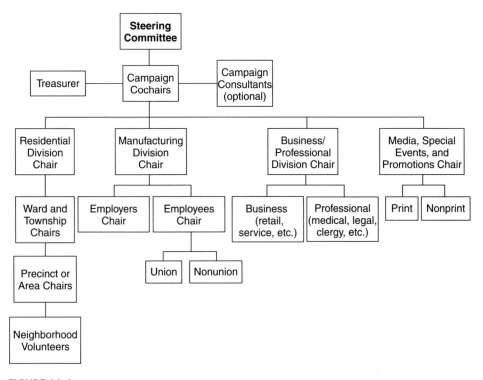

FIGURE 14–1
Organizational Chart for Funding Campaign Leadership

should be made to include some professionals on the steering committee (e.g., physicians, dentists, lawyers).

The *campaign cochairs* are responsible for the day-to-day direction of the campaign. They need to be dedicated, competent, and credible, but most important, they must have the time and schedule flexibility to involve themselves in:

◆ Recruiting chairs for other committees
◆ Recruiting and training volunteers
◆ Developing a campaign theme and slogan
◆ Approving all media copy
◆ Scheduling ads and promotional events
◆ Chairing the steering committee
◆ Speaking at public and organization meetings

Because of the time requirements, politicians, company presidents, or media and sports celebrities—individuals who have demanding schedules—may not be good choices for cochairing the campaign. They may, however, be called upon to endorse the campaign. The *treasurer* should record all financial transactions and expenditures, sign all checks for the campaign organization, and complete all forms and reports mandated by state law. This fiduciary responsibility is often overlooked.

Campaign consultants can provide valuable experiences and direction in situations where administrators have had little experience with funding campaigns. Because there are both political and economic dimensions to employing consultants, school officials should always carefully check references, the quality of previous work, and consultant philosophy before retaining these resource people.

The *residential division chair* is, after the campaign cochairs, the most important person in a campaign. This individual is primarily responsible for recruiting, training, and motivating the volunteers who address the following tasks:

◆ Identifying positive voters and getting them registered
◆ Arranging for absentee ballots to be sent to those identified as positive who will not be in town on election day
◆ Delivering, through personal contact, campaign literature to as many households as possible
◆ Covering the polls on election day, making phone calls to remind those identified as positive to vote, and providing assistance such as babysitting and transportation to get the positive voters to the polls

The individual who chairs this division must be well connected throughout the school district and have excellent organizational and interpersonal skills.

The *manufacturing division chair* interacts with two groups: employers and employees. This position requires an individual with accomplished negotiating skills because obtaining the endorsements and financial support of both groups can be a delicate matter.

The *business/professional chair* holds responsibilities similar to those of the manufacturing division chair.

The *media, special events, and promotions chair* must handle all advertising, letters to the editor, endorsements, videotapes, parades, and other promotional activities.

The Volunteer Army. Several hundred volunteers may be needed to support the campaign. Clearly, the residential division chair cannot contact all these people, but he or she can organize and manage the process. One method is known as the pyramid system. First, ward and township chairs are recruited by the residential and campaign chairs. The ward and township chairs are expected to recruit precinct or area chairs who assist them in recruiting volunteers.

The volunteers should be in place at least 1 month before the last day of voter registration. This permits time for them to canvass their assigned area to locate positive voters and register them if necessary. Each volunteer should be assigned 10 to 12 residences in their neighborhood. Assigning more may make recruitment difficult; however, some volunteers may agree to cover more homes.

Building Potential Support Through Positive-Voter Identification

Locating and Registering Positive Voters. Volunteers should be trained to identify positive voters, and they need to know how to register them. Volunteers should be taught to approach their neighbors with basic questions such as, "I'm the neighborhood volunteer for the levy (bond) campaign. Is there some information I can get for you, or are there some questions you have? What do you see as the issues?" Neighbors who make negative comments—such as, "I don't see how we can afford this since we're on a fixed income," "Don't the teachers make enough money already?" and "They never told us how they spent the money from the last levy"—are likely to vote against the levy or bond. The volunteer should be taught to write down these questions or concerns, and to respond by saying, "I appreciate your sharing these with me. I'll be back in a few weeks with some information to help you make a decision." The volunteers should be instructed to leave *without any further discussion or argument*. They should realize that the purpose of the initial contact is to find positive voters; campaigning comes later.

If the responses to the volunteer's basic questions are positive—such as "It's about time we fixed the old building for the kids," "I'm worried about losing business and industry if we don't improve our schools," and "How can I help with the campaign?"—it is likely the person will be a positive voter. If, however, the volunteer is still uncertain, he or she should ask, "Would you be willing to have a yard sign during the campaign?" Once the volunteer has determined that the person is positive, the question can then be asked, "Are you registered?" If the person is not registered, the volunteer can explain the registration procedure or perhaps actually register the person at that time (depending on registration laws).

At the training sessions, each volunteer should be given a stack of voter contact cards. These are 3-by-5-inch note cards, printed if possible, that have spaces for the name, address, ward, precinct, township, and phone number of the person contacted; the volunteer's assessment of whether that person is positive, negative, or undecided; and the questions asked or information requested. Negative comments or questions should be recorded on these cards. As the cards are completed, volunteers make one copy for themselves and return the other copy to campaign headquarters, where they will be arranged by precinct or township polling place.

Following Up.   Once the campaign is under way, volunteers return to their neighborhoods with promotional materials. They should make every effort to *achieve personal contact* with every assigned individual. Citizens who are positive need reassurance that their vote is important; those who are negative should be given additional information.

Some negative persons may have open minds and be willing to listen. Each volunteer should be challenged to convert one potentially negative voter. For each conversion, the campaign actually acquires two votes—one is removed from "against" and one is added to "for."

Getting the Positive Voters to the Polls.   In many states, a list of those who have voted must be posted at each polling place, usually by 4:30 p.m. A volunteer can be assigned to a poll site and, by using the list of positive voters obtained from the voter contact cards, will identify all who have voted. Anyone on the positive list who has not voted can then be contacted. The call should be in the nature of a friendly reminder. "Hello, this is (name) from the levy committee. I wanted to see if you have voted yet. We really need your support." Offers of babysitting and transportation can be made at this time.

ELEMENTS OF A SUCCESSFUL CAMPAIGN

Once an overall strategy is chosen, all elements of the campaign should contribute toward its implementation. Input from the market survey should be considered the "marching orders" for all phases of the campaign. Many general forms of campaign tactics can be fine-tuned into specific activities. The list that follows is suggested only as a menu from which campaign leaders can select the tactics that are feasible and affordable. Some of them are public relations activities; others are broader forms of promotion and marketing activities. All have been campaign-tested (Graham, Wise, & Bachman, 1990; Wise, Graham, & McCammon, 1994). They are not presented in any order of importance, cost, or effectiveness.

Testimonials

Prominent people in the community can provide testimonials for the media advertising program. All that is required is a formal request. Although accustomed to communicating, some of them may prefer endorsing a prepared testimonial. This not only makes it easier for the person making the endorsement, it also gives the campaign leaders an opportunity to address the major issues by speaking through the mouths of people who command respect in the community. One of the most successful types of testimonial is the "I've changed my mind" statement. Undecided voters may relate to such statements. These comments also suggest that becoming better informed leads to a positive position on the matter at hand.

Presentation of the Price

There is a price attached to the passage of a levy or bond issue—usually in the form of a tax increase. Voters tend to overestimate what they will have to pay, which serves to only heighten their resistance. To counteract this resistance, it is important to provide some perspective about tax increases. An effective tool is a tax table that compares one's increase in property taxes with the present level of *taxes paid* rather than with the current market value of his or her home. This table should be simple to interpret, but include detail so voters will be able to determine the actual tax increases for a wide range of tax amounts. The tax increase should also be broken down into cost per day. In this way, the cost is made to seem relatively small when compared with other daily expenditures. Accuracy is extremely important in constructing such a table. Input from the county auditor or treasurer will be needed to ensure that accuracy. Such a table can be used in different ways in the campaign. Certainly, it should be included in any campaign brochure and in media advertising. These data are especially influential when accompanied by a concluding message such as, "For such a reasonable price, we must say 'yes' to our schools."

The Audiovisual Presentation

An audiovisual presentation can be an effective tool for communicating campaign issues. It can be used to present a consistent message to the community, and it provides a virtual speaker's bureau for the campaign committee.

An audiovisual presentation should be produced well in advance of the campaign. Preparing the slides or videotaping the footage, plus writing and editing the narrative, are time-consuming processes that usually require technical assistance from a media specialist. The presentations should address all issues identified through the market survey.

Once the presentation has been developed, it should be shown first to campaign chairs and volunteers to ensure they have a full understanding of its contents, to answer any questions they may have, and to correct any technical errors. Once formal approval is gained from the campaign committee, the appropriate community groups should be made aware of its availability.

A Campaign Song

Developing a campaign song is a good project for students. The task serves as a creative activity and involves them in a tangible way. The song could be recorded by the school choir and used as background for TV or radio ads. Additional opportunities to sing the song may come if students are asked to present programs at community activities. School officials should obtain publisher approval if the song is adapted from copyrighted material.

The Question of the Day

Well before the campaign begins, campaign leaders should approach newspapers, radio stations, and cable television to see if these media would publish or announce a daily question and an answer provided by the campaign committee. If they agree to do so as a public service, no cost is involved. The same question should be distributed to all media on a given day. By arranging schedules, the most important questions may appear several times.

The Campaign Brochure

A good brochure should be the centerpiece of campaign strategy. It should be ready for distribution about 3 weeks before the election. It should be attractive but not so extravagant as to cause negative reactions from voters. One should be able to read the brochure in 5 to 7 minutes. It should include the tax table and a question-and-answer section that addresses the major positive and negative issues. State laws differ with respect to funding campaign materials; some states prohibit the use of public funds to support a referendum position.

Newspaper Coverage

The local newspaper offers several avenues for carrying the campaign message. Consider using the following:

- ◆ *General coverage.* Most newspapers cover school district news on a regular basis. Some even assign a full-time reporter to this duty. If the school officials have a good relationship with the education reporter or the editor, then the newspaper is likely to provide coverage.

- *Letters to the editor.* During the campaign, there should be a sequence of letters to the editor, from different constituencies, addressing key questions and emphasizing the benefits that the levy or bond issue will provide. Some of them may be unsolicited, but a contingency plan is advisable. Campaign leaders should designate respected persons in the community to write letters to the editor. Designated members on the campaign committee also should be prepared to respond to negative letters immediately, especially when they contain false or erroneous information.
- *Editorial endorsements.* Editorial endorsements are a powerful weapon in a campaign. Campaign leaders should provide the editor with information that facilitates a correct and objective opinion.
- *School page.* In many communities, the newspaper has a section devoted to student activities and student opinions. This feature presents another opportunity to publicize campaign issues. Students can be very persuasive when it comes to extolling the benefits they will derive from the levy passage.
- *Question of the day.* Mentioned earlier, this feature in a newspaper keeps the issues before the public on a regular basis during the campaign.
- *Paid advertising.* Postelection surveys have shown that paid advertising in newspapers is effective in influencing voters (Wise, Graham, & Bachman, 1986). A common type of paid advertising is an endorsement from business and civic leaders in the community. Another approach is to ask businesses to include a "slug" in their own ads near election time—for example, the slug "Vote yes for our school's future" could be added to an existing ad.

Radio and TV Coverage

Call-in Programs. Local radio stations and community cable television call-in programs are other outlets for getting across the campaign message. These programs should include panel members who are well informed about the campaign issues, including school board members, campaign leaders, and school administrators. Teachers, students, and parents also should be considered. Songs or promotional tapes can be infused if the medium permits. To ensure that important issues are addressed, having designated persons raise specific questions is an effective technique. If possible, school officials should reserve the right to screen questions because they are irrelevant or inappropriate. It is best to schedule call-in programs toward the end of the campaign when specific issues need to be clarified.

Special Programming. Local radio and TV stations may be willing to carry special programs that have been prepared in advance on audiotape or videotape. One program might introduce campaign leaders to the community; another might discuss the vital issues in the campaign; still another might focus solely on economic issues.

Public Service Announcements. Many cable television operations have a "weather screen" channel which, in addition to reporting the weather, carries other short messages. The campaign committee should investigate this option as a way to gain, at no cost, public service announcements.

Paid Advertising.   Buying TV time is expensive. If a decision is made to use it, graphics, sound, and narration should be of high quality. The ad copy should highlight the issues identified in any earlier market analysis. If there is a campaign song, it might be used as a lead-in or conclusion for the ad.

Town Hall Meetings

The tradition of the town hall meeting has long been a fixture of American politics and society. We have addressed it as one of the "elements in a successful campaign" in earlier editions of this book.

Unfortunately, the pace of activities of the 21st-century American, the precipitous decline in the proportion of households with children in public schools (or in any form of school), and the overall decline in public interest in schools have rendered the "old fashioned" town hall meeting a near-fatal blow.

If campaign leadership chooses to have some form of town meeting, it must consider "drawing a crowd" to be its most serious hurdle. Our 25 years of experience have convinced us that only select circumstances can create the setting for a well-attended town hall meeting. Those circumstances would include a campaign that must address issues of serious controversy (e.g., where school boundaries or attendance areas are being changed; where closing schools is proposed; where considerations or radical changes are involved). Sometimes the use of a highly popular and visible community supporter as host/hostess/moderator will aid in stimulating attendance.

Where any such attempt is made, the event must be given as much publicity as possible. Where a public access television channel is available, live and/or taped for repeated rebroadcast transmission of the event should be planned.

In recent years, we have favored the use of a live television call-in program on election eve (discussed under "Radio and TV Coverage") as a substitute for the traditional town hall meeting. This approach reverses the pattern and instead of requiring the public to come to the town hall, it allows the campaign to reach out and "come to" the public. Again, heavy promotion of the call-in program is required and this may require using some campaign funds designated for advertising.

Another variation of the concept of the town hall meeting is addressed in the sections that follow under the topic of "School Tour and Model Display."

A town hall meeting provides an open forum for anyone to ask questions about the levy or bond issue. Board members, administrators, and campaign leaders should be there to answer questions, to reaffirm the positive benefits to be derived from the levy, and to refute any misinformation being circulated. Such a meeting offers a way to neutralize any "We haven't been given all the facts" criticism. As with call-in programs, it is useful to have "plants" ask questions that the campaign committee wants to address publicly. Be sure to invite the media to cover the meeting since their reports will reach those who were not in attendance.

School Tour and Model Display

Those who have recently been inside a school building are more likely to be positive voters (Wise, Graham, & Bachman, 1986). Thus, giving the public an opportunity to see a model of the proposed new facility or the school renovation project is beneficial. Architects can provide such a model, and they can prepare a floor plan showing the number and size of rooms. A model and floor plan become even more meaningful when citizens are able to tour present buildings. At the conclusion of these tours, campaign materials may be distributed. Parent organizations and students can play a key role in conducting tours and distributing information.

The authors have identified a variation on efforts to increase attendance at school open house events. Our research continues to confirm the importance of having persons exposed to public school buildings as frequently as possible. Such exposure nearly always correlates with a greater willingness to support school funding issues. Following is a foolproof tactic for dramatically increasing adult attendance at the school open house. Such attendance is vital when the building, renovations, or repair of facilities is an important part of the purpose for requesting added school funding.

The tactic involves creating a contest among classrooms in the elementary (and perhaps middle school) buildings of the district. Students are informed that the class or classroom whose students can produce the greatest number of adults attending the open house will be declared "school champions" and will receive a bonus (class pizza party, trophy, etc.). The key is found in creating such a spirit of competition that students will invite or compel parents, grandparents, aunts and uncles, neighbors—ANYBODY—to attend the open house so that the student's class will get credit for that attendance. When persons arrive at the school they are given a map of the building with numerous places noted to be visited. In order for the adults' visit to be counted for the student's class, a space must be stamped at each location in the building designated for a visit. At each designated location, a student will greet the visiting adults and point out what happens at that location—with careful reference to any deficiencies in space, inadequate equipment, or whatever limitations are present. The visitors' map will receive the required stamp and he or she will be escorted to the next stop on the tour of the facility. We have seen increases of 500–1000% in attendance at school open house events where this tactic has been used with well-coordinated organization provided by staff who realize the importance of exposing community members to school facilities. Don't try this unless you are serious and can expect full cooperation from staff. Properly promoted among students (particularly elementary grades) and properly planned and coordinated, it can bring huge crowds into the schools.

Main Street Projects

Letters to Employees.   Often business leaders are willing to send a letter to their employees discussing the merits of the levy or bond issues. This may include highlighting positive effects on the local economy. Another possible action is to request permission to place a campaign poster on a company's bulletin boards.

Statement Stuffers.   Banks and utility companies often include stuffers on a variety of topics as a public service in their monthly statements. Officials at these companies may be willing to include a stuffer on the levy or bond issue election. If so, the stuffer should be prepared well in advance and designed to fit the company's mailing envelope.

Table Tents.   Businesses or firms in public buildings may be willing to have a table tent displaying campaign materials. If so, someone on the campaign committee should be assigned to keep the table supplied with materials.

Student Projects

Windshield Washing.   A unique way to involve students in a campaign is to ask service station operators to allow students to wash the windshields of customers, free. After cleaning the windshield, the student would give the driver a card that says, "We are pleased to clean your windshield. We hope you can see your way clear to vote YES on _____ ." The action may win more than a smile.

Parades.   If weather permits, a parade may be scheduled on the Saturday before the election. It might include the high school band, drill teams, and students groups who hand out campaign brochures to people along the parade route. It could conclude downtown where campaign chairs and other supporters can ask citizens to vote "yes."

Menugrams

Many schools distribute a weekly lunch menu, which ends up being posted on refrigerator doors. In many homes, the menu is the most frequently referred to piece of literature the school publishes. Reserve space on the menugram to place a brief message about the levy campaign that urges parents to vote "yes" on election day.

Lapel Badges

A distinctive lapel badge or pin carrying the campaign logo or slogan can be worn by campaign workers as they make their rounds in the neighborhoods. Many companies make these pins with only a short lead time. Ordering in large quantities keeps the unit cost low.

Announcements at Athletic Events

Campaign information or inserts can be included in the printed programs for athletic events. Many schools now have electronic scoreboards that can carry messages as well as the team scores. This technology can be used to present a brief message to a large audience. Another approach is to have campaign workers hand out brochures as people come through the gates.

POTENTIAL PITFALLS

There is no such thing as a sure thing in funding campaigns. The activities presented here are campaign proven, but since no two situations are identical, *victory can never be guaranteed.* Some pitfalls can generally be identified and overcome by timely and adequate planning, funding, and volunteer effort. The most serious pitfalls to a successful campaign include the following:

◆ A late start in getting input from the market or the scouting report. There is no time to gain input, which inevitably leads to "flying blind" in developing campaign strategy tactics.
◆ A lack of campaign workers. Troops in the trenches are at the heart of a successful campaign. Without them, victory is difficult.
◆ A campaign organization comprising only the elite of the community. A grass-roots campaign team will generally create the best image, deliver the most credible message, and turn out the hardest-working volunteers. Those promoting the campaign should be representative of the community.
◆ The presence of organized opposition.
◆ Division on the school board. When the school board members disagree, they transmit mixed messages.

Other specific negatives usually encountered in a local campaign include:

◆ Perceptions that teachers and administrators are too highly compensated.
◆ Perceptions that the district has too many frills.
◆ Negative feelings associated with the closing of a treasured school building or consolidation of schools.
◆ Past abuse, scandals, or perceived sins of earlier school boards, superintendents, or other employees.

USING THE WORLD WIDE WEB

The *Yahoo* education search engine is quite useful for locating sources on the Web that relate to levies and bonds. The address is http://www.yahoo.com. Once it is reached, at the white bar next to the left of the word "Search," type *school levies*. Then at the choice bars, click on "matches on all words" (and) "all." When we did this in 1996, about 500 sources were found. As of June 2002, 52,300 sites were available! You can find everything from newspaper articles to local school Web sites and campaign committee Web sites. Our suggestion is to get on and enjoy the ride; the exploration is fun and quite informative.

SUMMARY

The point has been made earlier, but it bears repeating here for additional emphasis: public relations *must* be a continuing effort. It must *not* be used just before a levy or bond issue campaign. Much of the content of this book is directed toward the application of public relations concepts and tools on a continuing basis.

This chapter has focused on one critical element of school administration: funding levies. Suggestions for planning and delivering a successful campaign were provided. Experienced administrators will attest that this political responsibility is among the most challenging they face.

CASE STUDY	Learning From the Market

Residents of a suburban school district defeated a $10.5 million bond issue by a vote of 64% against, 36% for. The bond had included the following components:

- ◆ An addition to the present middle school, which would permit all sixth, seventh, and eighth graders to attend one facility
- ◆ Removal of asbestos from the elementary buildings and the middle school
- ◆ Locker and training rooms for boys and girls at the high school
- ◆ Remodeling of elementary buildings to add classrooms and increase energy conservation
- ◆ Addition of a gymnasium/multipurpose room at the high school
- ◆ Additional instructional facilities—library/media center, art room, music room, science labs—at the high school

Before putting any further bond issues back on the ballot, the school board decided to conduct a market survey and use the results to guide a new campaign. A survey instrument was developed, and a sample of 300 households was chosen for door-to-door interviews. The survey question and results are shown in Table 14–1.

In analyzing the results, the district found that the top-five factors encouraging a positive vote were:

1. Explain *why* money is needed and *how* it will be spent.
2. Allow elementary school children to attend a neighborhood school.
3. Eliminate overcrowding at the elementary schools.
4. Prepare for growth in enrollment.
5. Avoid cost increases that will accompany a wait-and-see stance.

Analysis also revealed that the top-five factors encouraging a negative vote were:

1. Building now will increase property taxes.
2. The information from the last campaign was not sufficient.
3. New industrial property has been tax-abated.

TABLE 14–1
Survey Questions and Results

Which of the components from the previous bond campaign did you consider *Indispensable Very Important, Somewhat Important,* or *Not Important?**

Component	Indispensable	Very Important	Somewhat Important	Not Important
Addition to middle school	18	35	32	15
Asbestos removal	59	23	10	7
Locker and training rooms	7	25	42	26
Remodeling elementary buildings	22	43	28	7
Gym/multipurpose room	3	13	36	48
Additional instructional facilities	14	38	32	15

*All numbers in percentage form; lines two and six only total 99 percent due to rounding percentages.

TABLE 14–2
Projecting the Vote

Component Combinations	Cost in $ (million)	% For
All six components as before	10.5	28.6
Build new middle school	6.5	36.3
Build new middle school and asbestos removal	7.8	37.9
Remodel elementaries, build addition to middle school, and asbestos removal	5.3	40.6
Remodel elementaries and build addition to middle school	4.0	39.7

4. Renovation of the board of education building last year was unnecessary.
5. Operation of new or expanded schools is bound to increase property taxes.

When the district projected the vote for different combinations of the six bond components, they came up with the figures shown in Table 14–2.

QUESTIONS AND SUGGESTED ACTIVITIES

CASE STUDY

1. Which combination of components would you put on the ballot? Explain.
2. Design the strategies and tactics you would use in the campaign.
3. Prepare five ads to be used for TV, radio, and print.
4. Prepare 10 "questions of the day" to be used in a brochure and in the newspaper.
5. Prepare three letters to the editor addressing the positive and negative issues that were identified.
6. Prepare an outline for the scenes and write the script of a videotape presentation.

CHAPTER

7. What is the difference between marketing and selling?
8. Is it possible to project the outcome of a bond election? If so, how?.
9. What are the potential funding sources for a bond campaign?
10. How can positive voters be identified?

SUGGESTED READINGS

Bane, V., & Pride, K. (1993). The $325 million bargain. *American School Board Journal, 180*(10), 24–28.
Bauscher, R. H. (1994). School board election steps for winning at the polls. *Educational Facility Planner, 32*(1), 16–17.
Bohrer, S. D. (2000). Gaining rural community support for a bond issue: A superintendent's experience. *Improving Rural School Facilities: Design, Construction, Finance, and Public Support.* (ERIC Document Reproduction Service No. ED445860.)

Boschee, F., & Holt, C. R. (1999). *School board success: A strategy for building America's schools.* Lancaster, PA: Technomic.

Cannon, G., & Cannon, P. (1997). Tax strategies. *American School Board Journal, 185*(5), 35–36.

Carter, M. A. (1995). How to blow a bond issue—or not, if you'd prefer. *Clearing House, 69*(5), 289–292.

Fielder, D. J. (1995). A bond for the record books. *American School Board Journal, 182*(10), 35–37.

Flanigan, J. L. (1995). Pre-planning the next bond referendum. *Educational Planning, 10*(1), 27–34.

Fowler, F. J., Jr. (1993). *Survey research methods* (2nd ed.). Thousand Oaks, CA: Sage.

Friedenberg, R. V. (1994). Winning school-levy campaigns. *Education Week, 14,* 32–34.

Graves, J. J. (1998). *Winning the referendum battle in education.* Springfield: Illinois Association of School Boards.

Grier, T. B. (1994). Speak right up. *American School Board Journal, 181*(11), 48–49.

Kastory, R. C., & Harrington, S. J. (1996). Voter perceptions are key to passing a school bond. *Educational Research Quarterly, 20*(1), 49–58.

Kotler, P., & Andreasen, A. (1991). *Strategic marketing for nonprofit organizations* (4th ed.). Upper Saddle River, NJ: Prentice Hall.

Lifto, D. E. (2001). Lessons from the bond battlefield. *American School Board Journal, 188*(11), 50–51, 56.

Lindstom, D. (1994). Bond tip: Let's go to the videotape. *American School Board Journal, 181*(7), 33–34.

Mathison, T. R. (1998). Successful bond elections. *School Business Affairs, 64*(1), 30–33.

Morrison, G. (2000). Raising money, winning votes. *American School & University, 73*(3), 402–405.

Mulkey, J. R. (1993). Marketing your schools. *The Executive Educator, 15*(7), 32–33.

Planning Successful Bond Campaigns. (1998). Raleigh: North Carolina State Department of Public Instruction.

Simpson, J. B. (1993). The 81-cent solution. *American School Board Journal, 180*(10), 28–30.

Walker, P. A. (1996). Passing a bond referendum starts here. *School Business Affairs, 62*(9), 32–35.

REFERENCES

Graham, G. T., & Wise, G. L. (1990). Marketing for the school administrator: Tracking the variables that ruin the best-laid plans. *Record in Educational Administration and Supervision, 11*(1), 64–69.

Graham, G. T., Wise, G. L., & Bachman, D. L. (1990). *Successful strategies for marketing levies* (Fastback No. 310). Bloomington, IN: Phi Delta Kappa.

Wise, G. L., & Graham, G. T. (1993). Using the "scouting report" in a market-centered development of policy and programs for the schools. *Record in Educational Administration and Supervision, 14*(1), 54–56.

Wise, G. L., Graham, G. T., & Bachman, D. L. (1986). *Marketing levies and bond issues for public schools* [Monograph No. 7]. Dayton, OH: Wright State University.

Wise, G. L., Graham, G. T., & McCammon, C. L. (1994). *Marketing—not selling—the successful levy campaign.* Columbus: Ohio School Boards Association.

15

Evaluating Public Relations Programs

Doug Newsom

All constituencies of today's schools are increasing their demands for accountability, responsibility, and credibility. Keeping ahead of these expectations means that public relations research is essential for identifying and monitoring issues, anticipating and planning for crises, and preparing information for policy decisions and implementation.

Whether the educational setting is public or private, an individual school or a whole district, evaluating results in a measurable way is essential. Solid information is critical to maintaining support, not just financially but also in the opinion of the various publics to which a school or district is socially responsible.

Earlier claims that public relations activities are not measurable has been replaced in public relations practice by considerably more attention to research. The primary role of the professional public relations person today is offering counsel in strategic planning that delivers measurable results. Strategic planning originates with an organization's own mission statement—the core for decision making about what the organization does. Most accrediting agencies recognize such efforts when they review. An ongoing monitoring and evaluation program by the public relations office can generate the documentation needed by accrediting agencies and give direction to policy makers by identifying problems and opportunities as these arise.

EVALUATION OF THE MISSION STATEMENT

An organization's mission statement should undergo frequent review, as discussed in Chapter 10. If both the organization and its socioeconomic as well as political environment are relatively stable, every 5 to 7 years is an acceptable frequency. But if an organization undergoes dramatic change, then the mission statement needs more frequent review. Although this process requires time and effort, it can be a valuable learning experience for participants and can build morale.

One way for a school district to do this is to send the mission statement to each principal for study and feedback. However, this may not be very effective because of resistance to change in some schools, especially if authority or autonomy is threatened. Another way is to appoint committees in each school, such as administrative staff, general staff, faculty, and support groups. The support groups should include both student government and faculty governance groups as well as parent associations. These committees should carefully study the viability of the mission statement. Each word needs to be examined to see how every part of the mission statement can be translated to specific activities of the organization. Sample questions that need to be asked are: What does this statement mean? How is it now being interpreted? What is the organization doing now that demonstrates a commitment to the mission?

When these reports are done, a central committee consisting of members from each school committee should write a consensus critique. Selection for these committees is preferably done democratically, not only for credibility, but also for the participants to really "buy into" the result. The central committee's "product," their critique of the mission statement, should then be distributed to all of the schools.

Yet another way to arrive at a qualitative-quantitative evaluation of the mission statement is to use focus-group interviews (FGIs), followed by a questionnaire. (For more discussion of such processes, see Chapter 13.) The results of initial FGIs sometimes are accepted as substitutes for in-depth research, which is a serious methodological mistake. FGIs should be used only to gain insights into what questions to include in a questionnaire and how to ask those questions. Effective FGI techniques require careful selection of homogeneous groups within units and inclusion of enough groups to represent the diversity of the district. Participant selection should be dictated by an organization's characteristics.

Videotaping these groups of 12 or fewer participants often adds a second dimension to the communication—the nonverbal behavior. Often that nonverbal behavior contradicts what is being said. Videotaping may not be acceptable if members of a focus group prefer to remain anonymous. If the review of the mission statement is controversial, it is better to use only an audiotape of the proceedings. The key issue is to analyze results for adjectives and adjectival phrases that tend to reveal points of view sometimes beyond the language used by the participants to describe concepts. The analysis provides a road map that leads to posing survey questions that can be more easily understood.

Surveys built on the FGIs should use bipolar scales, thus allowing for degrees of intensity of responses. Pretest of the instrument with people like those participating in the focus group, but not the actual participants, checks validity of the questions and helps to spot problems for correction before the survey is used. FGIs can be used again to flesh out survey results in a qualitative way.

Another analysis technique for the mission statement is the Delphi process. Participants can be chosen randomly or by quota sample. (A quota sample may be chosen randomly but is nevertheless proportionally representative of the universe [the larger group].) Usually cost and acceptable sampling error are considerations. In this process, questionnaires that elicit open-ended responses are sent directly—not through supervisors—to participants. Whole paragraphs might be the responses to a question such as: "Is our mission to make students good citizens of the world?" Participants' responses are compiled without editing and sent back to them. After they have read everyone's response to the questions, participants are asked to rate the responses on a numeric scale. They might rank their own response below another's response to the same question. (For example, one might prefer, "First let's be sure they develop a sense of self-esteem and social responsibility" to his or her own response, "We need to make them good citizens of their immediate community first.") The respondents' rankings are totaled and a collective order is given to edit the responses. The response that receives the most first-place rankings is at the top of the list, and so forth. This collective rank ordering makes it possible to edit responses and arrange ideas into categories or statements. These statements then are sent back to the participants. The two-way process can go through several phases until ideas are clarified. Eventually, the results can help to mutually redefine or reaffirm an organization's mission.

EVALUATION OF POSITIONING STRATEGIES

Although a mission statement should be the focus for an organization's activities, the statement itself does not define how an organization wants to be seen by all its publics.

That is the purpose of a positioning strategy, which is also expressed as a statement. For example, a strategic positioning statement for a high school might be that it wants to be known as a leader in combining vocational and liberal arts, or it might want to be seen as offering the best opportunities for students with learning disabilities. The positioning strategy is drawn from an interpretation of the mission statement. It is usually written by district administrators, then sent out for evaluation by internal publics (e.g., employee groups). Fashioning a position statement is likely to be a more contentious process than drafting or modifying the mission statement because some constituencies within an organization may see the strategic position targeted to exclude them.

Existing position strategies should be reviewed qualitatively in the same way as mission statements, especially if priority external publics (e.g., community groups) are included. Although it is imperative for internal publics to agree about the mission, the primary advantage of having a strategic positioning statement is to focus the opinions of external publics. Proposed or existing positions can be reviewed quantitatively by a telephone or e-mail survey of internal and external publics. Such a process not only validates the positioning, but also gives some evidence of the effectiveness of the organization in communicating its self-image.

SIGNIFICANCE AND USE OF EVALUATION

The way publics see the organization living up to its self-defined role is critical to the financial and moral support the organization gets. Evaluating public perceptions of how well the organization has achieved its goals and objectives—inspired by its mission statement and focused by its positioning strategy—is as important as documenting its achievements. Many accrediting reviews, such as those required by state departments of education, attest to this in that they ask for the opinions of both internal and external publics, as well as hard evidence on such matters as promotion and testing results at the lower levels and retention and graduation statistics.

One use of evaluations is living up to schools' social responsibility. Although public schools don't have stockholders, they do have stakeholders which includes all of their publics. Private schools do have direct and indirect investors, indirect investors being those who may offer "gifts in kind," such as landscaping. Knowing what they got for their investment is important.

Initially evaluations are used for planning, either broadly or specifically. Planning may be for a district's entire focus for an academic year. An example might be to improve test scores a specific amount on a state or national exam throughout the district. Or planning could be more specific, such as to increase the number of students taking a certain exam by a number or percent. Another specific project plan might be encouraging more students to get involved in healthy activities and to make nutrition changes in order to lower the number of obese students. It could be that an evaluation of a previous project or activity may indicate a need for changes, and the direction of those changes. All of these are planning functions.

Evaluations are also used for monitoring plans as they are being enacted, and, once completed, for reporting the results of the plan implementation to the constituencies (publics) involved. Finally, evaluations are used for giving advice to management. Public relations counsel to administrators can be as important as the school or district's legal counsel. Although schools are "tried" in the court of public opinion daily, it is rare that they are tried in the legal system.

Planning

Planning for the district or for an individual school means making some decisions about emphases. That is what positioning is all about. An emphasis always has budget implications. Because funding is important at all levels—only the funding mechanism differs—it is necessary to monitor publics to locate problems that might have funding implications. Opinions of one public might correlate with opinions of another. For example, teacher complaints about broken, worn-out equipment may correlate with student complaints about inadequate classroom resources. The weight of such attitudes may result in complaints from parents about priorities.

Results of internal and external evaluations can help set priorities and establish systems for maintaining what is working well for a school. They also can validate aggressive leadership or risk taking on the part of administrators. Evaluations should not only anticipate problems that can be addressed in planning, they should also help substantiate decisions.

Planning for projects is another part of evaluations. It may be that a project, even a traditional one like an annual school picnic, has ceased to attract participation. Evaluations help to eliminate projects that are no longer viable or to modify them or replace them with projects that are deemed needed, such as "job fairs" in high schools, especially where many of the students are not college bound.

Reporting

Communicating the results of evaluations helps administrators and overseers, such as school boards, understand what the needs, concerns, and successes are. Also, it gives confidence to students, teachers, and parents who are investing time and energy. Evaluations also give authority to the official reporting requirements of all institutions. Such factors as dropout rates, drug abuse cases, and harassment situations all must be assessed and the results reported. On a more positive note, administrators who have invested heavily in computer equipment may be able to report increased research skills and an interest in "fact-finding" on the part of students.

School administrators must justify their actions to a plethora of oversight groups, from regulatory and accrediting agencies to special-interest groups. Monitoring and evaluating on a regular basis offers credible benchmarks for progress made and justifies action taken. Monitoring and evaluating activities also provide opportunities to communicate an organization's effectiveness to different constituencies. Survey results often generate responses from publics and influence opinions.

Counseling Decision Makers

Advice or counsel is a reasoned recommendation based on sound evidence, not necessarily experience. Counseling is a primary public relations function for strategic decision making, and it is not an "I think" process. Acceptable evidence must come from ongoing monitoring and evaluation. Counseling is most critical, of course, when there is a crisis. Crisis counseling, sometimes called "reputation management," is often needed when a reputation can no longer be "managed" because of prior action or inaction. However, sound counsel can come from evidence of how priority, and sometimes nonpriority, publics are likely to respond.

Evaluation often provides the critical evidence in emotional decisions, such as whether to allow students who are not getting a diploma to sit with a graduating class. One issue that got national attention was a mainstreamed student with mental disabilities who still had some more work to do but wanted to sit with his class at graduation. Evaluations can help here in monitoring what percentage of a class is likely not to graduate and whether there are some students with special problems or needs. Then decisions can be made and communicated early enough that crises, especially ones that draw national attention, can be anticipated and managed.

IDENTIFYING AND MONITORING AN ORGANIZATION'S PUBLICS

Every organization has easily identifiable publics. Consider at least 10 publics and multiple levels of each: media, employee, member, community, government, investor, consumer, international, special, and integrated marketing communication (Hendrix, 2001, pp. 16–21). This comprehensive list can be used as a guide to keep an administrator from overlooking a public as he or she compiles a list. Gathering information about each public on the list is part of an administrator's secondary research role.

Media publics fall into two large categories—mass and specialized. Mass media includes local and national print publications such as newspapers and magazines, wire services, radio stations, and television stations. Specialized media also include local and national. In the local category are trade, industry, and association publications; organizational house and membership publications; publications from special groups; ethnic publications; and specialized broadcast programs and stations. National specialized media include general business publications; national trade, industry, and association publications; national orga-nizational house and membership publications; national ethnic publications; publications from national special groups; and national specialized broadcast programs and networks. Most of these designations are clear, but specialized broadcast stations might be an ethnic station or a religious station or special programming within mainstream broadcast media for specific groups such as children. Another area that might need explaining are the publications from special groups, particularly support groups for various problems or crises. Many of these media, both print and broadcast, also have a presence on the Internet.

Employee publics generally fall into two categories: administrative and administrative employees. The former consists of district and school administrators. The latter includes all other district personnel (e.g., teachers, clerks, bus drivers).

Member publics are divided into six major categories: organizational employees, officers, members, prospective members, state and local chapters, and allied or related organizations. Four are related to schools. Organizational employees include all district personnel. Organizational officers include elected and appointed board members. Prospective members include individuals who may become part of the organization for professional or personal reasons. Related or allied organizations include those sharing the same interests, for example, the Teachers' Association.

Community publics include community media, community leaders, and community organizations. Community organizations include civic, service, social, business, cultural, religious, youth, political, and special-interest groups, as well as others. When considering community media, the local news media (listed under general media publics) are included, but so are other very special media such as neighborhood newsletters or newspapers and neighborhood Web sites. As an example, one all-American city had, in addition to city-wide events, celebrations planned by each neighborhood for that neighborhood, although others were invited. A school district celebrating a major anniversary might have districtwide festivities in a central location, but also encourage and help each school to plan its own festivities with class reunions and such. Another important consideration is a community's ethnic mix. Research must be ongoing to see what ethnic mix percentages are currently in a community and what projections or trends indicate in the way of change. For example, in many Texas cities, the Hispanic population is growing dramatically. In the Dallas–Fort Worth area in which the case study for this chapter is located, population estimates suggest that Hispanics will be the majority, not the minority, by the 2010 census.

Government publics are at the federal, state, county, and city levels. At the federal and state levels, the legislative and executive branches are listed by Hendrix, but there are occasions when the judicial branches also might be considered. For counties and cities, the major leadership, officials, commissions, and departments are each a separate consideration as a public. Organizations always focus on the government areas that have regulatory authority over them. Keeping them informed is critical and knowing what facts they need is a significant part of research.

Investor publics are less important for schools, except for private ones. For general information, though, investor publics include shareowners and potential shareowners, security analysts and investment counselors, the financial press and wire services, and regulatory groups.

Consumer publics include employees, customers (students and their families in the case of schools), activist groups, publications, community media, and community leaders and organizations.

International publics are host-country media—(mass and specialized), host-country leadership, and host-country organizations. Under leadership, Hendrix includes public officials, educators, social leaders, cultural leaders, religious leaders, political leaders, professionals, and executives. Host-country categories include business, service, social, cultural, religious, political, special interests, and others. Many schools today have students who are citizens of other nations. This has enriched our experiences, but broadened considerably the publics that even local schools have to acknowledge. A ruling in a district that prohibits a particular form of dress or hairstyle can provoke international attention of the unwanted kind.

Integrated marketing communications is the category identified most specifically by Hendrix. It acknowledges the blending of publicity and advertising to create an opportunity to ensure that organizations "speak with one voice." Although most public schools do not use advertising, private schools do. It is important that all messages from an organization are consistent to ensure credibility. Hendrix includes in this category customers, employees, media, investors, suppliers, competitors, and government regulators.

Unlike the categories for content analysis research, the typology of publics that Hendrix developed has many overlaps; few categories are mutually exclusive. Developing and maintaining a complete list of an organization's publics are important activities. But it is unreasonable to monitor all these publics carefully all the time, which is why most organizations prioritize their publics. Prioritizing works fairly well, but can create blind spots. Trouble may be brewing with a nonpriority public and go unobserved until it is a problem. For this reason, occasional monitoring of nonpriority publics is a good idea. If national trends in education seem to indicate an interest on the part of some of these publics, those groups should be given priority standing until the trend is understood. Homeschooling is a good example. Parents of children taught at home have opted out of the public school system. Knowing why they did and what opportunities exist to get them to return to public schools is important. One way of prioritizing publics is to use a PVI index ($P = VI$). It is simply an informal measure of a public in terms of the organization's ability to influence or impact that public (on a scale of 1 to 10) and the vulnerability of the organization to action by that public.

Although not a true "index," a PVI index can provide a rank for each public in its relationship to the organization. For example, some publics are always priority publics, such as the school board in a district or a board of directors for a private school. A board's impact is almost always in the 7 to 10 range because its approval is necessary for the district to function. However, in some districts with a strong superintendent and a weaker board, the ranking might be 7. If the school board is exceptionally strong or some members are likely to be activists for certain causes, the ranking may be 10. The same is likely to be true for special publics. In some school districts, groups that monitor what books are available in school libraries are very aggressive. In other districts that may not be the case, but they may have a group concerned about nutrition and the availability of "snack" foods in the schools. The more active such a group is, the more vulnerable the schools are to that group.

An easy way to figure this informal measure is to list the publics, assigning each a P value for that group's potential to influence. Add that to how much damage that group might do. A strong board might be able to protect a school district from book censors, for instance, or it may not. In estimating that influence, assign a value, 1 to 10, for that public's ability to have a significant impact. The result indicates how vulnerable the organization is to the group. The simple score of potential to influence plus vulnerability shows how important the public is and helps with prioritizing. With any given issue, especially one that could provoke a crisis, priorities must be reconsidered.

THE RESEARCH BASIS OF MONITORING A PUBLIC

Informal Research Methods

Three basic informal measurement methods are available: unobtrusive measures, audits, and publicity analysis (Newsom, Turk, & Kruckeberg, 2000, p. 148).

Unobtrusive measures are observations that do not intrude on the process of gathering data. One such measure might be color-coding tickets to a performance or lecture so you can see which publics are most responsive to that offering. Sometimes this helps determine whether it is worth doing again. Such measures are indicators, but not very reliable ones.

A ticket intended for one person representing a particular public might be given to and used by someone else.

Audits are more structured and reliable, especially if they incorporate some formal research methods as part of the examination. Public relations audits are not financial audits, but communication audits. What they have in common with financial audits is an examination of process. A communication audit begins with interviews among administrators. The purpose is to determine administrative objectives for all of communication processes, from putting announcements on the intranet to sending messages home with students. Then, certain groups (e.g., teachers, parents, students) are chosen to be audited; a methodology is approved for each group; the activities are scheduled; and then there are two separate processes—one dealing with secondary research and the other dealing with primary.

The secondary research means gathering and studying existing information about the group or groups to be audited; looking at communication policies, plans, and procedures; and collecting whatever information is available on measures of effectiveness, formal or informal. The primary research portion of the audit is where some formal research tools may be used. The first effort involves focus-group interviews with each of the groups to be included in the audit. These may be followed by some individual interviews. The result may be the design, pretesting, and implementing a survey for each group. Finally, in preparing the audit report, the audit data from formal and informal sources are compiled, analyzed, and interpreted. A report is prepared on the findings which are presented to management who may decide whether or not to make public the findings. A critical consideration in communication audits is confidentiality. Participants must be assured of anonymity. This is essential with employees, but in schools is also important for students and parents who are likely to be included in a communication audit.

Communication audits are a common public relations tool because education organizations should evaluate the effectiveness of their communication with their publics. The communication audit weighs what a district or school *intends* to communicate and what its communicators *think* they are communicating, against what some of their publics think they are saying and their reactions to those communications. Disparities among administrators and the groups are examined so recommendations for improvement can be made.

In analyzing publicity, organizations use print media clippings and transcripts from broadcast publicity to see how effective their efforts are to get recognition for the organization. Publicity analysis can be done according to audience, medium, message, frequency, and sometimes, context. Publicity about the organization also is examined for its positive or negative content. Often the analysis makes an effort to weigh the value of the publicity according to the prestige of the medium, the amount of time or space, and the significance of the medium to priority audiences. Table 15–1 shows the advantages and disadvantages of the three basic informal methods of evaluating a public's perception of an organization.

Formal Research Methods

Formal research methods may be qualitative or quantitative. Qualitative measures include the use of focus groups and panels; in-depth interviews that are fairly self-explanatory; and case studies, diaries, and historiography. Quantitative techniques are varied, but the most commonly used in educational public relations are content analysis and surveys. Whether

TABLE 15–1
Advantages and Disadvantages of Various Informal Research Methods

Method	Advantages	Disadvantages
Unobtrusive Measures	No "intrusion" affects the public.	There can be investigative error.
	They can yield physical evidence.	There can be recorder error.
	They can be less costly and more convenient.	They yield fixed data.
		They yield some physical evidence not appropriate to psychological or sociological study.
Audits	They make it possible to locate problems in the making.	They are especially sensitive to the "guinea-pig" effect; that is, awareness of the measure itself.
	They can detect breaks in the communication chain.	They can be insensitive to confidentiality.
	They help develop images held by different publics.	People with less formal schooling may give only socially acceptable answers.
		They can encourage responses to visible cues from interviewers.
Publicity Analysis	It shows evidence of efforts.	It has the same disadvantages as do unobtrusive measures.
	It suggests other opportunities.	It yields incomplete documentation.
		It is difficult to put into context.
		It is not a measure of audience impact.

Source: Adapted from *This Is PR: The Realities of Public Relations* (p. 148), by D. Newsom, J. V. Turk, and D. Kruckeberg. Copyright 2000 by Wadsworth Thomson Learning. Adapted with permission of Wadsworth Publishing Company.

the method used is qualitative and quantitative, researcher bias is always an issue (Newsom et al., 2000, pp. 153–154). Advantages and disadvantages of the various methods are shown in Table 15–2.

Ethical and Legal Ramifications of Measuring

Ethical and legal problems can occur during the research process. Ethical issues include honesty in the gathering of data and in consideration of subjects—not adversely affecting subjects or misrepresenting to them who wants to know what and why. Confidentiality must be preserved, if that is a factor, and there must be no misrepresentation of the results, or "cooking the data," which can occur with both qualitative and quantitative measurements. These are concerns whether the research is being done in-house or by a vendor. When the research is bought from an outside contractor, it is imperative that the public relations director or the coordinating administrator understands the methodology well enough to judge its validity and to determine if the conclusions drawn are legitimate.

Breaches of confidentiality can harm respondents and invite legal problems. For example, people identified in focus groups or through survey responses may be fired or transferred as a result of a disclosure of their identities. It is also important to be sure that in

TABLE 15–2

Advantages and Disadvantages of Formal Research

Method	Advantages	Disadvantages
Qualitative Focus Groups	Feedback can be quick and less expensive than other methods.	They are often used as giving conclusive evidence when they are merely tools used for subsequent research.
	They are flexible in design and format.	They can be mishandled by the moderator so that not all participants express opinions.
	They elicit more in-depth information and often point out "whys" of behavior.	They are not always representative of the research universe.
Panels	The advantages are the same as with focus groups.	They involve the same disadvantages as focus groups.
	They may be chosen to represent a specific population.	Panelists over time "learn" some of the reasons for difficulties and cease to be representative.
In-Depth Interviews	They allow ways to follow up on new lines of inquiry.	They are difficult to transcribe and code for content analysis.
	They permit respondents to describe in detail.	The interviewer may influence responses.
	They permit broader, more comprehensive questions.	Responses often include extraneous information.
Historiography, Case Studies, Diaries	They give insight into situations.	They are difficult to generalize from.
	They suggest further research opportunities.	They often lack the rigor of scientific methods.
	They provide detail that can put other research into perspective.	They are time consuming and often require searching for data that is then selectively presented.
Quantitative Content Analysis	They show what appeared, where, how often, and in what context.	They are costly and time consuming.
	They permit comparison with other data, especially about publics.	They provide no information about the impact of messages on the audiences.
	They can be useful in tracking trends and in monitoring change.	Some information may not be in the media.
Survey Research	They are flexible.	Respondents may not answer truthfully, either because they don't remember or because they are conscious of the socially expected response.
	They can be administered by mail, telephone, computer, or personal or group interview.	They are inflexible, allowing for no expression of true feelings.
	They capitalize on the enjoyment of expressing opinion.	The wrong questions may be asked of the wrong people in the wrong way.

Source: Adapted from *This Is PR: The Realities of Public Relations* (pp. 153–154), by D. Newsom, J. V. Turk, & D. Kruckeberg. Copyright 2000 by Wadsworth Thomson Learning. Adapted with permission of Wadsworth Publishing Company.

reporting results, such as candid responses to an audit question, respondents are not damaged in a way that might produce a libel suit.

The accumulation and storage of data can create both ethical and legal problems, so research results must be protected. If results are shared in industry, trade, or professional publications, the name of the organization as well as that of all respondents must be masked unless specific, written permission for disclosure is given.

Cultural Considerations in Research

One of the first things to remember is that not everyone living in the United States is a citizen. Citizens of other nations living here have a considerable impact on school populations. In certain parts of the country there are high concentrations of citizens from other countries who are working in multinational companies or in companies that need their skills or expertise. Their children attend local schools. Many ordinary processes taken for granted are unfamiliar and perhaps even seen as invasive by other cultures. Schools involved in research must be aware of this or alienate some of their students and their families.

Beyond that, some minority populations among U.S. citizens have a different world-view from the majority population and certainly from each other. What is accepted by one culture is not necessarily accepted by another. The biggest risk in doing research in a multi-national, multiethnic population as exists in this country today is assuming too much. Although it always is true that there is no homogeneity among publics, this especially needs to be considered in doing research among a mix of cultures. An administrator does not represent all Americans. A superintendent or principal does not even represent all employees. There is no "cookie cutter" for publics. Nevertheless, nominative typologies as discussed earlier can be used. They work well, as long as the researcher remembers to pretest survey methodology and questions with all diverse publics. For example, in Texas, there is some risk that a survey questionnaire sent to a child's parent will be completed by an individual who does not have a very good command of the English language. Often the child has to translate the questions for the parent. Strict translations are rarely accurate because vocabularies are incongruous across languages. Even professional translators often must search for the best word to convey meaning and intent. Relying on a young child or even an adolescent with a limited vocabulary to translate survey questions is obviously a precarious decision.

MONITORING ISSUES, PUBLICS, AND PROGRAMS FOR DECISION MAKING AND FINE-TUNING

The critical importance of monitoring is as a preventive device. Issues that have an impact on a school district, such as the new federal rules on tracking foreign students for enrollment and attendance, are potentially a crisis in the making. Administrators need to be watching what is going on in the world—socially, economically, and politically—so they can be prepared. Other reasons for monitoring are to intercept opportunities and to see how programs are being accepted. A principal might find an idea that could be applied in her school. Also, monitoring facilitates data collection for final program evaluations.

This portion of the chapter addresses how to identify issues and monitor them; how research about district publics helps administrators adjust to their perceptions of policies and actions; how administrators can use research to build a constituency among district publics so that a crisis may be averted or public support can be governed if it can not; how research can help administrators determine what policies are likely to create conflict with district publics, before they are promulgated; how to consider research costs in planning the district budget; how to use research in recommending and assessing policies; how to measure results of district activities, programs, or policies in relationship to goals; and how to use research to monitor collective perceptions among district publics.

Identifying and Monitoring Issues

Administrators typically identify issues and monitor them informally. However, a formal process is more useful because the ability to anticipate issues increases. Consider the topic of student apparel. Many school systems reacted to national studies of students wearing types of clothing or colors of clothing to signify gang membership. A number of school officials responded by instituting dress codes, but others pursued the possibility of having students wear uniforms. The latter group was influenced by the potential for uniforms to provide certain benefits. For example, students might gain a greater sense of identity with the school. Also, uniforms seemed to equalize social status, and many parents supported the concept because it reduced clothing costs for their children.

Issue identification comes through monitoring the socioeconomic and political scene to detect any topics that could have an impact, either positive or negative. Issue monitoring is a cyclical process that goes from identification, to analysis, to determination of policy options, to the development of programs, and then to an evaluation of the results.

Behind the issues identification is theory and research that aids the next step—issue analysis. After analysis, judgments must be made and priorities placed on which issues merit attention. The next move is considering policy options. This involves looking at existing policies, determining strategies, and then designing a program to meet the goals. Once the program is designed, it must be communicated to build trust and acceptance. After the program is implemented, the results have to be evaluated to see if any changes need to be made. Issues usually affect a number of publics, and they are important in considering strategies to identify each of these publics and attempt to determine how a proposed policy would affect each. Defining and delineating publics is the first act of any public relations effort.

Identifying, Adjusting, and Meeting Expectations of the Publics

Publics are generally defined as people who share a common bond of interest. For convenience, publics are often referred to as internal or external, but these are artificial boundaries. Through ongoing involvement, for example, many alumni make themselves members of internal publics and have to be considered as such. Alumni of schools, even elementary schools, have become active opponents to closing schools or to selling them.

Thus, although alumni are usually classified as an external public, they may include many who emotionally are members of a school's internal public.

Likewise, parents and grandparents who give public schools their time as volunteers, and are at the school almost as regularly as teachers and staff, see themselves as an internal public. Teachers and staff are often members of a school's volunteer or donor publics, as well as being employees of the institution. Keeping the vagueness of these classifications in mind when dealing with publics, and certainly in prioritizing and measuring them, is very important.

Public relations practitioners use research to identify publics and their characteristics. They also evaluate ongoing relationships these publics have with an organization, especially in particular situations such as crises. They then use the media to reach these publics. Media alternatives must be researched thoroughly to determine which one or which combination is most effective as a delivery system. Monitoring the media to see their effects on publics is also necessary (see Table 15–3 and Table 15–4).

A public has to be clearly identified before it can be conceptualized. There is no such thing as a "general public." A public does not exist unless a mailing list can be created for it. Even the mass media know exactly who their publics are and can give very clear descriptions of the audiences they are reaching. That is how they sell time and space; they are selling audiences of real individuals.

Educational institutions' publics generally have high expectations, which makes delivery sometimes difficult. Determining exactly what each public's expectations are is an important purpose of monitoring. Another is finding how satisfied they are with the match of their expectations with reality. A study of parents whose children have been in magnet schools is an example.

Building a Constituency Before a Crisis

When an organization—educational or commercial—is involved in a crisis, it is too late to shore up relationships with its publics. That is unfortunate because in a crisis, an orga-

TABLE 15–3
Prioritizing Publics

Internal Publics	External Publics	
	Direct (Marketing Communications)	Indirect (Institutional Communications)
Management (top and middle)	Customers	Potential customers
Staff and employees	Sales representatives	Potential investors/stockholders
Employee organizations	Traders and distributors	Financial community
Association	Suppliers	Community of institution
Union	Competitors	Government (local, state, federal)
Board of directors		Environmental community

Source: Adapted from *Public Relations Writing: Form & Style* (p. 12), by D. Newsom and B. Carrell. Copyright 2001 by Wadsworth Thomson Learning. Adapted with permission of Wadsworth Publishing Company.

TABLE 15–4

Media Alternatives

Internal Communication	External Communication
Personal	*Personal*
Person-to-person and person-to-group	Person-to-person and person-to-group
Audiovisual	*Audiovisual*
Specialized media: films, slides, videotape, closed-circuit TV, computer networks	Web pages with art and sound, films, slides, videotapes, CD-ROMs
Publications	*Publications*
Specialized media: books, newspapers, magazines, newsletters	Mass and specialized with controlled and uncontrolled publicity as well as institutional and commercial advertising
Direct Mail	*Direct Mail*
	Personalized, institutional, and promotional
Exhibits	*Exhibits*
Posters, bulletin boards, personalized items	Product packaging, displays, graphics, point-of-sale promotions
Critics	
Individual and institutional	
E-mail	
Fax	*Broadcast fax*
CD-ROMs	
	Listserv (e-mail)
Intranet	*Internet site (on World Wide Web)*

Source: Adapted from *Public Relations Writing: Form & Style* (p. 12), by D. Newsom and B. Carrell. Copyright 2001 by Wadsworth Thomson Learning. Adapted with permission of Wadsworth Publishing Company.

nization must draw on all its resources, including good relations with its publics. Priority publics are likely to shift somewhat in a crisis, and there is no way to predict the direction of the shift. A low-priority public in normal operating times might suddenly become critical to crisis survival. Evaluations can help guide the development of a strategy for building relationships where they are not as strong as they might be. (See Chapter 12 on crises.)

Special publics are ones to watch when auditing relationships. These publics often have some intense, though peripheral, relationship with an educational institution. Consider a decision to expand a school into a playground area that is also used on weekends and evenings as a neighborhood park. The expansion means losing most of the park area and cutting down a number of trees. Neighborhood groups get involved first and alert environmentalists, not usually a priority public for schools. A peripheral public can become a primary one over one issue or even an incident.

Through monitoring and ongoing evaluation, an organization can maintain a continuing dialogue with publics so there are no surprises on either side. An educational organization also can get a clearer understanding of how much its publics appreciate its goals and objectives, critical information in launching any changes.

Determining Levels of Acceptance for Policies

Even before a policy is put in place, the likelihood of its acceptance with various publics can be evaluated. If publics have been carefully described by their demographics and psychographics, a statement about the policy can be pretested on a sample to get reactions. A more common way among educational institutions is to form a panel of affected publics to review the proposed policy. The method is often dictated by organizational culture and an institution's relationship to the publics involved.

A survey of a district's teachers can determine what their reaction might be to year-round schooling, or morning and afternoon shifts of students in crowded districts. Rezoning schools to redirect flows through elementary, middle, intermediate, and high schools is something parents and even neighborhood associations need to consider before a policy is put in place. It is better to find out that a proposed policy may be opposed than to have to fight for an unpopular policy once it is put into force—or, even worse, to have to withdraw a failed policy.

These hypothetical policy issues have gradations of levels of acceptance. Focus-group interviews can provide a basis for a questionnaire that can then be sent to the larger public. Responses can help determine what sort of policy would meet the most resistance and what is likely to cause serious problems.

Budgeting for Research

Research always has an associated cost, and an administrator needs to plan for this in developing a budget. Look at each activity or goal for the year and determine what sort of research is indicated for each (see Chapter 10 on planning). Depending on district or school needs, it may be that most of the research can be done internally, but this does not mean that costs are not involved. The researcher may require released time and personnel costs may need to be increased. Also, cost increases for supplies, copying, printing, distributing, and so forth are likely. It's safe to figure about 10% of what is allocated for each project or activity to research. As a general rule, approximately 10% of a project's budget should be allocated to research and evaluation costs.

Research is an investment, not a luxury. High-visibility projects often require external evaluators, largely for credibility reasons. However, time is another consideration; often a consultant can complete the research more quickly than an internal team. Last, external reports provide a degree of protection for a superintendent or principal, especially if the results are not welcome by the school board and public. Often, people blame the messenger for negative news.

Remember that monitoring all publics all the time in great detail is generally not cost effective for a school district. Administrators force the problem of scarce resources, so they must be selective in making financial decisions. However, a communication audit should be done once a year for each high-priority public, just as audits are done for other aspects of the institution. Such communication audits produce longitudinal documentation for decision making. An audit of nonpriority publics on a revolving basis can then be budgeted.

Assessing and Recommending Policy

Public relations practitioners have to function as internal counsel or advisers to administrators. If there is no opportunity to affect policy, then what they are doing is *publicity*, not public relations. The evaluation of policy is part of the public relations counseling process.

Policies should be considered a fundamental part of the communication audit process. What are publics saying or doing that would cause some sort of new policy to be considered? What are some publics doing that may suggest the level of policy effectiveness? Some policies may not be working. Others may be working but are having a detrimental effect on attitudes and opinions among some publics. That could suggest a change. Information already accumulated for other reasons may be a rich research resource for public relations people. Information in routine record keeping sometimes reveals trends with policy implications.

One school district discovered, for example, that most of its teachers did not live in the district. Knowing that the city had once considered a mandate that all employees live within the city limits—or at least a salary consideration for those who did—the district's public relations officer suggested that hiring from within the city, all other considerations being equal, be instituted as a policy. The school board accepted that recommendation, after considerable debate, and though not precluding the hiring of those living outside the district, the new policy gave preference to those who did. Every new hire was encouraged to locate in the city, rather than the suburbs. A side benefit of the new policy was that minority recruiting improved.

Basic record keeping and fact finding are activities that the public relations person may have to do independent of other departments. An efficient retrieval system should be in place because the public relations person sometimes needs information at a moment's notice. In the public relations department, keeping easily accessible files on all forms of institutional communication is necessary. These range from news releases and annual reports to speeches by officials. The department also is expected to keep information on what is written and said about the institution.

Combining all this intelligence makes it possible to get a reasonably good picture of what the priority publics of the institution think about it—personnel, programs, and facilities. A review of this information is likely to indicate some gaps that additional research may need to fill.

Assessing Results in Relationship to Goals

Research should be ongoing and structured. As shown in Figure 15–1, routine research moves into developing and testing hypotheses, then revising and following up with additional research to fill in the gaps. The plan, once put in place, is monitored in all its aspects. The ongoing evaluation process is also monitored so that the final evaluation is complete enough to offer some suggestions for planning and policy making. Then the cycle starts all over again. This cyclical pattern can help any institution see if it is meeting its own goals and objectives. Most organizations attempt to do this. However, what they often do not do is to see how their publics are reacting to the way goals and objectives are being accomplished. Such knowledge is necessary if an organization is to fulfill its mission statement and meet the intrinsic goals of its positioning strategy.

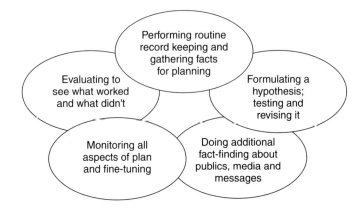

FIGURE 15–1
The Cyclical Pattern of Research
Source: Adapted from *This Is PR: The Realities of Public Relations* (p. 143), by D. Newsom, J. V. Turk, & D. Kruckeberg. Copyright 2000 by Wadsworth Thomson Learning. Adapted with permission of Wadsworth Publishing Company.

Evidence is sometimes available through unobtrusive measures. Chambers of commerce seek evaluations on their city's public school programs to entice companies to relocate. Real estate agents in a school district seek information about particular schools to use in selling homes in that school zone. Evaluations of the "best schools" often are purely opinion based. A system must be developed, therefore, to measure how publics, especially priority publics, are perceiving the institution.

Monitoring Collective Perceptions

Collective perceptions about an organization by its publics are based on what it says and what it does. These collective perceptions constitute the organization's image. If all these fit together, then public perception is fairly close to reality. The reason for that congruity is simple. What the organization says is consistent with what it does, and fits with the mission statement that has given people some expectations of what it should be. When this is true for most of the organization's publics, the image of the institution or organization is generally clear and accurate. That image may not fit a new positioning strategy statement. Also, it may not match what the goals are for the organization—but the image will be clear and measurable. If an organization wants to change the image to reflect a new positioning or new goal, it will be relatively easy to see when the image begins to change. However, if an organization has an image that is not clearly defined, it may indicate two problems. One is that the organization is not communicating very well with its publics. Another is that what it is saying does not match what it is doing or what various publics are experiencing in their relationships with the institution. When that happens, a problem profile for an organization may begin to appear.

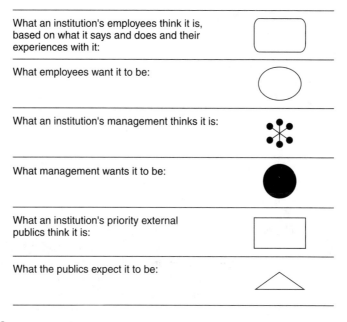

FIGURE 15–2
The Problem Profile
Source: Adapted from *This Is PR: The Realities of Public Relations* (p. 113), by D. Newsom, J. V. Turk, & D. Kruckeberg. Copyright 2000 by Wadsworth Thomson Learning. Adapted with permission of Wadsworth Publishing Company.

A problem profile results when different priority publics hold very different views of the organization (see Figure 15–2). The solution is to discover through research where the discrepancies are and correct them either through communication or policy changes that are then clearly communicated.

Anticipating responses from all publics, especially priority publics, is key to evaluating and monitoring the climate of public opinion, another responsibility of the public relations officer. Yet, this cannot be done effectively unless the officer has good evidence of the perceptions of relevant publics about the organization. The public relations practitioner (or anyone else in the institution) cannot create an image for the institution. But public relations officers can be effective in improving the way publics perceive an organization, a goal achieved only by monitoring public opinion, which is always in flux and highly sensitive to events and experiences.

USING EVALUATIONS FOR STRATEGIC MOVES SUCH AS CAMPAIGNS

Sound program evaluations tell an organization how it is seen by different publics, thus supporting the identification of and an analysis of shortcomings. These evaluations are especially critical when building a pre-crisis constituency. They also help to determine the persuasive level at which continuing campaigns are functioning. Evaluations can also be used to estimate the level at which new campaigns should be launched to be successful. When a campaign is over, a sound evaluation indicates what succeeded with whom and why, and the quality and depth of the residue of goodwill that is left for the future.

Determining Strategy According to the Persuasion Process

An organization seldom has only one campaign going on at once. Although there may be something that has a priority, such as a school district's bond drive, there may also be a campaign to get new computers in the classrooms—a co-op program with a local grocery store chain or other retail outlet. It may be a direct fundraising campaign. (See Chapter 14.)

The typology of campaigns mirrors the six steps of the persuasion process: presenting, attending, comprehending, yielding, retaining, and acting. Therefore, it is critical to know at which persuasive level priority publics are before structuring a campaign.

A campaign to create awareness, the first level of the persuasion process, may be required if priority publics are not aware of the issue, problem, or need. Whatever it is must be presented to them. Monitoring and evaluation processes can identify this for each public. However, since awareness campaigns are perhaps the most expensive to launch and maintain, resources can be saved if the priority publics for the campaign are already aware of the problem but are not really paying attention to it—perhaps because they are not convinced it is important.

A campaign to convey information, the second level of the persuasion process, is totally different in structure from an awareness campaign, both in using media and in crafting messages. A message has to be strong enough to gain their attention. Monitoring and evaluation of publics helps indicate where to start.

Suppose the knowledge of an issue among priority publics is such that there is no need to get their attention or to inform them about its significance. This does not necessarily mean the publics understand what they can do about the issue or, more important, what the educational organization wants them to do about it. Thus the campaign should be structured to gain the publics' comprehension, the third level of persuasion.

Yielding is the next level. Pitched at this level of the persuasion process, a campaign is likely to emphasize shared values as a way of getting compliance or participation. Such a campaign is a facilitating effort aimed at getting priority publics to act on whatever it is that they already have accepted and are ready to do. Say a school's library was damaged by fire, and the damage is widely known and the extent of it understood, many constituencies may help rebuild the collection, if only they are told specifically how they can help.

Publics must be encouraged to retain a desirable position, especially if that public has been encouraged to do something that is new. Suppose, for example, the library situation may attract some local bookstores that never paid any attention to the school before. It is easy to write off the bookstores as "one-timers" and be grateful for that. It is even better to change the bookstore owners' or managers' attitudes or behavior and convert them to regular contributors of one kind or another.

Priority publics may already be at the persuasive level of acting. But what they do now may not be exactly what is desired. If so, a campaign to modify behavior is needed. A school district might find new "adopt-a-school" or some other partnership opportunities from those who help with the problem. The ongoing campaigns of an organization are likely to be at all these different levels, depending on the issue or need, the priority publics, and their level of understanding.

Determining the Level of Success

All campaigns should have specific purposes derived from goals and objectives that are the tangible expressions of the mission statement and positioning. But evaluating a campaign is more than determining whether the purpose was achieved. A capital fundraising campaign can meet its goal and leave a path littered with hostile publics who not only never will help again, but will make negative comments about the organization every chance they get.

Evaluations should examine two outcomes: (a) what the organization did and how much it cost to do it; and (b) what the results were for each effort, tangible and intangible. First, the focus is on determining the actual productivity involved in the campaign and the real costs of each effort. Then the cost effectiveness of the various efforts is determined. Sometimes carefully contrived formulae are used to figure out something like the dollar equivalents of publicity if the same space or time had been bought. That sort of fiction is not very useful. What you want to know is who saw it and what they thought about it. Or if a campaign has focused on the introduction of a new core curriculum, for instance, no matter how much meeting time it took or how many publications were produced, the bottom line is whether students and teachers understand it and see it as an improvement. It is also important to know whether other evaluators, such as accrediting groups and professional associations, say good things about the school for making the change.

Glorious campaigns have introduced dismal failures. The commercial marketplace makes quick assessments, but the marketplace of ideas sometimes takes a little longer. Evaluations must judge results and offer predictive information for planning.

SUMMARY

Evaluating public relations activities is essential to sustaining support. Whether it is identifying issues and monitoring them, handling a crisis, or making policy decisions and implementing them, research by school public relations practitioners is critical for schools to be credible, accountable, and responsible to all their constituencies.

The primary role of the public relations professional is to offer counsel in strategic planning that offers measurable results. Research begins with a review of mission statements to be sure these are still viable. Some reviews are informal, but most use a qualitative-quantitative approach that begins with focus-group interviews. The mistake many people make is using the results of focus-group interviews for decision making. FIGs are only preliminary to other research, usually a survey. However, another way to review mission statements is by using the self-developed survey or the Delphi process.

In addition to an updated mission statement, research should assist schools and school districts in developing a positioning statement—something that describes how the school would like to be seen by all of its publics. Positioning statements help with setting priorities, so these are useful in planning, in reporting to oversight groups, and in counseling, especially in times of critical decision making such as in a crisis. One point to remember is that every type of research has ethical and legal ramifications, and confidentiality is essential.

All research has to begin with the organization's publics, which can be considered in 10 broad categories: media, employee, member, community, government, investor, consumer, international, special (such as activist groups), and integrated marketing communications. Often informal methods are used, such as unobtrusive measures, audits, and publicity analysis. Many times, formal research methods are needed. Qualitative research methods include focus groups; panels; in-depth interviews; and historiographies, case studies, and diaries. Quantitative methods include content analysis and surveys. Both formal and informal research are used for issues identification and monitoring, which is done to detect any issues that could have an impact, either positive or negative. The cyclical process offers an opportunity to position policy that the schools want to put in place and evaluate the success of that. Adjusting policies and meeting the expectations of the publics means ongoing relationships with these publics have to be monitored. Having built a solid support constituency is important in times of crisis.

Monitoring all publics all the time is not cost effective, but all communication projects should have a monitoring and evaluation component built into their budgets. Since public relations practitioners have to function as internal counsel to management, they should retain all information about such projects. As this suggests, research has to be ongoing and cyclical, with good assessment of collective perceptions, to get an idea of what the institutional image is. When using evaluation for strategic moves such as campaigns, it is important to determine what strategy should be used based on where targeted publics are on the six levels of the persuasion process. The levels are presenting or making people aware, attending or giving them information to which they will pay attention, comprehending or understanding the message, yielding or accepting, retaining the position, and acting on the persuasive message. Finally, the level of success has to be evaluated from the position of how all publics have reacted to the campaign.

| CASE STUDY | Measuring Support for a Fine Arts Magnet School |

The Keller (Texas) Independent School District's idea to create a small fine arts high school was built on research. The first research was secondary to examine the need for another high school in the district. Looking at the population growth and the demographics, Keller ISD officials decided that in the future they really would need more than four big high schools, but not five.

Superintendent Charles Bradberry said a smaller high school focused on fine arts would give the district an economical way to grow and fill an educational void at the same time. Art and music, including orchestra, would be included. Anticipated completion of the school is 2006. However, another part of this story is a campaign for the approval of bonds. This case just deals with research leading to the campaign.

Background

Keller ISD has 13 elementary schools, 4 middle schools, 4 intermediate schools, a learning center that typically has 60 to 70 students, and 2 high schools. Keller's elementary schools are K–4; the intermediate schools, 5 and 6; middle schools, 7 and 8; high schools 9–12. The Learning Center is an alternate education facility. The district is governed by a seven-person school board, each member elected to a 3-year term. There are only two private schools in Keller.

The city of Keller, located in Tarrant County, is southeast of Fort Worth and included in what is called the Dallas–Fort Worth Metroplex. Since 1982 it has grown from a city of somewhat fewer than 5,000 to 25,000 people in 2002. Although it is growing at a fast pace, the Keller Chamber of Commerce says the intent is to keep the look and feel of a small town. That has an impact on the way the citizens relate to the school district.

Keller was founded in 1881 after the completion of the Texas and Pacific Railroad connection between Fort Worth and Texarkana. Its original name of Athol was changed in 1882 to honor John C. Keller, a foreman on the railroad. The town wasn't incorporated until 1958.

The town's first educational facility in the 1800s was a subscription school built by the Mt. Gilead Baptist Church, with church privileges reserved. That site was abandoned and a new school built, which was used until 1898 when a new property was bought and the school moved to the site where Keller Elementary School stands today. Thus, the schools in Keller have always maintained a close tie to the history of the city's development, an important consideration.

Keller's location means that it has a population mix of Whites, Hispanics, Asians, and African Americans. Children from all of these ethnic groups are now attending schools in the district.

Developing the Survey

The survey has a core of questions that are administered by the Keller School District annually to gather longitudinal information. Each year a committee chaired by Superintendent Bradberry drafts other questions to include. Bradberry has a research background and does survey research for other school districts.

Administering the Survey

The school district has 18,000 plus students, and a copy of the survey was given to each student to take home to a parent. A note with the survey advised the parent that it was necessary to return only one questionnaire unless the responses were different for the various schools their children might be attending. The assumption was that there would be about 11,000 used due to the duplications. There were 4,000 surveys returned, for a response rate of 36%.

Reporting Survey Results

Two other issues were included in the survey. Parents were asked if they would approve a property tax increase. Nearly half of the respondents, 48%, said yes. Considering the national economic situation in June of 2002, that brought forth an acknowledgment of surprise from Superintendent Bradberry who said it demonstrated community support for education. He also said the funds raised from a tax increase would be primarily directed toward reducing class sizes. Another issue proposed for support was developing a sixth-grade center. The idea of having schools for sixth graders only is a national concept. In Keller, Bradberry said schools for sixth graders only would permit the offering of full-day kindergarten without redrawing boundaries. Although 50% of the parents were supportive, 36% said they were not, and 14% were undecided. This idea, the district felt, needed more consensus before moving ahead.

In evaluating parental approval of the district, the survey asked questions about whether the parents had a problem or concern about the schools and if they felt welcome in the classrooms. Results in those areas were especially meaningful to the district. Nearly all of the parents responding, 92%, said they felt welcome in their child's classroom and 79% said they had experienced no recent problem or concern about their child's school.

This is meaningful to evaluate the climate of public opinion for support of a bond issue. The results of the survey were posted on the district's Web site on July 1, 2002.

Updated information about Keller ISD is available on the city's Web site: http://www.cityofkeller.com. It also may be accessed directly at http://www.kellerisd.net if you want to keep up with developments in this case. Head of Keller ISD is Superintendent Charles Bradberry. Keller's communication director is Helen Williams, and the research director is Dr. Bill Newton.

QUESTIONS AND SUGGESTED ACTIVITIES

CASE STUDY

1. Name and explain the types of evaluation needed in this case.
2. Of what significance are a district's mission and positioning statements to decision making? What is the role of research in developing these?

CHAPTER

3. Identify the primary components of evaluating a public relations program.
4. Choose an issue that lends itself to creating an opportunity to institute a new policy, and determine what research needs to be done to see the policy through to a successful endorsement.
5. What is the role of public relations research in
   a. forming policy,
   b. advising management on policy issues, and
   c. evaluating district and school activities and programs?
6. What are the primary obstacles to evaluating public relations programs?

SUGGESTED READINGS

Babbie, E. (2000). *The practice of social research.* Belmont, CA: Wadsworth/ITP.

Center, A. H., & Jackson, P. (2002). *Public relations practices, managerial case studies and problems.* Upper Saddle River, NJ: Prentice Hall.

Culbertson, H. M., Jeffers, D. W., Stone, D. B., & Terrell, M. (1993). *Social, political, and economic contexts in public relations: Theory and cases.* Hillsdale, NJ: Erlbaum.

Cutlip, S. M., Center, A. H., & Broom, G. M. (2000). *Effective public relations.* Upper Saddle River, NJ: Prentice Hall.

Newsom, D., Turk, J. V., & Kruckeberg, D. (2000). *This is PR: The realities of public relations.* Belmont, CA: Wadsworth/ITP.

Stacks, D. W. (2002). *Primer of public relations research.* New York: Guilford Press.

Strauss, A. L., & Corbin, J. M. (1998). *Basics of qualitative research.* Thousand Oaks, CA: Sage.

Wilcox, D. L., Ault, P. H., Agee, W., & Cameron, G. T. (2000). *Public relations strategies and tactics.* New York: Addison-Wesley, Longman.

Wimmer, R. D., & Dominick, J. R. (2002). *Mass media research: An introduction.* Belmont, CA: Wadsworth/ITP.

REFERENCES

Hendrix, J. A. (2001). *Public relations cases.* Belmont, CA: Wadsworth/ITP.

Newsom, D., & Carrell, B. (2001). *Public relations writing: Form & style.* Belmont, CA: Wadsworth/ITP.

Newsom, D., Turk, J. V., & Kruckeberg, D. (2000). *This is PR: The realities of public relations.* Belmont, CA: Wadsworth/ITP.

Name Index

Subject Index